MODERN LAW ENFORCEMENT
WEAPONS & TACTICS

3rd Edition

PATRICK SWEENEY

©2004 Patrick Sweeney

Published by

 krause publications

An F+W Publications Company

700 East State Street • Iola, WI 54990-0001
715-445-2214 • 888-457-2873
www.krause.com

Our toll-free number to place an order or obtain
a free catalog is (800) 258-0929.

Library of Congress Catalog Number: 86-72618

ISBN: 0-87349-659-0

Edited by Kevin Michalowski
Designed by Ethel Thulien

Printed in U.S.A.

Acknowledgments

Every book, unless it is a work of fiction, requires a collaboration between the author and his sources of information. Unless you're Winston Churchill writing "A History of the English Speaking Peoples" or Isaac Asimov writing just about anything, you can't just do it all from memory. My friend John Farnam is far too modest, but he sums it up nicely "I just remember what other people have learned and pass it on."

Even when I carried and wore a badge I couldn't keep up on everything. Now that I don't (the phrase "There's a new Sheriff in town" is not just a cliché.) I have to depend on those who spend their waking hours in the front lines of the homefront. I would like to thank my long-time friend, shooting buddy and my personal nominee for modern Renaissance man, Law Enforcement Division, Jeff Chudwin, Chief of Police of Olympia Fields and President of the Illinois Tactical Officers Association. Also of great help was Ed Mohn, Libertyville Police Department and the NIPAS Emergency Service Team, and Multi Jurisdictional Team Advisor to the NTOA. And Ron Proudlock, Livonia Police, Ret'd. Last but not least, all my friends and associates in the Illinois Tactical Officers Association who have been so free with their hard-learned tricks, tips and information through the years.

On the medical front, I'd like to thank fellow Gunsite Graduate Anthony M. Barrera, MD, FACEP (aka Doc Gunn), and dedicate the emergency medical section to the late M-SGT William Chris Dwiggins, who spent so much time and effort imparting his hard-earned knowledge on emergency medical matters at Gunsite. And while he will not have his MD until after this book is out, I'd like to thank Jeff Gerak for his incredible patience in putting up with my seemingly endless stream of questions on basic medical details. James Etzin of the International Tactical EMS Association was invaluable for his insights, for pointing me towards info I hadn't thought of, and letting me know there are many more locations for law enforcement EMS training than I had ever thought there were.

In the category of "I can't believe these guys get paid for this" manufacturers and their reps who went out of their way to provide me with samples, information and help, (and in no particular order) are: Travis Noteboom of Benchmade Knives, Dick Swann of A.R.M.S., Ernest Emerson of Emerson Knives, Dave Skinner at STI, Gary Smith at Caspian, Greg Anderson at Blackhawk Industries, Jeff Hoffman at Black Hills Ammunition, Dusty Rhoades at London Bridge Trading Company, Radha Govind at BfR Boots, Deb Williams at Springfield Armory, David Johnson at Boonie Packer, Robert Castellani, President of North American Rescue Products, and Teressa Carter at Remington. And my apologies to anyone I might have left out due to poor memory or caffeine overdose.

Finally, as I do (and she deserves) in every book I write, I thank Felicia, for her patience, love and able assistance on the translation from "gunspeak" to the English language. For those of us whose first language is more concerned with ballistics and reloading, shooting techniques and tactics, English can be troubling. She makes the translation, and life in general, easy.

Introduction

A lot of people get into the shooting sports (or many other sports for that matter) for the gear. If you think a bunch of shooters sitting around discussing bullet weight and powder selection is strange, you haven't listened to dirt bike racers debate the merits of one brand of shocks versus another, or which weight oil is appropriate for what climate. Or in the old days, photographers discussing which film was "warmer" or which had "snappier" colors for fleshtones or landscapes.

When it comes to shooting, the activities of the special teams in law enforcement really bring out the gearheads. After all, the gear includes not only guns and ammo, but there are lights, body armor, uniforms, web gear, and such exotica as night vision gear, grenades of many kinds, radios and teamwork. And when it comes to writing, the task increases commensurately. After all, in order to write about gear, you have to handle it, test it, use it and compare it. Unfortunately, to handle, test, use and compare everything available in every category would take more than I have. More time, more manuscript, more publisher and editor patience, and more energy. And, it having taken several years of work, multiple volumes of books, and a mountain of gear, would be out of date before it hit the newsstands.

Gearheads are not just readers, either. There are definitely police officers that worked hard to get onto a team so they could not just get into the action, but get

the cool gear, too. Never underestimate the "cool guy gear" factor as a sales tool. There is a reason there are always more volunteers for Ranger and Airborne units than there are slots available. More applications for all the "high-speed, low-drag" positions in the military and law enforcement than there are slots available. And gear is part of it. But gear is more than just a substitute for a video game as entertainment. In a bad situation, quality gear can make the difference between succeeding and failing. Between coming home upright or feet first; between being cited and praised or being remembered and commemorated. To that end, I undertook the task of sorting through equipment, procedures, attitudes and information, and delivering it to you.

I'm only human, and do what I can. I'm sure I will fail to mention or test someone's favorite, or the issue gear of a big department, but I can't cover it all. I'm sure I'll praise something a reader has tested and disliked. Or criticize something a reader depends on. If we disagree, find out why and let me know. I want to know. In this project, as with all my others, I contacted as many of the manufacturers of each category as I could. And as with each prior book, I had many responses. Some immediately sent catalogs, suggested products, and called to ask if I had questions. Indeed, several shipped products when I simply asked for a catalog. Others promised, and shipped, and were happy to answer questions. A few promised but never sent anything, not even a catalog. But there are limits to the "Sweeney fun gear" budget, even when I get to write about it and theoretically justify it as an expense in some future audit. That said, there are products I've written about that I've spent my own money on. Usually products that I feel strongly enough about that I've bought them even before doing the book. And a few that I couldn't in good conscience leave out even though it meant reaching into my own pocket.

So, when you're reading through the chapters, don't assume that a missing product or brand is a bad thing. It just means that I can only devote so much time to getting gear, and have to spend time testing it and writing about it. And what about the stuff that didn't pass muster? That's a delicate question. Should I pan a product, knowing the book will be on the shelves for years? What if the manufacturer improves their product? What I did when faced with that dilemma was simple. If something didn't measure up, I contacted the manufacturer. If they took care of it, or replaced it with a new and improved design, then I wrote about the product and left the incident alone. If the tale is amusing or instructive, then I wrote about the efforts. If the manufacturer could not or would not make good on a faulty design or product, I dropped it from the book. If it is in here, you can depend on it. If it isn't, it may be as simple as I couldn't get to it, or as bad as the boots that fell apart in two weeks and never came back from their return trip to the manufacturer. I also have a problem with panning bad gear in that I only have so much room. Every page I devote to trashing bad boots, web gear or guns is a page I cannot get back on which to write about good stuff. And since my Publisher wants a book and not an encyclopedia (not that I haven't approached the Britannica people) I have to limit what I cover.

And what did testing entail? For the firearms, that's an easy answer. I shot them. I shot them from the bench to test accuracy, and then shot them in practice and in training sessions to check handling, durability and function. I didn't dunk them in water, mud or sand, I didn't abuse them by hitting them with hammers or sticks, and I didn't feed them bad ammo. Believe me, my practice sessions are hard enough on guns, I don't need to be abusing manufacturers loaners. For the knives, I cut stuff. Not me, but paper, cardboard, rope and twine, wood, cloth and webbing material. Again, no abuse. Yes, you can hammer a knife through plywood or sheet metal if you try, you can see if the blade bends or breaks if you clamp it in a vise, but why do it? If you need to climb something, they make tools for the job; they're called pitons. If you're worried about a knife breaking, buy one with a thicker blade. (And stay away from vises.) As for clothing, web gear, boots and the like, I wore them in practice sessions, training and testing. The best way to find out if web gear or a vest will stand up is to load junk magazines into the pouches and practice room entry or thick brush patrolling for an afternoon.. (Why junk magazines? Because I'm not deliberately subjecting my tested and reliable magazines to wall and doorway impacts if I can avoid it. Especially not for training.) Sometimes the testing got a little too real-world, as the inadvertent slash test of the Blackhawk gloves. But in all, gear testing gives me excuses to make sure that my range sessions do not become rare and infrequent events.

One question that comes up when the subject is training is; "How can you reveal our secrets?" Usually the question is put earnestly; sometimes it is put to me in an irritated and aggressive manner. The short answer is that "There are no secrets, the only secret is good training." You see, I first faced this question back in 1973, when I was quickly working up the ranks in United Tae Kwon Do. "How can you teach people the secrets to your techniques? Aren't you afraid they'll use it against you?" The only appropriate response I've been able to come up with was one I hit on very early in my training: "Yea, right." When the "secret" to a unbeatable side thrust kick is to do it correctly 500 times a day with each leg, just how much "catching up" is someone going to be able to do? I was better because I trained harder, not because there was some trick to be discovered and then hidden from others. The same applies to an

entry team, a tactical marksman, and a rapid response diamond. Knowing the different ways an entry team can handle the doorway isn't going to help you if they've practiced and you haven't. It still isn't going to help you unless the total of your hours of practice are greater than their hours of practice. (Let me point out here that most, if not all of the bad guys are bad guys in part because they are allergic to hard work.) Specific knowledge can potentially help specific people. If I disclose the patrol patterns and the specific variables considered by a particular police department, it might, just might, help a B&E team. Of course, that department would respond by assessing the situation, adapting to the problem, and soon corralling the bad guys. Or, if I were to disclose the Rapid Response drills to a Meeting Engagement that the Rangers use, why some dirtbag in a Third World dustbowl of a country might be helped. (If he reads English, If he got this book, If I disclosed the information, and IF he/they practiced, it might help. My money would still be on the Rangers.) A few pictures and some pages of description are not going to replace actual practice. But they will allow you, the reader and potential consumer of gear and training, to make intelligent choices. That said, I am not going to disclose how to defeat particular equipment or techniques. Those who teach and train with law enforcement know the weaknesses of equipment and training, and the hidden strengths of some items. I am also not going to reveal the extra capacities of certain gear, capacities that give law enforcement officers an extra advantage when dealing with the offenders who are their clients.

I also had to struggle with just how to present the material. Some publications get so breathless and sensational in their presentation that you wonder if you're reading a firearms book or magazine, or the tabloids by the cash register. "Gun Grab: Five ways to carve the Felon off your Sidearm!" or "React to an Ambush: Seconds to live or Die!" just aren't me. On the other hand, you can write to be too dry and clinical. I hope I've been informative, entertaining, and made you glad you stopped to browse the bookrack and found this title.

Table Of Contents

Chapter 1 .... Use Of Force 7

Chapter 2 .... The Uniform Ensemble And Convergence 19

Chapter 3 .... Web Gear, Vests And Holsters 29

Chapter 4 .... The Synthetic Revolution 51

Chapter 5 .... Foot And Joint Protection 55

Chapter 6 .... Gloves For All Seasons 62

Chapter 7 .... Physical Protection 68

Chapter 8 ...... Rucksacks 83

Chapter 9 .... Let There Be Light 87

Chapter 10 ..... The Beretta M-92 103

Chapter 11 ..... The 1911 In Law Enforcement 106

Chapter 12 ..... The Para Ordnance LDA 113

Chapter 13 ..... Check Out The S&W 99 116

Chapter 14 ..... The Kahr Arms Pistols 119

Chapter 15 ..... A New Idea For An Entry Pistol 121

Chapter 16 ..... Springfield XD 127

Chapter 17 ..... Light And Lighting In General 129

Chapter 18 ..... Multi-Tools and Knives 131

Chapter 19 ..... First Aid 152

Chapter 20 ..... Hydration 165

Chapter 21 ..... Ballistic Testing 172

Chapter 22 ..... The Patrol Rifle 180

Chapter 23 ..... Improving The AR-15/M-16 198

Chapter 24 ..... Pistol Caliber Carbines 222

Chapter 25 ..... Springfield M-1A Scout Rifle 233

Chapter 26 ..... Myths Of The Rifle 239

Chapter 27 ..... FN Special Police Rifle 248

Chapter 28 ..... Long Gun Light Methods 254

Chapter 1

Use of Force

LET ME START by telling you that I am not an attorney, I don't play one on TV, and the closest I've ever gotten to Law School is walking by and admiring the architecture. I've been in court a bunch of times, but in every instance my opinion was being sought on matters ballistic, not procedural or legal precedents. But, I have talked with a number of officers, lawyers, a few Judges, and been subjected to classes on Use of Force and its Legal Aspects. If you want the lowdown on what the situation is in your jurisdiction, pay your money and hire an attorney. But I do have opinions, unlike my friend Terry O'Hara, who told me "I have no opinions. The Queen does not allow me to." He's a Judge in Canada, and since his word is Law, he can't utter an opinion on a legal matter unless there are two attorneys in front of him in his courtroom. At the time I thought it was a scream. There he was, the professional arbiter and determiner of fates and the law, and he could not say "what was what" except during a case. I later figured out why. Since his word is

the law, offering an opinion without the written transcript can only get him and everyone who hears him in trouble. Offering his opinion can prejudice a case he later hears on the subject discussed. Better to avoid the Judicial Review Board and all the hassles, and not offer an opinion until paid to do so. Terry is a smart guy and a great shotgun shooter.

Hire an attorney. Get it in writing. Learn the limits. Then enjoy your mass-media entertainment options.

We've all seen it. The movie detective, having just gotten back to the station from his latest high-volume shootout, and just gotten the mandatory chewing-out from his supervisor, gets a tip from his street informant, and is within moments dashing out the door hot on the trail of the suspect. Or, only slightly more realistic, his boss has him turn his gun in to the crime lab. So, when he gets the hot tip, he grabs another gun from his desk drawer, jams it into his holster and dashes off.

These are just plain wrong, and on so many levels it isn't funny. (The high-volume shootout? We'll get into that later.) Gun wrangling and legal issues on the television and in movies are so bad, and so noticeably bad once you've learned to see them that it can interfere with watching the shows. My wife complained a long time ago (and many times since) "You've ruined action movies for me. I now see how badly some actors handle their guns, and boy does it irritate me."

While the bad gun wrangling is a problem, in that it conditions people to

Training and testing is the key. Unless you use gear in a serious training environment, or in a real operation, you don't know what it will stand up to.

Two knives, an elegant one for when the big serrated Emerson may not be appropriate. And the Emerson, when the smaller one isn't enough.

Weeks of academy, days of departmental Use of Force, state-mandated Lethal Force Use by a Peace Officer class, and you think he cares what caliber he has? You bet.

think that is how things are done, the improper depiction of the law is more so. Let's start right out with the big one, the Board of Inquiry.

Remember back in High School, when your Civics Teacher gleefully intoned the quote "a nation of Laws and not Men?" In case you weren't paying attention, or in case they've dropped Civics from the curriculum, what it means is this: No one is above the law. The Law is a set of rules, and an organizational framework of how to implement the rules. The Law is something we have decided among ourselves. As a result, there are variances in what is allowed. In one State you can have a folding knife with a blade up to 4 inches long. In another, length doesn't matter, but only folders are allowed. In still another, it is a felony to possess double-edged knives. And similarly with firearms. In Arizona, Open Carry is allowed. In California, only concealed carry, and then only with a local permit. In Michigan, a police officer from another state may carry, but should the same visiting officer then travel to California or New York City, he is committing a

major violation. (The quote given to me, in a brusque New Yawk accent was; "Yea, but you ain't the police here.") The higher the authority, the more likely the law is to be uniform. Not necessarily rational, but uniform. And the Courts enforce the laws. So, what of our cinematic police officer? He has to operate within the Use of Force guidelines of his department, and those guidelines have to take into account what the courts will decide should things get out of hand. ("Out of hand" defined as a prosecution or lawsuit ending up in front of a Judge.)

So, he knows the bad guys are in the building, and goes in, kicking down doors along the way, shooting a bushel basket of ammo, and then settles the whole thing by telling his boss "I got the bad guys, where's my medal?" Not likely. To start with there is a little thing called the Fourth Amendment. It seems our hero (using the term loosely) needed to go before a Judge, with reasonable proof of his suspicions, and acquire a piece of paper called a "Search Warrant." The warrant allows him to then enter the stated premises and search for the evidence in his case, evidence that he has asserted to the Judge exists. The part with which scriptwriters play fast and lose is the benefit of the doubt. You see, Judges assume that the officers presenting the evidence are good, upstanding citizens. (And they're usually correct in that assumption.) They give the officer more or less benefit of the doubt, depending on the circumstances, the officers' track record, the judges experience, prejudices (hey, he or she is only human) and knowledge.

So far, no big deal. Evidence gained unlawfully is deemed to not exist, the officer gets reprimanded (or fired, if it happens too many times) and life goes on. But then we get to the dramatic shootout. The Officer may fire only when his or someone else's life is in danger. He can't fire off a few shots to accentuate his questioning. He can't shoot because he knew the bad guy was going to put up a fight. To quote the US Attorney General opinion of October 17, 1995,

Sprinting through a course of fire is great fun, and sometimes even makes for a fun movie. But both are only a game, and not reality.

Before and after training and an operation, every aspect has to be discussed. Here Phil Singleton discusses the proper method of a bus assault.

An 82nd Airborne trooper, equipped with many items found on SWAT teams: kneepads and hatch gloves, a Camelbak, and an Aimpoint. Except for the rocket launcher, he could be a perimeter officer on a drug raid. (DoD photo)

If your department ever needs this kind of deployment, God help us. In a military context, a SAW 249 like this could be used for "area denial." Law Enforcement doesn't need that, at least not yet. (DoD photo)

making the Use of Force Policy uniform in all branches of the Department of Justice: "Law enforcement officers and correctional officers of the Department of Justice may use deadly force only when necessary, that is, when the officer has a reasonable belief that the subject of such force poses an imminent danger of death or serious physical injury to the officer or to another person." Seems clear enough. However, remember, we are a nation of Laws, and not of men. Even though the officer is given great leeway in the performance of his duties, and extra powers that the rest of us do not have, he still must account for his actions. And that is where the Board of Inquiry comes in. Another clichéd prop of the scriptwriter, the board of inquiry exists in a perfect world to make sure officers clearly know what the bounds of deadly force are. A shooting incident would be dissected, the officer questioned on all aspects, and then the rest of the force would have a newly clarified definition of what is acceptable. In an imperfect world, knowing that a board of inquiry exists can keep morally weak officers from getting themselves into trouble (and the rest of us at hazard for their willingness to cross the lines.)

The process differs in its details, but simply put, once the shootout is over, the arriving officers secure the scene, collect the evidence (including the involved officers' firearms) and interview witnesses. In order to protect his rights, the involved officer may or may not have an attorney present when he/she is questioned. The officer goes on Administrative Leave. He/she files paperwork, organizes the desk, works on other cases (without leaving the station) and packs a different firearm than the one used in the shooting. The officer most definitely does not go back out "on the streets" to continue working the case that got them into the shooting. Once the board of inquiry reviews all the evidence and issues an opinion, and assuming the opinion is to declare the shooting justified, the officer goes back to work. Some departments will insist on a psychological debriefing, or counseling. Other departments will leave that to the officer and his union agreement. And the rest of the scene described above? Well, anyone who keeps a loaded firearm in an unlocked desk drawer is asking for a written reprimand. And anyone who takes said firearm out of the desk and stuffs it in a holster without making sure it is or isn't loaded can go off to work without my help, thank you.

What of some of the other cinema staples? To quote once again the Department of Justice statement. (I select the DOJ statement not because it is the best, but because it is a Federal agency and the policy seems quite rational. There are some aspects of it I'm not comfortable with, however.) Fleeing Felons: "Deadly force may be used to prevent the escape of a fleeing subject if there is probable cause to believe (1) the subject has committed a felony involving the infliction or threatened infliction of serious physical injury or death, and (2) the escape of the subject would pose an imminent danger of death or serious physical injury to the officer or another person." Note the "and" between (1) and (2). Federal Agents can't gun down subjects because they are running away, regardless of how heinous the crime they've committed. Not unless the agents have probable cause to believe their flight would pose an imminent danger to others. So, our cinematic hero shoots at the fleeing felon, and then gets his supervisors congratulations? I don't think so. What about warning shots? Well, believe it or not, in some jurisdictions they are allowed. Again, the DOJ statement: "Warning shots are not permitted outside of the prison context." What about shooting the tires of a moving car? We've all seen that on the screen.

The Big Three
or the Big Four, which is it?

In order to legally use Deadly Force, you, the defendant, must be able to prove several things. The one-word descriptions are, Ability, Opportunity, Intent, and Preclusion. Some jurisdictions require that you demonstrate all four. Some only require that you demonstrate the first three. You will not be hailed as a hero until you can demonstrate them, and maybe not even then by some people. In most cases, the definitions will be viewed from the perspective of a "reasonable man." Not to slight women, but to define things from what a reasonable, rational, and moral man would see. This is only a summary, as I could easily spend half the book simply covering the categories, defining terms and demonstrating situations.

Ability

Simply put, did he, the deceased, have the ability to inflict "grave bodily injury or death" (GBID) upon you? And what does your state, county or city include in the list of physical acts that constitute GBID? "Your Honor, he had a big knife." Done, as a knife is a deadly weapon as any reasonable man can realize. What about a 70-year-old man faced with a professional wrestling school dropout? Done, as the disparity of force makes serious injury highly likely. A firearm? Yes. But ability must be tempered by....

Opportunity

And could he (the assailant) put the force to use? A big knife, on a balcony too far away to jump, does not meet the definition of opportunity. The same balcony poses no hindrance to an offender armed with a deer rifle. A tool without the opportunity to use it is no threat under the law.

Intent

How do you know he intends to use it? His spoken words, his body language, his location can provide the information. It can be spoken. "Your Honor, he said 'I'm gonna kill you' as he reached into the tool box and pulled out the biggest crescent wrench I've ever seen." That's one example. Walking into a party store at the corner, to see the man at the counter turning towards you with a shotgun in his hands and a snarl on his face is another.

Preclusion

Could you have done something else besides used deadly force? While the requirements of the previous three are much the same, preclusion, and the requirement for it, can vary greatly from one jurisdiction to another. Some require retreating from

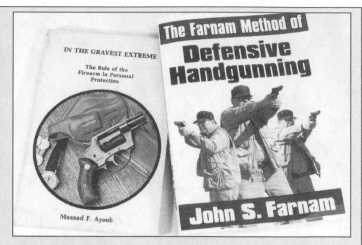

Even for police officers, Mas and John are useful references and good sources of information.

danger while in public. Others do not require it, and may even state retreat is not required if you are in a place you have every right to be. Many hold the home to be a no-retreat location. And all instances of retreat may be waived if you are defending someone who is unable to retreat. Preclusion is also a psychological consideration. If you could have retreated, but didn't (even if the law did not require it) how will you feel afterwards? Will you be consumed with doubt and depression? Will you have a few bad nights, and then live with it? Only you will know.

In the Law Enforcement context, much of this changes. For example, retreating is not usually an option. A tactical withdrawal may be called for to gain time or advantage, but the police can't let someone go because they might be "too tough right now." Once engaged, the police do not leave. They can't. First, they have a duty to the rest of us. In the event they did let someone go, and that offender then harmed another, how would you feel as the officers in the first instance? (Certainty of lawsuits aside.)

The first thing you should do is get and read "In the Gravest Extreme" by Massad Ayoob. For civilians will explain many things, and is a good foundation for those who will have or do have a CCW. And for a law enforcement officer, it is a summary of the basics of the laws. (and the restrictions civilians are under) Both can then use it as the starting point for your consultations with your attorney. The civilian should make margin notes for specifics in his/her home state, and the officer can use it as a bedside reminder of departmental policy and state law concerning arrest procedures.

First, it doesn't work. Tires that have been shot deflate slowly, if at all. They don't suddenly burst and shred, throwing the car out of control. Second, the vehicle is moving. It is hard enough hitting things with gunfire when they are standing still. But, curiously enough, in some jurisdictions, shooting at a moving car is permitted. (Something scriptwriters don't get right.) That situation is when the car itself is being used as a weapon. If someone tries to use a car to run down an officer, and there is no escape, then some jurisdictions allow it. Again, the DOJ policy: "Weapons may be fired at the driver or other occupant of a moving motor vehicle only when (1) The officer has a reasonable belief that the subject poses an imminent danger of death or serious physical injury to the officer or another, and (2) The public

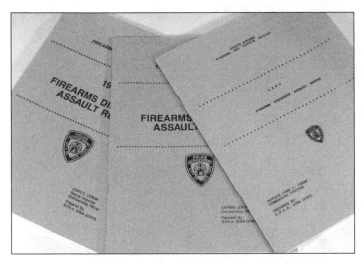

The NYPD SOP-9 used to be available to other agencies. It stopped being distributed, which is unfortunate. If you can get your hands on copies, do so.

The SOE Gear CQB vest, with ammo, tools, EZ-Cuffs, wound dressing and badge. Remove the badge and add fragmentation grenades, and it could be a military rig. The two jobs are overlapping a lot more than before.

safety benefits of using such force outweigh the risks to the safety of the officer or other persons." Why the extra line on "public safety benefits?" Simple. A car is not like a firearm. If the suspect outside of a vehicle is shot and disabled, the dropped firearm won't just "go off." But a car will keep moving. Shoot the driver, and the car can keep going down the road to crash into another car, a building, or strike a pedestrian.

And all of the guidelines exist to inform the officer of what to expect if the matter should end up in front of a Judge.

The climactic shootout

Every movie has one, and some TV shows do too. And through all the years, the statistics on police shootings have changed only a bit. Back when it was only revolvers, the numbers were something like (subject to regional variance) 'under three shots fired, less than 5 yards distance, and half the time at night." Now that everyone carries magazine-fed pistols instead of six-shooters, the numbers have ticked up a little. But still, six shots average at 5 yards average, and half the shootings at night sums it up. So why does our hero go through a case and a half of ammunition, fired through seven different firearms? Because the bell curve of skills applies to moviemakers, too. It is easier to sell tickets if the audience is entertained. It is easier to entertain with high-volume cinematic firefights than it is with suspense built to a 10-shot finale.

One reason there are not so many shots fired in real life as in the movies as that each officer is fully responsible for each shot fired. Unlike a military context, where a machinegunner may be assigned a street, field, building or enemy emplacement, and told "suppressive fire, an average of one four- to six-shot burst every 10 seconds, continue until told otherwise or you see yellow smoke on the objective" a police officer cannot fire unless the situation meets all the requirements listed in the sidebar. There are exceptions, but they are rare and fraught with danger. A miss is noted, searched for, the results

Teams take manpower, and manpower and training costs money. But not training, or having an under-staffed team can cost, too.

detailed, and listed in the report. Misses with unfortunate consequences will often result in legal action against the department or officer. For many years, the New York Police Department published their SOP-9 reports. They listed the statistics of all shootings of and by departmental personnel, and summarized the ones that offered examples to learn from. (NYPD stopped publishing the report, or at least making it available to other officers and departments. A great shame, as it offered valuable information.) For decades, the statistics were the same, reflecting the variances of time, location, experience and determination of those involved. And rarely (not even once a year) was there a shooting where all involved consumed as much as a full box of handgun ammunition.

So the next time you watch a movie and see the end of the climactic shootout littered ankle-deep in brass, realize that of the several thousand shooting incidents that happen each year, you've just seen a simulation of the once-in-a-lifetime incident. And an evidentiary job of mammoth proportions for the evidence techs getting that assignment. (Hey, you determine the exact direction and final resting place of every one of those two hundred shots fired in that scene!)

Special teams are no different. Yes, they crash through the door with four to six team members, who carry as many as eight to 15 firearms, but if even one of them fires a round, the whole process begins. The firearm involved will be tagged as evidence (and maybe all the others as well will be test-fired by the evidence team to provide ballistic samples) the individual involved will be rotated off the team until the board is done with its work. (And maybe the team put on desk duty until that members return.) Which can be a drain in a busy city with a tight budget. You can't send your team out on call after call, with one or two or more members or teams off for administrative leave due to last weekend being so busy.

No, real life isn't like the movies.

Why SWAT?

Back in the "good old days" police walked a beat, they knew everyone's name, and often didn't have to involve the courts in settling disputes. Uh-huh. And they also operated sometimes in a much more heavy-handed manner. As the citizenry became more aware of their rights, matters that might have been settled on the sidewalk were moved to the courts. The increase in crime we experienced in the 1960s called for more officers to deal with the volume, and a new approach; a more organized approach, to deal with the particulars. The beat officer may have been sufficient to deal with the relatively normal problems in his precinct, but a barricaded gunman or hostage situation calls for more officers and a different approach.

The different approach requires different equipment, training, organization and attitude. Uninvolved outsiders complicate the problem of team structure, organization, training and attitude. One might even be a bit condescending and consider administrative and political controls as coming from untrained and inexperienced observers who really shouldn't be involved. If you are going to get your blood pressure all worked up because a local ward representative or county commissioner weighs in with an opinion on tactics or training, then you aren't going to last long when the real pressure hits you.

The first change in law enforcement operations brought about by the adoption of SWAT (or SRT, EST, ESS, etc) is the Team. Some departments continue to

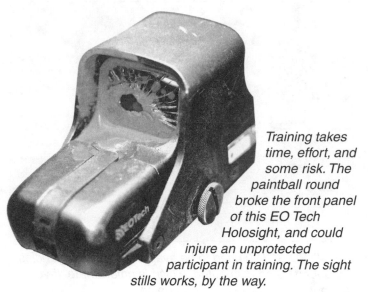

Training takes time, effort, and some risk. The paintball round broke the front panel of this EO Tech Holosight, and could injure an unprotected participant in training. The sight stills works, by the way.

send out two-man cars (only the heavily-urbanized cities still maintain beat cops) while others use one-man cars. For a patrol officer, help is back-up, called for on the radio, arriving sometime later. In the team structure, your back-up is standing right behind you. After all, since the team is there prior to the precipitation of trouble (the second change) you/they can have enough or more than enough help on hand. Thus four- and six-man teams (women, too, in some departments) are the standard maneuvering unit. However, the team approach increases the manpower costs very quickly. A barricaded gunman situation, with the manpower requirements of an entry team, a perimeter team or teams, a negotiator, a tactical marksman, the Scene Commander and his staff, and an EMS unit standing by can quickly run to 25 to 30 people. As a result, many departments have their SWAT team as mobile individuals on regular patrol, who collect to the scene when called. Otherwise, they simply conduct their every day patrol duties as a uniformed officer.

However, teams are of no use unless trained as teams. So, even the patrol officer, as SWAT on call is an officer who works fewer patrol hours a week than a patrol-only officer. For there must be weekly training sessions devoted to team drills, training for

The Sage Control SL-6 in a Blackhawk carry case, ready to go into the trunk of the car or back of the SUV. (Courtesy Blackhawk Industries)

If you need a bundle of flexible cuffs, or other stuff, the SOE Gear empty mag pouch works well as a cargo case.

As law enforcement requirements evolve, so do the manufacturers offerings. CTS offers a training-only NFDD (125dB) so teams aren't exposed to the 175dB of the regular NFDD, day in and day out.

Guns are sometimes the least of it. EZ-Cuffs, smoke, OC spray, fire extinguisher, entry tools, and they all require training. And practice. And certification. With all the paperwork and training requirements it's a wonder we ever get out on the street.

the specialized equipment and weapons, review of Use of Force policy and team action matrices. No, even the part-time SWAT officer must be more than just a patrol officer with a special "SWAT tab" on his uniform sleeve.

But what does the SWAT officer do? That depends. In traveling and teaching I end up in a lot of different jurisdictions, and see a lot of different teams and approaches. Some teams insist on going out on every drug raid, high-risk warrant service and barricaded gunman call. Other teams (or the jurisdiction they are in) separate those functions. The Narcotics Division has its own raid team, the High-risk warrant or Felony Arrest Unit has a team

(often multi-jurisdictional) to scoop up offenders, and the SRT (Special Response Team) is called only for hostage and barricaded gunman calls. Sometimes the differences are budgetary. Sometimes they are political. And sometimes they are partly a result of legal considerations. The catchphrase we all learned in school "A nation of laws and not of men" covers law enforcement officials as well as the rest of us. A department and its officers must operate within the framework of the law and its restrictions, or find themselves broke or imprisoned. The federal law covering much of our area of interest is USC Title 42, Section 83, describing "the seven deadly sins:" Negligent Assignment, Negligent Entrustment, Failure to Train, Failure to Direct, Failure to Supervise, Negligent Retention, and Negligent Hiring. If you as the Chief come to the realization that your team is not sufficiently trained in some aspect of raids or rescues, and you continue to authorize their activity in that area, you're in legal hot water. That's partly why some teams don't do certain things. If they do not have the correct equipment for a task, (budgetary restrictions) have not trained for or performed a task (no boats in the desert, so no waterborne ops) or have not been properly trained (one team member "read an article once" is not enough) then you as the Chief or Team Leader can be held legally responsible for any errors, accidents or injuries that occur.

The solution is to make a solid, logical and legally supported case for the equipment or training your team needs. If you are denied, then you are covered in the event of an accident or tragedy.

It is fashionable in some circles to decry the "militarization" of the police. Pointing to the Posse Comitatus Act of 1878, critics feel that that the blending of law enforcement jobs with military equipment and organization is an invitation to abuse and disaster. Perhaps. However, the jobs of both are changing. The police have to deal with seemingly

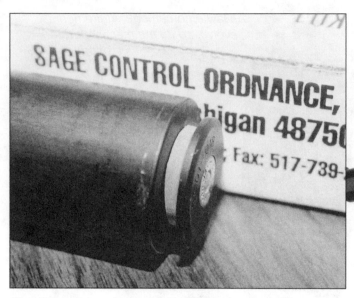

The Sage Control round extractor groove can be marked with a colored rubber band to indicate what kind it is.

If you carry spray, you must carry decon wipes. Otherwise you're risking exposure for which you have no remediation.

ever-greater and new threats, ones that were never thought of when beat cops were common. New problems and threats require new equipment, training, attitudes and organizations. For instance, if there is an overturned truck on fire, the first official on the scene is likely to be a police officer. It is his or her job to assess the situation, and call for assistance. But just what is going on? Just a bad driver who jack-knifed a semi for which the burning wreck needs a fire truck and an accident form for the daily paperwork? Or is it a toxic waste spill, and he'd better have a respirator along or be dead in an hour, week, day or month. Or is it the opening act of a terrorist cell using a Weapon of Mass Destruction? In which case he'd better have the respirator and a patrol rifle, for the offenders will be aggressive against attempts to stop the fire and contain the WMD. The problems for the military also flow into the law enforcement arena. Back when my father served, prisoners were disarmed and marched at gunpoint back to a collection point where the intelligence section could interrogate them. Now, they have to be restrained with handcuffs or cable ties, debriefed and their legal rights safeguarded (as much for P.R. reasons as legal). And just who are the combatants, anyway? Uniformed military? Para-military volunteers? Terrorists in civilian clothes? And not all situations are what the military had to deal with back when my father was in uniform: A group of protesters is coming ever closer to your checkpoint at an intersection in a third-World country. Can you use tear gas to drive them back? What if you spot an armed man in the group? May you fire upon him? A legal misstep could be cause for a court-martial, as well as causing the U.S. severe legal and public relations problems.

The police will adapt as needed, and as budgets and manpower allow. The military will adapt, also as needed, with less public scrutiny. And both will be adapting with legal oversight from the courts. After all, a degree in criminal justice or a state certification as a peace officer doesn't take a year (or more) of study and supervised training because handcuffing suspects is such a difficult task. No, the time is mostly spent learning the law and its specifics for your jurisdiction. Can you recite the requirements you need to justify a Terry stop? (do you even know what it is?) Can you recite the steps in the force continuum in the departmental Use of Force policy, the threshold of each and the allowed response? The Courts oversee the results, and refine their interpretations of the Law and the restrictions under which our police must act. As long as that happens, I'm not too worried about the East Podunk SRT mounting a coup. When I see National Guard troops manning the drunk driving checkpoints, then I'll find out what happened while I was chained to the word processor.

Less lethal

Not all force is lethal, or even has the potential. You are not going to talk someone to death (although you can talk someone into it.) because mere words are not lethal instruments. Sometimes persuasion,

Chemical irritants for restraint require training. And come in many sizes.

however, requires more than just words. For that, the miracles of modern science are working to produce improved persuaders. In discussion of these, it might seem to some that we're descending into "weasel word" territory. Not so. The reason a beanbag round, or a flashbang are referred to as "less lethal" instruments, and not non-lethal is because the Law and the citizenry expect words to have meaning. If you advertise your product as "non-lethal" and, after it has been used a million times, someone dies as a result of its use, you're in trouble. After all, you said it was non-lethal, right? And someone died, right? So were you trying to fool everyone in order to sell more product; or were you negligent in not testing it sufficiently?

So, since it is theoretically possible (and in some instances has happened) that someone might die as a result of the use of the product, anyone who makes persuaders other than firearms advertise them as "less lethal." And that's what police departments call them.

Tears, noise and light

Chemicals can be formulated to many wondrous things. They can clean our clothes, they can make our lawns green, and they can stop you in your tracks from noise, light or smell. On the chemical irritant front, the greatest thing since sliced bread is oleoresin capsicum, the active ingredient in OC pepper spray. Using the active agent in hot peppers it is so irritating that seeing is almost impossible, breathing is tough, and the pain is quite intense. The basic measure of a pepper's "heat" is the Scovill Unit, and the peppers you eat have ratings in the hundreds. OC pepper spray usually has ratings in the millions. In the early days we worried about who had higher numbers, who had a higher concentration, and which worked better. They all either work or not. Yes, there are some few individuals who seem able to shrug off (or at least keep active for a short while) when exposed to OC pepper spray. I'm not one of them.

There are a bunch of less-lethal impact rounds, left to right they are: twelve gauge pancake, twelve gauge sock, 37mm sock, 37mm soft baton. They all suffer in comparison to the Sage Ordnance rounds.

The hot ticket now (you'll pardon the pun) is a sufficient concentration of active ingredient, mixed with marker dyes, and or foaming agents to prevent quick washing. You can have your choice of spray or stream, mixtures of both, and varying size units. The basic unit that fits on a belt would be one like the Fox Labs FIVEpointTHREE in the 56-gram size. Small enough to fit in a belt pouch like the Uncle Mikes OD pouch, it has enough OC spray to get the job done on several people, or allow you to determine they aren't going to stop, and you need to be doing something else. At 5.3 million Scovill Units, and 2 percent active ingredient, it will do the job. The ultra-violet tracing dye will continue to identify the recipient even after the OC has been washed off.

For larger applications, there are larger units. In the top range for individual use is the 16-ounce bottle, the size of a medium thermos bottle. You can go even bigger, but when you get to measurements starting in the multi-gallon range, you need help handling it.

And if you carry OC spray, you must have a decon wipe handy. It will be a rare incident in which OC is used, where all involved are not sprayed to some extent. You can get backsplash just from an offender raising a hand and deflecting the stream. And if you

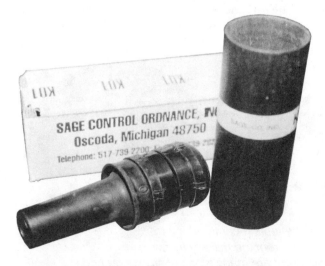

The practice rounds can be reloaded many times, for ultra-cheap marksmanship skills maintenance.

The Sage SL-1 and SL-6, with a Blackhawk carry case for ready deployment. (Courtesy Blackhawk Industries.)

The Sage round is 40mm, comes out of a rifled bore, and can hit like the hammer of Thor. I've been able to strike 80-yard targets with boring regularity with an SL-6.

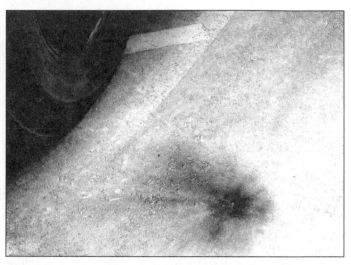

This is the flash mark of an NFDD on the pavement. They don't burst, but they're still hazardous.

One wag has joked "they can't make flashbangs any smaller, they couldn't get all the warnings on them." NFDDs are not backyard fireworks for the 4th of July. They are serious tools, and require training to use properly.

spray late, then you'll get tackled by someone who has just been hosed by OC pepper spray. Lucky you.

Impact

The basic impact tool is the nightstick, but they are falling out of favor. One wrong move, or an offender who reacts differently, and you could find yourself calling an ambulance to treat a fractured skull, instead of filling out a Use of Force report on the offenders bruised arm or fractured hand. Using a stick also forces you to get close enough to strike, always a drawback. The initial response was the development of the "sock" projectile. Using a shotgun shell, loaded with a much-lighter powder charge, a cotton or canvas sock (a "beanbag") full of lead powder is thrown at the offender at a low enough velocity to cause pain and require compliance. However, the shotgun approach has several problems. First, the projectile is relatively light, and has to be launched at a high velocity (for a non-penetrating projectile) to work. If it goes too fast, the injury can be severe. Too slow, and it doesn't work. Due to the high velocity, some targets are off-limits. The only

acceptable areas are the abdomen and the upper legs. One variant of the projectile is the flat beanbag. It is rolled into a cylinder to be inserted in the shotgun shell. When fired, it opens and unfolds. Except when it doesn't. And when it doesn't, it may penetrate the offender's body. The greatest drawback is the selective nature of the ammunition. That is, lethal and less lethal may be fired from the same shotgun. What if there is a mix-up? There have been. The result is either a less-lethal incident turning into a lethal one, or a lethal incident where the less-lethal ammo may cause more problems. Additionally, an offender who sees the shotgun, who may not know or believe it is loaded with less-lethal ammunition, may precipitate violence because he views the police as escalating the confrontation.

A better option is to use something intimidating but which is not viewed as a "gun" in the usual sense. Sage Ordnance makes two, the single shot SL-1 and the repeating SL-6. The projectile is a soft-rubber faced bullet the size of a small man's fist. Just looking down the wrong end is intimidating, and getting hit by one is not at all fun. But due to the

One of the tools recently come over from the military to law enforcement are many types of smoke grenades. Sometimes you have to hide, or hide something, from view.

Carrying an NFDD, you need more than pockets. This Blackhawk case snugly holds a training dummy. For the real thing, I'd tape the ring, but then I'm a belt and suspenders kind of guy.

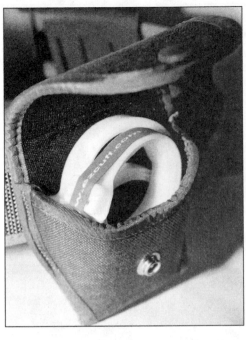

The single cable EZ-Cuff fits three to an Uncle Mikes handcuff case.

frontal size of the bullet, there is almost no chance of penetration. (Never say never, it may be brought up in court.) With six quick shots on hand, and the ability to reload the gun in a lot less than a minute, anyone who sees it will probably comply right away.

Grenades

Noise, gas, stinging smoke and combinations of these elements are available by just tossing a small cylinder. The basic grenade used by police is the "flashbang" or NFDD. "Non-Fragmenting Distraction Device" is the official term. Loud, as in 175 decibels (where a gunshot is "only" 145) and producing a million candlepower, the flashbang distracts and stuns just about everyone in the room. The non-fragmenting part of the title is important. There are fragmenting distraction devices, but they are too dangerous to use in a civilian context. It is bad enough being too close to an NFDD, but the FDD can cause serious harm. The NFDD body is very heavy and stoutly constructed, and the reactive chemical compound cannot generate enough force to break the grenade casing. Instead, the explosion is vented through the ports on top and bottom. The principle is simple: make a loud enough noise, and a bright enough flash,

and the offenders/suspects will be stunned for a few moments, long enough to conduct the raid in comparative safety. At 175 decibels (where a gunshot is 145, and 3 decibels is a doubling of the noise) a flashbang can be quite disorienting. At a million candlepower, it can dazzle your eyesight indoors even in day time. Outdoors, the flash isn't much. But flashbangs are still dangerous. There have been several incidents of officers being injured from a NFDD going off in their holder or hand, due to handling errors. Personally, I tape rings and insert the grenade into the carrier with the spoon on the inside. I have met many officers who do not tape the rings, but they all carry them with the spoon inside the pouch.

Handcuffs

If you don't think handcuffing someone is a "use of force" you've obviously never tried to restrain a non-compliant suspect. The traditional metal cuffs are

Grenades need carry pouches, even this rubber ball sting grenade used as a distraction device. (Courtesy Blackhawk Industries)

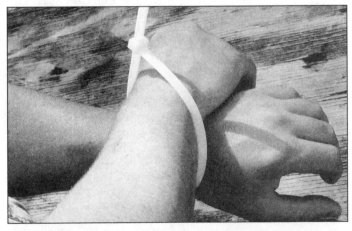

Electricians cable ties have nothing on EZ-Cuffs. The EZ Cuffs are larger, longer, less likely to cause injury, and virtually unbreakable.

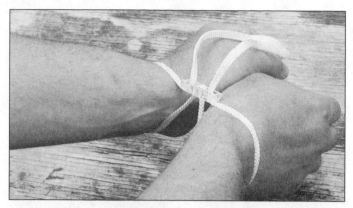

Tuff-Ties are flexible restraints that are ultra-compact.

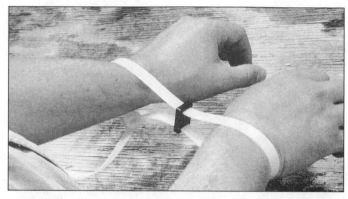

The modifieds are single-cable cuffs with an adapter that allows for hands-parallel cuffing.

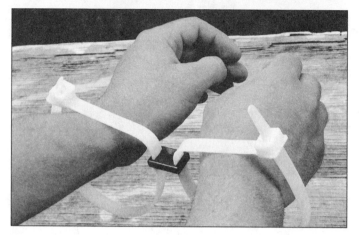

The double-cable EZ Cuffs.

You can fit four or more tuff Ties in a handcuff case.

heavy, bulky, noisy and can be used as a weapon if the suspect gets the upper hand on you. The newer alternative is plastic. One, the EZ Cuff, is made of synthetic and looks like the standard electrician's cable tie. Indeed, many use cable ties as cuffs, but you shouldn't. First, cable ties are made to hold wiring, and are not designed for more strength than wiring requires. Cable ties can be too easily abraded or broken. Second, cable ties are thinner, and it is more likely that a suspect who is restrained by cable ties can injure himself than with the thicker EZ Cuffs. The EZ Cuffs come in several styles, single-loop, single loop with a center bar, and double loop. The advantages are that the single loop is much more compact, the double loop offers a higher level of restraint (by placing the hands parallel, the offender is less able to offer resistance). The downsides are that the single loop affords the suspect more flexibility in hand location and movement (unless you tighten the restraint to the point of risking injury) and the double loop model is larger and bulkier. The single loop with the center bar is the compromise between the two.

The single loops are so compact that you can roll them up and secure them with a wide rubber band, and stuff three into an uncle Mikes handcuff case. Or slide a pair of each into the two slots in the shoulder suspension of an SOE Gear CQB vest. Yes, they stick up behind you unless you tuck them out of the way,

but you can have four restraints in your vest at no extra bulk or weight.

Another approach to the non-metallic restraint is the Tuff-Tie. Instead of synthetic cable ties, the Tuff Tie uses synthetic rope and plastic sliders. The Tuff-Tie offers less bulk, and greatly reduced possibility of injury.

No restraint system is perfect and all can be defeated. I've even heard of (and tested myself) methods of breaking metal handcuffs that could be done with relative ease and little fuss.

The future

Much budget, time and brainpower are being spent on new approaches to restraint and control. The ideal is the Star Trek "phaser set on stun" that could knock someone out from a distance. From microwave or radio wave transmitters that cause unbearable heating of the skin, to objectionable smells and audio barrages that would compel a crowd to leave an area, ingenious experimenters are seeking answers. And as soon as they come up with something, enterprising offenders will be seeking countermeasures. After all, we've been in this cycle of tool and countertool for as long as we've been out of the trees. It isn't likely to end anytime soon.

Chapter 2

The Uniform Ensemble and Convergence

HERE IN THE United States we have a tradition of the separation of the military from the civil law-enforcement operations. In many countries the police are the Judicial Police or the Railway Police or the Name-a-Category Police, while the "real" police are the National Police, who are part of the military. Indeed, there may be Soldiers, Marines or Sailors walking the streets enforcing the laws and keeping the peace. In some countries, there are only The Police, like Germany. There isn't a "city police" department, (except for a couple of the big ones) and an officer can transfer from one city to another without loss of seniority. But Germany is a small country compared to the United States. The start for us was our experience with the soldiers of the British Crown in the 18th Century. Those of you who

Coastal patrols require different gear than street cops, and the uniform identifies the officer.

remember history will recall that there are some seemingly strange things in the Bill of Rights. The Third Amendment prohibits quartering soldiers in private homes. Why? What? How'd that get in there? Simple, to stretch the budget, and keep an eye on locals who might otherwise cause trouble, the Army of King George III would quarter soldiers in people's homes. The homeowner was expected to feed the soldier or soldiers, and put them up each night. As a means of keeping the locals under control, it worked. However, after the Revolution no one wanted a repeat of that so it was prohibited. Later, in 1878 came the Posse Comitatus Act, which forbade the use of military personnel in the enforcement of civil authority. No Army troops were allowed to keep the peace in towns in the West. (Or, more to the point, in the Reconstruction South.) As a matter of fact, the Army (and the Navy and Marines, and later the Air Force) is very careful about not letting individuals build fiefdoms. No one can stay posted or in command of a unit long enough to build a personal following.

This is very much unlike police departments, where someone might spend an entire career in one department, or one division of a department. Why is no one worried? (Well, some are, but for reasons of efficiency, not political coups) Simple, no one is going to mount a coup on the City of Bellweather using the Bellweather Police Department as their stepping-stone. But the separation of powers is more than just something we insist on at the Federal level, it is something that happens at all levels. Thus we have the apparently crazy-quilt pattern of overlapping territory, jurisdictions and staffing. County, City and State Police, Federal organizations for every category, and even private security in some locales all have different jobs and jurisdictions because a unified department would be fraught with the potential of too much authority in one place. When you get down to it, we like our law enforcement entities small, fractured and under the control of the locally elected officials.

A company of MPs in Fallujah, Iraq, about to conduct a raid. The weapon pointed over the wall is a shotgun. Every soldier whose vest front we can see has handcuffs. How different is this from the bad parts of Detroit, Phoenix or Los Angeles? (U.S. Army photo)

job, why have it? Two examples would be the PEQ-2 (or PEQ-4) laser targeting designator, and handcuffs. The PEQ-2 is used to mark a target so it can be given the attention of something falling out of the sky, like that one-ton package of explosives. Or, painting a vehicle, bunker or machinegun position so someone with NVG can then whack it with a guided missile or cannon. It has no use in the law enforcement community primarily because you/we don't blow things up. And, it is too powerful to pass the eye-safe requirements for non-military use.

Handcuffs are a police thing. Once apprehended, the suspect or offender is to be controlled, searched, transported and detained. He is to be treated with dignity, and not allowed to harm himself or others. His Miranda Rights must be protected and the evidence safeguarded. In a military context outside of the special ops raid, prisoners can be detained in the short term by pointing weapons at them. Shoved behind a barbed wire fence, they are kept in place and quiet by the threat of getting shot. (I know, I know, it is a kinder and gentler age. But everyone involved knows what the situation is, and no one expects to be read their International Miranda Rights. But in a generation or two, who knows.)

The important thing is to know what the job requires, what the law allows and what the boss expects. And to square those three with what it takes to go home at night in one piece. As a bonus for some, looking good in uniform aids in the process.

Uniform ensemble

We need clothes. Besides preserving our modesty (trust me, there are some people you just don't want to see naked) clothing protects us from the elements and makes quick identification possible. Clothing, and its adjuncts, also provides us with pockets. Pockets are one of those "what do you mean someone had to invent them?" products that we take so for granted that we never think about it. Well, someone did, and we should thank them. The clothing of feudal Japan had no pockets. A samurai would have various small pouches or bags hanging from his belt, or things pinned to his clothes. The objects he actually carried were few, the rest were left to servants. There were no pockets on Togas, so those Roman Senators all required servants to carry "stuff" for them. Indeed, you could trace the development of pockets and their integration into clothing right along with the general improvement of the social structure, and the production and accumulation of small, valuable possessions. Until wallets, watches

And in the early days of the police, the jobs of cops and soldiers were very much different. Keeping the local thugs from forming and profiting from a protection racket in the slums of a big city is entirely different than making sure your infantry company is trained to receive a mounted charge. A century later, the job of raiding drug houses is still different than that of preparing your unit for an armored assault. The jobs stayed separate for a long time, until police departments started forming special teams to deal with a barricaded gunman, and the military started forming special teams to handle jobs requiring more delicacy than an infantry company could manage. Now, a raid team that goes into a slum to apprehend the operators of a meth lab has more in common with a raid team detailed to snatch a terrorist leader than either have in common with their parent organizations. But their parent organizations are still very different.

Which brings us to our present project. While the two teams have much in common, they still have many differences. For one, the city raid team will ride in panel trucks or vans, using streetlights and headlights for illumination. The special operations team going to snatch a terrorist will ride in helicopters, guided by GPS-aided navigation and night-vision optics. And should the special operations team get in trouble, they can count on artillery, air support or guided missiles, where the city team will have to get on the radio and call in their backup, which is another team. Whether the job is getting a 2,000-pound bomb dropped on target, or getting into a drug lab before the evidence can be destroyed, some things will be the same. Some things are very, very different, however, and as much as something might be "cool," if it doesn't serve a useful purpose for your

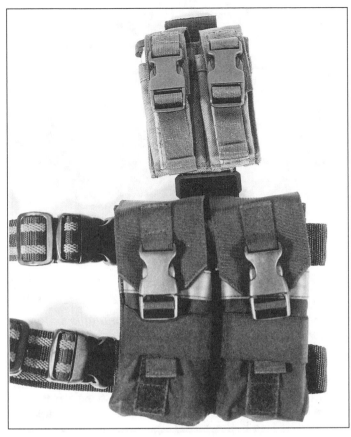

You can mix and match your web gear to build what you need. This Blackhawk thigh rig for 5.56mm magazines has an SOE Gear dual pistol pouch on top.

First-line gear includes the essentials: a sidearm, spare ammo, badge, things like that.

and keys became common, just what would you have carried in these new-fangled pockets, anyway?

Clothes in post-Roman European cultures also lacked pockets for a long time. But we now have them, and should use them appropriately. Belts have a longer history. After all, a belt is just an improved rope. Belts can hold many things, but belts have their limits. One limit is weight. Too much weight and your belt won't stay up without being too tight. And belts are not limitless. Those of us who have a discernable waistline find that a belt only holds so much, and then you are back to using pockets. A duty belt on my waist will comfortably hold a holster, magazine pouch, cuff case, light holder, OC pepper spray holder, radio and pager. If I'm to carry more, I have to use pockets or the gearbag in the patrol car. My friend Jeff Chudwin, who is shorter and has a smaller waist, can't even fit all that.

When it comes to the extra equipment that a tactical team has to carry, belts just aren't enough. Thus the use of web gear modified from the military, or equipment vests. From head to toe, the uniform and equipment is and must be tailored not just to the officer who wears it, but the climate, mission and threat. As a result, there is no single "standard-issue" even within departments or military units. A four-man entry team may have four different uniform ensembles on, and on the next mission some may change. And yet, some things will remain the same. To show the gear, I've modeled as many variations as I can, and described those that I can't.

The uniform ensemble consists of uniform shirt and trousers, headgear or helmet w/balaclava, web gear, gloves, boots and protective gear such as elbow and kneepads and ballistic vest, and eye and ear protection.

Uniform

Everyone needs a uniform. Whether you're one of the Pope's Swiss Guards, LAPD SWAT, or the newest guy on the recently formed East Podunk Special Response Team, you need a uniform. Yes, for the pockets, and for the prestige, but also for identification.

The origins of uniforms go back centuries in Europe, and much longer if you include the Romans. Each Legionnaire was issued a red cloak, and body armor, and each Legion had distinctive emblems for the shield, standards and totems. The idea was to build unit cohesion, and to make friend or foe identification easy on the battlefield. When warfare was you and the five guys from your tribe versus the six guys for the neighboring tribe, identification was simple. You knew everyone by sight. The Romans fought in battles with tens of thousands on each side. The SWAT uniform in the early days was blue or black, and made on the same pattern as the military Battle Dress Uniform. Blue, because it was a traditional police color, or black, to give the SWAT

Notice the pockets on the sleeves. Also, the Aimpoint sight, the multi-tool pouch and the weaponlight. (DoD photo)

The Blackhawk Talonflex tactical thigh carrier is super-fast for a reload, and lets you carry two spare mags along with a flash-bang. Modern, useful, and way cool.

team a means of unit identification. Recognizing climate and terrain differences, or wishing to differentiate themselves, many police departments have changed from the early standard. One path is to simply use woodland camouflage pattern sets. It makes sense, especially for rural teams. Some Sheriff's departments go with plain green, and use the black of the web gear to create a camo effect. One approach I've seen is to take white-background woodland camo pattern and wash them with a blue dye or black dye. The result is a "blue camo" or "black camo" effect. In all cases, the idea is to make the team instantly identifiable as both a team and a law enforcement unit. It also provides some small measure of concealment. A tactical team operating in a desert environment, or a desert city with a lot of stucco buildings, would be well-served having chosen tan or desert pattern uniforms. Emblazoned on the front and back are large patches with "SWAT" or "POLICE" or "SHERIFF" on them, as additional identifiers. In some cases it is not immediately obvious that a group of black-clad armed men are "The Police." In some cities, home invasion is a problem, and law-abiding residents have been known to resist entry by individuals lacking identification.

Uniforms are not all the same, either. They come in many sizes, and not all are readily available. Me, I need trousers in medium/extra tall. My friends Ed Mohn of Libertyville and Al Kulovitz late of the Cook County Sheriff Police each make me look like a skinny little point guard. At 6'6" and 6'8" respectively, their uniforms require yards of cloth. And they have heard all the jokes, as have similar large officers in every other department I've ever worked with. When selecting colors, a unit or department has to take into account the size of their officers and the climate in which they operate. Getting trousers custom tailored can be expensive, especially when you shred them monthly in training or operations.

The basic battle dress uniform (BDU) needs some modifications, and the new Marine Corps uniforms are a step in that direction. The pockets are not all useful. The two bellows cargo pockets on the trousers aren't much use (and can be uncomfortable) with tactical thigh rigs in place. With a holstered pistol clamped right over it, you can't do much with a cargo pocket. Ditto the upper BDU blouse pockets, with a tactical vest on over them. The lower pockets on the BDU blouse also aren't much use. Anything heavy will bounce around when you walk or run. Anything light will get crushed when you go prone. Units in

One essential for any uniform is identification.

Helmets are now an essential gear item. In the old days, a riot gear-up called for pulling motorcycle helmets out of the lockers. They never offered much protection, so now the PASGT gets the call.

many cases are now taking their uniforms to a tailor and having the trouser cargo pockets removed, and adding pockets on the sleeves. The BDU blouse/jacket is replaced with a uniform-type shirt in the same pattern or color as the BDU trousers, tucked into the trousers. If the lower blouse pockets aren't useful, why have them?

Headgear

At the simplest, a baseball cap with the departmental name or logo on it will serve as headgear. For some rural departments, a boonie hat, or a cowboy hat might be selected, since rain and sun are more of an environmental consideration than merely a comfort consideration. Some departments use the Army Ranger cap, and some use helmets.

Helmet

In the modern age of plastics (know called "polymer" for more panache) a steel helmet is out of date. In the early days of SWAT teams, helmets were either fiberglass motorcycle helmets, or the steel helmets left over from WWII. Neither offered a lot of protection, but they offered protection against the impacts an entry team was likely to face: blunt objects and stationary objects. A fiberglass motorcycle helmet will not survive a hit from a ball peen hammer, but the wearer will. And in the chaos and confusion of a raid, things get thrown and fall. If you are just wearing a snazzy hat or beret, and something as prosaic as a book falls off a shelf and hits you on the head, you could end up sidelined. However, a motorcycle helmet offers no ballistic protection at all.

The PASGT helmet is a great leap forward. While heavy, it offers protection against more than just impacts. That ball peen hammer that trashed the motorcycle helmet would bounce off a PASGT. The PASGT helmet is layered Kevlar bonded with industrial-strength epoxy. The shape was the result of a great deal of testing and offers added neck protection while not interfering with hearing. (Yes, it looks so much like the German helmets of WWI and

The pockets on this SOE Gear vest can be used for rifle magazines, or any other object that is needed and fits. Pockets are fine for wallets and money, but real gear requires web gear.

WWII that it was nicknamed the "fritz" helmet.) It is strong enough to offer ballistic protection. In almost every combat since its adoption, there have been news stories of soldiers whose helmets stopped rifle bullets, saving their lives.

If your department has helmets, authorizes helmets, or can buy them, wear them. Yes they are heavy. Yes they make it tough to fit radio headsets, hearing protection and the other communication essentials of modern police work, but I can tell you from personal experience that getting hit in the head is no fun. It hurts, it interferes with your performance, and if you bleed on stuff it can be tough to get the stains out. Seriously, it is the cheapest insurance you or your department can purchase.

In addition to helmets, teams that raid drug labs often wear a nomex balaclava. A tight-fitting hood, the balaclava protects from flash burns that might happen if the flammable vapors of the lab are accidentally ignited. They also cover the face from identification, a bone of contention in some circles. Team members who day after day raid drug labs are not happy with their faces always being seen. (Of course, when court testimony is required, the Judge won't allow a hood, but that is a different matter.) Civil libertarians and some tacticians object to anonymous teams, as they present a potential problem of accountability.

Web gear

The idea of web gear is to create more pockets. However, just more pockets isn't enough. Some equipment is so bulky a pocket won't suffice. And other equipment is so abrasive that a pocket would quickly tear. And, if your pockets are built into your uniform, and you are handed some new piece of equipment to carry that doesn't fit any pocket, what do you do? Change to a uniform with the correct pockets? No, change your web gear.

First, you have to consider what level of equipment is appropriate for each level of web gear. The military has refined the concept to First, Second and Third Line gear. Some units expand that to more levels, and carried far enough you can consider the precinct house as just another level of gear. (Although one you don't have to carry, thank God.)

In the military context, First Line gear is that which is worn daily, and should include the gear necessary for your survival in an emergency. Escape and evasion, a sudden attack, a downed chopper (for pilots) are typical emergencies. First Line gear is your uniform and boots, ID, personal medical equipment, compass and, if issued or authorized, a sidearm. Prudent troopers include, when able, a knife and or a

The SOE Gear empty magazine bag can serve many uses. And the elastic top makes it easy to access.

multi-tool such as a Leatherman. All this goes on when you get dressed in the morning. (If your job description precludes a shower and bed, then you probably don't take off the Second Line gear, either.) If you do not often go to Second Line gear (a firebase radio operator, for example) then some items that are often carried on the Second Line get shifted to the First. A wound dressing would be just such an item. It

Second-line gear includes the extras: the rifle, ammunition for it, wound dressing, etc.

My friend Bill Jeans with his vest design, all duded up for a raid or training. His vests, and his teachings, are both first-rate.

Night Vision Gear. Sometimes you have to have it. Most of the time it sits in its box and waits.

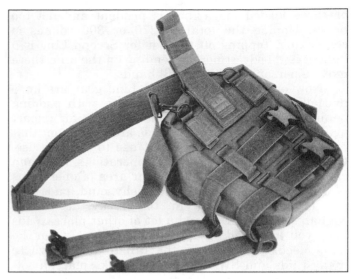

Blackhawk Industries makes a gas mask bag that works in four or five other capacities; it can also hold ammo, evidence, camera, lunch, first aid supplies or anything else that fits. And go on your leg, belt, vest or over your shoulder.

must be with you all the time, so it is best on your First Line gear, even if it is more comfortably lashed to your Second Line. Ditto a multi-tool. If your job is cutting open cartons, stringing wire and building or shelter maintenance, you have a toolbox. But faced with a problem that needs attention now, and a toolbox "over there" a multi-tool is a great thing to have. If you feel the need, a big knife is comforting. But many find a big knife gets in the way on base, and leave it attached to the Second Line. A compass, for many, is relegated to the same location as the big knife. Personally, having talked to too many people who've gotten lost, (and been "turned around" myself a few times) a compass is a First Line essential. A personal flashlight would go on First Line, with an extra weapon-mount light as Second Line. And let us not forget that ID includes a meal ticket, blood chit and other accouterments of civilization.

Second Line gear includes all the things you need to do your job in a firefight. For a basic Infantry trooper or Marine, that means web gear with canteen or canteens, a rifle, grenades, personal radio and more ammo. The grenade list would include several fragmentation, smoke, white phosphorus and CS/CN. For some squad members, it includes the unit radio. For others, it is all that plus the extra ammo for the squad machinegun, or rounds for the mortar, or explosives to be used when you arrive at your objective. The Second line also includes a canteen or two, with water purification tablets, strobe light, big knife, gloves, extra pistol magazines, map, compass (if you don't have it already) and a GPS unit. For the low cost, and extreme usefulness, a GPS is a modern essential. Even if not issued, personal purchase is prudent. In modern warfare and sweeps for terrorist units, the addition of "zip strips" is a new one. Tough plastic strips take the place of heavy, clanking handcuffs. Second Line gear should also include extra First Aid supplies, for yourself and for others. A useful item of web gear for units expecting lots of action is a dump bag or empty magazine pouch. Ammunition is relatively easy to get. Extra magazines are not. When

you expend a magazine, a designated bag or pouch is where you dump it. A spent magazine pouch makes thing so much more organized than the way my father did it in Northern France and Germany. He stashed the empty magazine down the front of his shirt until he could tend to it.

With a dump bag, when you get a chance, you can reload the mags without having to re-trace your steps and look for the magazines. One question that always comes up for Second Line gear is "how much ammo?" The only answer is "enough." The basic load of seven magazines in issue mag pouches totaling 210 rounds is a minimum. In Afghanistan when our troops went to rescue a downed chopper and ended up fighting through the night and the next day, one trooper involved fired more than 400 rounds of rifle ammunition. For the weight, an extra pouch with two

In hot weather, nothing beats a Camelbak for keeping you going.

or three loaded magazines is prudent and not too heavy. Upping the total to 270 or 300 rounds is comforting. Topping off the list for Second Line is a helmet and body armor. Depending on the unit, there may be personal radios for all hands.

New on the list for Second Line gear are knee and elbow pads. Some are composite, with padding behind and a tough plastic shell outside for impact against rocks and such. The pads are equipment that migrated from law enforcement use to military use. On a lot of locales for military operations, knee and elbow pads aren't needed. If your area of operations is composed mostly of soft, squishy mud, pads just get in the way. But in the rocky deserts of Afghanistan and Iraq, and a lot of other places, pads keep you from ending up on the sidelines when the team needs you. And in the urban jungles where many raids and SWAT operations take place, a soft place to kneel is a rare thing.

Third Line gear. The living stuff that keeps the elements off you, sustains you and provides extra duration for the unit once you arrive wherever you are packing it. All the Third Line gear goes in or on a rucksack or pack. In cold weather, a sleeping bag. In warm weather, a blanket, in the jungle, a mosquito net. Food, extra water, extra batteries for your gear like the GPS unit you have, unit equipment, all go in or on. Extra ammunition is placed in a bandoleer. Your entrenching tool, and if issued, saw, axe and machete (or divided among the squad) along with rope, 550 cord and tape. Extra rations, water and in cold weather a small stove go into the rucksack. In a rainy climate, a poncho or Goretex parka gets strapped to the outside. And last but not least, extra clothing such as socks, your personal maintenance gear, razor, toothbrush, soap, foot treatment powders, pads and tape.

Whew!

But wait, there's more. Add to all that the mission-specific team gear, not all of which goes on every mission. Night vision gear (NVG). (Some might be Second Line anyway.) One-time message pads, extra batteries for the radios, NVG, GPS, flashlights,

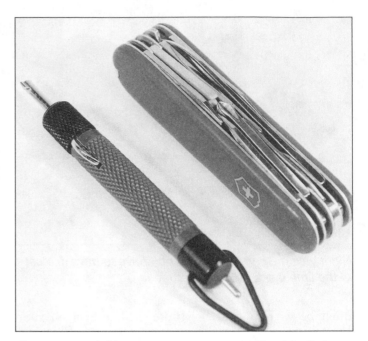

Some essential items are not very sexy, like this Swiss Army knife and handcuff key.

strobe, and PDA or laptop computer. Demolition equipment, explosives, blasting caps, tape, wire, blasting charts and initiators. Maps. Claymore mines (some of which may be in both Second and Third Line.) trip flares, trip wire kits, gas mask, parachute, dive gear, rappeling harness and rope, the list is larger than you'd think.

Fourth Line is an expansion of the gear a unit needs in the field, and is kept back at the base. In a deployment, it is kept in the tents or barracks. When you are not in the field, some may be stored in unit lockers or secured storage. Fourth Line gear includes extra uniforms, PT clothes and shoes, civilian clothes and personal effects. Obviously, in a deployment to some Third World location, PT clothes and civvies will be at a minimum. Fourth Line also includes duffel bag and barracks bag or bags, extra web gear

Even in daylight it can get dark in many places. Bring a light. Better yet, bring two.

Through a night vision device, the world appears green.

not used at the moment, (extra mag pouches, grenade pouches, etc) footlockers and padlocks.

And you are correct if you think that a lot of this is left behind at times. A prudent and experienced trooper will divest himself of all non-essential gear. One of my earliest recollections of my father's stories of WWII was when he knew they were going back to the front to relieve a brand-new unit: "The ditches were littered with gas masks, spare boots, BAR bipods, and all the other stuff that was too heavy and not needed." In today's warfare, there is less walking, and more helicopter transport. But still too much gear.

Law enforcement

How does all this relate to a tactical law enforcement team? The biggest difference is that for a tac team, the First and Second Line gear are pretty much one set. A team member is not going to spend very much time with just First Line gear on, except in a training environment. If they are gearing up, they go all the way to Second Line. However, some aspects of military gearing aren't relevant. When going on a raid, it isn't necessary to pack two canteens per man. (Unless you're doing a raid on a remote location in Arizona, for example.) Also, the extreme ammunition requirements aren't there. Prior to September 11, 2001, if I was assigned a raid team, and each one of them showed up for the first training sessions in full gear with 300 rounds of rifle ammo, and with 50+ rounds of handgun ammo, we'd have a little talk. If they included fragmentation grenades, smoke, WP and CS/CN, we'd have a serious talk. Police officers are not expected to become engaged in firefights with opposing units of infantry. If a suspect or suspects puts up enough resistance to require high volumes of rifle fire, we should have backed off and waited them out. However, in the modern age, who knows? It may well be that a tactical team rolls on a callout to find that the "barricaded gunman" is a terrorist cell attempting to take over a sensitive facility, and a full-out gun battle is called for. (I still wouldn't be too keen on the frags and WP, and would want a letter from the Chief authorizing them and outlining the Departmental Use of Force Policy.)

A law enforcement tac team will all have personal radios, and probably cell phones and pagers as well. The tactical team would have zip strips and handcuffs, and the dump bag would be used as a quick-reaction evidence bag. One instance would be in a raid on a drug lab. The bad guy makes a poor career choice and shoots back, gets shot for his troubles, and in the shooting the reactant glassware gets hit and begins to burn. The team must pick him up and hustle out. His firearm? Pick it up, make sure it is "on safe" and put it in the dump pouch. Then follow the team out, or if an extra one is available, grab a fire extinguisher and battle the blaze.

Law enforcement Third Line gear is not stuff you carry, but rather keep in the vehicles. And in some cases, your "Third Line" is a backup team. Ditto mission-specific equipment. If you need NVG, then you put it on before you exit the station or vehicle.

Law Enforcement used to be blue. Now a lot of it is green or black. Boots, gloves, pads, armor, all things not seen two decades ago.

Demolition gear is constructed by your explosive entry expert before you go on the raid, and placed where needed during the raid. A covert entry on a raid calls for wedges, mirrors, poles and cameras, rope and lock picking equipment, all kept in the vehicle. (No one in his right mind would make a high-speed entry while schlepping an 8-foot video boom.)

And the Fourth Line? That is your regular uniform, your dress blues, extra gear divided between the station house locker and home. From here, we go on to the chapter on web gear, holster, vests (loadbearing) and pouches.

Gloves and boots

Basic gloves protect your hands. Basic boots protect your feet. Both keep your extremities warm in the cold, and hot in the warm weather. Plain leather or synthetic gloves offer some protection, and improved materials protect from flash burns (nomex) cuts (Kevlar and other synthetics) and even chemical exposure. Boots protect your feet from hazards on the ground or floors like nails and broken glass, and protect your feet when you have to use them as impact devices on doors or offenders. Additionally, some boots (BfR) and some inserts (Second Chance) offer protection against puncture, and blast from small explosive devices.

Protective gear

Elbows and knees can be injured from falls, impacts and obstacles. Your eyes can be injured from blast fragments, firearms ejecta (powder, shot wads, splashback from impacts). Continued exposure to flashbangs and gunfire can injure your hearing. Comfortable, inexpensive, effective protection for all are available, and anyone who does not avail himself of protection will sooner or later be injured. It will be an injury that could have been prevented. And ballistic vests can save you from knives, bullets, and even the impact of clubs, sticks, batons and fists and feet.

Gas masks keep you safe. Find a good way to carry one.

Respiratory

What's in the air in a drug lab? Mostly bad stuff. Some toxic, some cancerous, some merely very bad smelling. In many cases you'll need protection for your lungs and eyes, and maybe even a full protective suit. And when there might be fire, smoke, or other irritants, a respiratory filter can be more than just useful, it can mean getting the job done and going home in good health.

The complete ensemble

I kept a close eye on equipment and uniforms in the last few classes, and asked some team leaders for their mandatory and suggested equipment lists, and the typical (if there is such a thing) SRT member steps out of the vehicle equipped off the list at right.

One interesting item my friend Ed Mohn pointed out was that entry team shield members commonly leave their long gun in the vehicle in favor of a pair of sidearms. The second gun is then carried on the load-bearing vest. Why? One arm is fully occupied holding the shield. In the event of a shooting incident where the shieldman runs his gun dry, how is he going to reload, and hold up the shield? After all, if he ran dry, there has to be a significant amount of incoming. Dropping the shield would be unwise. And handling a long gun is out, so the drill is to drop or holster the first handgun, and do a New York Reload. (Draw a second weapon. Named thus from the habit of NYPD officers back in the revolver days who often carried a second or third wheelgun, in lieu of reloading from belt loops.)

As mentioned before, gearing up for a call-out is definitely a mix-and-match process. In the middle of a hot summer, a prudent team will have full Camelbaks and a pair of canteens. In winter, the first things that go on are thermal long johns, wool socks and waterproof boots. If the suspects are known to be violent, and willing to fight it out, then there will be a call for extra magazines, NFDD's including chemical and rubber grenades, shields and a cover team of precision marksmen. If the idea is to recon and be quiet, the team scout will sneak in with minimal equipment, to reduce noise and the possibility of getting snagged while sneaking around. The scout will be in uniform, vest, helmet and sidearm. All the bulky and heavy stuff is left behind, for if he turns a corner and walks into trouble, the team is within shouting distance and will be there in an instant, to settle the altercation in favor of the team and not the offender.

And jurisdictional policy decisions will sometimes dictate equipment, along with climate. If the Chief feels an AR-15 or M-16 is "too much gun" then the team is going to be armed with H-K MP-5s, shotguns and sidearms. If he is more progressive, the team will be loaded up with ARs or M-16s. The sidearm may be the standard departmental issue, and it may be one selected by the team.

Whatever the gear mix is, the important part of the ensemble is the part you can't see: training.

Mandated Call-out Gear:
BDU with departmental ID (shoulder patches, "Police" or "Sheriff" panels, etc.)
Ballistic helmet
Eye protection
Radio
Two weapons with two lights
Load-bearing Equipment, with:
Two extra magazines for the long gun
Two extra magazines for the sidearm, unless it is a 1911, then four extra magazines
Two distraction devices (flashbangs)
One small smoke grenade
Individual Trauma kit
One set regular Handcuffs, one set flex cuffs or cable ties
Gas mask
Boots
Ballistic vest (entry teams often add a trauma plate)
Knee pads

Optional Gear:
Elbow pads
Camelbak (except in Summer or in hot climates, then it is mandated)
Hearing protection (Personally, I'd make it mandatory, but I'm not in charge of a team)
Tactical knife, folding or fixed
Multi-tool
Gloves
Balaclava
Advanced Trauma kit

Extra Options:
Extra pair of prescription glasses, in protective case
Special meds, such as insulin, bee sting antivenin, etc
Ballistic groin protector

Chapter 3

Web Gear, Vests and Holsters

AS THE JOB of law enforcement changes and expands, there is more gear to carry. A regular uniform only has so many pockets, and most of the new stuff doesn't fit in them anyway. (Find a set of

To carry it all you need more than just pockets. Web gear and/or a vest let you pack what you need. (You bet I look tired. When this photo was taken, it was 4 p.m., I'd been up since 5 a.m., and it was 92 degrees in the shade. And you can see how much shade I've got.)

uniform trousers with pockets that will accept a radio larger than a pager. Go ahead.) Since the special operations teams aren't going to be wearing standard uniforms anyway, the extra pockets on BDUs might be useful. But they aren't. Stuff a Motorola radio in a cargo pocket and try to run across the street. If your own radio doesn't leave bruises, the laughter from those watching will sting; especially if running slings the radio out of your pocket and across the street ahead of you. No, in order to carry it all, you need a system better than pockets. And there are limits to the duct tape approach. You need web gear or a vest.

You also need the best you can get. There is nothing more expensive than cheap gear that wears out or fails you. Even if you aren't put at risk, cheap gear simply has to be replaced again when it wears out, while the "expensive" gear just keeps on working. In the old days, we had a few choices; we could use USGI gear, or we could use even cheaper knock-offs and imitations. Why is GI stuff (at least in the old days) so bad? Thank the "Lowest bidder" acquisition process. Rather than construct mag pouches (as one example) to a high enough standard to make them last, they were simply made inexpensively and treated as if they were practically disposable. Ever looked over a table full of surplus, scrapped GI M-16 magazine pouches? I have. Once you get past the faded color, the torn flaps, the busted corners and the rusted hardware, you notice that even the ones that aren't broken are heavily worn.

The new gear makers all used stuff like that. The owners and staff at the three makers I look to first, (in the order I discovered them) Blackhawk Industries, London Bridge Trading Company and Special Operations Equipment, all used issue gear. And all hated it when it failed them. And all make new gear so tough you really have to go out of your way to make it fail. They sell to the people who took over their military jobs when they left, They know what the job entails, and They know what happens when gear fails. You, the consumer and law enforcement officer, can take advantage of that attitude and knowledge. No, you are not likely to ever have to bail out of an armored personnel carrier to assault an objective, or parachute to your area of operation, but you can be

The Tek-Lok from Blade Tech is a non-rusting attachment system to secure pouches or tools to belts, vests or web gear.

A MOLLE vest worn by an Air Force Sergeant, with a PRC-148 radio mounted on it. He doesn't have many ammo pouches on, but then his "main gun" is circling overhead. (DoD photo)

sure that any gear built to do those jobs will give you years of exemplary service. All top-quality gear makers charge well for their products, and all will be close in price. For example, a tactical thigh rig for M-16 magazines will cost you around $60 to $75. (2003 prices) You could save some money by finding someone who makes and sells them for only $40, but the money saved is not much. And a year after you bought your "deal" gear, when you're replacing your busted gear, the money you "saved" back then will have been spent on something you can't remember.

How is it that the new gear, more expensive as it is, gets past the "lowest bidder" process? Simple. The military Special Operations community, to avoid being bogged down in the glacially slow standard process, managed to get acquisition authority outside of the regular channels. (It happened in the early 1980s,

partly as a result of the debacle of the aborted Hostage Rescue in Iran.) One result was readily apparent in Afghanistan. Faced with the need to be mobile, the units involved simply bought a fleet of commercial pickup trucks. What would have taken months and months through the regular process took a week. Rather than draw issue gear from supply, and then have to draw more, or duct tape to repair it, those same military units just buy good stuff to start with. They tried new gear, and if it failed, either told the maker or stopped buying and using it. They bought more of what worked. The trickle down effect is that when the regular units see what the SpecOps people have, they start asking for it. Or just buy it themselves.

Web gear

The original (for our purposes, not historically) is the military method. A wide belt, with attached suspenders, and various pouches attached to the belt and suspenders. It is still a viable method. The introduction of plastics has made the gear slightly lighter, impervious to corrosion, and a little more comfortable. The Vietnam-era magazine pouch and canteen designs have some shortcomings. The material of which the pouches are made is a bit light (GI gear, not newly-designed by the makers mentioned), and quickly wears. The canteen pouch is lined with a synthetic "fur" that simply adds weight, especially when wet. Old-style suspenders are not padded well enough for the current heavier load of gear. If you go with the old style, get updated designs with better padding. Padding on the pistol belt (even though it won't have a pistol on it, that's what it is called) is also a great way to increase comfort.

The traditional web belt, suspenders and pouches is still able to do the job. (Courtesy Blackhawk Industries)

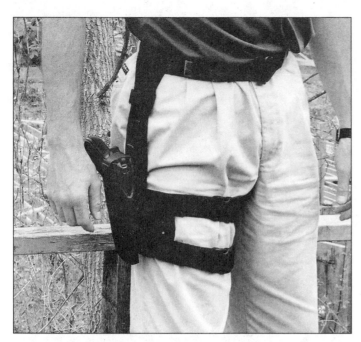

Sometimes you don't need much gear. For some work, this Blade Tech holster and a radio is enough.

A modular vest panel with pouches attached. (Courtesy Blackhawk Industries)

Blackhawk makes padded Alice gear that is much more comfortable to wear.

An old trick is to use electrical tape to reduce rattles. And to keep things from shifting. My brother Jim enlisted in the Army before going to College and signing up for ROTC. His plan was to get both an Education and a Commission. (He succeeded.) His description of the first ROTC formation was a scream: "There we were, 100 brand new ROTC cadets and three old hands. Their uniforms still smelled of the plastic bags they'd been stored in, and you could see the storage folds. Our uniforms were mismatched in the amounts they'd faded, and our gear had wrappings of electrical tape to keep it quiet. And darker sections on our uniform shoulders where we'd just taken off our old unit patches."

The belt and suspenders, with the pouches distributed comfortably, balanced and accessible, is then worn over the body armor. Somewhere on the armor or web gear, you need to mount a prominent "Police," "Sheriff," "Deputy" or "SWAT" patch for easy identification.

Tactical thigh rigs and holsters

What to do when you run out of waist space? This can be big problem for those of us who don't have a lot of real estate around our waist. In many cases a couple of mag pouches, a radio, some first aid gear and handcuffs pretty much use the length of a belt. With the even greater load carried by infantry or Marines, more storage is needed. The tactical thigh rig was an obvious solution. The thigh rig is not attached to the pistol belt of the web gear, but to the trouser belt. That way, even when you take off the Second Line gear you still have the pistol with you. Since a single pistol is sufficient, the other thigh can be used for first aid,

spare rifle magazines, grenades, etc. Which one you choose depends on your job description. If you are an infantry trigger-puller, the left thigh (assuming you're right-handed) is the place for four more rifle mags, or two more mags and a couple of grenades. Or a dump pouch. If not, then extra pistol mags and a first aid kit. A specialized application would be an explosives ordnance disposal (EOD) toolkit. A big toolbag is useful, but sometimes you don't need it all. So carry just the essentials on the thigh rig.

Two brands I've had very good luck with (and great durability, based on long-term testing) are Blackhawk and London Bridge Trading Company. I've had both a Shooting Systems and an Uncle Mikes tactical thigh rig on hand long enough to like them, but not long enough yet to see if they'll hold up. Based on the apparent durability of their construction, I'm betting they will hold up, but a year isn't long enough to be sure. When selecting a tactical thigh rig, you need to look at several factors. Does that brand come for the sidearm your department issues or authorizes? If you can't find a holster, using one that is "close enough" is a bad idea. It isn't just that your sidearm might fall out, but that it might fall out where someone else could find it. I don't know about you, but where I come from dropping a loaded pistol calls for review and perhaps even a letter in one's file. Second, is it comfortable? Unfortunately, comfort isn't something that can be measured with a ruler. You have to wear one to find out. However, there are some things that help. Are the leg straps wide and padded? Both help. Elastic straps are even better. Third, what kind of retention does it have? A thumb-break is good, but sometimes you need more. An airborne strap can keep your sidearm with you while traveling to the raid site. A flap also retains the pistol, and offers protection from the elements. Is there a spare mag pouch? There are few that don't have them, but if you like one that is lacking, you

A unitized load-bearing vest like this Blackhawk lets you carry lots of gear.

For training, this officer has removed his radio (note the loose wire) and gas mask. No point in beating up valuable and fragile items just in practice.

simply must find a way to attach a spare mag pouch to the holster or belt. Yes, you may never need one, but if you were optimistic about the odds, you wouldn't have a sidearm at all.

One aspect of tactical thigh rigs, holster or mag pouch, that not many users need to worry about is the length of the drop strap. I'm tall, with long legs. London Bridge makes their holsters with a long strap. Blackhawk holsters are proportioned for normal people, and to use theirs I have to add a drop strap extension. Not a problem, for once I add the extension I'm doing fine. Just be aware; if you're tall you can avoid the "tactical jock strap" syndrome by adding an extension.

Vests

The vest has a great deal of appeal. The big advantages of a vest are a more even distribution of the load (wider shoulders, wider weight distribution) and the easy-on easy-off design. And, some vests can be had with a pistol holster included. For someone whose job is to sit down a drive a car, truck, boat or aircraft, a thigh holster might not fit the seat.

Vests come in three types; unitized/modular, unitized/body armor, and chest/web gear. All those covered in this book are "load-bearing vests" that is, they are intended to carry gear and lots of it. These are not just a photographer's vests with a few pockets, or used to conceal guns and other gear. These are vests intended for hauling lots of ammo, a radio, water and other tools. The unitized/modular

vests look something like a photographer's vest or a down vest, but with lots of pockets. Modular vests differ in that the vest itself is just a set of attachment panels, and you can build your own by attaching the pouches you need. A modular vest is marginally heavier than a unitized vest, since you have to have the attachment system on the vest panels and on the pouches. On the unitized vest, the pockets are sewn on. The slight drawback to the modular approach is that in order to be configured for each outing, you or the department have to have a lot of extra pouches and holsters on hand.

Unitized/body armor vests incorporate soft synthetic body armor panels in the vest construction. If you want the lightest arrangement, use a unitized/body armor vest. The lighter weight (lighter than a modular over a body armor vest) is gained at the expense of having the vest non-alterable, and the extra cost of having it tailored to you. (A "one-size-fits-all" vest is cheaper, but you may come to regret the savings if your vest is so uncomfortable that you can't stand to wear it. Body armor in your locker is no good.)

Chest/web gear vests are designed to get the main weight, your loaded magazines and stuff, off your belt and up on your chest. The advantage is that you aren't moving that weight with your leg every time you step. The disadvantage is that with your waist open, you (or the people in charge of your job) may view it as an opportunity to add more gear. If you need it, and can carry it, you can pack an impressive amount of gear using a chest/web gear vest, and gear on a waist belt and tactical thigh pouches. Just don't try to walk across soft ground.

In a military context, the chest mount is good, since it allows room for gear law enforcement officers rarely need, like canteens and lots of grenade pouches.

One vest that your team must have, and no one wants to wear, is the entry tool vest. Someone has to carry the sledgehammers, rams, mauls and hooligan tools. If instead of a dedicated vest, everyone on your team each carries one tool by hand, who has a weapon out? So, some lucky member gets to pack the 50 pounds or more of the tools.

Accessory pouches and auxiliary gear

You don't always put pouches or extra storage on a vest to hold more ammo. Sometimes you need other items. (After all, the chances of getting into a running gun battle that will consume a basic load of 5.56 [200+ rounds] are very, very small) Sometimes you need to pack water, binoculars, a map or maps, radio, extra first aid gear or food. The SOE Gear first aid pouch is perfect for just what it is named for, or to stash a compact set of binoculars, laser rangefinder, or other gear. The Blackhawk medium pouch is larger and a little flatter, and will hold more stuff. For really capacious storage in a compact and removable pouch, use the LBTC SAW pouch or the SOE Gear empty mag pouch.

Testing

How do you test web gear? Three aspects must be considered; comfort, ease of use/access, and durability. For comfort, it was simple. I put one of them on each day when settling in for my writing sessions. Yes, I wore them to the range, but for a real gauge of comfort, daily wear is the only true test. The comfort test also inadvertently tested how quickly they could be doffed. Every time the doorbell rang, I had to get out of whichever vest I was wearing. Sometimes vest and holster. If you live in the kind of a neighborhood where you can come to the front door wearing a load-bearing vest and tactical thigh holster and not arouse alarm, I have only one suggestion: move. The FedEx driver loves our dog, but me wearing web gear is bound to alarm her. Ditto the mailman, newspaper boy and all the others. To test ease of use and access to the gear, only range sessions and training classes will do. Each practice session I'd pack the web gear along, and after going through the days intended practice I'd put on the web gear and practice reloads and weapons handling. As for durability, all the gear I tested passed. After months of range sessions and classes, none were showing wear. Oh, they were broken in and in some cases grubby, but they showed no signs of wearing out. I'd have to subject them to a lot more abuse than I was willing to, to see which failed first. Any will give years of service, unless your job involves swimming to work, or jumping out of perfectly good helicopters or aircraft. And then they'll still give you many times the service of issue gear.

Maintenance

For the most part, maintenance is easy. (That, after all is one of the things tested for any gear adopted for military service. Web gear and uniforms that require dry cleaning are not much use in the field.) For BDUs, a regular machine wash is fine. No bleach, no starch, and don't iron them, and they'll last. Starch and ironing wear them out a lot faster than use. If the powers that be insist on "starch and iron" then just resign yourself to the fact that you'll go through garments a lot faster than you otherwise would. Web gear takes more handwork but less washing. You can't just throw a tactical or load-bearing vest in the wash, then hang it up to dry or run it through the dryer on "low." For one thing, the buckles and snaps make the most God-awful noise. No, to wash web gear fill the laundry tub full of warm soapy water. Empty all the pockets. Slosh it around, and scrub the really muddy spots with a brush. Then rinse thoroughly, and hang in a warm and dry location so it can drip-dry. Unless you work in a really muddy place (Louisiana comes to mind) you won't need to wash web gear more than once a year, or once per spill into the muck. For rips and tears in BDUs, you can have any tailor or seamstress patch, repair or reinforce. For the web gear, the best thing to do is send it back to the manufacturer for repair. They have the heavy-duty sewing machines and the proper thread to make sure your repaired section is as good as new. For unit patches, name tapes and the like, just go the closest tailor. Yes, you can do it yourself, but the professional does a much better job, and the cost isn't enough to break the bank.

London Bridge Trading Company

LBTC is in contention with Special Operations Gear as the best tactical gear maker you've never heard of. Both have fanatically dedicated followings, and both make stuff that is tougher than you'd believe. Dusty Rhodes my contact at LBT objects to being compared to or mentioned as being in contention with SOE Gear. He feels that they compliment, rather than compete, with

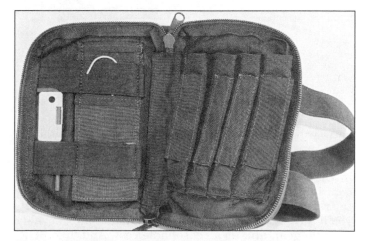

The London Bridge Trading Company tool pouch. Besides EOD, it is useful for entry teams and armorers.

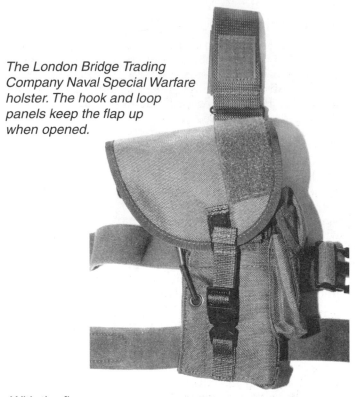

The London Bridge Trading Company Naval Special Warfare holster. The hook and loop panels keep the flap up when opened.

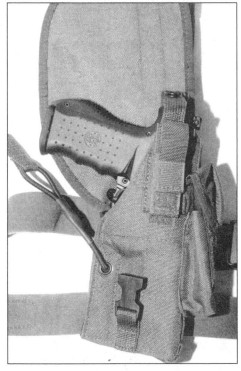

With the flap up and the airborne strap off, the thumb break strap now retains the handgun. In this case the SW-99 in a Glock-sized holster.

me down had I not made that clear. I have a number of LBTC holsters on hand, and include two in this book for your consideration. First, a rig for Glock pistols, and a second a holster for a 1911 with a mounted weaponlight. In addition, London Bridge makes accessory pouches, tactical thigh rigs and rucksacks.

The Naval Special Warfare holster I have on hand is made for a Glock 9mm/40. In a pinch you can tighten it down to hold a 1911, but it will be a loose fit and the pistol will not be happy about it. It does hold the Springfield XD and other pistols well. But you should specify which sidearm you want to use, and use that one only, in any holster you acquire. The first thing you notice about the NSW is the flap. Yea, yea, yea, "Flaps are passé, no one uses a flapped holster if they can get out of using a GI holster." Tell that to the troops in Iraq as they bundled up against the sandstorm. A flap keeps dust, dirt, rain and snow out of your handguns. (Well, at least it does better than no flap.) It also keeps the weapon with you when you bail out of a plane, exit a chopper or jump off a boat. The flap is backed with a hook-and-loop panel, and when you open it, it will stay up, stuck to the fastener panel sewn to the leg-drop strap. The flap is also detachable, so you can unsnap it and stick it in a pocket once you've arrived. The retaining strap is a thumb-break, with an additional fast-strap hook-and-loop panel. When you have time to reholster, snap it. If you are in a hurry, use the hook-and-loop for a quick-secure. Also, the NSW has an airborne strap. As extra insurance for vehicle exit, you can stretch the elastic loop up over the butt of the gun. It isn't going anywhere with the strap over the grip, so be sure you undo the strap once you're safely on the ground.

Up front, the holster body has a magazine pouch. The flap is full-coverage, so the spare magazine is protected from the weather, and has some protection from impact. It has hook-and-loop panels, and two snap fasteners, so you can snap it over two different magazine lengths. The snaps add security; the hook-and-loop panels make it a quick-close flap on a reload. A magazine pouch someplace else is faster on the reload, but with a pouch on the holster you always have a spare magazine with the sidearm. The leg-drop strap has plenty of adjustment for those of us with long legs, and the leg straps are elasticized for comfort, rubber-backed for no slip, and have securing panels on the front. You can clip a checklist, notebook or spare pouch there.

The 1911 holster is a bit different. It has the same long leg-drop strap, with plenty of adjustment. It has the thumb-break retaining strap, with fast-secure hook-and-loop strap. It has elastic and rubber-backed leg straps, but without the checklist straps of the NSW. It has a magazine pouch on the front, sized for a 1911 magazine instead of the Glock magazines of the NSW. (You can get an NSW for a 1911, just ask.) It has no flap. The Airborne strap is a webbing strap with a Fastex buckle. And this one is sized to take a 1911 with an attached weaponlight. The size this one will take is the Streamlight M3. It will take a 1911 with the Surefire bracket attached, but isn't big enough to take

each other. In looking over the respective catalogs, there are large areas where they do not overlap. He's got me there. But the competition I was thinking of was in the field of making tough, durable and dependable gear for those who have to have the best and are willing to track it down. Of course now that the word is out, you'll have less tracking to do. Both make unbelievably durable gear, and at a reasonable cost. And, like SOE, all LBTC gear is 100 percent made in the U.S.A. I got the distinct impression that Dusty would have tracked it with bracket and light. (If you want your 1911 to fit with the Surefire light on, tell LBTC which model you have mounted, and I'm sure they can cut one to fit.) It is the same hell-for-tough design and construction, and will give many years of exemplary service.

One note on tactical thigh rig holsters, and other gear: leg straps come long. LBTC (and other makers) don't know if you are a lean, mean, airborne machine, or as Richard Davis so politely termed the larger shooters at his pin shoot, a "stable weapons platform." Leg straps come big enough to fit most anyone. You can cut them short, but a better solution is to make sure you get the elastic bands to bunch up or secure out of the way the excess strapping. The elastics are an inch wide, and collect the extra strapping without being in the way. Unlike electrical tape, they won't leave residue behind, and don't have to be cut off when you need to expand the straps. Make sure you get some for each item of gear you get that has straps.

To fit the LBTC, or any holster, takes a bit of time. Once done, you don't have to change the adjustments unless you go from winter to summer uniform or back. Note that the top of the drop strap is a hook-and-loop flap assembly that does not require you unfasten your belt to attach or remove. You may have to loosen your belt a bit to get finger room, but you don't have to undress. First, adjust the leg drop for your body. Let it out enough so the upper leg strap of the pair is low enough to not be a "tactical jock strap" and bind you in embarrassing places. You can mount it too low. You should not (unless you have short arms and a long body) have your arm straight down to draw the pistol. Too low, and the holstered pistol swings as you walk, and makes walking a lot harder than it needs to be. Once it is low enough (but not too low) then cinch up the leg straps. "Tight" keeps the holster from flopping around, but "too tight" can cut circulation and be uncomfortable. The elastic bands have a lot of give, and the buckle is easy enough to adjust that you can adjust through the day, changing as you need to. I prefer to attach the leg straps by running the free end through the securing loops on the back of the holster, from the back to the front. That way I can slide the buckles and the excess strap up against the holster, and keep them from binding or clanking against the buckles of the spare ammo/empty mag/gas mask pouch on my other leg.

In addition to holsters, LBTC makes a wide range of other gear. Their catalog seems a bit thin simply because they don't think that many people are interested in items like a 500-round belted .30 caliber ammo bag for a helicopter-mounted machinegun, so they don't list a lot of the very specialized gear they make. They're probably right on that one. If you need something, ask. It may very well be that LBT makes it, but except for the special operations unit that asked for it they haven't had any other requests. With that in mind I have some of their other gear that you'd be interested in.

First, an EOD tactical thigh tool kit. EOD is Explosive Ordnance Disposal. It means arming things to blow up, and disarming things that didn't or

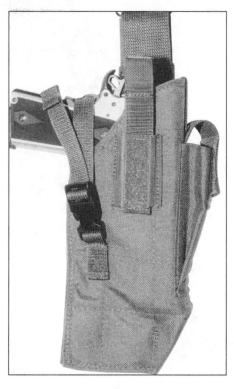

The LBTC tactical thigh holster for 1911 with light attached. Not much more bulk for a handy way to keep illumination with you. Note the buckled airborne strap.

haven't yet blown up. Sometimes EOD work is very simple: you see the explosive, you clear out a safety radius, then shoot it with a rifle or machinegun, and it explodes. But you can't always do that. Sometimes you have to deal with it. For that, the EOD tech needs tools like pliers, screwdrivers, wire cutters, jumpers and other arcane goodies. Goodies like an electrical meter and ohm meter, and electrical tape. Yes, there is a toolbag. There is always a tool bag. But the most commonly used and handy tools are in his pockets. That is, if he doesn't have a bag like this. Pliers, cutters, screwdrivers, knives all fit into the tool bag with room to spare. "All fine and dandy," you say, "but I don't go around defusing bombs." Fine. For entry teams, not every door gets the hammer treatment. Sometimes you have to deal with doors or gates wired shut, screen doors latched with little hook latches, and cheap locks that can be dealt with by using big sidecutters, instead of using a 3-foot long cutters, or prying the latch off with your big, expensive knife. If your entry team has one member with a tool kit on his leg, you can deal with the unforeseen problems of wire, duct tape, chintzy locks and screen doors. The pouch has the standard first-class LBTC elastic leg straps. The leg straps, like all LBTC gear, slide through their retaining loops so you can position the buckles where you want them. Or remove the top strap and use just one leg strap, if you find the top one rides a bit too high on your leg. The leg-drop strap is not as long, nor as heavily constructed as the weapon or magazine pouches are, but that is a good thing. You aren't packing heavy gear, and you want it a little higher so you can see what you're grabbing. The pouch has a hook-and-loop fastened pocket on the outside, perfect for gloves, a wound dressing, or a notebook or laminated cards. The pouch opens completely with a

The LBTC universal SMG pouch can be fitted to a modular vest, web gear, a rucksack or a vehicle.

zipper running around three sides. Inside on the flap (or forward for right-handed, left leg wear) side are elastic loops for larger tools. Sewn behind the elastic are three deep and narrow pockets for tools. On the inside strap against your leg, are four deep and narrower pockets for other tools. When I'm working as a class Armorer, I find the tool kit is perfect for the range work. I can stash the tools needed to pop open a recalcitrant AR, adjust sights, tighten scope mounts, pistol grips and lights, all from the tools in the EOD pouch. And best of all, I can see what I'm grabbing, and don't have to select by Braille.

For those who are not playing with things that go boom, LBTC makes tactical thigh rig magazine pouches and accessory mag pouches that can fit on a vest. The SMG crowd will be pleased with the three-mag 9mm pouch. The thigh-mount I have on hand is the FBI style, designed by and for those Agents. It rides higher than some, looped directly to the belt instead of being a drop rig. The individual pouches are long enough for Colt 32-round 9mm mags, and have hook-and-loop fastener panels as well as snap fasteners. For maximum security you fasten the snap and use the hook-and-loop, and when you need to quickly stash a magazine just pressing the hook-and-loop will keep it fastened against anything but a parachute drop.

The same pouch body is also available as an Alice-clip back or belt-loop pouch. You could attach it to a belt or vest. A tactical rifleman who is using a .30-caliber bolt-action or semi-auto rifle as the main gun could attach the mag pouch to his vest for mags for the backup 9mm SMG. A 20-round mag in the gun on the rucksack, with three, 32 round magazines in the pouch, will get you through a lot of emergency.

If, instead, you want more ammo capacity in your vest, then LBTC has rifle mag pouches, too. For those who want hook-and-loop, there are rifle pairs like the 9mm pouch described above. Or, you can have the plastic fastex buckle. The rifle pouches are double-pair, holding a total of four, 30-round AR/M-16 magazines. If you need real volume, the SAW pouch will handle your needs. The SAW (Squad Automatic Weapon) is primarily used as a belt-fed light machinegun, using 200-round belts in a plastic drum. The drum rides in a 6-inch x 7-inch x 3-inch pouch, which happens to be the size you'd need for a seven-magazine AR/M-16 pouch. And LBTC has that covered for you. Inside the pouch is a hook-and-loop fastened strap assembly. With the strap pulled loose and pushed to the front, a SAW drum drops right in. Pull the assembly to the back and fasten it, and you have separate loops to keep your AR/M-16 magazines stored in an orderly fashion. Attach an LBTC SAW drum to a vest (like the SOE Gear CQB vest) and you've nearly doubled your ammo load. If you don't need that much ammo, the Saw pouch can also double as a binocular pouch, or hold a laser rangefinder, extra first aid supplies or equipment, or be used as a quick-dump evidence pouch.

Meth lab on fire at the conclusion of a raid? Fire extinguishers aren't enough? Grab the evidence (at least enough to present to the ADA) stuff it in pockets and the SAW pouch, and get the hell out of Dodge.

If you need a vest, London Bridge makes those, too. Theirs are integrated, with magazine and gear storage pouches.

All LBTC gear has edges that are double folded and sewn down, or are taped. Everything is stitched tightly, and the thread used is heavy-duty. Everything is made of heavy-duty cordura or tougher material, with no cheap fabric fill, pack cloth or other shortcuts or economizing. All of the LBTC gear is tough, a lot tougher than you might ever need unless you are going to be drawing a salary for the "work" of jumping out of planes or helicopters, or swimming ashore loaded for bear. But the best of the London Bridge Trading Company product line are the holsters. If you get one, you will not be disappointed.

Blackhawk web gear

If you want a catalog full of "to lust for" web gear, get the Blackhawk catalog. You'll be treated to 130 pages (2003 catalog) of gear, more than you and your department could buy unless someone wins the Lotto big time and decides to shower you in ballistic nylon. The owner of Blackhawk is Mike Noell, and he served his country as a Navy SEAL before retiring to make good gear that he would have used when he was on the job. All Blackhawk gear is tough, well designed and offered in the usual colors; Black, OD, tan and woodland. One thing Blackhawk offers that others don't is variety. You can get lost in the models, options and features. Take as an example the typical tactical thigh magazine pouch. You can buy three or four or five different ones from some makers. From Blackhawk, you can select from 20 different ones, and that doesn't even get into color and caliber

The LBTC four-mag rifle pouch comes in a Velcro and snap version.

And LBTC also makes a Fastex buckle version

The winner for multiple-cargo capacity is the LBTC SAW gunners pouch. Closed, it can carry, magazines, evidence, first aid, etc.

Open, you can see the dividers for seven 30-round magazines.

The Blackhawk Omega VI holster can be had for many sidearms and several colors. (Courtesy Blackhawk Industries.)

Blackhawk Omega VI assault holster

The latest Omega holsters come in CQB, airborne, bungee and Special Operations models. The differences are how the airborne retention operates (Fastex-buckled strap or bungee) whether the holster is stiffened with a plastic insert, and on the Special Operations holster, a flap. You can also get a holster that attaches to a modular vest.

The Omega holster is a tactical thigh holster, with a drop strap from your trouser belt. The holster can be worn as a high-ride or low-ride. High ride puts it on your belt with no drop, and for that you remove the leg straps. Dropped, you have two non-slip leg straps to keep it secure. The Omega leg straps have a non-skid backing, and elastic near the buckle to allow expansion as you walk, run or sit. On the front is a spare magazine pouch, secured with a Velcro panel. The thumb-break snap keeps the sidearm in while you are moving, and for quick securing after reholstering you simply flip the outer strap over and secure it with the Velcro panel. Your sidearm will stay in until you can take the time to re-set the thumbreak. Available right- or left-handed, Black, OD and desert tan, and for all the common pistols, Omega will serve you well. As for fit, if you insist on something different, you'll find many uncommon pistols fit common holsters. For example, the 1911/Browning 9mm holsters will also take a CZ-75. The holsters for the big Glocks, the 20 & 21, and the USP 40 and 45, will also accept the S&W 99 in 45. For the S&W 99 in 9mm or 40, use a Glock 9mm/40 holster.

Omega M-16 Enhanced drop-leg pouch

If you need extra ammo, or your vest is already dedicated to other items, the thigh rig offers a place for storage. The Omega Enhanced differs from other leg rigs in that you can stash four 30-round magazines in a compact space, and not lose them. The Enhanced stores the mags two per pouch, with internal dividers to keep the magazines apart. The exterior of the pouches have a wide elastic band that retains the remaining magazine when you've pulled one out. No worries about losing the second one if you don't have time to fasten the buckle. The pouch has the

options. (I don't envy the warehouse or inventory people at Blackhawk, keeping track of nearly 100 tactical thigh magazine rigs alone.) Ditto vests, web gear, packs, drag bags and holsters. Blackhawk makes their own vests, the R.A.C.K. and S.T.R.I.K.E. that are compatible with the issue M.O.L.L.E. vest, and components and pouches that will fit all three.

And everything Blackhawk makes is guaranteed. Burns, cuts, abrasion holes and normal wear and tear are not covered. Otherwise, if you manage to bust it, and it fails due to manufacturing, construction or material failure, they'll repair it or give you a new one free. Having a pocket rip off because it couldn't hold the weight of the flashbangs in it will get you a new one. Getting dragged down the street by an offenders vehicle will not. Dropping your lit cigarette onto your gear (shame on you for smoking, it cuts your wind) is not covered under warrantee.

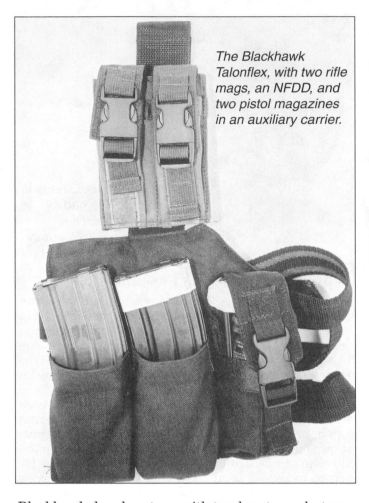

The Blackhawk Talonflex, with two rifle mags, an NFDD, and two pistol magazines in an auxiliary carrier.

Bad guys lock their doors, too. Not always, but when they do, you can count on the ability of these "keys" to open any door. (Courtesy Blackhawk Industries)

Blackhawk drop leg strap, with two leg straps, but you can also remove the drop strap and leg straps and secure the pouch to your belt or a modular vest. If retention of the second magazine is not a worry, you can get the regular drop pouch without the elastic. In the regular pouch, you can specify two or four magazines total. Why ditch the elastic? It is strong enough that getting magazines into the pouches is a definite two-handed job. You don't just slip a loaded magazine into each slot, you have to wrestle each one of them in. Some don't like to work that hard. I don't mind, as I would rather not lose a tested and reliable magazine if I can avoid it, and getting magazines into the pouch is not a timed event.

The two elastic leg straps keep the pouch secured without cutting off blood flow. The weight of four loaded magazines can be too much for some straps, especially when running. Having the pouch flopping around on your leg while sprinting after someone is uncomfortable and slows you down. The non-slip elastic construction of the Omega pouch keeps the magazines under control.

Omega M-16 Talonflex/Flashbang pouch

It has the looks and speed of a competition rig, but solid magazine retention and a flashbang as well. The Talonflex pouches are open-topped, with the magazines retained by a plastic flex panel that clamps them like a spring. I have not yet been able to eject a magazine by running or jumping, but for a fast reload they are as fast as a competition pouch. The flashbang pouch is secured by a flap with a Fastex buckle, with room to slide the spoon into the pouch for safety. The flap is adjustable and removable. (Why you would want an open-topped flashbang pouch is beyond me) It has the same excellent leg straps as all the other Omega pouches, which can be removed to allow the pouch to be attached to your belt or modular vest.

If you don't pack flashbangs, the pocket can take a tool kit, small water bottle or medium sized chemical spray canister.

Vests

Blackhawk makes a huge variety of vests, too. They make unitized, modular and semi-modular vests. The unitized ones come with magazine pouches or gear pouches, and fasten on the front with zippers. The semi-modular unites use Fastex buckles and have loops on the bottom for attaching a pistol belt. The Modular vests (the M.O.L.L.E. and S.T.R.I.K.E.) can fasten (depending on the design) in front or back, and take all the pouches and attachments from the M.O.L.L.E. system. One feature that will make many customers happy is that all unitized vests have an integral pouch on the back for the Blackhawk

Hydrastorm system. Many of the others have attachment points for a hydration cover. You don't have to add anything to the unitized vests, or make sure you order the correct letter suffix product code, to be sure you get a vest that will hold drinking water. (You will have to ask for a reservoir, however.) Blackhawk makes all the usual tactical and patrol vests (patrol in the military context, as in sneaking through the woods looking for bad guys) as well as specialized vests. Like the entry tool vest, to hold sledges, hooligan tool, lock cutter and prybars. And to fill those vests Blackhawk also carries tools. If you're tired of going down to the local "big box" hardware store to buy yet another sledgehammer with an "unbreakable" handle, buy tools where you buy your vest. Blackhawk can send you a vest with tools. All you need to do is find someone who can carry it. If you load up a Manual Entry Vest, or a U.K. M.O.E. vest with sledge, maul, hooligan tool and a couple of smaller prybars, you have a 50-pound load. Add to that a bulletproof vest, weapon, ammo, helmet, radio and all the other miscellaneous gear, and your entry mule is not going to be running to the door very quickly, weighed down by 70-80 pounds of gear.

On the unitized vests, Blackhawk has a non-skid panel on the right hand collarbone area, called the Sniper Shoulder. It prevents movement of the buttplate of the shoulder weapon when you're in a firing position. They also come with a drag handle.

As with all manufacturers, Blackhawk will do custom orders. If you need enough of them, you can have your vest done pretty much any way you want. If you only need one or two, then pick carefully form the catalog, because you won't be wearing them out any time soon. As with all the other gear, vests are available in other than black, except for the tool vests. If you want to pack entry tools for the soiree at the door, you have to be dressed in formal black.

Blackhawk accessories

The first thing to consider is your height. If you are like me, tall, lanky and with long legs, you'll find that Blackhawk leg drop straps are almost too short. I can usually adjust them for enough drop to avoid the dreaded "tactical jock strap" effect, but sometimes there isn't a lot of Velcro holding things together once it is adjusted. Blackhawk makes two drop extenders. One is a Velcro loop with metal band to extend the strap. The other is a quick-release buckle. The D.L.E. adds up to 5 inches, while the Q.R. adds 2 inches. I find the quick release so useful that I have used them on other maker's gear. (Yes, I mix and match sometimes.) I find the QD very useful in a class environment. Rather than nearly undress each time I need to transition from the range to the classroom (and lose time I should be spending on the lesson plan) the QD lets me take off a holster and tactical thigh rig as fast as taking off a vest. If I happen to have all three, then divesting myself of the holster, thigh rig and vest is a moment's work.

One accessory I find very useful is the Blackhawk shotgun pouch. Rather than a looped pouch (like the G.I. pouch that held a dozen rounds) or a bandoleer

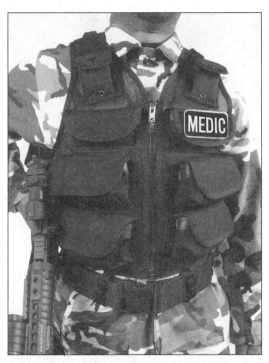

Load-bearing vests can carry others things besides ordnance. (Courtesy Blackhawk Industries)

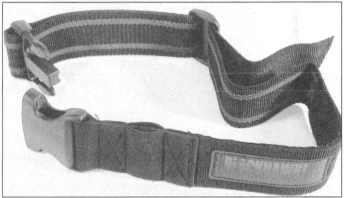

Blackhawk leg straps are very comfortable, easy to adjust, and can be retro-fitted to other gear if need be.

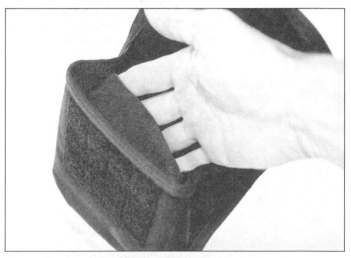

The Blackhawk shotgun pouch has an elastic opening under the flap, so the shells don't fall out when you move. It can also be used as a first aid pouch or laser rangefinder/binoculars case.

The SOE Gear CQB vest, loaded and ready to go. Total inventory: eight 30-round rifle mags, three pistol mags, one Surefire light, One Leatherman Crunch, one wound dressing, four EZ Cuff ties.

of loops, the shotgun pouch is a tough fabric box with an elastic opening on top. You dump the rounds in, and then when you need one reach in and extract it. You can't keep a mixture of rounds in it, but that isn't a problem. If you're using a shotgun, you'll have a main supply as your ready reload. The specialty rounds you keep in special stashes, such a breeching rounds on a Sidesaddle on the breaching gun. Or if you carry buckshot as your main supply, then slugs in a separate belt pouch.

To round out your ensemble, Blackhawk makes a dizzying array of magazine pouches (from one to six magazines, handgun or rifle, for thigh, belt or vest) grenade pouches (frag, smoke, sting, pepper, gas, flashbang) pouches for your cell phone, pager, PDA, medical kit, handcuffs, lights, radios, gas masks, canteens, keys, gloves, batons, maps, notebooks, pepper sprays, suppressors, knives and shotgun shells. For long-distance carry, they make a line of rucksacks and their Hydrastorm water carriers. You can get cargo bags, carry bags, storage bags and discreet transport bags, too. If you cannot assemble a complete rig from Blackhawk gear, you are either way too picky, using something totally oddball, or are too cheap to buy good gear. With the amount of stuff that is needed, and the amount of additional stuff that it is prudent to carry, you are almost neglectful if you haven't added a few pouches here and there for the extras.

The SOE Gear CQB vest, with two mag pouches devoted to OC pepper and smoke.

Special Operations Equipment

John Willis knows what it takes to make gear tough enough to stand up to real-world use. And what it takes to make gear comfortable enough to wear all day without feeling like your own equipment is punishing you. While you won't find a huge catalog full of variations on equipment, what you will find are plenty of designs to see you through. Being a small shop, and offering specialized gear in a variety of colors (Black, Tan, OD, Woodland and Tri-color desert) John and the sewers make your gear once you order it. Needless to say, they are all made in the U.S.A. As a result, if you want something a little different, they can do custom work. For example, if you want to substitute a particular kind of pouch on one side of a vest, they can do it. One substitution that is apparently common for military users is to swap the pistol magazine pouches on the rifle mag bodies on their vests for pouches to fit 40mm grenades. While there is not much call in law enforcement use for a 40mm HE from an M-203, in the military context, there is. One complaint of the

The SOE CQB vest side, showing the attachment panels and the belt loops. If you need to add pouches, there is room here.

issue vests for 40mm gunners is that they don't hold enough grenades. By adding storage of grenades on other vests in a fire team or squad, the grenadier can have additional supply close at hand. Be aware that substitutions and specialized orders will cost more. However, considering how long your investment will last, the cost is worth it. John kindly sent me a selection of mouth-watering gear to test and evaluate. First up, the CQB vest.

The CQB vest, along with its 10 other vest variant siblings, is a semi-modular vest built on an "H" harness skeleton. (Eleven vests, five colors, custom pouch substitution available. No wonder they make them as you order them!) The magazine pouches ride up off of your trouser belt, out of the way of any gear mounted there. The rifle magazine pouches are sewn directly to the vest front panels, and on the CQB (and some other models) the side panels are left open, but with attachment straps to hang or secure extra pouches or gear. You can secure whatever else you need there that fits; canteen, first aid kit, more ammo pouches, tool kit, etc. The tops of the chest panels have hook-and-loop panels that also are securing points for other modular pouches, or to keep the flaps open if you wish. In its basic form, the CQB holds eight AR magazines in four pouches, and each pouch has a side pouch for a pistol magazine, flashlight, OC pepper spray can, or knife. The rifle pouches hold two 30 round M-16 magazines, or one 20 round M-14 or FAL magazine, or three MP-5, Colt SMG or Uzi magazines each. The rifle pouches are

roomy enough to take a set of clamped 9mm magazines, should you want to carry them in their clamped pairs arrangement. The magazine pouches are also roomy enough to take a pair of 37mm rounds, although some rounds may be short and you'll have to dig for them in the pouch. For instance, the Sage Control Ordnance baton rounds sit so deep getting them out may be a hassle. If you press the CQB into service as a 37mm round vest (or use a pocket or two to carry extra rounds for the 37mm gunner) you would be well-served by putting a chunk of foam rubber or a plastic block in the bottom of the pouch to raise the 37mm rounds higher. Additionally, the pouches are large enough (but it is a snug fit) to take a smoke grenade up to 2-5/8" in diameter. As with the 37mm rounds, the grenade will ride low in the deep pocket, so a chunk of foam or a plastic filler block is called for to make it easy to grasp. The buckle and hook-and-loop fastener panels have plenty of reach, so you don't have to worry about your smoke falling out at an inopportune moment. The pistol pouches fit every size magazine I had on hand to test, except for the overly long 25-round Beretta M-92 and Browning Hi-Power magazines and some STI magazines longer than 126mm. The pouches are roomy enough to swallow both a Leatherman Crunch and a 1911 single stack magazine at once. The rear vest panel has attachment points for a buttpack. The shoulder straps have securing loops and hook-and-loop flaps to tie down gear or a hydration tube. On the back, between your shoulders and below your neck is a drag strap. The drag handle is secured to a huge hook-and-loop fastener panel that adjusts the gap between the shoulder straps. The fastener panel seems large enough to tow a Buick. It is large enough, in fact, to hold the weight of a Marine and his gear, while another Marine held him off a set of stairs. The photo is in the catalog. Everything is adjustable, from the fit of the vest around your chest and waist, to the drop from your shoulders, to the Fastex buckles that hold down all the cargo flaps. Even the hook-and-loop panels do double duty, in that you can secure the pouch flaps up out of the way if you want to. Or, attach a knife scabbard to the front of the vest. The "cool commando" way of attaching a knife to your vest or web gear is to secure it upside-down from one of the suspenders. The only problem with that is gravity. If the attachment comes lose, the knife drops off. If the snap, catch or whatever else is holding the knife comes lose, the knife drops out. (A big, sharp, knife, dropping out of its scabbard or sheath, onto you or one of your team members? Or falling into running machinery? Does anyone else see a problem here?) The hook-and-loop panels let you secure the knife horizontally (my favorite) or vertically with the point down. And the front panels on the mag pouches themselves are built to hold pouches. If you want to secure a small pouch under the flap, you can. Just let out the Fastex buckle adjustment enough to cover the extra pouch, and secure the extra pouch in the webbing slots. Or, keep the flap up, and the pouch open, for fast access,

The back of the SOE Gear vest has attachments for a buttpack, Camelbak cover, patrol pack, or anything else you might want.

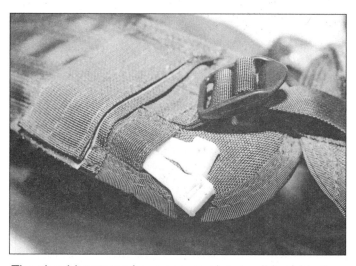

The shoulder straps have access slots to slide cable ties or EZ Cuffs up into the structure.

and secure another pouch to the front of the mag pouch. Or secure a knife under the flap, attached to the hook-and-loop panel, and covered by the magazine pouch flap. At the bottom of the vest are loops to attach a pistol belt, in case you need more real estate to secure more gear to. On the back, you can secure a buttpack to the vest, using the lash panels, or the fastex buckles. SOE makes buttpacks, too. Depending on just where you secure a buttpack, and what you put in it, you can pack a rucksack while wearing this vest. (It may seem obvious, but it

isn't. Equipment makers who make more hiking and backpacking gear don't always address this problem.)

You can attach a Camelbak to the vest, or put the Camelbak on and then put the vest on over the Camelbak straps, and route the drinking tube over the CQB shoulder straps.

Three Fastex buckles on the front secure the vest, so it is easy on and easy off. One interesting manufacturing detail is the front of the shoulder straps. One of the panels of their construction is folded and sewn, but left open on the tops and bottoms. And ends up being a perfect place to insert and carry cable ties used as field handcuffs. The 10-inch length of the panel makes it a bit short, but

Magazine fit

The rifle pouches on the SOE CQB vest would take any pair of 30-round AR-15/M-16 magazines. The 20-rounders also fit, but there was a lot of extra room up and down. Were you in the position of being on a department that only issues and authorizes 20-round magazines, there are two options: Use a filler of rolled cloth or a plastic box. Or ask SOE to cut the pouches for 20-round magazines. Personally, I'd use filler. All my AR mags, the magazines for my AR-180, and the Ruger Mini-14 magazines all fit just fine. Steyr AUG magazines, being bulkier, would not fit two to each pouch, nor would clipped Sig 552 magazines. If you want to stuff a pair of either of these in a pouch, you'll have to order a triple-M-16 mag pouch vest. The CQB pouches easily swallowed 20-round M-14 or FAL magazines. The MP-5 or Colt/Uzi SMG 32-round magazines required loosening the Fastex strap from the AR setting, and there was not enough slack to accommodate my 40-round magazines. There was even a little bit of room with the AR mags, enough to get my fingers in to snatch a magazine. The pistol magazine pouches are what everyone is concerned about. First, consider how web gear or a vest is made. Many layers of cloth are laid down flat on a cutting table, (how many depends on the intended production volume and size of the cutting instrument.) and the pattern is drawn on the top layer. Then the cloth is cut out following the pattern. A huge manufacturer can use a computer-controlled cutter to make sure all patterns are absolutely identical. Otherwise, there will be small variations in each cut. A particular cut may be just inside the line, on, or just outside the line. There might be a slight bunch in the cloth stack or intermediate layers. Then, when it is sewn, the stitching may run just inside, on, or just outside of the intended sew line. (Everybody tries hard, but they're all human) On a rifle mag pouch, the variations are so small that you won't notice. If they are large enough to notice, you just might want to switch to a different brand. Pistol pouches, being much smaller, can have the variances make a difference. When you start expanding the envelope, figuratively or literally, you can end up with the mag you want not fitting.

The pistol pouches on the CQB vest would take any double-stack 9mm pistol mag of standard capacity. Beretta, Sig, Glock, EAA, S&W, Browning Hi-Power all fit without a problem. I could even, if I let all the slack out of the buckle strap, fit an STI 126mm magazine in, or two 1911 single-stack magazines. It would not, however, take a 10-round 1911 magazine. (I'm sure SOE could make them should you ask for them.) The Patrol pouch for belt mount, however, would not take the larger mags. It would take all the standard 9mm mags, but I could not get it closed on the STI or on a pair of 1911 mags. The Double Pistol pouch would take all the 9mm, a pair of 1911 standard mags, even a 10-round 1911 mag, but would not buckle shut on an STI 126mm. While the mag pouches would fit a pair of 1911 magazines in each pouch, I'm not sure I'd want to carry them that way. There is the risk of losing one of the pair while getting the other out. However, the pouches on the vest are probably backup storage to other pouches, on the holster or the trouser belt. And since I'd be able to store an extra mag, I think I'd be willing to risk the potential loss of one of them, After all, even if you use three pouches for other stuff — Leatherman tool, OC spray and flashlight — you'll still have a pair of pistol mags tucked away. The variations in just what magazines would fit when I tried to wrestle the biggest one possible into a pouch is not something you or I should blame SOE or any other manufacturer for.

If what you desire is that your pistol pouches fit a particular magazine, you need only ask. If your department issues Para Ordnance hi-cap pistols chambered in .45 ACP, make sure you tell SOE when you order your gear. That way they can make sure your mags will fit and you will not be disappointed. If you just assume that the pouches will accommodate "my .358 Thunderzapper Magnum" magazines, you might just find they don't. And when that happens, only your closest friends will have any sympathy for you.

While I love the 1911, I can get by using just about anything. Also, when I teach I have to adapt to what the departmental issue or authorized sidearm might be. So getting specialized gear wouldn't be wise for me.

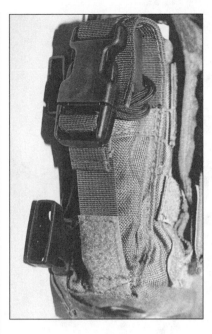

By unscrewing the cap enough to prevent illumination ("white light AD") the SOE Gear pistol pouches on the CQB vest will take a Surefire light.

six rifle magazines in the Land Warfare vest. The Patrol vest increases that to 12 M-16 magazines (8 M-14/FAL) plus the pistol pouches. Not enough? The Surefire Instructors' vest has all that, and a sewn-on 6-inch x 6-inch zippered utility pouch on one side panel of the vest. Finally, the Lightfighter (light compared to what?) vest holds 12 M-16 magazines, four pistol magazines, and has two 6x6 zippered pouches. What if you carry something else besides an M-16 or M-14? Then the MP-5 vest holds six MP magazines and has six pistol pouches. The SAW gunner's vest is the real weight-packer. (Any police department whose team is so active that they need a SAW gunner is a place I don't want to go. However, a security team for a sensitive installation, such as a nuclear plant, might need just this.) Two pouches each hold a 200 round pre-loaded SAW drum, plus pouches for four more M-16 magazines, and four pistol magazines. By my count that is 520 rounds of 5.56 ammo and up to 60 rounds of pistol ammo.

If you need less instead of more, the Direct Action vest only holds eight M-16 magazines, but the pouches are cut low for fast reloading. The AK vest holds eight AK mags and four pistol mags.

And the Medical Technician vest has two medium pouches, one large pouch, a dedicated IV pouch, and an instrument pouch. The Med Tech vest does not have pistol magazine pouches on it. However, if you wanted them on it, for storing a flashlight or Leatherman tool (heaven forbid that a Med Tech actually have a defensive weapon) all you need do is ask for them and pay for them.

In use, I have found chest-mount vests in general, and the SOE vest in particular, very comfortable. I can wear a vest all day, day after day, and not be worn down or beaten up by the gear I'm packing. And, the chest mount makes prone a viable position. With the regular web gear, I find that all the stuff packed around my waist makes prone difficult. The various pouches rest on my abdomen and bear on the

we're talking about a means of keeping a spare or two at hand, not a means of storage for handling a crowd of rioters or a frat party gone bad. Both front panels have secured edges sealed with hook-and-loop panels, but easily opened to store maps, or to insert flotation foam. If you are assigned to the power squadron, but don't want to add a bulky (or inflatable) vest to your gear, adjust the straps for comfort and slide in flotation foam.

And if all this isn't enough, then you can have more. For starters, the Land Warfare model bumps the magazine capacity up to 10 AR/M-16 magazines plus the four pouches for pistol mags, light, Leatherman tool, etc. And since the Land Warfare vest has two of its four pouches built for three AR/M-16 magazines each, those pouches will also hold a pair of .30 caliber rifle magazines. Meaning M-14 or FAL users can get

The SOE Gear Patrol mag, in the belt mount version. This one holds two rifle mags and two pistol mags.

diaphragm, making breathing tough and shooting real work. The chest mount props up the ribcage, and lifts (at least for me) the diaphragm off the ground. In the latest class, I was able to shoot a 300-28X score on the Patrol rifle qualification course without a problem. The prone fire stage was almost like shooting from a sandbagged rest position. I do find one small quibble using a chest-mount vest, and that is due to my peculiar physique. I'm tall, but it is all in my legs. When I have the geared-up vest on, anything on my trouser belt is tough to get to, as the vest rides just over the belt. I've learned that if I mount anything on the trouser belt, and expect to have any hope of digging it out, I have to belt mount it horizontally. Those of you with a longer torso need not worry.

All SOE Gear vests are made of 1000 denier Cordura. All seams are heavily stitched, sewn with taped edges, and any location where something is attached is attached to stay. Nothing that is load-bearing is sewn on with just a line of stitching. All panels of hook-and-loop fastener are wide and heavily stitched, then stitched again at right angles and sometimes cross-stitched as well. All the vests have integrated buckles and attachments points for a buttpack, SOE's own Lite Pack or a Camelbak cover. All the vests also have routing straps and loops for communications gear (microphone, handset, earplug) or your hydration tube. All vests have 3/8-inch closed cell foam padding in the shoulder straps. That alone should get John Willis a great big hug, or at least an "atta boy." You haven't lived (or felt like you were dying) until you'd spent a day carrying/wearing something heavy that had lightly- or un-padded shoulder straps. All the vests also have long adjustment straps. For me, not being (In the words of Richard Davis, founder of Second Chance) a "stable

weapons platform" i.e. fat, adjusting vests is always interesting. I usually end up with enough extra strapping to lash down a vehicle in a cargo plane. SOE vests are designed to have enough adjustment to fit even the largest person while they are wearing chemical protective gear, a MOPP suit, cold-weather clothing, or body armor. When I had the vest tightened up, I had lots of extra strapping left over, almost down to my knees. Rather than cut it off (and not be able to adjust to cold weather, for example) I just folded the extra strapping and taped it.

If you don't need a full-house vest, but want to have spare ammo for your patrol rifle on a perimeter deployment, then the belt-mount Patrol mag pouch will serve you well. It holds three (depending on which you ask for) M-16 magazines, and has two pistol mag or tool pouches on the sides. The fastener is a hook-and-loop belt loop that is flapped, so you don't have to take your belt off to put on the pouch. The loop is wide enough to fit over a uniform belt. With the pouch pre-loaded with rifle magazines and two magazines for your sidearm, it takes only a moment to grab it along with the patrol rifle as you leave your vehicle to go to the assigned perimeter location. Once relieved you can gear up with more from the trunk of your patrol car. The CQB mag pouch offers the same in a smaller package, holding only two M-16 magazines.

One aspect of equipment that gets overlooked is what to do with empty magazines. In the law enforcement context, it is not much of a problem. In the rare event of a high-volume shootout, the empty magazines are simply dropped and replaced and the fight continued. Afterwards, the evidence technicians can locate, identify, photograph and recover the magazine or magazines. In the military context, dropped magazines are lost magazines, rarely recovered, especially in a dynamic fight. In a static position, dropped magazines that aren't damaged can be recovered and re-used. In the 1993 Somalia raid covered in the book and movie "Blackhawk Down," the Rangers were in fierce combat so long they began to run short of ammo and magazines. Having been on the move for much of the fight, they could not recover dropped magazines once they'd left a particular position. Even when they were supplied with more ammo, it had to be loaded into the limited supply of remaining magazines. It is highly unlikely that a SWAT team will be in such a predicament, but a spent mag pouch as other uses. It can be used to carry extra ammo, tools, evidence (in the event of the need for a speedy exit) medical supplies, binoculars or a laser rangefinder, or lunch. (Hey, even high-speed, low-drag guys have to eat.) The SOE Gear pouch is tough, and big enough to hold seven M-16 magazines. The flap is secured by hook-and-loop fasteners and has a slot on top. The slot is mostly closed by an elastic strip on each side. You can easily slide an empty magazine in, but it is unlikely to fall out. If you have a spare moment when there are some magazines already in it, you can open the flap, organize the ones in there, then continue inserting spent mags by sliding them in and then rotating them into the correct orientation. This pouch

The SOE Gear empty mag pouch will take many magazines. It also will hold grenades (right) spare equipment (gloves on the left) and many other items can be attached to the loops sewn on the outside.

The empty mag pouch can also have other pouches or tools attached to it. Then, use it as a thigh or vest-mount pouch.

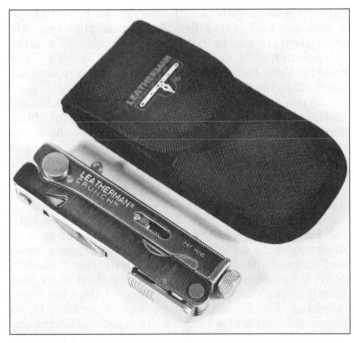

Sometimes the best or most useful tool is one everyone else also has. Don't get out of the car without a Leatherman.

came with optional grenade pouches on the sides. The grenade pouches are adjustable (like just about everything else SOE makes) and can hold smoke or flashbangs. They are too large to hold HE/Frags. The outside of the pouch has hook-and-loop strips to secure extra gear, such as a multiple pistol magazine pouch or a multiple 40mm grenade pouch. The pouch is also useful in a training environment. While on the line going through rifle or handgun drills, you expend many magazines. Rather than drop them on the ground and risk damage, or stuff them in your pockets and become uncomfortable, just stash them in the empty mag pouch. You can keep track of the training, care for your mags, and not get distracted by fishing in your pockets sorting loaded and spent mags.

Some departments/users will not require a "dump bag" for empty magazines. But if you want extra storage for items you need to pack, the SOE Gear empty mag pouch can be a great way to carry items. If you use the open slit on top, you can carry and easily access a pair of compact binoculars or a laser rangefinder. If you use the flap, you can pack a pair of large binoculars. The pouch holds enough disposable handcuffs (cable ties or mission-specific brands) to secure a whole block full of frat house rioters. If you need a large and readily accessible supply of OC pepper spray decon wipes, you can clean your whole shift with what you can stuff in the pouch. If you use it for something other than an empty mag pouch, be sure to label it as such.

To attach it to your person or web gear, there is a buckle at the top, and a webbing strap that fits the buckle. You can attach it to your trouser belt, or you can use the webbing strip to fasten it to a vest or web gear with Alice fasteners. On the bottom rear are two slots for the thigh strap. If you're wearing it as a tactical

thigh rig, then the supplied leg strap goes through the slots and secures the pouch to your leg. The leg strap is wide, with a big Fastex buckle, an elastic expansion section, and enough length to go onto anyone smaller than a sumo wrestler. If you secure it to a modular vest, then use Alice clips or 550 cord to secure it through both the buckle and lower strap.

If you need to secure more pistol mags to your gear, the Dual Pistol Upper give you lots of options. Built to go on the SOE vests over the rifle mag pouches, you can secure it anywhere you can find hook-and-loop or Alice clips. The rear is the hook part of the combination, with the panel sewn on to accommodate Alice clips. You can slap it on the loops portion of your vest, or use clips to secure it to a vest, belt, pack or other pouch. You can also use it to store particular tools you might need, or a Leatherman tool. One option is to secure it to the front of a rifle magazine pouch, and use the hook-and-loop fastener above the rifle pouch to keep the rifle flap up and open. The only problem with this approach is that a stumble or fall might spill the rifle mags. Were I taking that approach, I think I'd use some elastic around the pouch to give some friction to the rifle mags in the open pouch. Another approach would be to secure it above the empty magazine pouch. Used to carry spare pistol magazines, or a knife and Leatherman tool, it would readily accessible and out of the way. The hook-and-loop faster panels are good to keep it secured, but not sufficient by themselves to keep it attached. You must lash it down with 550 cord or use Alice clips to attach it.

The First Aid pouch measures 6 x 5 x 2 and can hold a lot of gear. You can either stuff it full of the daily personal first aid stuff you need, or use it as a capacious wound dressing holder. If you already have a compact and tested first aid pouch, then use the SOE Gear pouch to hold small binoculars, a laser rangefinder, tools, or lunch. (OK, a small lunch.) While called a First Aid pouch, it can serve in many uses, as it is just as tough as the rest of the SOE Gear.

If you need extras, SOE makes them. In addition to the gear covered here, they make tactical thigh rigs, both for magazines and handgun holsters, magazine pouches for rifle and handgun, grenade pouches for 40mm, smoke, flashbang and HE, canteen pouches (1 and 2 quart) buttpacks, slings, belts and smaller pouches for handcuffs, radios, lights, knives and three different gas mask covers.

The real test of gear is to wear it daily, test it in the field, and see where it breaks, wears out or fails under load. To do that takes more time than I have, and more chances to abuse equipment than I want to have. When something new shows up, I sit down and look it over closely from every angle. I then try it on, checking for fit, adjustment and function. It so happened that while I was in the middle of giving the SOE Gear vest and accessories their trial fit, the doorbell rang. I was able to unfasten the buckles and slide out of the vest and spent magazine pouch before I was halfway to the door. (I don't answer the door wearing stuff. The neighbors might start to gossip even more than they do.) I wore the gear as much as I could for many months, at the range and on training sessions, giving them as much use as I could without actually abusing it. It not only has not failed, but some of it (once I wash the mud off) looks practically brand new. That's where SOE, as one of the new generations of web gear manufacturing have an advantage over the old, and offers you better gear. Based in Southern California, John Willis deals directly with team members on military units such as Marine Recon and Navy SEALS. If he makes or designs something that is sub-standard, he'll hear about it. Most likely he'll hear about it when a disgruntled customer kicks open the front door and throws the busted gear through as a conversation starter. I'll be the first to admit that he doesn't make everything. But what John Willis makes, you can depend on.

Uncle Mikes Duty Gear

One of the original nylon holster and equipment makers, Uncle Mikes has expanded their line through the years to cover most of the market. I still recall the outrage of the traditionalists, back in the late 1970s, when we started seeing nylon gear to replace leather. There had always been nylon, cotton and other stuff, but the Uncle Mikes worked and lasted. They don't do the military end of things, the really aggressive vest, mag pouches and the like, but for duty gear and gear that will blend with your vest and tactical gear, Uncle Mikes has lots of items. And new on the scene is OD Green. Uncle Mikes has been making all their gear up to now according to the Henry Ford plan: "Any color you want so long as it is black." For those who dress in something other than blue or black, OD is a welcome addition. The start of the line is a complete outfit in green, a duty holster with selections for all the most popular models, belt, double mag case, pager case, chemical agent case,

The Uncle Mikes duty belt, with its Velcro backer, doesn't require extra lashing to keep it secure. No more "loopers" to keep the duty belt on.

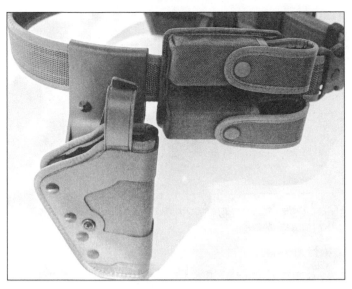

The Uncle Mikes Duty Pro-3, mounted on the Uncle Mikes duty belt with the dual hi-cap pistol pouch.

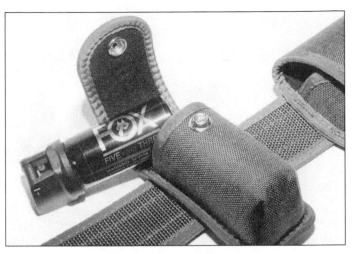

The Uncle Mikes Duty Belt and OC spray pouches are snap-fastened.

universal radio holder and single handcuff case. Which is just about all that will fit around my waist comfortably. In addition, there is a tactical leg drop harness that you can attach the holster to, swapping it from belt to thigh or back again.

Uncle Mikes Duty Pro 3 holster

The holster is the Pro 3, with three retention features. One is the thumb break strap, the second is the tension screw on the bottom outside of the holster, (the only one that is a screw on my holster, the other attachments are rivets) and the third is the retention device latching on the trigger guard. If you look down into the empty holster, you can see it. To release the pistol on the draw, you must rotate the butt of the gun in towards your body. To do so consistently requires practice, so you must drill and do nightly draw and dry fire practice until you can draw smoothly. If you do not, the retention device will defeat you just as surely as it would an attempted gun grab by an offender. The one sent to me was for a Beretta M-92, and it only took an evening of practice to get the draw mastered. While I would not take the Uncle Mikes Pro 3 off to the Steel Challenge match, it is fast enough for duty work. (And were there a Duty category at the steel Challenge, I just might consider the Pro 3.)

The back of the holster has (on the standard duty holster) a drop and offset jacket-slot hanger. The loop of the hanger has clamping screws. Once you have settled on a belt location for your holster, tighten the clamping screws and it will not wander off on you. To change a duty holster to a tactical rig, you need the load-bearing accessory harness. Simply remove the three locking screws on the back of the drop loop, and then attach the load-bearing harness. Then adjust drop and leg strap tension.

The Uncle Mikes Pro-3 in OD Green, for the Beretta M-92, has been adopted by, and bought in (you'll pardon the pun) boatloads by the U.S. Navy

Pacific Fleet for use by Force Protection units. Since the standard-issue uniform for many units is now woodland green camo(even the Navy) then the Uncle Mikes holster would fit right in. One question that comes up, and one I put to several people at Uncle Mikes is: Where's the 1911 holster? The problem is the retention lock. The mould for the retention lock apparently runs on the order of $30,000! Mike's has got to sell a lot of holsters to get that money back. However, with the increase in interest in the 1911 in Law Enforcement, it will be coming soon.

Duty belt

The duty belt is synthetic, no great surprise to those familiar with the Uncle Mikes line. The adjustment for fit is the Velcro backing, with two sliders to keep the fit where you set it. The Velcro backing also secures the duty belt to an inner belt that runs through your belt loops. In the old days we used to use "loops," leather bands with a pair of snaps that encircled both the duty belt and a trouser belt underneath. Velcro works much better. The belt has a stiffener inside to keep its shape. To install any pouches, mark your comfortable adjustment, then slide one of the sliders away from the buckle and strip the end off the Velcro. Slide the pouch or pouches on, close the belt to the Velcro at your setting, and push the slide back to lock it down. Once everything is locked in place, you simply wear the underbelt, and attach the duty belt by locating your holster on your side, then pressing the duty belt down to the Velcro of the underbelt and fasten the buckle.

Accessories

All the Uncle Mikes accessory pouches secure closed with a snap. For the regular cases, the snap is black to match the nylon. For the OD Green gear, the snap is a pretty close match to the green nylon.

Double mag pouch

The Double Magazine Pouch comes in two models, a double-stack magazine and a single-stack magazine.

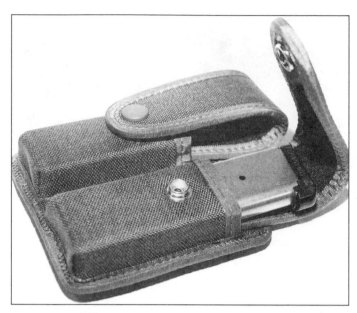

The Uncle Mikes pistol pouch also comes in a single stack version, for those who use the 1911.

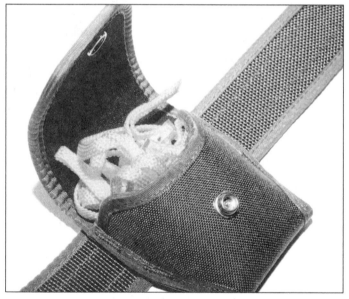

You can use the uncle Mikes cuff case to hold more than cuffs. Like a fist full of Tuff Ties, or gloves.

The double is for all the high-capacity 9's and 40's. The single is for those who can carry a 1911, and the single-stack S&W pistols. The double will not take the magazines from the S&W99-45ACP, they are just a bit too large. There is no hope of fitting a Para Ordnance, STI or other high-capacity 45 pistol mag in them. The single comfortably holds 1911 magazines and anything else that is similar. Single-stack S&W 9mm magazines have some play in them, but you can adjust the flaps to hold the magazine securely. The slots are stiffened with plastic tubes securely attached to the pouch body. They won't collapse when you remove a magazine. The backer of the mag case is robustly stitched on at the corners, so you can slide it on the belt to ride vertically or horizontally.

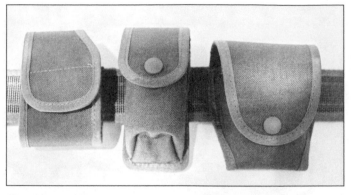

The Uncle Mikes pager pouch, chemical spray pouch, and handcuff case.

Cuff case

The cuff case is not lined with a plastic box, but the whole idea of a one-handed reholstering of a set of handcuffs is just a bit too mysterious for me to grasp. The cuff case is folded and sewn, and holds one set of cuffs, or a couple pairs of protective gloves, rubber or plastic. If you depend on cable ties or one of the new designs like the Tuff-Tie, then this case will easily hold gloves for searches and protection while treating bleeding victims. The backer is slotted for the wide duty belt and a smaller trouser belt, up to an inch and a half wide. It only rides in the vertical position.

Chemical case

The aerosol case is stiffened with a plastic tube with a tuft of foam at the bottom. You simply remove the foam if your issued aerosol is longer than the foam needs to fill. The backer is a simple sewn tab that lets the case ride vertically.

Pager case

One of the changes in law enforcement is the huge variety of communication options available. It is a rare police officer that doesn't have a pager and a cell phone on duty or off. Special Teams are no different. (They just have stricter team rules about leaving everything on "vibrate.") If you're gearing up in raid uniform, you don't want to leave the communications gear behind. For your pager, anyway, you can have an OD Green Uncle Mikes. Unlike the others, Velcro secures the pager case flap. The overlap and adjustment lets you accommodate the case to your pager. You can also fit a Motorola Walkabout in it. To press the talk button you have to leave some room under the flap, but the radio isn't going to fall out if you leave just a little room. The backer is the same simple tab as the chemical case, and only allows vertical carry.

Universal radio case

There are a whole lot of radios in law enforcement use. While many are similar in size (The designers all had the same batteries to chose from, and the same radio technology to work with. It is no surprise they are similar in size.) they are not

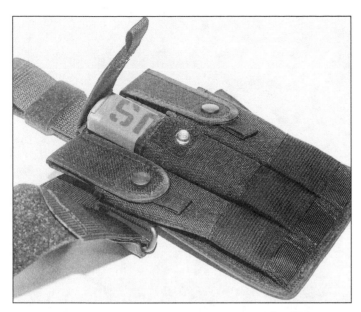

Uncle Mikes also makes tactical thigh carriers. This one holds three SMG magazines.

identical. A leather case will fit one radio model only. Synthetics allow for a design that can be adjusted to fit many different radios. The Uncle Mikes case is actually a strapping assembly. The belt loop fits the duty belt, and would be a bit loose on a trouser belt. It can easily be secured to a tactical or load-bearing vest. The straps are adjustable and secured by Velcro, and can be set to hold any radio smaller than a shoebox. The top straps are elastic cords, snapped to the middle strap. Once in, the radio is there to stay, but you can easily work the controls. The open design allows easy access to volume and frequency settings or knobs, and microphone or earphone jacks. If you need to remove it, or change the battery, you can unsnap and lift the radio out.

One easy way to integrate all these pouches and the Uncle Mikes belt is to secure them to the bottom of a vest. The Special Operations Equipment vests (and many others, too) have straps on the bottom for attaching a belt. With all the Uncle Mike pouches

attached to the belt, it is an easy thing to then secure the belt to the vest. Rather than lashing the pouches on here and there, wherever you can find some spare room, just secure them on the belt and the belt on the vest.

Web gear adaptability

Some items are made for one purpose, and you can't get anything else to work. A pager pouch, for example, won't work as anything else. But some others can be very useful in unintended roles. And you should always adapt your gear to your job. Anything you do to improve your gear for your job or your comfort, short of cutting things off, is good.

You can mix and match parts of holsters and vests. You tall operators can attach a Blackhawk drop-leg extension for more height. Or, if you work on water (many departments here in Michigan have a Power Squadron. We have four big lakes close at hand and thousands of small ones that are still big enough to drown in) you may want the drop leg extension in case you have to ditch your gear when you go overboard. You may want to swap older leg straps for new ones, or go to elastic and rubber-backed straps like Blackhawk or London Bridge Trading Co.

One recent discovery I made, and one that can be useful to you, is that a gas mask pouch can hold a huge amount of gear. I just finished shooting at the Factory Gun Nationals, and found that the Blackhawk gas mask pouch would hold my spare camera body with motor drive and zoom, a spare lens and a fistful of film. Were I needing ammunition and not film, it would hold a bunch of magazines, several bandoliers of ammo, enough wound dressings to take care of a night at the music hall after a headbangers concert, or a huge lunch.

Pouches intended for expanding a rucksack will work on a vest (with the correct attachment points on the vest, of course). Pouches for smoke or flashbang grenades can hold a flashlight, compass or wound

In attaching your gear, the Blade Tech Tek-Lok can be very useful.

The versatility of the newer gear allows you to pack specialty items like sunblock, insect repellant and 550 cord, and have it when you need it.

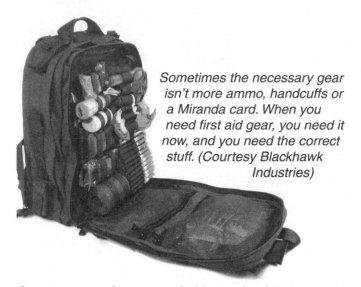

Sometimes the necessary gear isn't more ammo, handcuffs or a Miranda card. When you need first aid gear, you need it now, and you need the correct stuff. (Courtesy Blackhawk Industries)

dressing pouches can hold medical gloves for searches, and many of them can be used for flexible cuffs or cable ties.

Your imagination is the real limit here. Knock yourself out.

Storage and transport

SRT members do not sit around the station house with their feet on the desk, reading the latest gun magazines, drinking coffee and downloading pictures of guns and cars off the Internet. Many are at the station on call, while performing other duties. Some are on the road on patrol. And some are at home, on call, waiting for the pager to go off or the cell phone to ring. The first thing you learn when on call as an SRT/EMS/police officer/ fill in the blank, is that if your equipment is not all in one place you'll forget something. You have to have it ready to go or you'll lose time and forget something trying to load it all once you get the call. You could go to the big box store and buy duffel bag, but the weight of firearms, ammo, and the other gear will wear it out quickly.

One supplier I've had good luck with is Thor Defense from Illinois. The owner, Swen Swensen, is yet another one of the "Huge Chicago Guys" I run into in teaching. There must be something in the Lake Michigan drinking water, because I've met more guys bigger than I am in the Chicago area than anywhere else. Thor Defense offers tactical gear made to their specifications, and it is tough gear. I've tried Swen's Thunder Tac Bravo Gear Bag, Large, and I can easily stuff everything I need for on-call in it. (If it were any bigger, I could stuff more, but then I'd have to drag it to the truck instead of carrying it.) I can easily wrestle a tactical vest, holster, thigh mag pouches and ballistic vest into it, and have room left over for other gear like a med kit, respirator, lunch and ammo. The main cargo compartment is large enough to take the vest, holster and respirator without problem and the two side pockets can hold all the rest.

By adding a Blackhawk Discreet Carry rifle case, I can have all my gear ready to go in bags that don't attract too much attention.

The Thor Defense bag, with its contents on the outside; SOE Gear CQB vest and contents, Blackhawk gas mask bag, with Survivair respirator and filters, Camelbak, Hatch knee and elbow pads, LBTC pistol case with sidearm, windbreaker, rope, LBTC tactical thigh holster, North American Rescue Products BattlePak, personal first aid pouch, NARP First Responder kit.

The Kel-Tec SUB-2000is so compact it can fit into a sample case, gear bag or large attaché case.

Chapter 4

The Synthetic Revolution

IT USED TO be so simple: holsters were made of leather, and web gear was made of cotton. Then we got plastics and things began to change. In web gear it meant better designs made of cloth that didn't rot or support mold or mildew. In holsters there has been a divergence of paths. One is the "substitution" path. You can see it in the Uncle Mikes and Shooting Systems holsters, where more-or-less standard designs have been improved with synthetic construction. (The typical tactical thigh rig is a better design than the old cotton, but is for the most part just a substitution of nylon for cotton.) They feature synthetic stiffeners, security latches, and paddles, drop loops and fasteners. But for all the use of synthetics, they are evolutionary designs and the real revolution is in designs that use the properties of the synthetics to change the gear. For that, we go to three makers; Blade-Tech, G-Code and Fobus.

Blade-Tech

Blade-Tech is Kydex. Mention one and you will probably get a reaction mentioning the other. Kydex is a synthetic commonly found in sheets, and can be crafted into form-fitting holsters, sheaths and equipment pouches. Kydex is so tough I'm not sure you can drive a knife blade through it, but it still will not deform under heat or solvents. (At least not at levels you can survive.) Their tactical thigh rigs are

very secure and comfortable. The security is mechanical, not tactical. That is, your sidearm won't come out when you're running, but they won't preclude a gun grab. The shell is fitted to secure the sidearm even when the attached thumbstrap is open. The drop strap, the legs straps and the thumbreak strap are all conventional designs, but the holster is not. Formed of a clamshell of Kydex, it will withstand impact and not close up when it comes time to re-holster. The form-fitting design acts as the retention, keeping the pistol in place when running, climbing,

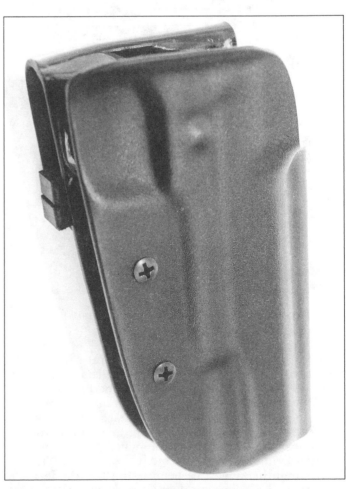

The Blade-Tech holster that everyone desires. Compact, durable, fast and comfortable for most.

Part of the synthetic revolution is this battery case from Surefire. You can step on it and your batteries are safe.

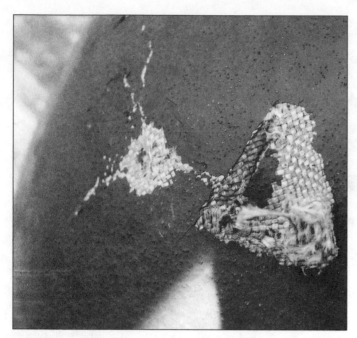

Part of the synthetic revolution is greater protection, as demonstrated by this tested PASGT helmet.

Not all synthetics are up to the task. Be sure to test before depending on anything.

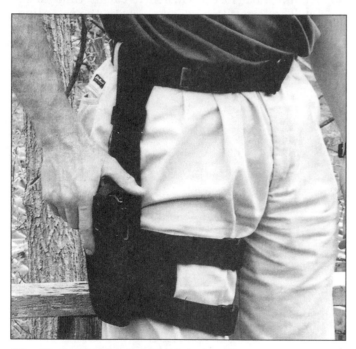

The Blade-Tech tactical thigh holster is durable and protective, and plenty fast.

jumping or kicking. My only complaint (and it is a small one, more the nature of my leg than anything) is about the leg straps. I find they tend to grab me, or my trousers, and after a few turns of going prone I have to re-position them. I'm still working with the existing straps, while considering how to remove the old ones and replace them with Blackhawk or London Bridge Trading Co. straps. Time will tell, and in the months since I've been using the Blade-Tech, the straps have become less of a problem. But that won't keep me from experimenting.

For a less tactical-oriented environment, Blade-Tech makes belt holsters. The same Kydex goes into a holster with several nice features. First, the belt loop is large enough to fit over a duty belt or a military pistol belt. So if you wanted to wear the Blade-Tech on those, you could. The holster comes with two rubber spacers to fill the gap if you use a belt not as wide, like my Galco instructor's belt. You can use one or both depending on how wide your belt is. And, by using the spacer either above or below the belt you can rig the holster to ride higher or lower on your belt. The belt holster does not have the thumbreak strap (although you can get it if you ask) but retention in activity is not a problem. What I like about the Blade-Tech is that it doesn't ride as tight to the body as many others. An advantage, you ask? Yes, for those of us with a discernable waistline. I find that many holsters designed to ride "high and tight" end up simply wedging the grip safety or tang of a handgun into my floating rib or kidney. The worst for me are those so loved by the International Defensive Pistol Association. Any holster on their approved list is one I cannot wear for any length of time without back pain. But for off-duty, training or

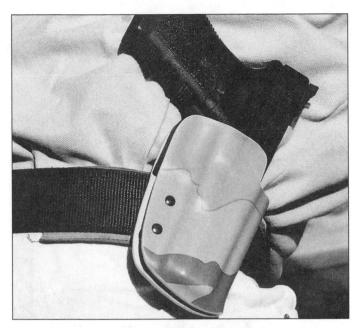

Blade-Tech can even be had in colors.

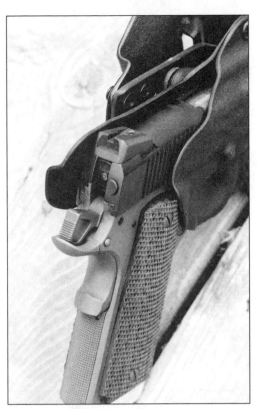

The shirt guard keeps the safety out of the cloth, and the sights out of your kidney.

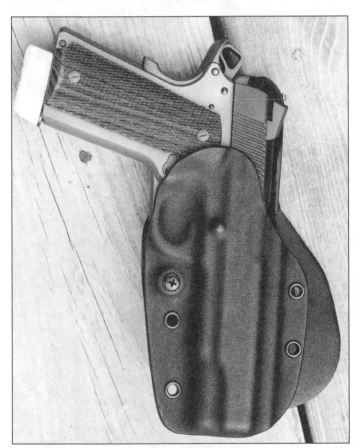

The retention is molded into the design.

non-tactical gear situations, the Blade-Tech rides low enough that it works great for me.

G-Code

Those who set out to design or manufacture a holster have to decide not just what to make it of, but what features it will or won't have. One feature that

The G-Code holster, showing the shirt guard.

all G-Code holsters have is a shirt guard. If you're using an in the pants holster, or a belt holster with a jacket over it, you have to deal with your shirt. Since it has been a long time since fashion dictated a skin-tight fit of a shirt at the waist (and many among us are glad for the change) there will be extra fabric of your shirt at your waist. The shirt guard does two things; it reduces the chance that you'll grab and draw shirt along with your sidearm, and it reduces the amount of sweating you'll do onto same. All G-Code holsters use tight molding as part of the friction fit to keep the handgun in the holster. In addition, there is an adjustment screw to tighten fit and keep your pistol with you.

The shirt guard adds comfort for me. As I mentioned, many approved IDPA holsters are very uncomfortable for me to wear. (I can only conclude

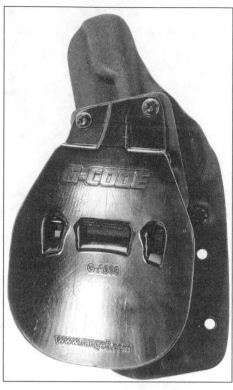

The back of the G-Code paddle design. Slip it into your waistband and it stays.

that the holster approval committee is composed of members who do not have discernable waistlines, else this problem would not exist.) The shirt guards of the G-Code holsters gives the gun and holster enough upper bearing surface that it rides on me rather than digs into me even though it rides higher than other holsters. G-code also makes magazine holders and other necessary items for carrying a defensive sidearm and spare ammo.

Fobus

Fobus holsters are a slightly different path of the synthetic revolution. Instead of being made of stiff Kydex sheets, they are moulded of a softer synthetic. The individual components are then riveted together and secured to the belt adapter. The result is a durable and incredibly inexpensive method of fabrication that creates a holster more than up to the task of keeping your sidearm with you.

The riveted design of the Fobus holsters has lead my friend Ned Christiansen to wonder if they could be torn apart. To find out, I wrapped my Galco Instructors belt around a tree, with a Fobus holster secured in it. I then placed a Glock 22 in the holster, and tried to tear the holster apart using the pistol as a lever. The short answer is; yes. However, it took a couple of minutes, and I was dripping in sweat by the time I was done. And I had to use the slide as a lever, as I was afraid I'd mangle the polymer frame of the Glock using it as the lever. So, if you're worried that your Fobus will come apart in a struggle, leaving you defenseless, don't. The effort it takes to tear the Fobus apart is great enough that it isn't going to come apart from some incidental stress. And if the bad guy does focus his efforts solely on the Fobus, well, your job just got easier.

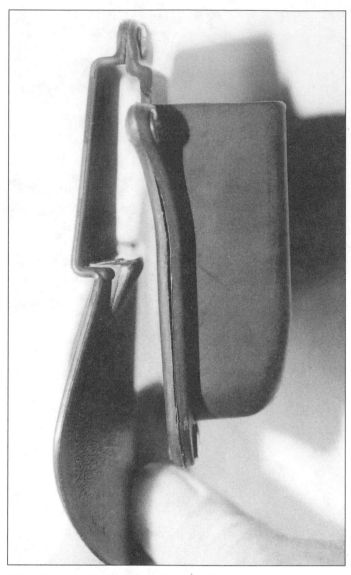

The Fobus belt clip works best with a belt to catch and not just trouser waistband.

The Fobus riveted design, with softer, flexible polymer construction.

Chapter 5

Foot and Joint Protection

YOU WOULDN'T THINK that boots were hi-tech, but they can be. As with other protective devices, good boots do more than just look good and keep that part of your body dry. A good pair of boots offers a non-skid tread, with an oil-resistant sole and insulation from electrical shocks. They should not squeak, except for the unavoidable squeak when your soles are wet and you are walking on a smooth floor. Waterproofing is good, and so is warmth, but both must be considered in the context of use and climate. Wearing waterproofed boots when working in Phoenix may not be the best thing. Ditto for insulated boots. If you're working in the swamps and bayous of Louisiana, waterproofing may not be as useful as boots that drain quickly. Here in Michigan, where it can be wet underfoot for long periods of time, (and a cold wet, at that) a waterproof pair of boots must be in the rotation.

What about Gore-Tex? A trademarked product, Gore-Tex as a component of boots, lets water wick out, but not seep in. While nice, you can get much the same

effect with Gore-Tex booties, and still have a durable leather or synthetic upper. (What can I say, I grew up buying, wearing, and caring for boots before Gore-Tex was invented. Some habits/prejudices die hard.)

Boots come with two types of sole assembly, molded and sewn-on. Danner refers to them as cement and stitch-down. In the molded, or cement, method, the sole of the boot is cast onto or glued to the mid-sole or shank. The advantages are that the boot is lighter, narrower and less expensive to make. If you have big feet, a stitch-down sole boot can be so wide it seems like the soles are constructed of sheets of plywood. The disadvantage to the cement or molded style is that when the sole is worn, there isn't much you can do to repair it. You can try building it back up with adhesive products, but the results aren't very good. Even if you have a belt sander to shape the blob into a sole, you often as not will find your repair flying off when you take a sharp turn on pavement. Stitch-down soles have the wearing surface sewn to the mid-sole. In order to do that, the

If you're going to get good protection for your feet and joints, you should also invest in good protection for your hands.

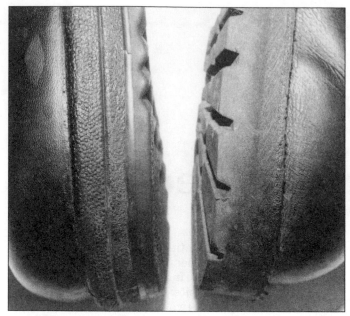

The BfR boots are molded sole design. They have speed lace eyelets and a padded collar.

A stitchdown boot (right) has a replaceable sole. It costs more, weighs more and makes a larger sole than a molded boot, left.

assembly has to be wide enough to provide a secure stitching platform. When the sole wears, the stitching is removed, and a new wearing surface is sewn on. Stitch-down boots can last as long as you maintain them and nothing cuts or abrades the shell. They cost more, weigh more, and are larger. My feet are narrow for their size, so a stitch-down boot doesn't end up too large. But there is a big difference between my 13B and a more common width for size 13 of C or D. (Not that size 13 feet are common.) I've known officers whose feet are so wide that if they wear stitch-down boots they can't work the pedals on a stick-shift car or truck..

BfR

Some applications require additional protection. One brand of boots, BfR, offers protection from small land mines. The amount of protection they can offer from explosive charges of the hand grenade size is amazing. (Not that I personally tested that application, mind you. There are limits to what I'm willing to do in the interests of scientific curiosity and practical application of writing projects.) I know what you're thinking: "Yea, so what? The druggies in my jurisdiction don't protect their drug houses with land mines." Yes, but what about broken glass? The meth lab you're about to raid stands to gross the operators tens of thousands of dollars (or more) in a few weeks time (or less). Can you be sure they haven't heard about punji sticks? Broken glass? Nails? Even if they don't go to any extra efforts, broken glass and chunks of rusty metal are common at many urban locales. And the sloppy, and hasty, scumbags sweating away in the drug lab sure aren't spending any time being neat. Busted labware is likely to be just tossed into an unused corner or

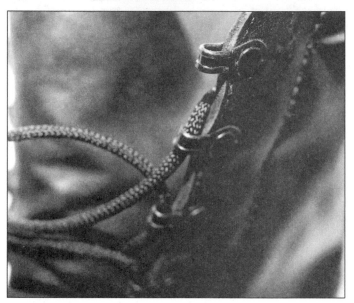

The eyelet design allows fast lacing without a lot of work.

room. Or out the window. The urban (and suburban) jungle is not manicured, especially those locations being used for criminal purposes.

In the interests of finding these things out for the book, I obtained a pair of BfR boots and tested them. From the outside they appeared to be standard boots, with a formed sole as an integral part of the boot. The toe section of the upper is formed from a single piece of leather. How do the boots protect? The soles have two shock plates, one on the heel and one on the ball, and the layer between the soles and plates and your foot contains multiple layers of Twaron®. Twaron is the new Kevlar, and the protection precludes penetration. The shock plates spread impacts over the whole sole, so a blast would not have the chance to apply differing leverages to the various parts of your foot. As I said, I'm not going to test them by stomping explosives, and the instructions that came with them tells you not to deliberately test them by standing on land mines. (I

The soles are not designed for thick, gluey, sticky mud. Good, since you don't often see that in the street or in buildings.

Nails, glass, knives all fail to do more than scar the sole pattern of the BfR boots.

can only surmise that someone did, and that is why the manufacturer added the extra warning, as a precaution against blame.) For the first test, I took the laces out and slid one of the boots over a section of 2x4. I then took a 12- penny nail and a carpenters hammer, and proceeded to try to drive the nail through the sole to the 2x4. I gave it a couple of hits and quit. Once the tip of the nail had penetrated the composite of the sole, it stopped against the shock plate. Additional hits simply dulled the tip of the nail. I wasn't about to sacrifice one of my knives (nor risk cutting myself) when the nail test failed. Since the nail test failed, jumping on broken glass seemed (dare I say it?) pointless. So, instead I walked on some sharp rock edges to see if the sole had enough flex to make the edges uncomfortable to my feet. The sole is stiff enough that the edges did not press hard enough to cause discomfort on the sole of my foot. Whether the ball or the arch, I could stand comfortably. The only other test I could think of was to let a large dog chew on them. However, the tops aren't armored (the toes are protected with a polymer cup, lighter than steel, for impact protection) so the dog's teeth would penetrate the top. Hardly a fair test. What was left was to test for comfort. How heavy, and how comfortable, are they? In order; not very, and quite. I wore them on my daily walks, a 3-mile hike with a rucksack, and found them quite comfortable. A few minutes of heavy bag work determined that they were not too heavy for unarmed work. (And very hard on the bag, but the effect shoes have on a heavy bag is old news.) Some boots with steel shanks can be so heavy that any kicking at all risks knee injuries. The BfR boots were light enough to do bag work without risk.

I have worn them in a couple of classes, where I alternate pairs of boots on odd and even days, and

have found them comfortable enough to wear all day without a problem, and offer support and protection. The sizing may be a small problem for some of our larger brethren. My feet are 13B. The largest size BfR makes just fits. As an international manufacturer, they are much more accustomed to dealing with clients ordering hundreds or thousands of boots in the range of 5-8. After all, how many troopers in the Singapore Defense Forces have feet larger than 10? If you don't need boots larger than I do, you can get BfR's in your size.

The uppers, being leather, can be treated with liquid silicone (more old-fogey technology) for waterproofing, and polished. Once I'd treated them, wet days are not a problem for my feet. I only wish they had sewn-on soles, so they could be resoled when the tread wears down in a couple of years.

Danner

If you are going to wear your boots all day long, and you have feet that are not "average" you should investigate custom-fit boots. Danner can make them to fit you. I have large, narrow feet, and in some brands by the time I get boots big enough for my toes, I have enough room side to side for another half a foot. If you're going to buy Danners, you must make the acquaintance of a Brannock Device. It is that black and silver "slider-foot-measure-thingie" that better shoe stores have. Measure your feet (both, not everyone has identical-size right and left feet) for overall length, width and arch length.

Danner boots come in all the options; all-leather, Gore-Tex, synthetics, jump boots and upgraded running shoes. The model I tested was the Fort Lewis, designed with the input of customers from the Infantry School at Fort Lewis.

Not only are the boots made to the size of your feet, the Danner crew can rebuild your boots years from now when you've worn them down. They can

The Danner Ft. Lewis boots are stitched-on soles, with laces going closer to the toes. The collar is padded and there are pull loops on the spine to make it easier to get them on.

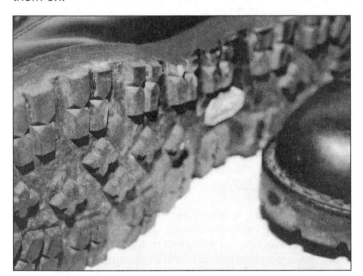

The Vibram lugged sole is aggressive enough to offer good traction but not as large as extreme mud requires.

Halfway up the eyelets, they change from traditional to speed loops.

The heelcups provided adds support, comfort, and aids in making the boots ready to go without needing breaking-in.

(Danner boots only, please) re-stitch the various sections of the assembly back together, re-line your boots with Gore-Tex, and with sewn-on soles, resole your boots. The price is as much as some cheaper boots, but you're rebuilding boots that already fit and are broken in. If you liked them enough to wear them out, then why not get some more life out of them?

The Fort Lewis boots I received were unlike many other boots in that the breaking in period was much shorter. I often find that I have to start out wearing most boots only a couple of hours each day to break them in. After a week of the "daily hour" routine (sounds like a soap opera) I can then wear them for half a day or a day and finish breaking them in. The Danners didn't produce any "hot spots" on my feet after an hour, so I just kept wearing them. At the end of the day I didn't have any sore spots, and could have worn them the next day. I added them to my class rotation, so they got alternate days wearing for

the weeklong classes, and put them into the rotation for range trips. The Fort Lewis model laces down closer to the toes than many other boots do, a "look" that is a bit different. Combined with the speed-lace loops on the uppers, it takes some work to get the laces tight and properly tensioned. But once done, they stay comfortable all day long.

Second Chance

Richard Davis is well known to many, since he originated the idea of soft-concealable body armor. What many of you don't know is that Richard is not one to let the grass grow under his feet. Second Chance makes insoles for your boots that offer puncture protection and a limited amount of blast protection from small explosive devices. As with all such approaches, there is a trade-off. More thickness offers more protection. You can make inserts only so thick before they become too thick to fit in the boots, or to thick to walk on comfortably. But if you want protection that you can swap from boots to boots, then the Second Chance insoles are your choice. Be sure to size to your feet, and make sure you have boots with enough extra room to take the insoles.

Plain leather generics

You can find plain boots at any surplus store, and some "fashion" stores in university towns. Unlined, lacking steel shanks, steel toes or other amenities, they are best used only as hard-duty training gear. That is, put all the hard wear and abuse on your cheap "surplus" boots, and save the expensive ones for real work. If your team is doing a practice recovery, and you're the designated casualty, it would be a real shame to be grinding your $250 custom boots through the gravel as the team drags your limp body out of the line of fire. Make sure your custom boots are broken in, and then use the generics for training. My friend Ned Christiansen found a pair of French Foreign Legion boots in his size (lucky him, few Frenchies have size 13 feet) for $15, and delights in the cheap protection they offer his feet for training and weapons classes. A quick look around town turned up a number of Asian knock-offs of name boots in the $29.95 range. For a limited protection item for your feet, at a very low cost, they can be a wise investment.

Running shoes/boots

One trend in boot design and fashion (oh yes, there are fashions in boots for special operations teams) are boots that are grown-up running shoes. The idea is to take a comfortable running shoe and "grow" the upper until it is 6 or 8 inches, or more. Customarily of synthetic fabric and synthetic leather construction, with a rubber or composite sole, they are comfortable. And they are quick to run in. However, they are running shoes in disguise. For those of us brought up in more traditional combative arts, shoes are weapons, and running shoes are just padded foot protectors. Also, the fabric does not offer as much protection to your feet, ankles and shins as leather does. If you anticipate using your feet as impact weapons, you might want to reconsider the running shoe/boot as an option. I know from personal experience that kicking a large individual with running shoes on your feet can dampen the intended effect. However, the running shoe/boot is quite popular.

Boot and shoe care

Boots should last years if they are properly cared for. The running shoe style boot, with fabric uppers and glued-on or molded soles will not. The soles can't be replaced, so when the heels wear you are done. I regularly wear a brand of shoes where each pair lasts me only six months. The sole is molded, and when

With proper care, boots can last a long time, be reasonably waterproof, and look good.

the heels round, I toss them. The uppers are still good at that point, but for the $25 they cost, replacing the shoes is easy enough. But good boots for my feet cost $165 to $225, and at that price, six months of use is not enough. You'd think something as prosaic as shoes or boots would be a subject everyone would already know all they need to on, but you'd be surprised. With running shoes now the standard shoe, there are a lot of people who have no idea what it takes to keep shoes or boots going. First, you should treat them as soon as you get them. Each manufacturer uses their own process to waterproof the leather, and for best results you should use their own products. Waterproof your boots if you expect any water at all. For generic use, I just use the liquid silicone that you apply with the applicator that looks like cotton on a wire. A couple of applications are good enough for Michigan. When you first apply it, remove the laces and get the waterproofing down into the seams around the tongue. You'd be surprised how much water can leak in if you neglect those areas. After that, keep them clean. Clean means that you occasionally suds up a cloth with saddle soap and wash the grime off. (Just rinsing isn't enough) Once the dirt is off and they've dried, polish. Rub polish on, let it dry then buff it. If your department insists on a spit shine, then you had better make the acquaintance of a former Marine and learn the intricacies of that arcane process. Every few washes, renew the waterproofing.

You should rotate your footwear. Wearing the same shoes day after day is bad for the shoes and bad for your feet. Without a chance to dry, the shoes or boots can become a perfect breeding ground for all kinds of bacteria and fungus. By rotating through a pair of shoes or boots, you give the leather a chance to recover from your feet and the environment, and thus last longer. There is no reason two pairs of good boots, rotated and kept clean and polished, shouldn't last up to 10 years. At full retail for two pairs, $500, that works out to $50 a year. Not bad. Of course, that doesn't count

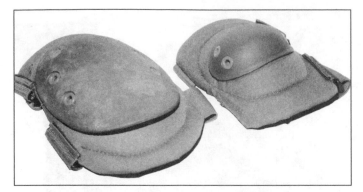

Hatch elbow and knee pads. The hard cover over the padded body offers greater protection and durability.

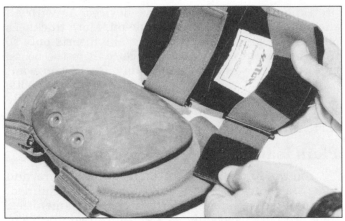

The Hatch elbow and knee pads are secured with two straps and Velcro sections.

the cost of many sets of laces, but you'd be going through them regardless of which boots you wore.

Elbow and Knee protection

In the modern world, your environment can injure you. Diving for cover, or kneeling behind a wall for cover or concealment, can get you injured. While the risk exists in daily patrol work, it is even more likely on special operations. Armando Valdes is a Sergeant on the Miami Police Department, the pre-eminent Glock shooter in competition, and a nice guy. And he was off the streets and out of competition for several years due to a knee injury suffered from a fall during a foot pursuit. (Desk work, yes. But nothing else.) Photos of troopers in Afghanistan and Iraq showed many with knee and elbow pads. When working in an urban environment, going prone is not always useful. For working and firing through doors and windows, kneeling is often more useful. But getting laid up from a knee injury isn't. I injured a knee in training once. I was at Gunsite, and we were doing draw and drop to one knee for 3-yard head shot drills. I drew, dropped, and heard a loud noise and felt a sharp pain in my right knee. The next thing I knew I was surrounded by concerned staff. They quickly looked me over, and took my .45 from me, all the while asking if I was all right. Their concern was that I had drawn and fired an accidental discharge and hurt myself. What had happened was that something had been on the ground under my knee, and struck me right under the kneecap as I put my weight down on it. The intense pain had caused me to clutch my hands, thus firing the 1911 into the dirt. In no time my knee swelled up to the point where I thought I was going to have to cut my jeans to get them off. During the rest of the class, I dragged my leg around like Deputy Festus in the old TV show Gunsmoke, trying to keep up. Learn from those who've been there, protect your knees. And elbows.

Hatch pads

The elbow and kneepads from Hatch are padded and hard-shelled. The exterior center is a plastic shell, bonded to a padded cover with straps. The straps are elastic, with Velcro panels and hinged to

the body of the unit by being looped through sewn-on buckles. On the back, there is room to write your name, a useful addition. In use, they are simple. Open the Velcro, slide the padding on, then pull the strap and secure the Velcro. Resist the temptation to get them "good and tight" for you will find they can easily be too tight. Also, test your motion once they're on, to make sure you haven't trapped part of your uniform sleeves or trousers and thus restricted your motion. Pads are not just for operations; they are for training, also. You can easily become injured from empty brass on the range. Kneel down on an empty 9mm case, and you will feel it. You could even be injured severely enough to require medical attention.

A problem I've found with many pads is they "walk." It doesn't do any good for your knee or elbow if the pad has slipped down to your forearm or shin, or rotated around. I've found the elastic bands on the Hatch pads to be wide enough to keep them in place, and when tight enough to keep them from rotating they don't cut off the circulation. The combination of hard shell center with wider padding makes them flexible enough to wear without restricting movement.

In settings other than riots, shinguards can be very useful.

Hatch shin guards come in three sizes, and can save you a lot of pain and bruising. (Courtesy Hatch Corp.)

So, you charge into the bus, and one of the passengers aluminum attaché case is sticking out in the aisle. Aren't you glad you wore your knee and shin guards?

Now, having protection does not make you invulnerable. Padding isn't ballistic protection. And padding only keeps you from being harmed by rocks, glass, brass and other debris. You can still go to your knees hard enough to hurt yourself, due to the force of the impact. Take some time to practice and see just how hard you can fall without it hurting. Then see if you can regulate your motions, and their force, to not exceed that level. It isn't easy, but in the long run it will pay off.

Extra protection for your legs can come in the form of shin guards and instep protectors. Originally designed for use in riot situations, I've seen some teams using them for entry work. In a crowded hallway, or with a resistant suspect, knowing your shins and feet are protected can make the job of control and entry a lot easier. The trick is finding a set that is light, comfortable and fit. They can be difficult to fit. Unlike elbow and knee pads, which are a one-size-fits-all proposition, shin guards and instep protectors are almost a custom fit addition. After all, you really can't expect the same guards to work with one officer who has a 29-inch inseam and size 8 shoes, and an officer with a 36-inch inseam and size 13 shoes. Hatch makes combo shin and foot guards in three sizes, measured by the rise in the shin area.

Chapter 6
Gloves For All Seasons

GLOVES ARE NOT just for keeping your hands warm. In fact, in many climates, a glove is something that makes your hands sweat while it is doing its real job, protecting your hands. The problem with most gloves is that while they protect your hands, they impede your ability to do much with them. The standard G.I. leather shells are a good example. If you're using them to keep your hands warm, or protect your hands while doing something hard, rough or dirty, fine. But don't try to do any delicate work while wearing them. They are stiff, clumsy, and only offer a small amount of protection. The gloves I recently tested, however, are none of those. I tested four models from Blackhawk Industries under their "Hellstorm" label. The four models were their Nomex Aviator gloves, Special Operations Light Assault Gloves, Navigunner Water Operations Gloves, and their Special Operations Light Assault Gloves; Kevlar. The Hellstorm gloves are made of the best materials for the job, whether synthetic or natural, with durable stitching, comfortable design and laden with custom features. I also tested four gloves from Hatch, their Elite Marksman, Specialist Airprene, Operator, and Friskmaster Max.

After months of daily wear, the Blackhawk nomex aviators show some pilling (all nomex gloves will) but they still have many months of use left in them.

First thing I did upon receiving them was to make sure they fit, as some gloves don't, even when they are listed as the proper size. They all fit just fine. Next, I tested them for dexterity. With any of the gloves I could dial a cell phone, work a PDA, change frequencies on a radio, and handle a firearm without problems. I could adjust clicks on a riflescope, and turn battery-operated sights on and off. While wearing the Blackhawk Aviator gloves I happened to need a particular form, and found I could pick up the paper without having to wrinkle it. I then tried the others, and found I could read a newspaper while wearing any of them. At the range, my hunt-and-peck field typing (one of the guys described it as "more like search and destroy") on a laptop went smoothly and without more than the usual number of typos. Once I got home from the range I tried a further experiment; touch-typing on the computer wearing each of the gloves. With a little practice I could type wearing the Blackhawk Aviator gloves and the Hatch Elite Marksman. The Hatch Specialist Airprene, Operator and the Blackhawk Navigunner worked fine for radios and such, but for touch-typing they caused a spelling error per sentence. The rest of the gloves were just a bit too thick and stiff to be able to type without making my spell check function go crazy. Considering that I couldn't even get single keys struck while wearing G.I. shells or winter gloves, these aren't so bad. If you do happen to use a keyboard while wearing gloves, test the gloves and practice until you've gotten used to them. For those who don't touch-type, none will be a problem. From now on, my definitive test of a glove's functional dexterity is picking up and reading the daily paper. All four Blackhawk gloves have their newly-patented index finger stitching. The four circles of stitching allow you to shorten the glove on your trigger finger and not worry about the glove fraying. Provided you don't cut the last one off, that is. I didn't test that feature, as I have not needed the tipless glove option yet.

At the range, I was able to wear any of them and still manipulate firearms. For the long-term test I left the gloves hanging by the back door, and each time I left the house I've put a pair on. Yes, people do look at you a little funny if you're at the grocery store

The Blackhawk Aviators fold up and fit compactly in the spare grenade pouch of the SOE Gear empty mag pouch. Gloves don't do you any good left behind in the vehicle or gear bag.

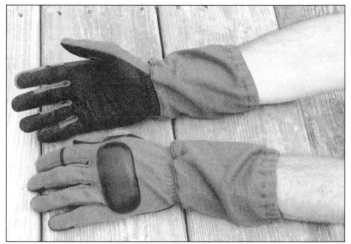

The Hatch Aviators have longer cuffs, comforting to those of us with longer arms who are tired of having our forearms exposed. They also have knuckle padding and a non-slip palm and fingers.

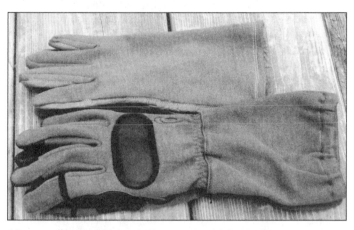

You can see how much longer the Hatch gloves are than the G.I. flight gloves above.

while wearing gloves. At least in warm weather. In the winter they don't stare much. A few test sessions at the range is a nice test, but there is nothing like the daily use of something to see how it really holds up and functions. After four months of daily use, they are all holding up well.

Blackhawk Nomex Aviators

Nomex is a heat-resistant synthetic fabric used to make flight suits and racing coveralls. The gloves are meant to protect your hands while not impeding the use of controls and instruments in the cockpit. (And ground crew handling potentially hot objects.) While Nomex is not heat-proof (nothing is) it will protect from flash burns and withstand momentary heat exposure. If your job takes you into a location where flash burns may be a problem (drug labs with vapors from flammable solvents would be one such possibility) or you may have to handle hot objects, Nomex gloves will protect you. My previous use had been with G.I. gloves, and I always found them to not quite fit. Often the fingers would be a bit too short, or the width of the palm restricted my hands. And the durability sometimes wasn't there. I've had G.I. aviators fall apart after a few weeks of use. The Hellstorms are still fine after four months of being in the rotation. The leather palm and fingers seem a bit softer than G.I. gloves, and have stayed "sticky" longer, too. While they don't actually stick to things, the surface gives you a little friction that helps in getting a good grip. The Hellstorm Aviators are also longer than G.I., coming up the wrists farther and offering more protection. Combined with a Nomex undergarment and a balaclava, you can have complete flash burn protection. The Hellstorm Aviator gloves have elastic stitching at the wrist to keep them snug and on your hands.

Hatch Operator

The Operator is a flash burn resistant glove made of Kevlar. The Kevlar construction also offers some resistance to cuts, but not as much as slash-resistant gloves would. The Operator should be thought of as a product-improved aviator's glove. First, it is a lot longer in the cuffs then other gloves. While most gloves will come 3, maybe 4 inches up your wrist, the Operator is a full 5 inches up. The cuffs have elastic both at the wrist and the end of the cuff up on your forearm. On the palms, the leather is kangaroo, cut and sewn in a complex pattern to accommodate the flex of your hand as you grasp something. The base of the palm has a padded panel. On the backs are a lightly padded panel covering the knuckles. While not positioned to pad for a punch, they do offer protection to your knuckles from inadvertent impact. The trigger finger has a sewn band around it, so if you cut off the tip of the glove for your finger to protrude, the fabric of the glove will not unravel.

I'm not quite sure how to go about testing the flash-burn resistance of Nomex or Kevlar gloves, so I wore them while handling hot objects. As expected, the offered momentary protection from the heat of hot metal objects and sun-baked tools. However, hold the hot objects for more than a few seconds and you'll start to notice the heat. These are heat-resistant, not heat-proof gloves. Don't expect to be able to handle red-hot objects without penalty.

Hatch Elite Marksman

The Elite Marksman gloves are synthetic backs with kangaroo palms, a snug fit and light glove for general use without loss of "feel" and dexterity. They are wrist-length, and while the Velcro closure strap pulls them snug so they won't slide off, it does not offer any support to the wrist as the Hellstorm gloves do. The backs are plain and the palms are relatively plain, with some shaping and stiching around the thumb. The materials are light enough that the construction does not require elaborate shaping to be comfortable and unobtrusive. For cool weather and light protection, they are very good gloves, with the added bonus of not looking like shooting gloves. If you want gloves for driving, riding or general range and duty work, that don't look like aggressive "combat SWAT gloves" then the Elite Marksman will serve you well.

Hellstorm/Blackhawk Special Operations Light Assault Glove

The SOLAGS are made of several synthetics, with a wrist strap and palm tension adjustment tab, both Velcro secured. The gloves end at the wrist strap, but getting a glove that had the strap and also went further up the wrist would probably not work. The synthetic is washable, so if your gloves get funky from sweat or something you'd rather not have on them, you can wash them and let them dry, and be back in business. The wrist strap takes some getting used to. To adjust any of the Hellstorm gloves, undo both the wrist strap and the palm back strap, and put the gloves on. Adjust the wrist strap to offer support to your wrist at the end of its range of movement. It is easy to get the wrist support too tight, and you'll find it uncomfortable and restrict your movement. Once you have the wrist strap set right, then close the palm flap, again, making sure you don't get it too tight. Since they are both Velcro, it is easy enough to re-adjust them.

As an additional test of the SOLAGS and Elite Marskman, I used them at the range, and in several classes, where I had to deal with doors and windows. One window was obviously in need of maintenance, as after the drill I found I had to extract some splinters from the left glove of the SOLAG. Splinters that would have been in my hand, had I not been wearing the gloves. (Then again, I probably would have spared my hands by going through the window in a more cautious manner, sans gloves.)

While the SOLAG gloves are not rated as being heat-resistant (as the Nomex ones are) they do offer protection from hot objects. As an impromptu test, I heated a small saucepan of water to boiling, then picked it up and placed it in the palm of a gloved hand. Then took my hand away when it got too hot. (Look, I'm not saying this is a definitive test, nor am I saying you should do this at home. I just had to know.) The two SOLAG gloves offered a few seconds more protection than the Nomex did, and the Nomex offered more protection than the Navigunners, elite Marksman or Airprene did. All protected my hands long enough that I could realize the pan was hot and pull away before I got burned.

Blackhawk Navigunners secured in the belt loop of the SOE Gear CQB vest. Quick and handy, and out of the way.

Hellstorm/Blackhawk Navigunner

The Navigunner is meant for water operations. The back is made of neoprene (a very thin neoprene, but plenty tough enough) with the palm and fingers made of HawkTex. The tougher and rougher HawkTex offers durability, and the edge of the palms and the tips of three fingers are covered with an extra layer of rougher HawkTex.

I don't scuba dive, and when I was with the Sheriff's Department I was not on the power squadron, so for me waterborne ops meant dunking my hands in a bucket of water at the range, and washing dishes. The range portion went just fine. As for washing the dishes, don't snicker about it. Consider the task: you're handling things not just slippery from water, but from soap, too. They are oddly shaped, smooth, flat, and if you drop one you can't avoid the penalty. Dropping some issue gear into the surf gets it wet and perhaps sandy. Dropping a china dinner plate breaks it. I did not break anything. And the gloves kept my hands warmer at the range, and cooler at the sink, than my immersed wrists got.

Hatch Specialist Airprene

The backs of the Specialist are made of Airprene, a bonded synthetic constructed of a layer of neoprene

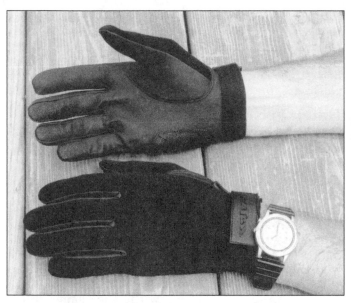

The Hatch Airprene gloves are light, comfortable, and offer a good grip in wet conditions.

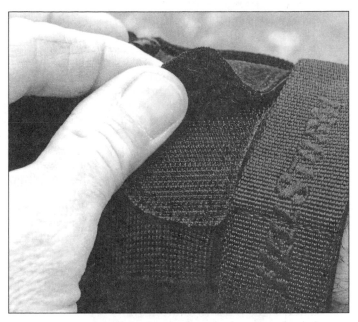

The Hellstorm gloves all have a Velcro adjustment flap, and a wrist brace cuff that is also Velcro secured.

and a layer of an open-weave synthetic. The palms are synthetic leather. The tips of the three off fingers are covered with a non-skid synthetic. The result is a good-gripping synthetic for wet operations that go on easy and wear well. While the wrist strap is larger than that of the Elite Marksman, it still does not offer the wrist support of the Hellstorm SOLAG. If you want support, go SOLAG. If not, the Hatch gloves will fit and work. Testing in wet weather and at the sink proved the synthetic leather and non-skid fingertips work well, and provide a secure grip.

Hellstorm/Blackhawk Special Operations Light Assault Glove, Kevlar

A Kevlar-lined glove offers protection against sharp objects. More protection than a non-Kevlar glove would. (And I ended up needing the protection.) The design is the same as the standard SOLAG, but the exterior of the Kevlar version is mostly leather. The palm and finger gripping area is leather. On the back, the knuckle area is leather, extending back along the seams of the upper and lower body, back to the wrist strap. The wrist strap and palm flap are the same, and you have to fuss a bit to get it on with support, without binding. The results of putting leather and Kevlar into the glove make it a bit stiffer and thicker than the standard SOLAG, but not much. But still less bulky and stiff than other gloves of this type I've tried. For testing, I did the same range and class sessions where I used the standard SOLAG, switching them back and forth. When I really needed them, the luck of the rotation had the SOLAG Kevlar on my hands.

I was (of all things) walking the dog. Our dog is a standard Poodle, 55 pounds and sharp as a tack. Good size, athletic, smart, and no idea in the world about fighting except to protect me, my wife, or the house. In our neighborhood there is a dog of Chow/ Shepherd mix with a bad attitude. At 70 pounds, it

usually gets "walked" by dragging its owner around the block, snarling at other dogs, people and random objects. Baxter and I were walking past a house getting re-roofed, and what with the noise of the generator and nail guns going off we didn't hear the Chow coming. I saw the blur of brown out of the corner of my eye, and the next thing I know there is a snarling fur ball at my feet. I spent the next few seconds yanking Baxter's leash to keep him out of the Chows path, and getting a few good kicks in. Despite my size 13 feet, I was not having much effect. One of the workmen came running up, so I yanked the leash hard enough to extract Baxter out of the fight again

The Hellstorm SOLAG Kevlars, after months of wear, multiple classes and one dog encounter. Years of wear left, and they aren't going back to Blackhawk Industries.

and threw the free end to the workman. I then dove on the Chow, aiming for the collar, and throwing my weight on top of it. I twisted the nylon collar it was wearing to choke the dog, and kept shifting my weight to stay on top. (I should point out this is not as dangerous as it seems. I'm 6'4", 205 lbs, a Second Degree Black Belt, and went to the State Finals in High School wrestling. Of course, if I didn't have 135 pounds on the dog, I would have found another way to solve the problem.)

Once the Chow started slowing down, I jumped off, watching to see if I needed to dive in again. When it got up it was obviously staggering, so my choking had had the desired effect of cutting off its oxygen supply. I chased it home and gave the owner a dressing down. He was apologetic, "She must have slipped out when the door was open ...." And on and on. I gave him a lecture, pointed out the size-13 shoe prints I'd put on his Chow during the struggle, and told him next time the police would hear of it.

When I got back to Baxter, the workman handed me the leash and pointed to my right hand. The palm of the glove was scored from a couple of Chow teeth, and covered with dog spit. Obviously the dog had gotten its teeth on me in the first moments of my diving in, but the Kevlar of the glove had kept me from noticing it. Once the adrenaline wore off, I could feel where the impact had been on my hand, and where the dog collar pressed against my hand. But I was not cut, and the glove, while slightly marked, is still functional. As a result of the experience, I conducted a test I had not wanted to try; I tried to cut the glove with a knife. With a freshly sharpened Buck lock-blade I tried to get through the leather. No luck, and even less marking than the Chow had done.

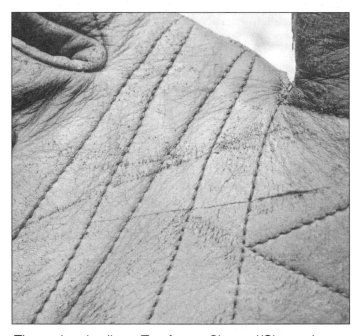

Three abrasion lines: Two from a Shepard/Chow mix loose in the neighborhood, and one knife tip test I did afterwards. Tough gloves, good protection, and constant companions.

Blackhawk isn't getting these gloves back, unless they want to replace them under warrantee. What is the warrantee? They will replace or repair anything they make that needs it, up to and including bullet holes. They don't need to repair or replace these, as the gloves are fine. The scars actually add a little character.

Hatch Friskmaster Max

These are some fine looking gloves. As with the Elite Marksman, if you want gloves that don't look like "combat SWAT" gloves, the Friskmasters are it. They look like a first-class pair of driving or light winter gloves. The lining is Hatch Powershield X3™ that is a blend or mixture or layered combination (they won't say) of Spectra®, fiberglass and polyester that offers 10 times the cut resistance of 100 percent Spectra® of the same weight. After my experience with the Chow, I was not looking for a rematch just to test another pair of gloves. (My Mother did not raise any fools.) So I tested with the same Buck pocketknife, trying to cut the lining on the inside. No go. Even placing the glove against a hard backer and trying to cut with force had no effect. I tried a sewing needle on the cuff, and was able to easily press it through. However, that is not a fair test, as the Friskmaster (nor any of the other gloves) is not rated nor offered as a puncture-resistant glove against needles. If you want a glove that will offer protection against needle punctures you have to go with something specifically designed for the job.

For cool weather, for good looks, and for cut-resistance, the Friskmaster will serve well as SWAT, duty, and off-duty gloves.

Sizing and selection

What size are your hands? Every manufacturer must know your size, for gloves truly are not a "one-size-fits-all" garment. On the Hellstorm box is the sizing chart, but for those who don't already have a box, here are the sizes:

Measured across the knuckles, from edge to edge while your hand is flat on a surface, Medium is 3-3/8 inches, Large is 3-7/8 inches, X-large is 4-1/4 inches and XX-large is 4-7/8 inches. If your hands fall in between these sizes, I'd suggest getting the next size up. You can tighten the wrist strap and palm flap to tighten an otherwise too-large glove. But a too-small glove is too small. As for the flap on the back of the hand, I just called it the palm flap. "Back of the hand flap" is too clumsy, and I have to call it something.

Hatch measures from base of the hand to the longest fingertip. X-small, 6-3/4 inches, Small, 7 inches, Medium, 7-1/4 inches, Large, 7-1/2 inches, X-large, 7-3/4 inches and the XX-Large, 7-7/8 inches.

What type do you need? That depends on what you are doing. For those who raid drug labs, the Nomex Aviators, Hatch Operators or the Friskmaster or SOLAG Kevlar gloves would work well. While leather and Kevlar don't offer the flash burn protection that Nomex does, they should do well enough at keeping you from getting burned that they are worth it for the extra protection from cuts. For

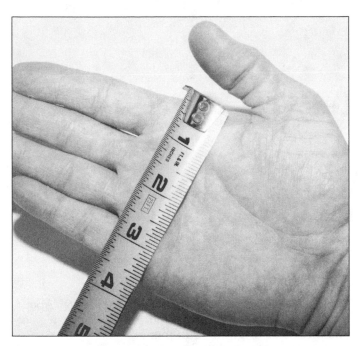

Some glove makers measure across the knuckles,

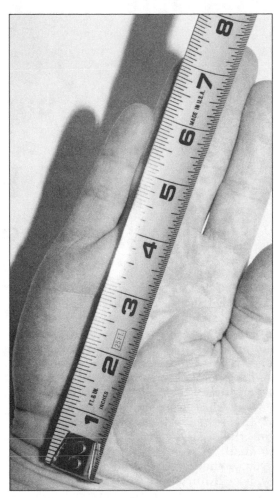

Other glove makers measure the length of the hand. Know what you need to order the correct size.

any kind of defensive work, I'd go to the SOLAG Kevlar or Friskmaster. Knowing that you at least aren't going to get cut on your hands makes the job of dealing with an assailant or offender so much easier. For those with specialized needs, like the deputies on the power squadron, or those rappelling, get specialized gloves for just what you need. Neoprene or Airprene for the Power Squadron, and all-leather and stout construction for rappelling. But remember, correct sizing. Brag about wearing a shirt a size larger than you actually do, but order your gloves the right size for you.

Medical gloves

Medical gloves made of rubber, Nitrile, or various generic plastics, can protect you from infectious diseases. Lest the readers who haven't done it think police officers are a bunch of squeamish sissies, it is a real concern. And in addition to infectious diseases (of which there are many, and in some areas of the country, prevalent) many suspects and offenders are low on the scale of good grooming habits. Grubby does not begin to describe some law enforcement clients. A pair of medical gloves stashed in a belt pouch, either uniform or tac gear, is a prudent item to pack.

Testing gloves

Once you've got your size nailed done, you have to test or train with your gloves to be sure they are the proper ones. You must gear up and do your range and team training with the gloves on. It won't do to "save" the wear and tear of training, only to find out in a raid that you can't work a radio, phone, or optics knobs with gloves on. For practice when not training, try wearing gloves while reading the paper or taking care of administrative duties around the precinct

house. Yes, you may seem a little affected wearing your gloves at your desk, but what better way to find out just how dexterous you are while wearing them? And if you type much of the time, as I do, then typing while wearing gloves will very quickly sort the dexterous from the protective.

Should you clip the fingertips for feel? That's a personal choice. I don't, but I select gloves lighter than protective so I don't lose too much feel. If you do, don't clip past the retaining stitching, or the gloves might unravel. For someone in a high-volume precinct or city, where gloves get worn out once a month anyway, the loss of a few days or use from a pair of gloves is not a big deal. Cut them if you like. For those who expect six months or more out of a pair of gloves, unraveling fingers are a big deal. But then, none are so expensive that a little testing will flatten your wallet. Try both ways and see which way you prefer.

Carry and wear

Where to carry them? For patrol, given a suitable climate, wearing them is the best solution. If you're not wearing them, keep them in a belt pouch. For a tac team, where gloves are part of the gearing-up process, just tucking them under a magazine pouch flap works.

Chapter 7

Physical Protection, Eyes, Ears And Body

UNTIL THERE IS some great big breakthrough in medical science, you only get one set of everything. One pair of eyes, one pair of ears, etc. etc. If you lose, damage or diminish any part, you cannot replace it. There are some repairs that can be done, but as we all know from automobile accidents, repaired is often not as good as original.

Your eyes and ears are particularly vulnerable, since in order to do their work they have to be right out there in the data stream. Your eyes are vulnerable to dust, grit, debris and whatever else is thrown at you. Whether thrown deliberately or inadvertently, it still hurts and still causes damage. Your ears must be exposed to the outside world in order for you to hear what is going on. Damaged hearing is more than just a joke. Two old-time shooters meet. One says to the other "I've got this great new hearing aid. I hear just like I was a kid again." The other old shooter asks, "What kind is it?"

Looking at his watch, the first shooter says "About quarter to Two." A hearing aid helps, but is a poor substitute for original equipment.

My father, as did so many of his compatriots, got the government-sponsored walking tour of northern France and Germany from 1944 through 1945. I noticed that he would turn his head to his right when something interested him. I asked him if that was a common trait at the reunions, and after a moment's thought he said yes. Well, you fire a .30-06 BAR while inside a small stone building for an afternoon, and your left ear will ring for six months, too.

In the old days many took eye and ear protection lightly, but my father didn't. I recall one instance when my brother and I were in our early teens, and we went with Dad to the rifle range at the private club while on our vacation. We were shooting .22s, and while there one of the other club members showed up and began attempting to sight in a deer rifle. A .300

Glasses are good even in training. But in real operations, they are essential. Firing from this distance is certain to create backsplash, and glasses are a must.

Savage. Dad, seeing the fellow didn't have hearing protection, offered him some. "No thanks, after a while you get used to it." Walking back, my Dad muttered, "Yes, you get used to it by going deaf."

Eye protection

Some of us go through life with armored eyes. I cannot remember a time when I did not have to wear glasses. I was one of those unfortunate kids who had to leave their glasses with the gym teacher during dodgeball. I got really good at interpreting the fuzzy blobs, their intent, and the direction and velocity of hurled objects, without optical correction. When it came to shooting, I was already ahead of the curve. My Dad, being an Engineer, insisted on glasses that met impact standards. (Yes, I was one of those unfortunate kids in school who wore big, thick glasses.) When I got contacts, I found I had some real bad habits. After all, my eyes had always been corrected, and had always been protected, so I would often get close to peer at stuff. The first time I was leaning in to a lathe to watch the cut, and had a metal chip hit my cheek when I wasn't wearing glasses, I realized that even with contacts I required safety glasses.

Shooting requires glasses. Every time you fire a round, or someone else does, stopping the bullet is only part of the problem. A short shooting distance means the bullet fragments, target fragments, and even dust, dirt, rocks and spent bullets can be bounced back at you. Long-range shooting doesn't pose that particular problem, but there is still the empty brass, powder gases and splattered oil and grease to contend with. I've had old-time shooters complain that us "combat shooters" ruined it for them, that they wouldn't have to put up with protective glasses and muffs if we weren't "shooting those steel targets" and "shooting excessive amounts

Getting injured on an operation is regrettable. Getting injured in training is inexplicable. Get protection, wear it, and don't be lazy.

of ammo." The polite term for that attitude is "B.S." I've gotten bouncebacks from shooting where there wasn't a steel target in sight. Some of the worst hits I've taken were on police ranges, and not on "run 'n gun" combat courses. As for shooting volume, if you wanted to reduce your risk of bouncebacks to the absolute minimum, the only way to do that would be to not shoot. That strikes me as a counter-productive solution to the problem.

As a shooter and deputy I was always equipped with eye protection. But not all of those lucky enough to have 20/20 vision were so equipped. Sometimes they had to be coerced into wearing protective lenses. Today the idea of protection is so heavily stressed that you'd think no one would go without. Guess again. If you run a range, you'll find you have to remind, insist and sometimes even threaten shooters

Were this a real operation, and not a training walk-through, there'd be dust, mud, brass and shouts flying. Eye, ear and body protection is a must.

to get them to wear their glasses. And this at a time when glasses have reached new heights of protection, comfort and good looks. (It is sometimes easier to get them to wear glasses if the glasses are "cool." I kid you not.) So, for you non-prescription wearers, what do you want in glasses?

Comfort

Eye protection is just like a ballistic vest, if it isn't comfortable, you won't wear it. You'll leave them behind, in the car, at the station, at home. Comfort in glasses comes from proper fit, and for that you need to concern yourself with three things: frame width, temple depth, and nose pad size. Get a frame wide enough for your face. Too wide, they tip, Too narrow, and the temples squeeze your face. The temples (sidebars) must reach your ears. If they are too short, the frames pitch down, or your ears feel like someone is trying to saw them off. Too long, and the frame slides down your nose. And nosepads rest on your nose, and provide a solid base. You want frames and lenses that sit high and tight to your face, without being so tight your eyelashes brush the insides. (Trust me, as a life-long wearer and one familiar with the feel, the sensation can make you crazy in just a few minutes.)

Durability

You'll get many years of use out of durable glasses. And a few weeks out of cheap ones. None will survive being sat upon. Do not balk because good lenses are a few dollars (or 10 or 20) more than cheap ones. You will regret buying the cheap ones.

Protection

Look for polycarbonate lenses that meet ANSI impact standards (American National Standards Institute) and look for protection for the lenses themselves. Good lenses will have anti-scratch and anti-fog coatings. The best will block both UV-A and UV-B rays. UV (ultraviolet) rays are bad for your eyes. Your eyes work by reacting chemically to the light, creating electrical impulses fed back to the brain. UV over-stimulates the rods and cones, and can damage them. If you get lenses that block only A or B you are still exposed to the other. Get protection from both. UV protection is particularly important when you use tinted lenses. When you use tinted lenses your pupil will dilate to gather enough light to see. If you use lenses that lack UV coatings, your dilated pupils will allow even more UV light in than they would have had you not been wearing lenses at all. Also get protection for the lenses. Only buy lenses that have anti-scratch and anti-fog coatings. If you can, buy lenses that have anti-reflection coatings. The cost of a good pair of glasses is sometimes a lot. But if you're already paying (for example) $80 for good glasses, and the coatings add another $10 or $20 to the cost, don't hesitate. (The last time I bought prescription glasses, the frames and lenses cost well over $500. Adding UV, anti-scratch and anti-fog added less than $100. Don't be cheap.)

One thing shooting glasses do, that most prescription lenses do not, is wrap around your face. Side protection is important. If you happen to be facing to the side (talking to another shooter, taking guidance from the instructor) when the bounceback is incoming, your eyes may not be protected. Wrap-around lenses offer protection. If your lenses do not wrap around, you should use side shields.

Wiley X

My introduction to Wiley X glasses was through Jeff Chudwin. I arrived at a class range for a rifle class to find him shooting at the ground out in front of the firing line with a shotgun. "OK" I thought "He's

Wiley-X lenses, having been pasted with #6 and 7-1/2 shot. The frames and temples came off, but the lenses are not perforated.

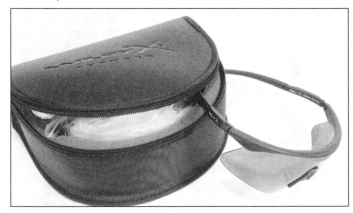

Case, extra lenses, cleaning cloth, all in a padded case. Toss this in your gear bag and be ready.

Wiley-X lenses wrap around to give side protection

test-firing a shotgun, and taking advantage of some class downtime to do so." Then I saw what he was shooting at, a line of shooting glasses on the ground. I thought to my self "They can't be out there accidentally." Correct, Jeff was testing a box full of Wiley X lenses to see if they would stop birdshot at ten yards. The answer is yes. After that, I had to have some, but the problem was correction.

For those who have uncorrected 20/20 vision, the Wiley X line includes regular-framed glasses, as well as their single lens and dual lens interchangeable frames. The PT-1 has a comfortable and adjustable nosepiece, nearly unbreakable nylon frame, and the lenses exceed ANSI Z87.1 and ANSI Z80.3 and the

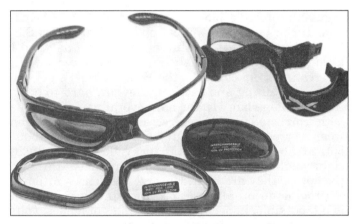

The SG-1 goggles, with replaceable lenses and head strap.

You should insist on 100% UV protection. The SG-1 lenses deliver.

You can replace the tinted for clear in a few moments.

military fragments standard MIL-STD-662. And the Jeff Chudwin shotgun standard of low-brass #6's and #7-1/2's. But I need correction. For that, I go with the SG-1, a goggle/glasses design. The lenses are made to fit lens cups that press into the frame openings. The cups have a foam backing ring to press against your face and preclude the intrusion of dust and fragments, but with small notches in the foam guard to allow airflow. For training and daily wear you can use the regular temples. For tactical use, remove the temples, install the headband and they become goggles. For all-day wear, they are great. And having two sets of lenses, one clear for indoors and one tinted for outdoors, allows you to switch easily without the cost of two complete sets of goggles. And the Wiley X lenses meet the same protection standards that the earlier ones do. If you plan to replace the lenses in the SG-1 with corrective lenses, make sure the ones your optometrist installs also protect from UV-A and B, and meet or exceed ANSI Z87.1 or Z80.3.

Uvex

One manufacturer I've had good luck with is Uvex, from Bacou-Dalloz. Their Genesis model offers all the features we look for in glasses. The lenses wrap around, they are multi-coated, the nose pads are large and soft, the temples adjust for length, and they also adjust for tilt. If you need to tilt the frames to keep the lenses close to your cheekbones, you can easily alter the pitch. For the fashion-conscious the frames can be had in a number of colors, and the lenses are available in clear, amber and tinted.

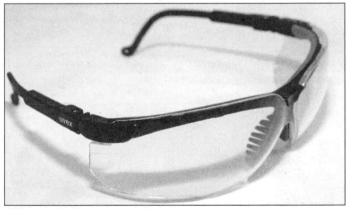

Uvex lenses offer protection and comfort.

You can get Uvex in clear and tinted. They ride high and tight, so splatter won't get around.

Goggles

The problem with many goggles is that they stand out from your face too much. This creates a problem when you try to get your face close enough to the rear sight of a long gun to use the sights properly. They can even interfere with acquiring a good cheek weld. The Hatch B.O.S.S. 6000 are protective goggles that are a close fit to the face, and minimize sight or stock interference. The polycarbonate lens rides close, and the aluminum frame prevents flex. The lens is protected from debris and wear and tear by an adhesive-backed tear-off sheet. You can apply clear, yellow or tinted to protect the lens and adjust for the lighting conditions you face. The drawback to the close fit is quickly apparent to us prescription wearers. To use the Hatch goggles you have to use the prescription lens insert integrated with the nosepiece, and have a set of lenses ground for your use in the goggles.

The Hatch goggles are compact, and do not interfere with other gear or equipment.

Unlike mil-spec goggles the Hatch rides under the PASGT, and won't be bumped as the helmet moves around when you run.

Once that is done, they are comfortable. Smaller and lighter than other goggles, they don't have to be as tight to stay put. They also don't bear against helmets. Some officers find the goggles and the helmet both want to be in the same place on your face, and getting them to play well with each other can be troublesome. The smaller B.O.S.S. 6000 is much less likely to give you that problem.

Al these glasses and goggles fit under a PASGT helmet, and do not interfere with communications gear.

Optical correction

Those of us who need corrective lenses schlep a lot more gear around than the rest of you. If I'm wearing contacts, and doing range work, I'll wear regular protective lenses like the Wiley X or Uvex. Sometimes I'll wear contacts and the Hatch B.O.S.S. 6000, especially if it is a full-gear training day and I need the goggles and a helmet. But for the days when I'm resting from contacts, the Wiley X SG-1's get the nod. For training and tactical, they are hard to beat. And my range bag always has several pairs of lenses both corrected and uncorrected. Those of us who wear corrective lenses all the time know about optical aberration, but you lucky dogs with 20/20 sight might not. When the light rays pass through the optics, they are bent. Uncorrected lenses attempt to provide an un-altered optical path, but perfection is not possible. Especially at the edges of lenses, your sight will be slightly altered. Straight lines begin to appear curved, and proportions of objects can become distorted. If you haven't noticed it before, pay attention to someone who wears glasses for correction; they will almost always turn to face you directly to talk to you. They have learned subconsciously that the center of the lens offers the least distortion. You should always check your protective lenses for distortion. Cheap ones will have more, and more of it at the edges. Good (read: expensive) ones will have none in the center and very little at the edges.

Even if you don't find shooting or tactical operations compromised by the optical aberrations of cheap glasses, you may find yourself getting headaches from wearing them. As with so many items, there are more expensive things than quality lenses.

Protect your glasses by storing them in the soft bags they are shipped in, and in hard cases. Without a hard case, your glasses could all be crushed simply by having a hard case or heavy gear topple over on the soft bag with your glasses in it. And prescription wearers should have a spare set of glasses on your web gear or load-bearing vest, in a hard case, just in case the pair you're wearing gets broken.

Hearing protection

For a guy who has spent decades shooting, years as a radio broadcaster, and lots of time around internal combustion engines (dirt bikes, four-wheeling, aircraft engines) my hearing is pretty good. That's because I have always protected it. I can count

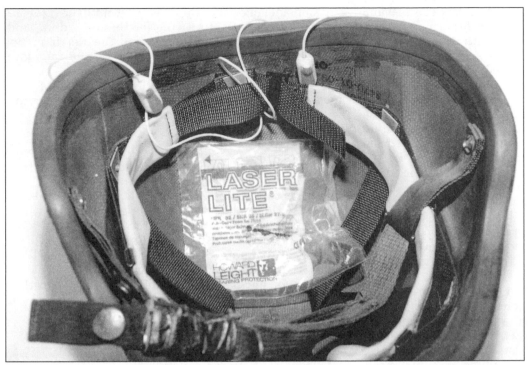

Hearing protection is so cheap (and hearing aids so expensive) that you should have plugs attached to every piece of gear, and in pockets all over you. These plugs tied to the helmet ensure there is always something for protection.

on the fingers of my hands the number of times I've been exposed to gunfire with my hearing unprotected. I can count on both thumbs the times I've been exposed to flashbangs without protection. And I was not one of these DJ's who cranked the headphones up to "11" on the amp. You cannot be too careful of your hearing, as even the best hearing aids are poor substitutes for the real thing.

Your ears work in a fascinating, and complex way. Inside what you think of as your ears is a diaphragm, the eardrum, which looks like and acts like a little drum. The diaphragm vibrates when sound strikes it, and the linkage of the small bones inside of it transmits that vibration to the inner ear, the cochlea. The cochlea is a spiral tube filled with fluid, lined with tiny hairs of different lengths. (Cilia) The vibrations compress the fluid, and each tiny hair responds to the wavelength of the compression corresponding to the hair's length. Thus, each cilia is responsible for reporting to the brain a particular wavelength of noise, and reporting just how intense (loud) that noise was. There is only so much stress each hair can take. Excessive stress, over a particular volume, over-works the hair, it dies and is not regenerated. You become deaf to that frequency of sound. As your hearing becomes stressed over time, you lose more and more hairs in the frequency of sounds you are exposed to. Smaller hairs seem to be more sensitive to stress, so you lose your hearing earliest in the upper frequencies. As a result, men who lose their hearing tend to not be able to pick up the subtle differences in women's voices, and spend a lot of time using "Huh" as an interrogatory when talking with their wife or girlfriend. Higher frequencies also correspond to the band where many words are differentiated; leading to the "time/kind" confusion of the joke we started with.

The audible range is from 20 to 20,000 hertz (cycles per second) with the human voice dynamics falling in the 500 to 6300 Hz range.

Noise is measured in Decibels. The decibel is a measure of the compression of air caused by the shockfront of the noise. The decibel scale is not linear. That is, going from (for example) 100 to 110 decibels is not a ten percent increase in energy. The scale is logarithmic, and each increase of 3 decibels is a doubling of the compression energy. (So going from 100 to 110 is an increase of 333% of noise intensity) In a similar fashion as poison, dosage creates the damage. You can be exposed to a low enough decibel level that your hearing is not damaged. After all, that is how you hear. But how intense, and for how long, matters. A quiet room still has some noise, 10 or so decibels, and normal conversation is around 65 dB. You can listen to conversation all your life and not suffer hearing loss. Depending on the speaker you may die of boredom, but your hearing will be fine. At the top end, where firearms noise exists, a one-time exposure can cause damage. A 5.56mm rifle can have a muzzle blast measured a 145 decibels, which is well into the one-exposure damage range. Flashbangs can be up to 175 dB. A suppressed firearm can operate in the 120-125 decibel range, which is just below the damage threshold from a one-time exposure. Firearms exposure is different than industrial exposure. Each cartridge fired is an individual, or impulse, exposure. Even a machinegun is a series of individual exposures. If you have a firearm that creates a 145 dB report, and your hearing protection offers a 26 dB reduction, you are exposed to momentary incidents of 119 Db. An industrial plant offers continuous noise. There is no respite, and thus the maximum exposure for an eight-hour day that is allowed by OSHA is 85 Db. From 85 to 89, they recommend protection, and above 90 they mandate it. There is a big difference between 119 and 85, but the momentary nature of a firearms report is what allows you to get away with the (protected) exposure. Were it not, we'd be scrambling to find hearing protection that offered 60 Db reduction instead of 22-26.

Distance also diminishes noise. If you are far enough away, noise is diminished enough to not be a hazard. However, closer makes things worse. And an enclosed space is even more damaging, from compression and reflection. Compression is the increase of the shockfront intensity of the noise caused when the space is so small the usual expansion of the noise cannot happen. Volume is the key, smaller makes it harder on your ears. And reflection? In an outdoor environment, you get one hit from the shockfront, as it passes by you. Indoors, you get a reflected shockfront from the walls, sometimes two or three waves, as the noise comes off adjacent walls, the ceiling and even the floor.

The bad news is, once gone, the hairs cannot be replaced or regenerated. All you can do is prevent their loss in the first place. The latest medical news as I write this is that scientists have managed to re-grow cilia in lab rats in controlled circumstances. However, it may be years (or never) before that process can be applied to people, and when it does you know it will be expensive. The good news is, it doesn't take a lot of cost or hassle to protect your hearing. The simplest protection that works are soft foam plugs that fit the ear canal. By compressing them and inserting them, and waiting a few moments for their expansion, you dampen a lot of the noise you are exposed to. Foam and plastic plugs offer protection from 26 to 33 NRR. (Noise Reduction Rating) Ear muffs "only" offer NRR from 22 to 28. The differences between the various plugs, headsets and dynamic headsets are more than can be measured by testing equipment. For example, many shooters notice that headsets are quieter on the range than foam plugs, even though foam plugs have higher noise reduction ratings. Some noise comes to your ears via bone conduction. Noise that strikes your jaw or skull can be conducted as vibration to the inner ear, and perceived as sound. Measured in a test ear canal, foam plugs block noise, But they do not block bone conduction. Earmuffs block some bone conduction, but being measured on test ear canals they do not block as much measured noise as plugs. Muffs are better at blocking noise, it is the test that makes them seem different. The important part is to find what is comfortable, and not get hung up on a point or two in rated noise reduction. For example, ear plugs that have an NRR on "only" 26 but are comfortable enough to wear all day, are better than plugs rated for 33, that you are constantly pulling out when they get uncomfortable, and re-inserting "when you need them." For you'll certainly miss an occasional "need" and be standing there talking to someone when another shooter lights up a loud rifle.

While protection is paramount, comfort is a must.

Considering the low cost, and the severe consequences (loss of hearing for the individual, and increased disability payments for the department) any department that does not provide, and mandate the use of, hearing protection is negligent. (Let us, for the moment, overlook the stupidity of the individuals who participate in firearms training and willingly decline the use of hearing protection.)

Availability

There are four types of hearing protection that work: foam/plastic plugs, custom-molded plugs, passive muffs, and dynamic muffs. There are also a whole lot that don't work, including empty brass (I've seen shooters using empty 9mm and .38 brass as "hearing protection") cotton tufts, cigarette butts or filters, ear-warming garments like flapped hats (I kid you not) and ski bands. Using your fingers to plug your ears works, but it is awfully difficult to shoot in that position. Don't be cheap (how much cheaper can you get than disposable foam plugs?) use what works.

Foam/plastic disposable earplugs

They are called disposable, but I've met many a shooter who was so cheap as to save the plugs and run them through the wash wrapped in an old pair of pantyhose. I don't know if the EPA has done any testing about continued hearing protection of laundered plugs, but it doesn't seem to hurt them any. Foam plugs come two ways, loose and detectable. The loose ones are just that, a pair (you hope) of plugs that you squeeze, insert and wait to expand. The detectable ones are those that have a string or headband, so manufacturing plant workers can wear them and be seen as wearing them. For us shooters, the detectable ones can be tied to a hat, so when you pull them out you don't lose them in the dirt. Are any better than the rest? They have differing NRR values, but the important factor is comfort. Find

There is no such thing as hearing protection that costs too much, or takes up too much room. Find a brand or style that is comfortable, and buy a bunch.

comfortable ones, buy a bunch (they're dirt cheap) and use them. I've got a bale of various plugs from Bilsom, and a cubic foot of them is a lifetime supply. Don't be cheap, spend the total that two boxes of premium handgun ammunition would cost you, and have a many-years supply of hearing protection.

Custom molded

The custom plugs are individually molded to fit your ear canal. Starting with a clean ear canal, the fitter mixes the plastic then goops it into your ear canal. Once it sets, it is removed, finish-shaped and has strings attached. Custom-molded plugs offer very good protection, better than many foam plugs. However, they are not for everyone, and I'm in the group of "not suitable." What I found, after trying them several times was that my ear canals are long and narrow, and I had too much wax buildup. If I fitted the plugs when there was no wax, then when I had some wax I couldn't drive them in with a rubber mallet. If I had them fitted with wax, when my ears were clean they didn't seal and didn't protect my hearing. With regrets I have to decline the use of custom plugs. For those of you who do not have my peculiar problem, custom plugs are comfortable, colorful (that fashion thing again) and offer good protection. With the miniaturization of electronics, you can even have custom plugs with dynamic microphones built in.

Foam plugs and custom molded plugs offer protection when you are wearing hats that preclude earmuffs, or helmets that don't fit over muffs. They are also unobtrusive (if you don't wear bright-color ones, with fluorescent strings attached) so a plainclothes officer getting ready to support a raid can have his hearing protected and not attract attention while standing on the sidewalk outside the building prior to the start.

Passive muffs

Ear muffs are molded plastic cups with insulating foam inside, that protect your hearing by diminishing sound to the ear canal, and diminishing the surface area around your ear that is subject to delivering noise via bone conduction. Muffs offer very good protection, but at a cost. They are bulky, you can't wear some hats with them unless you have a neckband model, they won't fit under a bunch of different helmets, and your ears sweat. But for inexpensive and comfortable protection, they are hard to beat.

Bilsom Compact

The Compact is a neckband muff designed to fit under a helmet. Intended for construction workers who have to wear a hardhat, it fits easily under a PASGT helmet. The neckband provides the compression to keep the individual cups tight to your head, while a plastic strap that rides over the top of your head provides the suspension. When wearing the PASGT, you simply put on the Compact first, and then tighten the top strap. Once set, you put on the PASGT. The Compact "only" offers 17 NRR. However, adding protection is easy with plugs. The EPA method of calculating added protection is to take the higher value rating, and then add 5 to the number. Put plugs with an NRR of 33 in, then add 5 from the Compact, and you're up to 38. Plus, the helmet is also going to diminish bone conduction from your skull. Your hearing will be well protected even from flashbangs.

Dynamic muffs

Dynamic muffs are the latest, and as the prices fall, will become the standard hearing protection. A dynamic muff has built-in microphones on the outside and speakers on the inside. Sound experienced by the muffs below the speaker volume is amplified to the set volume. So, if you have your muffs turned up to (for example) 65 dB, a sound next to you that is only 50 dB will be heard in your muffs at 65 dB. The least expensive models simply direct the sound from a mic to the speakers, and when the sound exceeds a certain level, the speaker momentarily shuts off, clipping the noise before it can harm your ears. As you move up in expense and complexity, dual mics feed dual speakers for stereo sound (and thus directional capability) and the best do not just clip off the sound peaks, but clip them off faster (the response time) and compress the curve down under the maximum safe level. It won't be long before dynamic muffs can block and compress sectors of the sound spectrum, offering even more protection.

Dynamic muffs offer protection, but that protection comes with electronics. You must select what is comfortable, but also you must take into account the response time, the speed at which it cuts off or diminishes sound, and the volume setting. Try all you can get your hands on and see what works.

The advantage of dynamic muffs is that you don't have to take them off to talk to someone at the range, as the conversation is picked up and fed to you at the set volume. If someone fires a round, you lose the part of the speech that happened at the moment of the shot (or only part of it, with the best) and the human brain can usually fill in that momentary loss of a word fragment. And you get the benefit of that amplification. I've stood in a hallway, with my dynamic muffs cranked up, and heard my training opponent breathing around the corner.

The trick is fitting the muffs under a helmet. If you are geared up, with a balaclava and helmet on, getting a set of muffs can be tough, and getting a set of dynamic muffs under the helmet can be real tough. The simple method is to open the helmet band enough to accommodate the headband, and then use the chin strap to keep the helmet secure on your head. The more complicated method, but more comfortable and helmet-secure method is to remove the headband from the muffs and secure the individual muffs to the headband and chinstrap of the helmet. But it is a lot of work, can be expensive, and any maintenance for one or the other requires the whole unit be sidelined.

Pro Ears Linear Elite

While the Linear Elite is not the latest model from Pro Ears, I have extensive experience with them. (They were recently replaced by the Dimension series.) I obtained a set a few years ago for an earlier project, and liked them so much I sent Ridgeline a check. They are very comfortable, and the batteries last a good long time. However, if you leave them on between range sessions you will find the batteries are dead. No problem for range work, as even when dead they still work like dumb muffs. The slim-line model fits under a PASGT helmet. As with all dynamic muffs, the foam rubber over the microphones can be rubbed off. When it does, you'll get some wind noise from the exposed microphones. It is a simple matter to glue a tuft of foam over each one (keeping the glue off the microphone opening) and eliminating the annoying wind noise. The linear Elite has individual switches and volume controls, so if you already have hearing damaged by noise you can adjust the volume for each ear. I've dropped them and knocked them off of tables, benches and tailgates. I've even dropped them in water (not something the manufacturer recommends) and they've still worked. If you and they take a real soaking, the batteries will quit sooner than if they'd stayed dry, but brief immersion hasn't harmed them yet. For really loud exposures, plugs and muffs offer protection, while still hearing the environment in which you're working. The new models of Pro Ears are even better, but my Linear Elites work so well I haven't felt the need to change. One advantage the new Dimension series has is that you can have them built with a plug for radio or cell phone.

Bilsom 707 COM

These are not tactical muffs. They are big and yellow, and you have no hope of fitting them under a

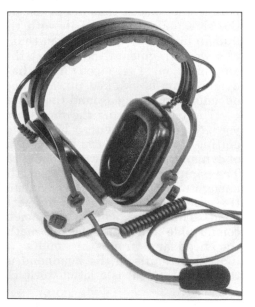

Big and yellow, they offer protection and communication.

PASGT helmet. They are best used in training and instructing. However, they have a number of attractive features. First, they have an automatic power-down feature, to save battery life. After four hours they turn off. If you need to keep using them, turn the switch off, wait five seconds and turn them back on. They'll patiently wait another four hours before turning off again. They have a built-in microphone, and a jack to plug in a radio, cell phone or other electronics. The incoming phone call rings in your headset, or if you are on a radio, the transmission comes right through. Just plug in the adapter, and then plug the adapter to a suitable location on the phone or radio. While walking the line, observing students, you can still be in radio communication with other instructors. (One facility at which I work on has four separate ranges spread across half a mile of firing line. Radio is the only way to stay in touch.) You don't have to peel the muffs off to try to use a radio handset, exposing your hearing to the gunfire. Or, as an inexpensive training alternative to regular radio communications gear, use the Bilsom and a Walkabout radio. That way you don't have to worry about using your dedicated communications frequencies in training. (Not to mention the stress of the rest of the department, if they should stray onto the training frequencies and wonder if the "Officer down" call is real or training.)

The boom mic is flexible enough that you can get it out of the way to fire a rifle or shotgun, and the volume control lets you adjust the speakers so you can use it to do an "auditory search" by cranking it up and listening to see what the microphones can discover.

They are so useful I've wondered about finding an electronics wiz who can take the guts out of it and install them in a dynamic headset that fits under a PASGT helmet.

And as a piece of equipment for the home, it fits right in with one of the essential portions of the tactical and legal plan Mas Ayoob lays out for home defense: electronic muffs for searching and hearing protection, and a cell phone to call for help. With the jack, you have them together. You can search, your hearing is protected, and if you need to make a call to 911, hit speed-dial and slip the phone in a pocket. Then, everything that happens is recorded (at the 911 center) and you have your hands free to deal with the problem.

Bilsom 799 Com

And for those training-only sessions, where you're just at the range working on your rifle zero, or working on your drills, the Bilsom 799 Com offers entertainment. And communications. The built-in microphone lets you communicate on a radio or cell phone. The dynamic microphones let you hear what is going on "outside" while protecting your hearing from gunshots and other noise. And the built-in FM radio lets you tune into your favorite station. If something happens "outside" the microphones pipe it in over the FM. When your cell phone rings, or the

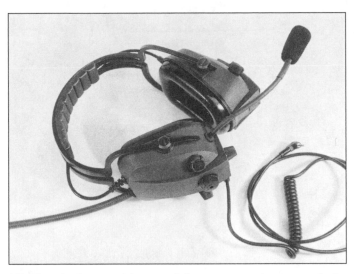

If yellow isn't your thing, and then you can have comfort and communication in basic blue.

radio you've attached receives a broadcast, it is also piped in. If only it fit under a helmet....

One thing I love about Bilsom products: they are shipped with batteries. When your muffs arrive, you'll have what you need to put them on and start using them.

Respirators

Sometimes fashions that got dropped are best left as curiosities of history. My Grandfather carried a gas mask. My father didn't. As I write this, I have one on the table next to me. It is new aspect of the law enforcement officers list of equipment, and one we all wish had stayed in the history books.

My Grandfather ran away from school to join the Army. Not an unusual career choice for an Irish lad in the late 19th Century. He spent nearly 20 years in the Philippines under Pershing making sure the peaceful settlement of the "Philippine question" stayed that way. From there he got shipped to cold, wet, muddy France to deal with the German troops. He was issued a gas mask. For those who remember their history class (for schools that still have it) and you recall those photos of the doughboys, the gas mask was that big boxy bag they wore high on their chests. Most of the bag was the filter. They wore it high on their chests because when they weren't in the trenches they were lying flat in the mud. On the belt it couldn't be easily reached and used, and would be in the mud. On the back it couldn't be reached at all. They needed them, as Artillery doctrine in the German Army called for the regular use of chemical shells. In typical methodic fashion, they had determined the most effective timing and selection of chemical artillery shells in the mixture and schedule of artillery fire on the French, British and later, American forces. After the Great War, armies kept their gas masks, but politicians determined not to use them.

In WWII, my father remarked that the first item of gear to be tossed into the ditch by G.I.'s arriving in Europe to lighten their load was the gas mask. In the Wehrmacht, the gas mask container was retained through the war, but I don't know how many actually held gas masks. A required item of issue, it was distinctive, and if you didn't have it you would be in trouble. And it was, after all, a useful container. But how many actually held gas masks by 1943 or 1944? I don't know.

After WWII, no one carried gas masks as a regular item of issue. They might be carried on operations where the intel indicated they might be needed, but as general issue they were not common. Units stationed in Europe during the Cold War had gas masks, but they were part of the MOPP gear, a full body suit intended to protect from chemical and biological agents. Today? Today a respirator or gas mask is something that should be in every squad car, should be issued to every officer, and should have training devoted to its use and care. Why? We live in a different world than our fathers. (Or for those younger, grandfathers.) A police officer who drives up on a traffic accident may suddenly find himself confronted with a tanker truck overturned, spilling who-knows-what. Yes, the placard on the side of the tank will tell you what it is, if you can see it and if you can recall all the codes. Knowing doesn't help much if there are people to be rescued from the accident. A respirator in the trunk can be a godsend at that moment. Or, an entry team making a raid on a clandestine drug lab may need to wear respirators just to keep from getting an inadvertent buzz, or to protect their health from the solvents being used. Called out for crowd control (like clothing of the 1960s, civil unrest goes in and out of fashion) a department should issue respirator/gas masks, if for no other reason than errant breezes. It is most embarrassing to try to quell the unruly mob with an industrial-sized OC pepper spray container, only to have the breeze blow it back in your face. And who knows what else you need to be protected from. Smoke from fires, the crowd's own pepper spray, water, and other fluids you'd rather not identify. A mask can protect you. But, in order to be effective, a respirator has to be comfortable, you have to know how to put it on and utilize it, you have to be able to work in it, and it must protect you from the common dangerous agents.

Protection

Gone are the days of a handkerchief over the mouth and nose. A paper filter will protect you from paint while spraying the garage and sawdust while sanding the stairs. A cloth one might reduce exposure of patient and physician, but for anything more you need real protection. That means full face and airway protection. You are just as vulnerable if only your eyes are closed from OC pepper spray as you are with your eyes closed and your breathing restricted. You need a face shield. The best, and only choice for law enforcement, masks have detachable filters. The filter can be discarded when its effectiveness has diminished, and you can select filters for agents blocked, cost and weight.

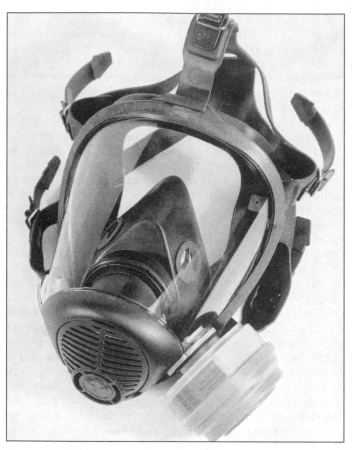

The Survivair by Bacou-Dalloz, is a two-filter full face respirator for better vision and a voice diaphragm, so your commands and communications can be heard.

Two buckles, and a few seconds later your lungs are protected.

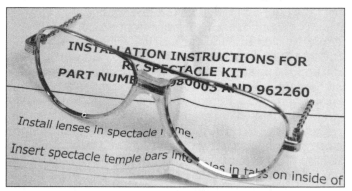

Those of us with prescription lenses need the insert that the Survivair was designed to take.

Mine is the Survivair, by Bacou-Dalloz, and can be fitted with one or two filters that will filter out many things. One of the first things you learn about respirators is that none of them are intended for use in an atmosphere containing less than 19 percent oxygen. As you all remember from high school chemistry, the air we breathe is mostly nitrogen, with a bit more than 20 percent of the mixture being oxygen. A respirator does not replace missing oxygen in the mixture. So if you walk into a cloud of gas that has displaced the atmosphere, and thus has no oxygen, you won't be able to breath anything useful. That said, it takes a lot to displace enough air to drop the oxygen to or below 19 percent. You have to set off a case of smoke, chemical and irritant grenades in a small room with no drafts before you can get the oxygen below 19 percent.

The Survivair is a full-face respirator with dual-filter capability. It has face seals all around, and adjustment straps to keep it snug to your face. Front and center is a voice diaphragm, so you can be heard when telling the smoke and chemical-breathing offenders what to do in order to comply with your wishes. It also helps in communicating with others on the team. One useful feature that many do not think of (mostly because they were born blessed with 20/20 vision) is the capability to accept spectacle lenses in an insert to the mask. Those of us with corrected

vision quickly find that respirators guaranteed to seal around the temples of our glasses, usually don't. With the spectacle inserts, you simply leave the inserts with a set of lenses (I just use the previous prescription from an old pair of glasses) in the respirator. When you need to breathe, off go the glasses, and on goes the respirator with glasses built in.

The Survivair is comfortable, it fits under a PASGT helmet, and if you wear only one filter and seal the other filter point you can easily use a long gun while wearing it. The adjustment straps allow it

On the assault, laden with gear, including a gas mask bag. Better to have it and not need it, than the opposite. (DoD photo)

The gas mask bag is vest-mounted. (Courtesy Blackhawk Industries.)

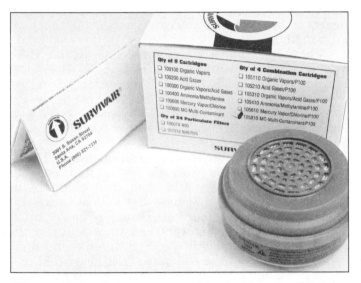

Filter selection is important, and for that you need to take chemical agent school.

to fit just about everyone. I haven't found someone yet, other than children, who can't get the Survivair to adjust to fit.

All respirators need and use filters. A replaceable filter allows you to continue using a proven mask once the filters become clogged. And it lets you select filters according to the risk you'll be facing. The selection of filters for the Survivair include organic vapors, acid gases, ammonia/methylamine, mercury vapor/chlorine, and the ever-popular multi-contaminant. In addition, you can select for particulate size. The N95 only filters larger particles than the P100, but lasts longer. If you've only one to stock, it would most likely be the multi-contaminant/P100, which will filter out a laundry

list of organic vapors as well as 99.97 percent of all particulate aerosols. You can spend an entire class (and there are many) learning the intricacies of chemical exposure, particulate size and how to deal with offenders who have plunked down their hard-earned cash to buy a surplus gas mask. And those particulars and intricacies are best left to said class, rather than lay out all the details. (This is one subject on which I prefer to leave information in the law enforcement community, and not turn it into a chem lab for miscreants.)

If you have a mask, you have to have a way to carry it. For the patrol officer, the choice is simple; where to keep it in the vehicle? Unless you're driving a big SUV, the trunk is your only choice. There isn't room in the front, and you can't leave it in back where your handcuffed suspect rides. Teams typically wear it on the vest somewhere, with many electing to use the rectangular carry case on the back. Another bag is the tactical thigh bag. Or, a multi-use bag like the Blackhawk Industries bag they sent me. Greg Anderson of Blackhawk does a good deal of training with respirators, including a lot of physical restraint training. He told me that after trying all the carry methods Blackhawk made (and they make a bunch) he found the tactical thigh bag was best. With its multiple straps and loops, as well as a shoulder strap, it can be worn on the thigh, it can be worn on the belt, it can be secured to a vest, and it can simply be carried over the shoulder like a purse. Best of all, it is big enough that you can use it for other things as well. Even if you never have to carry a respirator, this bag can be very useful in carrying a host of other items.

Body protection

When Richard Davis came up with the idea for soft, concealable body armor, everything changed. For a long time he tried to keep it a trade secret,

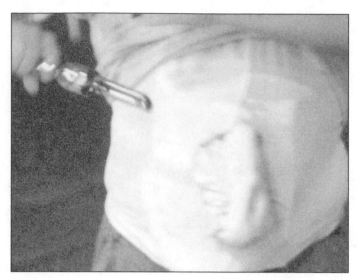

Full-power .44 Magnum at point-blank range, and the vest stops it. (No surprise there.)

something that only law enforcement knew about. The cover was blown a long time ago, so here's the skinny on the Davis Doctrine: If it isn't comfortable enough to wear, you can't depend on having it on when you need it. Comfort matters more than cost, level of protection, or brand. It just so happens that Second Chance, Richards' company, makes the most comfortable vests around.

The rumors and myths of vests rival the rumors and myths of Richard himself. Not the myths by Richard, he doesn't deal in them. The rumors and myths about Richard. Like the biannual one I hear through the grapevine; "Did you hear? The latest production lot is faulty, one failed, and Richard is in the hospital because his vest didn't stop the bullet." Oh, you didn't know? Richard Davis feels so strongly about his vests, and has such faith in them, that he will put one on and shoot the vest to prove it works. I've seen it a bunch of times in tape, a few times in person, and it never ceases to amaze me. Despite Richard's best efforts at getting the word out for 30 years, there are still a lot of old wives' tales about body armor. Lets take them one by one:

It won't stop a knife. All vests will stop most knives. Some do a better job of it than others. The

worst-case scenario is you lying flat on your back, and some miscreant is trying to stab you with an icepick. No fabric vest or woven vest will stop that. But for all the rest, the slashings, the stabbings while you're trying to dodge the blow, a vest will stop those. Richard Davis has done a number of videos attempting to demonstrate the strengths (and dispel the myths) of vests. I even got to be the bad guy in one of them. While attempting to kill Mike Jarabek, save number 500, I "die" a dramatic death. In one of the videos, he places all the variables against a vest: he lays it flat on a firm surface, he stabs directly downwards with both hands on the knife. The knife is a Gerber Boot Knife, a knife with a sharp, stiff and pointed blade meant to penetrate. Even with Richard's 230 pounds slamming straight down, all he can manage is to get the very tip of the knife through the vest. The knife wouldn't have hurt nearly as much as the impact. You are very safe from knives in your vest.

The impact will kill you. B-S. Ask one of the thousand-plus officers who've survived shootings. It can take you by surprise, but many never noticed they'd been shot until it was over. The impact can hurt. It can even be a significant injury itself, if it has stopped something much more energetic than it was rated for. But the impact won't kill you, or stop your heart, or stun you so you're immobile for the bad guys to finish you off.

They don't work when they're wet. More B-S. They lose some effectiveness, sure. But they only lose it when they're soaked, as in under water. If you've been under water long enough for your vest to lose (2 percent or 5 percent) of its effectiveness, you've got bigger problems than wondering if your vest will stop bullets.

Kevlar disintegrates after five years. No it doesn't. The problem with Kevlar is that no one knows how long it will last. And some things will degrade it so quickly that time matters not nearly as much as Do Not Run Your Vest Through The Washing Machine. The manufacturers had to come up with some kind of a service life, or face the likelihood of being sued in the future because "You never told me my vest wouldn't last 20 years." The last time I met Richard, he had a storage building full of turned-in vests that were past their five-year build date. We amused ourselves by pulling vests out at random and

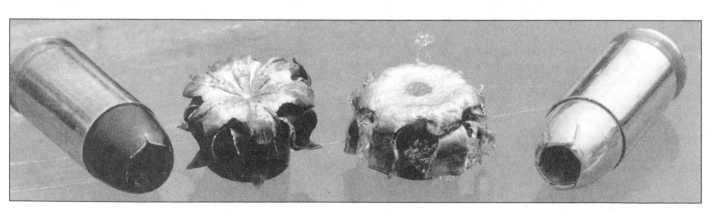

High-tech hollowpoints do not penetrate body armor. They are even less effective than other designs.

shooting them. They all stopped what they were supposed to stop.

You have to buy the thickest you can get. While I don't want to discourage anyone from buying a vest as good as they think they need, this runs counter to the Davis Doctrine. You should buy a vest that stops what you carry. After all, many police officers are shot with their own gun. It would be a shame to wear a vest that protects you from everything but what you carry. But once you'd got your own sidearm covered, you shouldn't go adding layers for more protection. You can quickly end up with a vest so heavy you don't wear it. It doesn't do you any good hanging in your locker.

The newest hollow-point designs penetrate vests. The theory goes something like this: the new hollowpoints are so sharp, and the edges so ragged, that they cut through the synthetic fabric of the vest. Actually, just the opposite is true. The better a bullet expands, the faster it gets tangled up in the fabric, and the sooner its energy is dissipated. Hollow-points stop sooner. Richard has a large but dwindling supply of the original Black Talon cartridges, which he expends in vests to demonstrate the point.

Cop-killer bullets had to be banned. Ahem. To quote Richard himself: "I can get a bullet through any vest, and I can make a vest to stop any bullet." The big stink about vest-piercing bullets overlooked several inconvenient facts: The originators of the first specialty rounds were themselves police officers, and sold only to departments and officers. The handgun rounds so vilified were actually less effective at piercing vests than common deer hunting rifle rounds. And lastly, no police officer has died from his vest having been pierced by such rounds. In all, it was a fabricated "emergency" made for political gain. A greater problem for a long time was the imported 7.62X39 ammunition, AK ammunition. Since the early imports had steel cores or steel jackets, they would penetrate just about everything. But that was corrected, and they now only penetrate as well as common hunting cartridges.

One size fits all. Sometimes written as "we need the standard sizes, small, medium and large" it is a parsimonious approach to negating comfort, the primary consideration. Fit is all-important, as an ill-fitted vest won't be worn, and thus won't protect. In order for your vest to give you maximum protection, you must have it fitted. The fitters who measure you up have done it for years, and have feedback from thousands of satisfied customers. If you have a question, or don't like the fit, ask and they'll answer your question. You may save yourself from extra cost and embarrassment, like the State Police agency that insisted they knew more than Second Chance when it came to fitting vests. They insisted (apparently quite strenuously) that the vests be made an additional two inches longer in front. They didn't want the gap between the vest bottom and the belt, a gap that might lead to someone getting shot under the vest. Soon after the shipment went out, vests started coming back. It seemed that when

In the old days, riots called for motorcycle helmets (right) or G.I. steel helmets. Now, many operations call for a PASGT Kevlar helmet (left).

sitting in a car (imagine that, a State Trooper who spends time seated in an automobile!) the vests would hit the top of the belt, ride up, and wedge against the Troopers Adam's apple. It only took one pothole in the road to discover the exquisite pain of that arrangement.

Get your vest properly fitted. Treat it well. It will treat you well.

Head protection

One of the minor points of the adoption of military gear that seem to irritate some observers is the adoption of the PASGT helmet for SWAT teams. I don't know why, but it seems to drive some observers up the wall. In any entry scenario, head protection is a vital aspect of the uniform and protective gear. It only takes one thrown kitchen utensil, falling object off a bookshelf or display cabinet, or low doorway to injure a team member, require medical attention, and a minimum of five added forms to the paperwork load.

All of which could be avoided with some kind of head protection better than a baseball cap or snappy beret. But why the PASGT? The "P" helmet was the culmination of the desire for better protection by the armed forces, and the advent of synthetics capable of offering ballistic protection. The "P" helmet is

The PASGT shrugged off a 9mm fmj with only surface damage.

Left, the exit 9mm, right, the exit .45 ACP in the motorcycle helmet.

A motorcycle helmet offers absolutely no ballistic protection. It wasn't designed to. Centered is a .45ACP jhp entry hole.

And as a final touch, the face shield of the motorcycle helmet offered no protection against #8 shot at 15 yards. Leave these behind and get a PASGT helmet!

somewhat heavy, something it has been faulted for in the services. Compared to the protection it offers over the old steel helmet, the weight is a minor problem. The P helmet also comes in several sizes, allowing for greater comfort. The helmet covers can be had in a variety of colors and patterns, or you can just paint it whatever color you desire. Many teams just spray paint theirs flat black to match their uniforms. The P helmet also is roomy enough to accommodate hearing protection, radio headsets, or a respirator.

An item that increases comfort is the "donut" a circular foam pad that you stuff up above the suspension straps, that gives the helmet a softer ride on top of your head.

And it offers protection. The traditional riot gear for law enforcement has been a motorcycle helmet. While motorcycle helmets offer good protection against accidents (I have a couple of friends who owe their lives to helmets and padded/armored riding gear) they offer nothing against firearms. To test, I sacrificed an old motorcycle helmet and a busted PASGT helmet. First up, there are incidents in every military encounter of soldiers whose lives have been saved by their PASGT helmet, so my testing is nothing new or groundbreaking. I tested first with 9mm ball. Known for its ability to penetrate well, I figured it would be a good test without making a complete mess of the test subjects. The 9mm Zero Ammunition 147-grain full metal jacket bullet sailed through the motorcycle helmet without any apparent slowing. The PASGT was a different story. The impact knocked the helmet off the table, and the bullet was re-directed 90 degrees, striking the side berm of the range with vigor. If you attempt this test yourself, I strongly suggest you fire from behind cover. The 9mm bullet still had sufficient force to cause injury after deflecting off the PASGT helmet. It would be a shame to hurt yourself in the pursuit of scientific inquiry. I then tried a .45 round, the Zero Ammunition 185-grain jacketed hollow-point. It also defeated the motorcycle helmet handily. Seeing the deflection of the 9mm, and having no cover from which to fire, I declined the risk of trying the 45 on the PASGT. I'm certain the result would have been even less than the minimal penetration of the 9mm round.

Next up, I tested the faceshield of the motorcycle helmet with shotgun pellets. We know from testing that good polycarbonate protective glasses like the Wiley X will stop shotgun pellets. What about the common windscreen of a motorcycle helmet? The test was the lightest possible load, a skeet load of #8 shot at 15 yards. As the photograph shows, the faceshield offers no protection at all. If you were wearing a PASGT and good glasses, your eyesight will be saved provided you aren't too close. The plastic surgeon can always extract the individual pellets from your face, and sand you smooth, but if you don't save your eyes, you haven't saved much. I didn't even bother firing the shotgun round at the PASGT, as it would have been a waste of ammunition.

The best thing you can do is to invest in a good helmet, and until they improve it, the PASGT is the best.

Chapter 8
Rucksacks

OK, A RUCKSACK is not a regular uniform issue item. Maybe a gear bag, for notebooks, reference materials and extra forms, phone and lunch, is a regular item in a patrol car, but not a rucksack. Then again, not every officer or deputy steps onto concrete when he (or she) gets out of the patrol car. Some rural jurisdictions just might call for a packed rucksack in the trunk. What to carry? Well, you could go with a high-tech backpacking ruck; super-light, gaudy colors, made to carry lots of gear. If you can stand the ribbing from the rest of the shift, that is. A puce and fuchsia rucksack may call for some good-natured comments. Or, you can just settle down with catalogs from Blackhawk and London Bridge Trading, and get yourself a pack that is so tough it will outlast you. And in proper black, green, tan or camo colors.

First question to answer is, how big? The four sizes to consider are; daypack, medium ruck/alpine, big alpine, and expedition. The daypack is just that. It holds enough gear for you to walk the day, perhaps stay overnight if it is warm enough, and is very handy. Light and comfortable, a daypack can be fine for a shift on perimeter at a call-out, or to keep you going while searching for a lost child or cutting trail to look for an escaped prisoner. A daypack volume will be in the range of 1,000 to 1,500 cubic inches. A medium ruck/alpine starts at 2,000 and goes up to around 3,500. In the medium, you can carry enough stuff to stay overnight, food and water and shelter for several persons if searching, and if it has lash points, more gear outside. The Big Alpine category goes from 3,500 to 5,000 cubic inches. With one of these you can stay overnight in a cold climate, or do two or three days in warmer areas. Expeditions go 5,000 to 8,000 cubic inches. You can carry almost everything you own in one of these. An expedition pack is what mountain climbers use to get to the big peaks, or special operations units in the military use to carry all their living gear and enough explosives to make a dent in anything.

You can expand most any pack by adding extra pouches and lashing things to them. A medium ruck, for example, holding 2200 cubic inches of gear, can be doubled in capacity by using straps and lashing extra pouches or sacks to it.

Sometimes you need extra gear, and want it right on your vest or web gear. The buttpack serves that need well. Just large enough to hold gear, not so large it gets in the way. (Courtesy Blackhawk Industries.)

The competition Electronic Dynamics shooters backpack is extremely useful as a range bag. But what makes it useful as a range back works against it as an operational pack for SWAT.

The monster ruck is capable of being packed with enough gear to live for weeks, and blow up anything that needs demolition.

The important thing to look for is padding. It doesn't matter how small a ruck is, if the shoulder straps aren't padded you will be in agony in short order. With enough padding, even a monster pack can be carried, at least for a while, and when you need to quit it won't be because it feels like your collarbones are being sawed off. When purchasing a pack, you should not get one that has no provision for a water reservoir. You can get top-notch gear that will last a long time, and will also let you transport water, for the same cost as lesser gear in flashy colors. Insist on being able to take water.

Two packs I've gotten to like a great deal are the Force 5 from Blackhawk, and the Ranger Backpack from London Bridge.

Ranger backpack

Designed for the 75th Ranger Regiment by the London Bridge Trading Company, it is a medium ruck, with extra pouches already sewn on. There are three external pouches with buckled flaps for pop flares. I can see having those for a rural department. Having found the lost hikers, you can use the flare as a final approach signal, once you've radioed the GPS position, especially if you are short of time. Also, there is a radio pouch, with a buckle and hook-and-loop fastened flap. Perfect for storing water, or a med kit, if you don't have a radio that fits. Many Motorola units fit with room for extra batteries, a map or other small flat items. Inside, the main compartment has lashing webbing to secure a large radio in place (Rangers need lots of radios, as do many other military units). The webbing can be used to secure a first aid supply container, extra water, or any other rigid container. For your own hydration, there is a compartment for a water reservoir, and it will accept a Camelbak unit or a Blackhawk Hydrastorm bladder. You can route the drinking tube out through any of the three secured flaps on the top. (Or use them for radio antennas.) The main compartment is plenty large enough for extra gear. There are two other zippered compartments on the back of the

pack, and lash webbing to secure extra pouches to the exterior. The external pocket is big enough for binoculars, a laser rangefinder, and lunch all at once. Also, there is a lash webbing attachment panel on the bottom, where you can secure a sleeping bag or other cargo. Tactical marksmen who have to build a hide can roll up camo netting for later use. The shoulder straps are well padded, and have both a chest strap to keep the shoulder straps where they belong, and a waist strap to keep the pack from shifting around as you walk. If you feel the need for more pockets, the "Devil Radio Backpack" made for the 82nd Airborne, has an additional storage compartment on the right side, under the pop flare pockets. Designed as a tactical pack and not an expedition pack, the 75th can be expanded enough to serve as more than just a patrol and assault pack.

If you don't need pop flares, you can use the pockets to store items kept in tubes. A plastic tube an inch and a half in diameter will slide in and can be used as a storage container. On top, there are straps to pull the pack tight, or to store a rolled poncho or jacket.

Were I designing my own ruck, for use other than as a Ranger or Airborne trooper, I'd use a shell from the London Bridge Trading Co 75th Ranger as a start. I'd leave everything else as-is but swap the pop flare pouches on one side for two (if they would both fit) of the cargo boxes/pouches that LBTC makes for their 82nd Airborne ruck: The Devil Radio Backpack. The radio pouch on the 75th is still useful as a radio or first aid pouch, but for those of us who don't use pop flares that much, swapping the right-hand pop-flare pouches for some more cargo space would be useful. I would then replace a pop-flare pouch by mounting it outboard of the radio pouch on the left side. Then again, it wouldn't be a 75th Ranger ruck after that.

The London Bridge Trading Company 75th Ranger pack. It can hold more gear than you can comfortably pack.

The Blackhawk Force 5 ruck has an integral hydration system, and expansion capacity.

Compression sacks don't hold heavy gear, but they keep light gear compact and protected. (Courtesy Blackhawk Industries.)

Blackhawk Force 5

The Force 5 comes from the Hydrastorm division of Blackhawk, and is a medium ruck (2,250 cu in) designed with expansion n mind. The inside main compartment has a division to hold a water bladder, with the drinking tube routed through the top covered panel and then down a shoulder strap. There are two zippered compartments for flatter gear. The sides have compression straps, so if you don't have the pack stuffed you can tighten it. If you do have it stuffed, then you can use the compression straps to hang light items. The rear of the pack has a webbing strap to secure other pouches or gear to, and the bottom has a rigid plastic panel for straps to secure a sleeping bag. (or something similar) the thing I like best about the Force 5 is the back. The back panel is a contoured foam-filled synthetic construction attached the bottom. The back, their IVS™ for cooling, allows airflow to keep your back from getting as sweaty as it otherwise would. The shoulder straps are well padded, as is the waist belt. The chest strap

is an easy-adjust design, so you can quickly tighten or loosen it as you change clothes to adjust to the temperature. The waist strap on the Force 5 is padded. The side straps to compress the Force 5 are useful to secure extra pouches, but they have two limitations: The pack has to be full for the straps to be secure, and they are not designed to hold much weight. But you can expand the pack using them as anchor points for extra pouches or gear.

Specialty packs

An EMT or medic can't do much with just what he (or she) carries in pockets. Even the pouches on web gear or a vest can be quickly consumed. For large-scale incidents, or extensive care in the short term, a backpack loaded with extras is needed. One item that is heavy, bulky and when needed, needed right now are IV bags. You can't carry more than one (or if you're a large person, two) on a vest. To pack more you need

If you need extra gear, but not all the time, pack it in an accessory pouch, label it, and keep it in the trunk of your car. You can clip an accessory pouch onto the side of any pack, like this medium on a Force 5 Blackhawk.

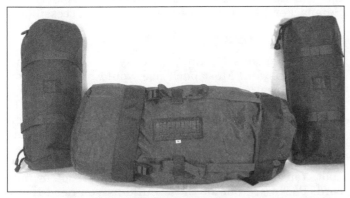

Compression sacks can hold tarps or ponchos, or in the winter a sleeping bag. (Courtesy Blackhawk Industries.)

a big and solid pack. The shoulder bag like a camera bag is fine for short distances, but to haul large amounts or over any distance you need a pack.

The contents would depend on what the individual is trained and or certified for, and the nature of the expected injuries. A combat medic would do a lot of work at the extremes: a lot of cuts and scrapes, and hopefully not too many gunshot wounds. A Special Forces medic would be treating infections and diseases in the local population. An EMT assigned to an area covered in freeways would expect to treat a lot of crushing injuries. But for extensive work, a big pack can be very comforting.

Pack expansion

Sometimes you need more. Blackhawk (and others, I'm sure) make clip-on bags and pouches that increase capacity. A compression sack for a sleeping bag or high-tech poncho, a clip-on bag for a med kit, or a bag for a water filter, all make packing easier. One approach to pack construction/assembly is to have the accessory gear in Blackhawk modular add-a-pouch bags. A small is 2 inches x6 inches x 9 inches, for 108 cubic inches of storage, while the large, at 6 x2 x16 offers 192 cubic inches. For med kits, the med pouch splits the difference at 123 cubic inches. You could easily take a Ranger Backpack or a Force 5, both medium alpine packs, and put a large modular add-a-pouch on each side (384 cubic inches) a compression sack on the bottom 29 x9 (1845 cu in), and a med kit pouch or two (246 cubic inches for the pair) on the back, you've more than doubled the capacity. However, the compression sack is not meant for heavy gear. You can stash a sleeping bag, poncho, poncho liner or tarp in it, but not anything heavy.

For a rural deputy, the basic pack could rest in the trunk of the car (or back of the SUV) with the accessory pouches next to it. In case of a call, you can quickly grab the pack with basic gear, and if you need more, secure the extra pouches to it in a few seconds. Need to search in cold weather? Lash the compression sack with a sleeping bag and insulated poncho to it. A call for multiple injuries? Grab the extra med kit and clip it on.

Or, just keep a monster ruck loaded with everything you'll possibly need in the trunk of your patrol car or SUV, and drag it out when you need something. If you have to carry it any distance, you'll wish you hadn't skipped your gym work during the last month or two.

The Wilderness

A specialty accessory is the Safepacker. On the outside it looks like a map case or some padded pouch to hold a flat object. Open it up, and there is room for a handgun and spare ammo. (And a map, too.) Secured to your pack it can be a relatively unobtrusive means of having a firearm at hand. Rather than bury your insurance deep in a pocket (Which pocket is it in? This is not the question you want to be asking when you need a vital rescue tool)

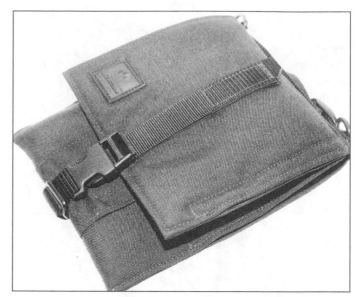

The Safepacker, by The Wilderness, looks like a map case. Inside can be the sidearm of your choice, with spare ammo.

you secure the Safepacker on the outside of your pack. If you're worried about it being obvious, secure a compression sack holding a poncho or tarp over the Safepacker, hiding it but not making it inaccessible.

What goes in a pack?

That depends. (I know, the easy way out, and the obvious answer.) Most pack use would be in rural or remote location operations. You'll need extra batteries, water, food, medical supplies and ammo. If it is a search and rescue, you'll need medical gear for those you find, and protection from the elements. You may find them just in time to erect a quick shelter from the coming storm, or get them out of a tight spot. You may need a shelter or tarp, or rope or 550 cord. Packs are one of those build-as-you-need-them arrangements. Location, job, climate and season all influence what goes in.

Chapter 9
Let There Be Light

AS IT HAPPENS, half the time we spend "down here" is in darkness, or relative darkness. And a good thing, too, or the weather, the seasons and the phrase "putting in a good days work" would all change. In the city, darkness is a relative thing. Even in the middle of the night it can be light enough to make out shapes and see movement. And in the middle of the day, you can walk into a windowless room and be in pitch-black surroundings. Realizing this, NYPD requires even officers working the day shift to have a flashlight with them. At "night" with the light of streetlights, advertising and automobile headlights, you can see objects and people. But can you identify them? In a military context, firing into the darkness at sounds, movement or in a direction away from your unit may be allowed or even a good thing. But even that is changing. In the modern age of public relations, "collateral damage" can end a career or result in a prison sentence. You simply must know what you are firing at, regardless of the circumstance.

My friend Mas Ayoob described perhaps the most chilling and relevant situation: You awaken in the middle of the night to hear sounds of movement downstairs. Fumbling, stumbling and occasional muttered curses allow you to track the person moving towards the bedrooms. With a light, you can startle, and identify, the person: Your drunken (fill in as you feel the need) a) brother in law, b) teenaged daughter's boyfriend, c) Next-door neighbor. Your brother-in-law or the boyfriend is there because friends don't let friends drive drunk, and they are sleeping on your couch. The neighbor is there because he's mistaken your door for his. Any and all

are looking for the bathroom, and not finding it. Do you really want to be comforted by the fact that the night sights on your defensive handgun allow you to shoot without needing illumination? A powerful enough light will not only identify the intruder, but startle and cause him to reflexively turn away from the light should he prove to not be so benign as the examples mentioned.

How much light do you need to trigger the avoidance reflex in someone? It depends on how adapted to night their vision is, how surprised they are by your appearance, and how concentrated the light is. If they've just walked in from a lighted area, you're going to need more light. If they are expecting someone, you'll need more light. And diffused light hardly helps. If you were to turn on a neon sign, it hardly matters that it pumps out a thousand lumens, if it is the size of a wall. It will be too diffused.

Now that I've used the term, just what is a lumen? Briefly, light is measured in two terms, lumens and candlepower. The word lumen is the contraction of "luminous flux" and to measure it takes more than just a calibrated eyeball. It is the total light output of a source. Candlepower is the measure of the brightest spot of a beam, compared to a calibrated reference of one candlepower. Can you directly compare the two? Can you say that 10 candlepower is equal to one lumen? Five? One hundred? No. It just doesn't work that way. You could have a neon sign that at its brightest part puts out a million candlepower, but the diffusion of the sign swamps the brightest part in diffused light. The total output? I don't know, but when a neon sign turns on in Vegas, you don't turn away. Conversely, a

The Surefire M6 is a whole lot of light for not a lot of bulk, weight or batteries. (photo courtesy Surefire)

The M3 is a step up from the G2s, without being a whole lot bigger.

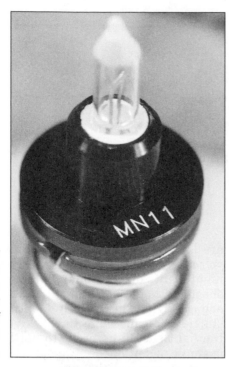

The heart of any light is the lamp assembly, and the Surefire assembly puts out a lot of light for such a small part.

You need more than one, so pack bigger ones than you carry as backup.

began looking at the options offered. Wow. From jewel-like little lights to lightsabers capable of bringing an alien mothership in for a landing, Surefire has them all. And once hooked on the lights, I had to know what made Surefire different.

The differences come down to reflectors, filaments, lenses and lamp assemblies and durable construction. The reflectors are pre-focused, and the surface of the reflector is stippled and vapor-coated. The rough appearance of the reflector is what produces the smooth even light. On regular lights, the shadow you see is the filament itself, reflected off the smooth surface of the reflector. The rough finish of the Surefire cancels out the image of the filament. The Surefire filament is tungsten, sealed in either a Xenon or Halogen gas environment. Filaments break from rough handling, or they burn out from oxidation. Remove the oxygen and you eliminate burnout. Shockproof the lamp assembly, and you reduce the breakage from rough handling. The extra shock-proofing on lights meant for the big guns, 12-gauge, is even more rugged. The lenses on Surefire lamps are Pyrex, highly impact resistant and nearly scratch proof. And the construction is tough. The metal bodies are machined from aluminum. If you want even more toughness, you can get them finished with Mil-spec type III hard anodizing. The synthetics are even tougher, as the Nitrolon they are made of will give slightly on impact, dampening the impact and making the light even tougher.

If it sounds like I'm sold on Surefire, it is because I am. I used a bunch of others through the years, all name brands, and as soon as I get my hands on each Surefire model I retire the old ones, not to be used again. (Well, I do keep some around. I've still got my five C cell light in the truck, but it is also an impact weapon and spare tire iron, as well as a light.)

What do you need?

Well, as the man said, that depends. The smallest light that won't get lost in your pocket, and puts out enough light to be useful as a combat tool is one of the 6 models. "6" as in six volts, starting with the original, the 6P, and include the E2, the Z2, the M2 Centurion and now the G2Z. The six-volt lights, using a P60 lamp, put out 65 lumens, and run for an hour on a pair of lithium 123 batteries. Whether you go with a Nitrolon personal light, a machined aluminum Executive or a Z2 Combat light, you have plenty of illumination. The Z2 is so well thought of (and has been for many years) that each graduate of the FBI Academy gets issued one. How bright is 65 lumens? Bright enough to read a license plate a block away (assuming your eyes are up to the job) or to force the reflexive turn from the light being shone in your eyes. If you want more, you can have it. Installing a P61 lamp into one of these pumps the output to an impressive 120 lumens, but at a cost. The batteries get sucked dry in twenty minutes. (You can almost hear them groan as you switch the light on.) And it gets hot if left running for more than a few seconds. The G2 Nitrolon or the G2Z are my first

seemingly small lamp with a 60-lumen output, properly focused, can make you see stars if it is shined in your face at night.

I have used just about everything to provide illumination in the last 25 years, and I must admit I resisted the siren song of Surefire lights for a long time. Why? Those of us old enough to remember the throaty roar of a big-block V-8 engine on a muscle car can remember when the Soviet Method of engineering held sway: bigger is better. No puny little "illumination device" is going to put out more light than my big honkin' D-cell flashlight, no sirree. And the cost was another reason. Why, if I were to ditch all my existing lights, and spend more now for new ones than my current ones cost, it would cost me... But the first time I turned one on, and saw the smooth, white beam, I was hooked. Once hooked on the light, I then

A little Executive or Outdoorsman, and spare batteries. You're set.

The G2Z is so highly thought of that every graduate of the FBI Academy gets issued one. (Courtesy Surefire)

Who'd a thought we needed a lanyard on our lights? Surefire. (Courtesy Surefire)

A bigger reflector gives you a hotter center to your beam. If you want a wider beam, you need a diffuser filter instead of a larger head.

choices here. And my wife's, too. As soon as I had returned from a training trip, she insisted that I get her one, also. "Baxter and I would not have had the run-in with the skunk, if we'd had your light." Baxter is our dog, and rather than subjecting the two of them to the skunk decon routine again, I gladly laid hands on another G2 Nitrolon for her.

If you need more light, you really should be looking at a bigger lamp, rather than giving a pocket-sized light the illumination equivalent of a boost of nitrous oxide. Next up in size would be something like the M3 Combat light. Running on a pair of lithiums, it puts out 125 lumens and runs for an hour. An hour may not seem like much, but in a tactical setting you are going to be turning it on and off with the hesitation switch, running it for a few seconds each time. Look at it this way: at three seconds per "burst', you've got the equivalent of a 1,200-shot magazine in that light. Twelve hundred bursts of 125-lumen light get a lot of dark places inspected. The beauty of the M3 is that it isn't that much larger than a personal light; it puts out twice the light, and lasts as long. However, if you want more, it can be had. You can put a Turbo head on your M3, for a sharper or "harder" beam. The larger head gets you more light in the center. Go up in lamp numbers for the M3 and get more lumens, or go to the M6.

The M6 offers either 225 lumens, or with the M21 lamp, 500 lumens. At 500 lumens you'll deplete the six lithium batteries in it in 20 minutes. But anyone lit up by it will have no choice but to turn away.

More? More, you say? There are more, but when you go beyond 500 lumens you run into other problems. For one, the backsplash of light off of the object you're illuminating, and other nearby objects, can cause you to look away. Or at least squint. The bigger lights are not a good idea for up close and personal use, but instead are best used to search distant places. Need to see what's in that alley? Is that an overturned boat in the water? Hit it with an Arc light high-intensity discharge lamp. This is a lamp that can blind, if someone was stupid enough to stare at it for a few minutes. Called The Beast, the B1 has an estimated rating of 2,500 lumens. The B1 runs on 20 lithium batteries that last 80 minutes,

If you need or want a whole lot of light, The Beast can deliver. Just be ready to pack the weight and put up with the comments about signaling the mother ship. (Courtesy Surefire)

an E2 Executive drops the output to an eye-easy 17 lumens for 15 hours of map reading! The drawback to LEDs is output. With the regular lamp, you get full output almost up to the moment the batteries die. You'll get an hour of output, a minute or two of yellow, then darkness. With the LED, the amount just tapers off, and off, and off, until you finally have to swap batteries to read the map. (Ten or 15 hours of continuous light later!)

Map reading may be thought of as a military requirement, but in the law enforcement arena low-light reading of information is also needed. You go out to raid a house in the middle of a tract development. Did you check the street name? Did you check the house number before going in? You can with a low-power navigation light, but you can't with your 120-lumen combat light, not without blasting your night vision and perhaps warning the suspects. But the E series, or an LED on the E series, allows you to check.

and weighs 3-1/2 pounds. The B2 uses a rechargeable Ni-MH battery and weighs almost 6 pounds. After an hour, you'll need fresh batteries, while you recharge the old batteries.

Moving backwards

You don't always need enough light to knock your socks off. Trying to read a map with a Z2 is an exercise in masochism. Even if you can squint enough to read the map (and the light doesn't scorch the paper) when you're done you have no night vision left, just a blob in front of you. What you need is a smaller light, or an LED head, or both. The E1 models only run 15 lumens, enough to see all the detail on a map without your eyes feeling like the mothership just landed. And you get that light for an hour and a half. If you want more life, then the LED head on an E1 generates 17 lumens for 10 hours! If you want more size (you can almost lose an E1 in your pocket, it's so small) then take something like the E2 Executive and swap the standard head for an LED head. The standard head gets you 65 lumens for an hour, but the LED head on

How many lights?

My friend Ed Mohn has a mnemonic on this subject: "Two becomes one, One becomes none." You should have at least one light with you at all times. Two is better, but carrying two lights on your person can be tough. After all, there are only so many pockets, and so much real estate on the belt. The easy way to get a second light is to have it mounted on a weapon. You have the spare, but you also have a light that isn't attached to a weapon. I was forcefully reminded of the need for a solo light while coming back from the 1999 IPSC World Shoot, held in Cebu, Philippines. Based on the assurances of the Hong Kong Regional Director, many of us had routed our flights to the Philippines through Hong Kong. "No problem" was the assurance. The actuality was just short of strip-searches. We found ourselves on the tarmac, with our luggage lined up (mine mysteriously absent) showing our paperwork. One member on our flight even had his ammo counted. The trip to the Philippines was bad, but at least it was in daylight. The trip home had us in Hong Kong

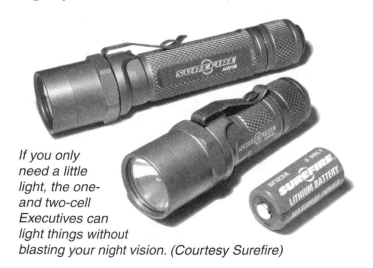

If you only need a little light, the one- and two-cell Executives can light things without blasting your night vision. (Courtesy Surefire)

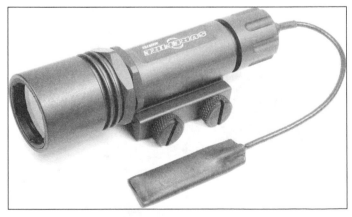

M951 SU 05 For military use, extreme durability is asked for. The Millenium series with a pressure switch will probably survive things you won't.

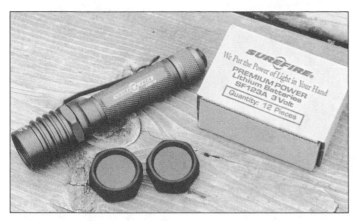

Sometimes you don't need white light, you need red or blue or green. The hand-helds take press-on filters.

at night. There we stood, paperwork in hand (we'd been clever enough to make copies, so we could simply hand them copies so they didn't need to take our paperwork off to makes copies) when I realized that the reading light the lead officer was using came from the weapon mount on an MP-5. One officer was holding it over the shoulder of the lead officer, and pressing the momentary switch on the forearm to light up our paperwork. If you aren't creeped out by the thought of that scenario, then you aren't going to be on any team I go through doors with. An AD at that moment would have all of us in a Hong Kong prison for who-knows-how-long while the matter was investigated and settled.

No, sometimes you need a light by itself. So keep one in your pocket, and one on the weapon. And more, as needed, like that cute little E1 for reading maps, street signs, apartment numbers and the like.

Always white?

For suspect control, you want white and lots of it. But for navigating, tracking, map reading, you may not. Filters allow extra control. Red filters cut down on light sensitivity outside of your area of operations. Blue filters allow blood to be more clearly seen and tracked at night. Under blue light, blood sparkles as a shiny black substance, standing out from the background. Green light also controls outside notice of illumination, and allows some map colors to show up that would be invisible under red light. One tidbit of info I got back from the Afghanistan ops was that colored filters could at times be counter-productive. Out in the hinterlands, an occasional flash of light is part of "what happens." A lamp left on when someone opens a door, or a glimpse of a campfire, these are white lights. However, only the Americans used red, blue or green lights. A flash of color at night was identifying.

Using the handheld light

There are many ways to keep illumination on target and under control, while also handling a weapon. Perhaps the easiest is to have a weapon mount, but that comes up in a bit. First, solo lights

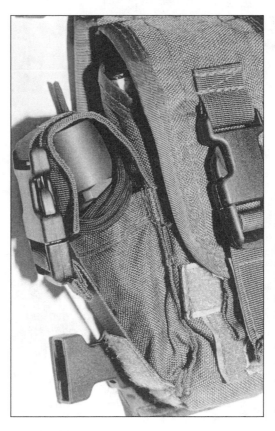

This Nitrolon G-2Z fits comfortably in the pistol magazine pocket of the SOE Gear CQB vest. And it will be ready for years, thanks to the Lithium batteries in it.

and handguns. Hand-held lights offer the option of not having a weapon at the ready. You may need one, or have one handy, but you don't necessarily need to have the light and weapon pointed at the search area. First, there are two basic and traditional ways to hold a light: saber and hammer. In the saber hold, the illuminated end is between your thumb and forefinger. You can use either the thumb to press the light switch,

In the old days, we used the "Interview" light method. The problem with it was it led to a natural reaction to use the light as an impact weapon, striking the forehead. Flashlight concussion is often an inappropriate Use of Force escalation.

The oldest of the flashlight two-hands methods, evolved from the quickly-obsolete "cup and saucer" shooting style.

The FBI style of illumination is awkward, and no one believes that you are 7 feet tall.

or the forefinger. In the hammer, the lighted end is pointed out of your fist from the little finger end of your hand. You can use your thumb, but traditionally you would use the forefinger or second finger. Both methods require a side-switch light. The tailcap of the Surefire lights can be pressed wit the thumb in the hammer hold, but the saber hold is useless. Through the decades we've tried a bunch of methods, and some have names. In the techniques, there are "hands-apart" and "hands-together" methods. Some techniques will work with either hold, saber or hammer, and some will only work with a specific method. For instance, the FBI and the Harries can be done both saber and hammer, while the Chapman and Ayoob are saber only. First, the hands-apart methods.

FBI

The oldest. Hold the light saber-style, and hold it out away from your body, at or above shoulder height, and slightly in front of you. The idea was to keep the bad guys from using the light as a target. As a decoy, it fails. As a method of illuminating things, it succeeds. The shortcomings are that you must shoot one-handed (as with all hands-apart methods) and that indexing the light is not easy or natural. It is common to turn on the light and have it pointing slightly off of where you intended. And using it for any length of time turns a night search into aerobic exercise. Holding any light out there is work. One advantage not often mentioned is the three-dimensionality of the light you see. A light source directly in line with your eyes produces a flat image, where the screen of brush (as an example) you're trying to see through is brightly lit and precludes seeing through to the intended object. By moving the light source off the axis of your vision, you can see through the intervening brush better.

The neck-hold method is fast, and easy to index. But you do risk lighting up your own gun using it.

Neck hold

Instead of holding the light out, you hold it next to your ear. Hold it hammer-hold, not saber. The light is easier to hold and easier to line up before you turn it on than with the FBI style. However, you are back to the flat light and brush problem. You also must be careful you don't light up your extended handgun, reflecting light back into your eyes and informing anyone who is looking that you have a gun out. The neck hold for a Surefire comes out of the old "interview position" of holding a big metal multi-cell flashlight by resting it on your shoulder. It used to be quite popular, until the Courts held that a big enough flashlight is an impact weapon and can be considered lethal force. As the most common target struck from this position is the head, it can get you in legal trouble. The same position with a Surefire won't get you in trouble. After all, if you can fracture someone's skull with a Nitrolon

In hands-together techniques, the light is centered on you; so don't leave it on any longer than you need to.

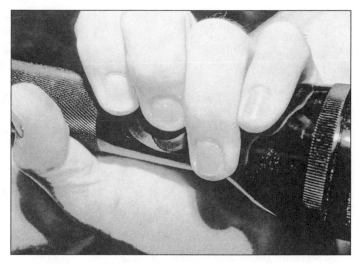

You can use your fingers or thumb to light, with the Harries method.

or Z2 from the neck hold, you probably didn't need a flashlight in your hand to do it.

Hands-together

There are two big disadvantages to the "hands-together" techniques: Your light is centered on your body, making the light an aiming point unless it is bright enough to force the involuntary turn. And by having your hands together, you increase the chance of "interlimb interaction." With interlimb interaction, when you clutch one hand, the other sympathetically clutches as well. Not as hard, but it can. If you trip and fall, and reach out with your gun hand to catch yourself, you can clutch the light hand and discharge your weapon. If you use a hands-together light technique, you must practice with it enough to make sure you keep straight which hand is the light and which hand is the gun. That way you won't shoot when what you wanted was to illuminate.

The Harries technique

The Harries was developed by Michael Harries, and taught first (that I know of) at Gunsite. The Harries depends on your using the Weaver stance. To assume the Harries, hold the light hammer style. Extend the handgun, then bring your left hand under your right (assuming a right-handed shooter) and up, and bring the backs of your hands together. Once in contact, you can rest a long light on your right forearm. The Harries is quite tiring, but you don't have to hold your hands up in front of you all the time. Bringing the gun and light down, you lower them as a unit. You can keep them together and pivot your arms

If you have a flexible wrist, you can search in Harries without covering with the muzzle. But it is work.

The Harries method. With a long light, you can rest it on your forearm. But you must shoot Weaver to use it.

In Chapman, press the hands out isosceles.

down to rest. The disadvantage, as mentioned, is that it is work. And, you cannot search without pointing the firearm at the search area. You also must shoot from the Weaver stance to use it. Isosceles shooters cannot use it. The advantage is that gun and light are together, and bringing your hands up brings up both. Commonly done with a side switch light, the Harries is easily adapted to a tailcap light.

Chapman

Ray Chapman was one of the first Combat Masters, back when IPSC was something done at the Southwest Combat Pistol League. The position is best done in the isosceles shooting position, although you can make it work in Weaver. Using the saber hold bring the light up next to, and in contact with, the gun hand, on the fingertip side. To best align the light, do not hold the body down into your palm, but keep it propped up on the fingertips and thumb. It is fast and natural, and you can separate your hands to search without also pointing your handgun at the search area.

Ayoob

Developed by Mas Ayoob for Isosceles shooters, the method is simple; use the saber-hold, and let the light rest in your palm. Use your light hand

In Ayoob, use the fingertips of the left hand to stay in contact with the handgun.

fingertips to grasp your gun hand. The result is a bit more secure than the Chapman. The pitch of your wrist tends to point the light slightly upwards, but at most distances that simply means it is pointed right in your opponent's face. You can search using the light, and have the muzzle pointed slightly down, and then when you need to shoot, a slight pivot to line up the sights gets you on target.

Rogers

Seen from above, Rogers uses left hand pressure for illumination.

The Rogers method depends on the ring around the middle of the G2 or Z2 lights. Clutch the light in your left hand, with the barrel of the light between the second and third fingers. The tailcap presses against (and is activated by) the heel of your thumb. You have to shoot from isosceles for the Rogers method to work. Using Rogers, you get light and sights aligned. You also get some position bracing from your light hand fingers being on your gun hand. And, by using a different motion (push to heel of hand instead of finger flex) you reduce the likelihood of interlimb interaction. The drawback is the light jammed between your fingers. Some find it quite uncomfortable.

Marine Corps

The Marine method uses a large light with a side button. Using the saber hold, press the bezel of the light forward next to your gun hand until the fingertips of the gun hand can lock into the ring around the bezel. Another isosceles method, as traditionally done. However, you can use it in Weaver if you switch from saber to hammer hold. The advantage is that the light and weapon are locked together during the search, although recoil will cause some separation.

Which method should you use? That depends on your physical type and flexibility, your shooting stance, and the area in which you work. The locked-

Marine technique, keeping the light indexed with the handgun.

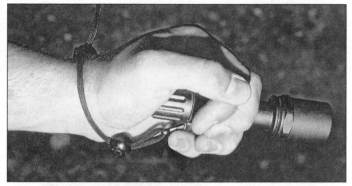

The basis of the Rogers technique, pressing to light.

together Marine method works well on a moving boat, as your light and weapon will stay pointed together despite the moving deck. Searching a warehouse, you need not worry about the floor moving, and a less-tiring method will be needed if you're to finish the search. Try them all. You may find you have need of several.

Searching

Not all illumination situations will require a firearm in your hands. You may be searching for a lost child, it may be a frequent search of a location that has a high rate of false alarms (in which case I hope your department is charging enough for the hassle) or you may be walking the dog. Searching without a weapon is a good time to practice either the FBI or the Neck Hold methods. The tailcap of the Surefire lights doesn't lend itself to the waist-high "thumb on the button" search methods that many of us got used to in the old days. The tailcap of the Surefire, and the lanyard on the Z series, led me to develop another method, one I call the "Mr. Casual" method. Adjust the lanyard and its two locking tabs so you can slip your hand into the lanyard,

"Mr. Casual", which can also be used as Rogers.

but it won't fall off if you let go. Hold the body of the light in your off hand, between your trigger finger and second finger. Hold it at the first joint of your trigger finger, and the second joint of the second finger, with the lanyard around your wrist. Use your thumb to press the button and light your subject. Unlike the FBI method, indexing the light to illuminate what you want is quickly learned. You can let go of the light to grasp or grapple, and not lose it. And, the motion is close enough to the style of the Rogers method that your nightly dog-walking sessions (for one example) reinforce your firearms handling method.

You can also use the lanyard-equipped Z lights in the Neck Hold, but instead of pressing the tailcap button, adjust the endcap so a squeeze of the body (tipping the end cap) lights the light. If you let go, the light goes off, but the lanyard keeps you from dropping it. To apply the squeeze, you brace the light body so the tailcap rests against the heel of your thumb. Crushing your hand closed flexes the cap and lights the light, once adjusted properly.

Long gun solo light methods

If you don't have a weapon light, but have a long gun, you need some way to use both light and rifle. The simplest, if you have hands big enough, is to hold the light against the forearm of the rifle. This method works best with a sideswitch light. However, you can adjust a tailcap light by screwing the cap to the right location, that when you squeeze the light hard enough it turns on. The method is a bit tricky, but it does work. Otherwise, you'll have to use a hammer hold, and simply rest the forearm of the rifle on your left wrist. On AR rifles you can gain some stability by pressing your left hand back until it rests against the front of the magazine well. A third method, for those with very good arm strength, is to simply hold the rifle with one hand (shouldered) and the light with another, usually in hammer hold. It isn't easy, but in a pinch it will do. The best method is to go to a weapon light.

Accessories

If you have lights, you need batteries. And if you depend on lights, sooner or later you're going to need extra bulbs. And since we all know it as Murphy's Law and not Murphy's Suggestion, you are going to

You need batteries, and buying them at the local party store, camera store or big-box hardware store can be costly. Better to just buy a couple of boxes right from the people who make the lights.

need them on the proverbial dark and stormy night. The best way is to carry and store them in a Surefire container. Waterproof and shockproof, each holds six batteries and a spare lamp assembly. You can pack a same spare, or a brighter spare lamp. Tucked away in your gear, you'll have a continuous supply of light for many hours. If you're running two or three lights, six may be just enough to get you through a night's busy work in a hardscrabble city. And what batteries should you pack? Why, Surefire, of course. Lithium batteries have a very long shelf life. Left alone and not subjected to light, heat or water, they will still be good in 10 years. But they have traditionally been expensive. In the beginning (Hey, wouldn't that make a great opening line for a book?) Surefire had a contract with Duracell that did not allow them to sell

A night's work might use up a lot of batteries. Better to have them and not need them.

'loose batteries." Surefire could only sell batteries installed in their lights. So, Surefire produced the "Hurricane lamp" which was a housing with a tiny led and a dozen lithium 123 batteries. That's right, buy the lamp, take out the batteries and toss the housing, and you had batteries cheaper than buying them at the drug store, camera store or hardware store. Surefire got tired of their customers struggles and grumbling, and contracted with a big battery maker to make batteries for Surefire. Packed in cardboard boxes of a dozen, your per-battery cost is dirt-cheap. The current suggested retail is $15 for a dozen Surefire batteries, which is less than half of what they cost at the local "big box" hardware store.

Weapon lights

In the old days, we mounted flashlights to firearms with hose clamps, duct tape and wooden or plastic spacer blocks. Ugly? You bet. Clumsy? Ditto. Did we all ditch our cobbled-together rigs just as soon as we could lay hands on proper gear? In a heartbeat. Even in the old days, trying to juggle a light and rifle with only two hands was not fun. We just didn't have cool gear back then. Now there are several models available for handguns, duty rifles and shotguns.

Handgun

The slickest piece of gear to come across my desk in a long time just emerged from its protective cocoon. Hot off the R&D and prototyping benches at Surefire, the P117C is so cool I almost can't send it back. However, it is promised to a service branch as soon as I send it back, and the fellows it is going to (I cannot

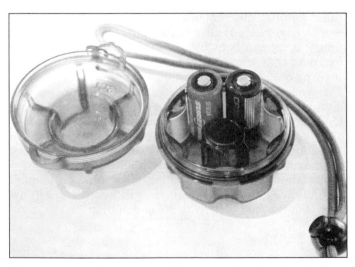

To carry spare in your gear bag or rucksack, what better than a Surefire case? It is waterproof, nearly unbreakable, and can also carry a spare lamp assembly.

The new 1911 weaponlight, with pressure switch as well as cross-bolt on switch.

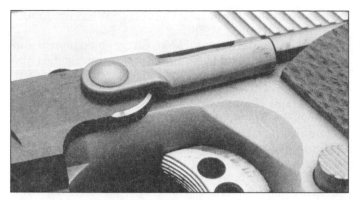

The mounting plate uses a new slide stop lever. I did not have a change in the point of impact when switching slide stops.

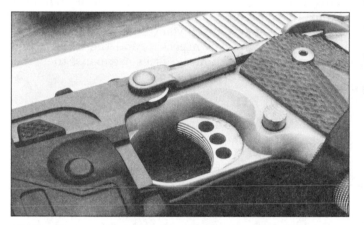

The pressure switch offers momentary on. The button in front of the trigger offers constant on.

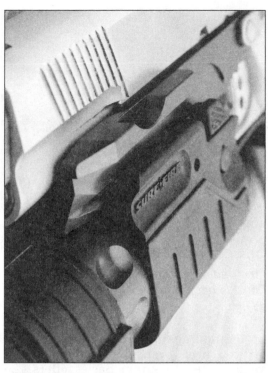

The rails fit the Safariland holster.

say whom) are people I do not want to annoy. The previous Surefire handgun mounts clamped to the front of the trigger guard, or some few pistols, such as the Beretta Vertec, Springfield Armory XD and newer Glock pistols that have integral weapon light rails on the receiver. The light itself then slid onto the clamped-on rail. This P117C (a Nitrolon with slimline switch and shuttle switch) has a different mount. The adapter is a machined aluminum bracket that fits under the dustcover of the 1911 (did I forget to mention that this is a 1911-specific adapter?) and is held in place with the slide stop. The light comes off of the adapter via the usual Surefire spring paddle. The switch, in this case a slimline pressure switch, comes back to the frame and rides right under the trigger guard. The bracket has two rubber pads, one that rests under the dust cover, and the other is spring-loaded and bears against the trigger guard. The pads keep the bracket from marring your finish, and the spring keeps the bracket tight to your frame. To install it is simple, if a bit fussy. Remove your slide stop. Now press the bracket into place, and insert the new slide stop. You'll have to do it in two steps, first to get the slide stop started into the bracket and frame, then to line the barrel link up and get the slide stop the rest of the way through. The springs of the mount ensure a tight fit, but also make wrestling it together a bit of a

task until you get the hang of it. Once in place, you can have the light on or off without any trouble. The bracket has rails and a cross-slot to lock the light in place, and two upper rails with scallops in them. The upper rails are to lock the holstered pistol into the Safariland holster for weapon lights, when the light is not in place. (Otherwise the holstered pistol would move in the holster.)

Now the real fun part: With the bracket in place but the light not installed, you can still force your 1911 into some tactical thigh rig holsters. If it is a sewn-webbing holster, and not a form-fitted kydex or multi-layer assembly (that is, a snug fit from design and construction) you can fit it in. I managed to get my Caspian race-ready 1911 into the LBTC Naval Special Warfare tactical rig with a little forcing. I can't guarantee it will fit all holsters, but it comes close enough that it is often a bonus, and worth checking. Lacking a Safariland holster, and using this weapon light, I'd be very tempted to simply mill the extra rails off. That way I could use my regular holsters, have the light available to be installed in a few seconds, and not have to force it, or acquire the Safariland rig. However, it must go back, so this one escapes the mill.

The light uses the standard pair of Lithium 123 batteries, and with the installed P60 lamp assembly delivers 65 lumens for an hour. Changing the lamp to a P61 would bump that up to 120 lumens, but then it would only have a 20-minute run time. The Nitrolon series are the lightest weapon lights for a handgun that Surefire offers. If you need more durability and are willing to put up with more weight, you can go with the Military Series. Offered with the same switch and lamp options, the Military Series lights are made with anodized aluminum bodies instead of the Nitrolon synthetic. The extra durability comes at

The 117 sent me had a red filter attached. This filter, like many larger ones, is hinged to pivot out of the way when you don't need it.

the cost of adding half again the weight, from 5.5 to 8.2 ounces. If you need even more light, and can stand the weight, the Millenium Series offers 125 lumens (MN10 lamp, 60 minutes run time) or 225 lumens (MN11 lamp, 20 minutes run time) but to get it you have to almost double the weight of the Nitrolon series, at 10.2 ounces.

The basic Nitrolon with a 65-lumen lamp is plenty bright. The sample I was sent had an FM 15 filter on it, for red light when closed. The filter element is silvered, and in daylight appears as a mirror. At night, with the light on, you get enough light to easily navigate by. It is not a stealth mode light, however. At close range, with night-adapted vision, it is still bright enough to dazzle the unexpected. If you want to be navigating stealthily, you need to be using the navigation lights on a shoulder weapon light. The filter has a clamp to make it easy to install, and the filter is hinged to expose the white light when you need it. The filter alone is more hi-tech than a lot of lights out there, and yet durable enough that you needn't worry about it failing you just because you accidentally whacked something with it.

Any Surefire handgun light is tops in the "cool guy gear" index, and essential when operating at night. But for those who use a 1911, this new mount is the slickest yet. Put it down in the "must have" category.

Rifle/SMG

Using a handgun one-handed with a light is clumsy, but it can be done. To try to use a shoulder-stocked weapon one-handed while lighting things with a hand-held light is more than a lot of shooters can handle. Yes, it can be done. But the risk of dropping something (usually the light) or missing a shot because you're trying to keep track of too many variables is too great. Weapon lights for long guns fall into three categories: The built-it-yourself

Millenium modular series, the integral mount M500, and the detachable M900.

The Millenium is durable, adaptable, heavy and can offer many options. To build one is simple. Get the Surefire catalog. Determine what weapon you wish to light, where you want to mount it, and then select the light, mount, switch and battery capacity options to build what you need. Designed and built at the request of military units that wanted complete modular adaptability, the Millenium series can be overwhelming to those who want a light for the one weapon they'll use. With four lamp bezel sizes, eight lamps, three switches, two mounts and three laser heads, the permutations are huge. For those who don't need the vast options or modular capability, or begrudge the weight, the pre-selected or custom-built lights are a viable options. The pre-selected or custom use simpler clamps to mount on the barrel or forearm, and are only six- or nine-volt systems. If you want a light for not a lot invested out of your own pocket, and the department won't allow modifications to issue weapons, then the pre-selected lights are a great choice.

M-500 and 510

The M-500 is a dedicated light that replaces the handguard(s) of the rifle. Offered for the CAR-15, the AR-15, H-K G-36 and G-36K, and Sig 551, you can have anywhere from 125 to 500 lumens of night-blasting light at the touch of a finger. The light options come from voltage selection and lamp/bezel selection. With the A series you can use an MN10 (125 lumens/1 hour) or MN11 (225 lumens/20 minutes) lamps. The AB series use the MN15 (125 lumens/1 hour) and MN16 (225 lumens/20 minutes). You can swap from one lamp assembly to another within the options for a bezel size. You can't, for example, run an MN16 lamp in an A series bezel. Won't fit. Both A and AB use three batteries, and differ in reflector size. The larger AB reflector produces a tighter center beam, with a brighter "hot spot" to produce the dazzling effect on an adversary. For the maximum light, the B series uses a

The M500 set up for a right-handed shooter, with the switch on the left and the light on the right.

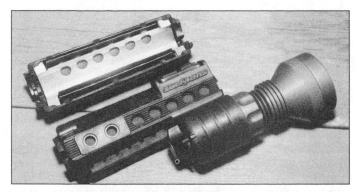

The M500 hand guards are lined with heat reflectors, as all good forearms are.

The forearm housing is cast as a single piece, no seams to let in water or flex and break. The lockout switch index, which can be felt in the dark.

Turbohead (2.5 inch bezel) nine volts produced by six Lithium batteries for 225 lumens (MN20 lamp/1 hr) or 500 lumens (MN21 lamp, 20 minutes). At 500 lumens you have to use the B series carefully in close-in terrain, otherwise an inadvertent light shot

will blast your own night vision for a few minutes. The handguard housing is the same for all models, so if you feel the need for more power, you can always upgrade bezel. Swapping from an A series, to a B series, you'll need everything forward of the handguard: that includes bezel, lamp, lamp housing, battery carrier and batteries. In addition to the high-intensity light, the newest Surefires have "navigation lights." Small LEDs installed in a "snout" in front of the rocker switch, the LEDs provide enough light to navigate at night with night-adapted vision. The LEDs are dim enough that you can maneuver with a reasonable assurance that your adversary isn't going to be instantly alerted to your presence.

To prevent the "illumination AD" all the 500 series have a rotary disable switch on the back of the lamp housing. Rotate to "off" and you turn off all switches, both for light and LEDs. With the rocker switch on, the momentary switch on the right side, and the rocker switch on the left, are enabled. The momentary switch is a long rubber tape that you press to light. Let go, and the light goes off. The rocker switch is a constant-on switch. Rock "on" and the light stays on until you rock it "off." The LED navigations switch is a momentary pressure switch that rides behind the housing lump for the rocker switch.

Installation is a snap. Remove the handguards. On AR/M-16s, you need to press the delta ring back towards the receiver, and then pivot each handguard out and away from the front sight. Depending on fit, spring pressure and hand strength, you may need assistance. To install the weapon light, first hook the front edge of the new handguard in the front sight ring. (Do the handguards one at a time, not both at once.) The light mount customarily goes in as the top handguard. Press down until it comes in contact with the delta ring, then press the delta ring back until the new handguard will snap into place. Once both handguards are in place, you can begin installing the

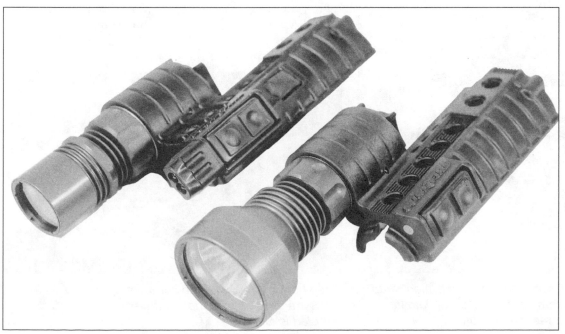

The navigation lights are small LEDs in front of the constant-on switch. Bright enough to move around in the dark, but not so bright they can be seen from much distance, so you're less likely to give your location away. The larger reflector does not give you a larger beam. Instead, it gives you a hotter central "spot" and greater dazzling potential.

internals. Install the batteries in the battery rack, positive ends towards the red end with the + mark. Hold the rifle muzzle up, drop the battery rack in negative end first. Then screw the lamp housing assembly into the handguard. If you are going to switch to the other lamp, you need to unscrew the bezel from the lamp housing. Once assembled, check switch function. Press the momentary switch, then release and press the rocker switch. Press and release the led switch. Turn the rotary switch, and then repeat the tests. One item that may be a bit of a mystery is the plug assembly. The plug goes into the handguard in place of the lamp housing assembly for training. For example, if you are going to be practicing door entries in the bright daylight, why risk damage to the light? Unscrew the housing assembly and put the plug in its place. Ditto weapon retention drills, and any other hard-use training where you won't need light. Put the light back on after training, run your illumination and switch checks, and then set it to rotary lockout.

While the customary method of assembly is to place the light housing on top, so the momentary switch and the light are on the right side, and the constant-on, LED switch and LED are on the left. Right-handed users then use the tips of the left hand for momentary, and the thumb for rocker or led. Left-handed shooters can learn to use their thumb for the momentary, and the tips of the right hand for the rocker and LEDs. Or, just turn the unit over. Install the light assembly on the bottom, and you can now use the tips of your right hand for the momentary, and thumb for rocker and LED. The rotary switch can be turned by the tip of the index or second finger. When the rocker is in the "off" position, you can turn it to "on" without taking your hands off the rifle. However, to re-lock it, you have to let go somewhere. No problem. After all, you may be in the predicament of having to turn the rocker to "on" quickly, but you won't have to worry about locking it to "off" fast.

The only difference between the 500 and the 510 is that the 510 is longer, built to replace the handguards of a standard-length AR-15/M-16. Except for the housing, all other parts are the same between the 500 and 510.

The H-K G36 and Sig 551 weapon lights differ only in the housing needed to fit their respective weapons. While the switches are in the same locations, assembly to the weapons will not be the same.

The MP-5 lights have more in common with the shotgun weapon lights than they do the 500 series. The housing is a duplication of the H-K forearm, and the light assembly uses the P60 or P61 lamp assemblies in the L60 module, and the P90 and P91 in the L90 module. The four models are the 628, with a momentary switch on the right side, the 628F with a right side momentary and a left side constant-on rocker switch, the 629 with momentary on the forearm and a momentary tape on a cable, and the 629F with additional rocker on the left. To install the weapon light is simple. Pull out the front pin on the forearm and pivot the forearm down and forward out of the receiver. Push the rear of the Surefire into the receiver, and pivot up until you can reinsert the cross pin. Done.

Shotgun

Shotgun weapon lights replace the forearm on the operating tube of pumps, and the entire forearm on autos. The model for the Remington 870 is representative of the group. The housing is encased in a soft synthetic for a non-skid grip, with a momentary pressure switch on the left side, and (new for 2002) a constant-on rocker switch on the left. The light assemblies are either the 6-volt L60 (P60 or P61 lamp) or the 9-volt L90 (P90 or P91 lamp). As with all other Surefire lights, you can install a laser in place of the lamp and reflector assembly. However, the lasers require the A12 adapter in order to fit. You see, due to the recoil of a 12-gauge shotgun, the battery is a unit, and not the standard Lithium 123 battery. The L60 takes the SF223A and the L90 uses the SF323A. Otherwise, your batteries would get hammered back and forth by not only the recoil of the

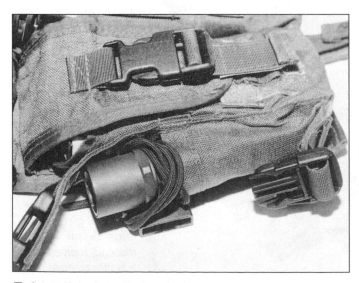

To keep the pressure button from being activated, wrap the lanyard around the lamp before inserting into the pouch. That way it won't rest on the button.

The shotgun light, with the constant-on switch on the left, for activation with the left thumb, raised is On, dimpled is Off.

The throw lever of the quick-release clamp.

The M900 light. This one has a diffuser filter, for searching. The lockout switch is on the bottom, and the constant-on is behind the lamp assembly. The pressure switch is on the bar in the column.

shot, but the inertial forces of being pumped. To install the forearm takes special, model-specific tools. The Remington 870, the Mosssberg 500 and 590, and the Winchester 1300 all have to have the regular forearm removed from the action bar assembly. For that you need a special wrench or the supplied installation tool. With the wrench, the easiest way to remove the forearm is to leave it on the magazine tube. Slide the wrench down over the tube, and holding the forearm, use the wrench to loosen the retaining nut. With the Surefire installation tool, remove the forearm and clamp the installation tool in a vise. Grasp the forearm with both hands, place it against the installation tool, and turn the forearm to loosen the nut. With the nut off, slide the old handle off, and slide the Surefire unit onto the hanger tube. Screw the nut back on (be careful it is easy to cross-thread it) and tighten.

M-900

For those who have a picatinny rail or accessory rail on the bottom of the lower handguard, or a picatinny rail on a shotgun forearm, you can get the M900. The 900 is detachable, powerful, has the same kinds of switches as the 500, and also acts as a forward vertical handguard. At the top the 900 has an A.R.M.S. throw-lever mount, allowing a quick on and off selection. You can rack the rifle with the light off, or stash the light in your gear bag for when you need it. One puzzling omission I noticed, both with Surefire and the tactical gear makers, is no pouch or holster for the M-900. When it is off the rifle, but you want it with you, where to store it? The best I've come up with is to use a Blackhawk pouch for the M3/M6 series as a field-modification holster for the M-900. At the bottom of the handle is the lock-out switch. By turning it parallel to the bore you turn off the unit, preventing inadvertent lighting, or depleting the batteries by pressure in your case or the trunk of a car. The bottom front of the handle has the battery port lock. Press and hold the lock up, and you can unscrew the bottom

to replace the three lithium batteries. Behind the handle is the pressure switch for the navigation lights. The nav lights are a pair of LEDs on the front that give just enough light to move around without stumbling, but (hopefully) not enough to let the bad guys locate you. And behind the light itself is the constant-on switch. Rotate the switch and your light is on all the time. (unless the lockout switch is preventing it) Since it is removable, the 900 can be used alone. My experience at the Hong Kong International airport convinced me that separate lights are a good idea; a very, very good idea.

With both the 500 and 900 series, you can get more light at the expense of battery life. In the 500 or 510, the model A and AB series offers you 125 lumens for an hour, or 225 lumens for 20 minutes. The B series gets you 225 lumens for an hour or 500 for 20 minutes. To get the extra power or battery life of the B series requires six batteries versus the three of the A or AB. The 900 light offers only the A and AB, since there just isn't room to stuff six batteries into the vertical foregrip. So, the tactical price you pay for the cool vertical foregrip, is that you are "limited" to selecting from 125 or 225 lumens.

One advantage to the vertical grip is operator comfort. At the latest patrol rifle class, one of the officers stood about 5 feet, 2 inches and had a barrel chest. He had to have the stock on his departmental M-4 collapsed down to its storage position, just to be

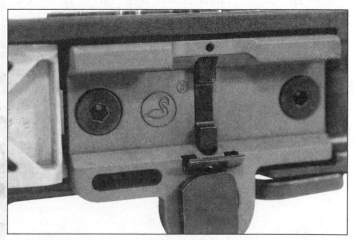

The Swan mount from A.R.M.S. that clamps the M900 to any picatinny rail.

The lockout switch.

The clamp-on filter housing. This one is a diffuser for a broad beam for searching.

The red led navigation lights underneath the lamp assembly.

The constant on switch on the M900 is directly behind the lamp housing.

able to shoot it. To hold the forend, he locked his Surefire M-900 all the way back, so it was just in front of the magazine well. With his large arms (proportional to his barrel chest) he couldn't reach any farther forward with comfort and control. So he had better control of his rifle, and a light as well. Cool.

For the operators who have night-vision optics, all Surefire lights can be fitted with an IR filter cover. When the cover is closed, the light emits IR only, to illuminate your little part of the world. Do remember, however, that IR light and night-vision gear works both ways, just as tracers do. If the bad guys have it, you're lighting the world for them, too.

Chapter 10

The Beretta M-92

MANY SHOOTERS VIEW the Beretta M-92 as the new kid on the block. Compared to the pistol it replaced in military service, the Model 1911, it is. But its lineage is longer than many realize. The locking system is directly descended from the Walther P-38. Beginning in the 1950s as the "Brigadier" when imported to the United States, it evolved from a steel-framed single-stack 9mm with a push-button safety and a heel-clip magazine retention, to the aluminum-framed hi-capacity double-action pistol that won over the U.S. military in the 1980s. Adopted with much wailing and teeth gnashing, it has proven to be a reliable, reasonably durable, 9mm and .40 caliber pistol. Its good points haven't kept its detractors from beating on it at every opportunity.

Those good points are accuracy, reliability in function (except for some extreme conditions) ease of use and comfort. The M-92 is plenty accurate, as competitors in the USPSA Production Division have proven. Fit a match barrel to it, and it is fully capable of winning at Camp Perry, the national Bull's-eye championship. Given good ammo it will perk along for as long as you care to stand on the range and shoot it. And it will not bite you, jab you with sharp corners, or abrade parts of your hands.

The bad points? It is big for its caliber, it is not the most rugged pistol around, the magazine springs seem to give problems, and most damning of all, it isn't a .45. For ruggedness, the aluminum frame is perhaps a bit lightly designed. I've heard of bunches of Berettas giving up from frame cracks. I've personally seen one stop working from the frame breaking behind the locking block recess, instantly turning it into a source of spare parts for the rest of the Berettas in that class. The magazine springs are

The Beretta, in an Uncle Mikes duty rig like this OD Pro-3, is suitable for many jobs.

The Beretta M-92and one of its larger groups fired that day.

a sore point, as some issued in Iraq have proven to either be too old and tired, or simply not strong enough to work in the dusty conditions. Daily cleanings are a must, and they are not sufficient to ensure some magazines continue to function. Since most American cities do not suffer such conditions, it isn't a problem here. The M-92 not being a .45 is not something that can be fixed, although Beretta does offer other models that are chambered for .45 ACP.

Since its adoption in 1985 as the military pistol to replace the 1911, the Beretta M-92 has been adopted or accepted by many police departments. The ease of use, the large capacity and the visible safety make it a popular choice. For those who can make the reach to the trigger, qualifying with the 9mm is a snap. The .40 caliber Berettas are a bit tougher, but the added recoil is nothing a little correct practice can't overcome. In military use, all those who are able have resisted the change to the Beretta. The Marines are famous for holding on to every 1911 frame that can be made to work, rebuilding each again and again as needed. I've even heard of depot surveys being conducted to uncover and requisition 1911s that have been languishing some place less useful than in a Marine weapons depot. Given a chance, the Recon community in particular would relish the chance to accept shipments of newly-manufactured 1911A3s.

The one problem that captured everyone's attention was the infamous broken slide period. For a short time, slides on government M-9's (the armed forces designation for the M-92) were cracking. A few even left the frames when fired, and there were a few injuries. The manufacturer blamed the ammunition, saying the government was using over-pressure ammo. The armed forces blamed Beretta, claiming the slides were defective. The whole matter was dropped (or so the story goes) when both sides found out they were right. And wrong. The ammo was over-pressure, and the slides had been made of a different alloy. (Apparently for one particular client who asked for it, and some ended up being used in the U.S. contract assembly.) The slides were replaced, and for a while military armorers were instructed to replace slides at absolutely insane intervals, like 3,000 or 5,000 rounds. (Many a 1911 owner laughed out loud on hearing this, as no one had ever heard of a 1911 slide breaking off. Replace in 3K? There is more than one owner with 100K through a particular 1911.) Problem solved. But if you really are the worrisome type, Beretta makes the MkII, with a reinforced slide at the area where the old ones broke.

One area that came in for continual improvement was the locking block. The latest version is the fourth design, and is now nearly indestructible. Ernest Langdon is a former Marine, IPSC competitor, and worked for Beretta for some time. He and I sat next to each other on the long bus ride from the airport to the range in South Africa for World Shoot XIII. I took advantage of the opportunity to find out a lot about the Beretta design, and found that my accurate and reliable pistol was not an anomaly. He can supply

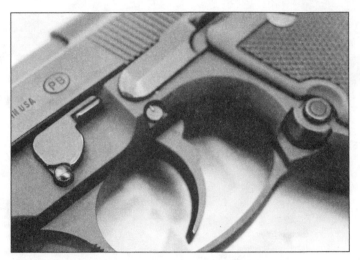

The magazine button is reversible, the disassembly lever (left side) easy to operate. The trigger is a reach for some shooters, though.

The M-92 safety can be a spring-loaded hammer drop.

Or the original hammer drop and safety design.

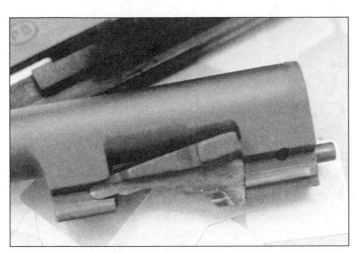

The locking mechanism is taken from the Walther P-38 of WWII fame.

You can obtain the newest design locking block from Langdon Tactical Technology.

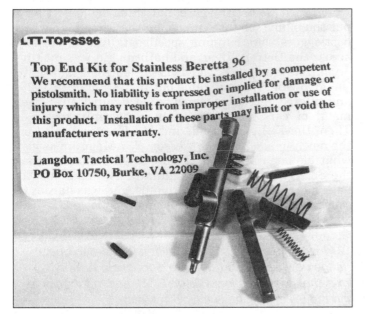

Spare parts are easily obtained, and best kept in the small bag they were shipped in.

you with a brand new fourth generation locking block in case you're worried about yours not standing up to high shooting volumes. He can also improve the trigger pull and provide you with the small odds-and-ends parts that you should stock in your spare parts pouch of your maintenance bag. Keeping spare parts on hand is not an indictment of the Beretta. There are few pistols as rugged and reliable as the 1911, and I keep spares for my 1911s with me. There are few gunsmiths, competitors or writers with a greater appreciation and love of the 1911 than myself, and I own and have been known to carry, a Beretta M-92.

Chapter 11

The 1911 in Law Enforcement

AND YOU THOUGHT police only want the newest, latest, high-tech tools? Guess again. In many instances, a known track record is better than high-tech "cool gear" stuff. And when it comes to fit, function and performance, older can many times be better. And the Model 1911 pistol is the phoenix that proves that point. (If I may be allowed to hopelessly mix my metaphors.) And, while I'm mixing, I will not spend a lot of time fastidiously trying to separate the 1911 from the 1911A1. I will just use the generic "1911" to mean all metal-framed single-stack pistols designed by John Moses Browning and accepted by the U.S. Government. When I mean differently, I will say so.

A lot of shooters might ask, "Didn't the 1911 almost disappear?" Yes. For some time, revolvers were the only "suitable" sidearm for police officers. For a while, such wasn't the case, but things change, and I put the blame for that change on the FBI. Back when bootleggers were running speedboats full of whiskey across the Detroit River, and bathtub gin was making organized crime rich, the 1911 in .45 ACP had quite the following. When it came out in .38 Super in 1929, and offered increased penetration against the sheet metal of cars, it was even more warmly received. Then, the FBI got armed, and Mr. Hoover settled on the newly-made Smith & Wesson .357 Magnum as just what his agents needed. (Ignore for the moment that the S&W N-frame .357 Magnum M-27 was/is just as heavy as a 1911, held fewer rounds, and was harder to conceal.) Where the FBI went, many followed. By the

The 1911, with an extended magazine, holds ten rounds of .45, while a fatter one holds eight or nine. Make the fat one a 40 and you can get 11.

The 1911 is back, but for some it never left. Starting upper right, is the new S&W 1911, left is a Springfield Armory, bottom is the most-excellent Wilson CQB, and in the middle, wearing the Surefire light, is a Nowlin Match.

It took years of competitive dominance by the 1911 for many to realize that it should not be relegated to the dustbin of history.

1950s, what the FBI did was practically gospel. If it came from Quantico, it was accepted as received wisdom. And what Quantico taught was that a double-action revolver, fired from the "combat crouch" the best option for police work and, most importantly, pistols were unreliable. Quantico also said the 1911 pistol was inaccurate, to boot.

What changed? A little thing called IPSC and a Marine Lt. Colonel named Jeff Cooper started getting people's attention. In the 1950s the quick-draw craze was hot. So hot even movie stars and recording stars did it. (Yes, there were movie stars who were practicing with guns, not agitating for their control.) But the fast-draw and quick-draw competitions were no more suited to the real world than Bull's-eye competitions were. Jeff Cooper started his experimentations with a style of competition called "Walk and Draw." They were held in Big Bear, California, in a series of matches called the "Leatherslap." In Walk and Draw two shooters began walking side by side towards their targets (usually balloons) and on the start signal drew and fired. The first one to break his balloon or knock down his target was the winner.

Where Jeff Cooper differed from the rest of the pack was in adjusting the rules to encourage relevant change. He opened it to any gun. After all, if you hit, who cares if you're using a cowboy revolver, a police revolver or a pistol? This immediately outraged the cowboy purists, but they still won, so who cared? Then he allowed any shooting position or sighting method. More heresy, but then a curious thing happened. Shooters started winning using other methods. Instead of hip-shooting with single-action revolver, guys were winning with other guns, and actually aiming. And most unsettling of all, they were using both hands. Jeff Cooper himself was one of those who resisted this new method developed by his friend Jack Weaver: (Yes, the "Weaver Style" you have all heard of.)

"I just knew it couldn't be right," said Cooper. "For two years I persisted in one-handed shooting because I knew it had to be faster. And for two years Jack beat me. I then switched and he never beat me again."

From there the experimentation expanded. Why always have side-by-side competitions? Why not set up a slice of life, and see how shooters solved the problem? From there things kept evolving and expanding. Later they expanded not to Jeff's liking, but life is sometimes like that. The result of the IPSC experiments was to create a body of knowledge that depended not on some authority handing down knowledge, but determined and tested through action. For many years in the 20th Century, pistols were derided as "inaccurate" or "unreliable." So much so that there were quite a few Bull's-eye competitors in the 1950s who spent inordinate amounts of time learning to thumb-cock a double action revolver. You see handgun competition back then was done one-handed. Revolvers were more accurate, more reliable, and had better triggers. So, thumb-cocking was the only thing to do. In the pre-IPSC days of "combat shooting" revolvers were fired double-action. Unless the match consisted of just one round fired for pure accuracy, double-action was always faster than single-action. Pistols were faster, but who wanted the loss of accuracy or the unreliability? After all, you couldn't have both accuracy and reliability without using a revolver.

The Southwest Combat Pistol League changed all that. The SWPL was the bridge from the Leatherslap to IPSC. Unlike the rigid rules of Bull's-eye, dictating shooting positions, distances, times and technique, the SWPL had a simpler philosophy: Solve the problem safely. If you had a malfunction you had to deal with it. Big deal, you say? In Bull's-eye, you could ask for an "alibi" round. One of the fellows who taught me shooting could "limp wrist" his pistol into a malfunction on demand. Should he see that he'd thrown a bad shot, he would limp wrist his gun, cause a malfunction, raise his hand and get a re-

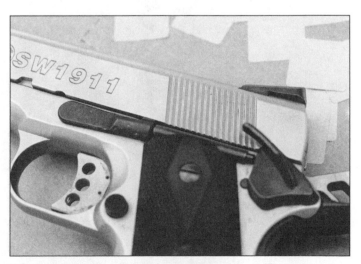

The S&W 1911 is in all respects a 1911, and not just a copy or knock-off.

The one change S&W made that shows is the external extractor. No need to worry about extractor tension with the S&W pistol.

shoot. (Was he cheating? You bet. Could he be caught? Not a chance. Did the rules "allow" it? Until recently.) In the SWPL, a malfunction just cost you time. And maybe the match. You, the shooter, were expected to deal with whatever the match designer came up with. It could require shooting from a sitting position at a target at 10 yards, then moving through a doorway and shooting a target at 50 yards. Quit whining, it's the same for everyone. And since the equipment was not rigidly controlled, you could use any handgun you wanted. And in the early days many did. However, the limits of reality soon closed in. Yes, a single-action revolver can be fast from the holster, but past five or six shots your time suffers from reloading. A double-action revolver reloads faster than the single-action does, but not as fast as a

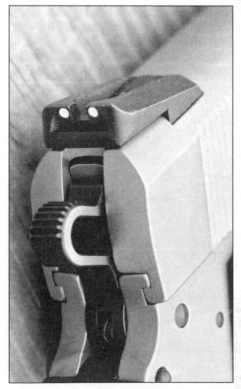

Three-dot sights, Novak pattern, commander hammer, the S&W folks did their homework.

pistol. Oh, those objections to pistols being unreliable and inaccurate? No one had asked gunsmiths to solve both problems. It had always been the custom (due to competition rules) to ask for a reliable pistol; or an accurate pistol, but not both. Once paying customers started asking, pistolsmiths started producing.

How does this get us to the 1911 in Law Enforcement use? Simple, the easiest to shoot, most durable, most common large-caliber pistol was the 1911. In the early days of competition shooters would use anything and everything. The late Frank Paris, a gunsmith in the Detroit area who built many Bull's-eye guns and was one of the first to start building "combat guns" and "pin guns" built up his very own MAB-15 for competition. He wanted a hi-capacity 9mm that was more durable than the Browning Hi-Power, and settled on the MAB. (It didn't catch on.) The Browning didn't catch on, either. One drawback was the insistence by many shooters on .45 caliber. The scoring favored it, and most right-thinking shooters who depended on guns in real life agreed. Many didn't, and later years saw the "wonder nine wars" where manufacturers scrambled to get high-volume 9mm pistols into the hands of police officers. But competitors went with the .45 ACP and the 1911. And went through many designs, improvements and changes to produce an utterly reliable pistol.

How reliable? I have a Kimber that was sent for my first book, back in the nostalgic old pre-Y2K days of 1997. It worked 100 percent, it shot small groups, it was stainless steel, and I could get it at a discount. (Sometimes a gun writer gets a deal. Most of the time we have to ship everything back.) Since then I have taken it with me on just about every range trip, and each time put at least a magazine through it. It has sat frozen in a car for weeks, been dropped (not intentionally, and not by me) rained on, fallen into snow banks, been sweated on, and has a grand total of seven malfunctions in more than 30,000 rounds. And those seven came from one aftermarket magazine I tested for a magazine article. I have others with more time and ammo in them. My main bowling pin gun started life as my one-and-only IPSC/pins/carry/whatever gun, and I've owned it for a quarter of a century. It has over 120,000 rounds through it. Granted, it is on its third barrel, but the first one was the pitted Government barrel installed when it was made in the Ithaca plant in 1943. The second died a sudden death from a hard chrome job that made the barrel brittle, before we knew about such problems. The third is still going strong. I have a half a dozen others that each have fired more rounds than the Kimber. And they all work reliably. In the event something breaks, or I win the lottery and can afford enough ammo to wear them out, they can all be rebuilt.

And my experience is not unusual. Jerry Barnhart, the top shooter, National Champion and all-around nice guy, used to shoot at our club before he built his own range. His practice regimen for the Steel Challenge when he won the title back was to show up with his steel targets (our club didn't have

This was still the taught and approved FBI "combat shooting stance" as late as the early 1980s. Paul is smiling because he never had to qualify this way, nor shoot that way in competition.

them then) and a bucket of ammo. A five-gallon bucket of ammo. He'd set up the steel, throw out a tarp, practice, practice, practice, then police his brass and go home. His main gun had over a quarter of a million rounds through it when he sold it in a moment of weakness. And it still worked fine and shot accurately. (He managed to buy it back some years afterwards, and it still works fine.)

But the 1911 and LE, you ask. In the early 1980s, the paragon of law enforcement wisdom and virtue, the FBI, was not so cutting edge. In the early 1980s, they were still teaching their agents the "combat crouch", with their left arm folded over their chest to protect their vital organs from incoming bullets. They were behind the times, so much so that their training methods got them hauled into court. The methods and acceptance standards were causing otherwise qualified women recruits to be washed out of training. Once the dust had settled and the FBI was forced to update, the IPSC shooters flowed in. Some were active agents who had sought better methods on their own. Others were retired agents who had found a better way of shooting. And some were the top competitors, showing up to teach the new methods. And they all brought 1911s with them

In the 1980s we spent good money to get a magazine well chamfered not as well as this. Now it comes standard.

to teach. In 1986, three cars of FBI agents in Miami tried to apprehend two bank robbers. When it was done, the robbers were dead, as were two of the eight agents. Of the other six, five were wounded. The FBI had been hanging onto the 9mm cartridge until that day, but made a short, expensive and acrimonious detour immediately afterwards to the 10mm before settling on everything else; 9mm, 40 and .45. The 1911 steamroller continued, as of those cartridges, the .45 is best suited for use in the 1911. You can get compact DA pistols in 9 and 40, but when you try to make a double-action pistol in .45 you end up with something too big for many agents.

Having blamed the FBI for the shift from the 1911, I have to give them credit for the shift back. In quick order the FBI Hostage Rescue Team went with high-capacity 1911s, then the Bureau as a whole went with the classic 1911, built by Springfield Armory for all SWAT teams. I had the lucky occasion of getting one on loan for the time I was doing my book, *The Gun Digest Book of the 1911.* A beautiful gun, it is well suited to the sometimes messy job of dealing with bad people doing bad things. Recently, LAPD SWAT went with purpose-built Kimber pistols. They had been using rebuilt confiscated guns as their issue guns, but keeping so many guns of so many vintages going had to have been a real headache for the LAPD armorers (or the pistolsmith they contracted the work to).

And we should never underestimate the "cool gear factor" when it comes to equipment selection. I once had an experienced police trainer tell me "if you want to sell something to police, paint it black and stick some Velcro on it." The rest of the group, police officers themselves, nodded and chuckled. The 1911 is the epitome of cool guy gear if for no other reason than it isn't standard issue. So, lets go through the strengths and weakness of the 1911.

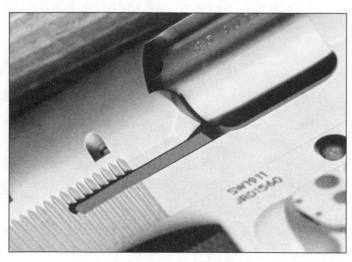

The extractor had no problems with any ammo fed it.

The hammer of Thor

Or as Jeff Cooper calls it, "The Yankee Fist." The 1911 is the smallest and most compact package containing: the biggest cartridge you can effectively use, enough rounds to do the job (whatever the job is) enough weight to keep from beating you up, but not so much you can't pack it, a frame you can wrap your hands around, a frame that doesn't punish your hand for shooting it, and is durable from its design and not its alloy. In that package you get a trigger that is easy to control and master (perhaps the most important aspect of marksmanship) and controls that are where your hand can use them.

On the down side it has a 19th Century extractor and locking system, and the headache of having been built continuously for a century, on four continents and in God knows how many factories.

The 1911 frame

The grip was designed in the first decade of the 20th century by a shooter, for one-handed shooting. At the time, the average man would have been 5 feet, 7 inches tall. The grip of the frame can be easily grasped

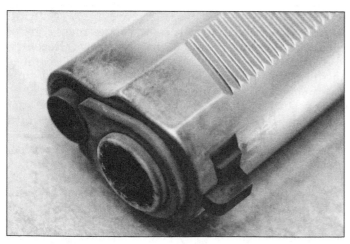

Despite getting good and dirty from shooting, the SW1911 never failed.

by anyone over 5 feet, 2 inches. With a little work (thinner grip panels, mostly) even really short people can hold it. And when you go to two-handed shooting, it gets even easier. The front-to-back and side-to-side dimensions are much less than those of many high-capacity pistols. One that compares favorably is the Glock. But there, the polymer of the frame allows for radical design changes. Where the 1911 really shines is in trigger reach. Trigger reach is the distance your finger has to go forward in order to get in contact with the trigger. In DA pistol, the reach is long, sometimes really long. I wear gloves sized Large, and for me the reach can be long on DA pistols.

The downside to the compact frame is capacity. The 1911 magazine only holds seven or eight rounds of .45. The 9mm and .38 Super variants hold nine or 10 rounds. (nine only in the 9mm. You can't get a flush-bottomed mag to hold 10 9mm rounds.) Mostly the capacity "problem" is just an arguing point. Unless you're in a competition where capacity matters, and you're stuck with a single-stack, a hi-cap isn't a big deal. That said, if you find yourself in the statistical oddity of a gunfight where capacity makes all the difference in the world, sorry about that. If you were to worry about that rare a problem, you'd also have a fire extinguisher in your pocket. (I do know officers who do raids on a regular basis who would not give up capacity. Curiously, they carry fire extinguishers on raids.) But for the great majority of gunfights, eight or nine rounds in the gun, with another seven or eight ready to go in two seconds, is plenty. And the cost of greater size of high-capacity frames often makes the grip too large or accurate shooting and easy carrying.

When first shooting a .45, many new shooters are warned of the excessive recoil. Properly held, the 1911 is not onerous to shoot. In fact, it is easy. You have to get a lot more hostile a cartridge than the .45 ACP to make a pistol hard to shoot.

Durability

Competition shooters put more ammo through guns than almost anyone else. There are some who exceed what IPSC, bowling pin and steel shooters consume, and they complain about the durability of the 1911. They also complain about the durability of everything else, too. With proper maintenance and a lack of abuse, you should be able to get in excess of 50,000 through a steel-framed 1911. The alloy ones will deliver less. How much less? Hard to say. If you're willing to accept barrel replacements as a standard long-term maintenance item, and you don't spend time in an environment where frame rails are ground down by fine, powdery, abrasive dust, a frame can last a lifetime. Over 250,000 rounds.

That said, I've heard that some in the Marine Recon community feel that operators should be issued two 1911s, one for training and one for going to war. But the problem there is not just that they put a lot of ammo through their sidearms. They also put a lot of wear and tear on their sidearms from training and operations. Whacking the frame of your sidearm against the doorframe of a building, armored personnel carrier or helicopter does not do good things for it. "Service life" encompasses more than just rounds fired. Luckily, the steel frame of the 1911 stands it in good stead.

Trigger and ergonomics

The trigger is the best part of the 1911. You can have it built to as light as you can handle (or even lighter) for competition. I strongly recommend against light, competition triggers. A clean, 5-pound trigger pull is light enough to be as accurate as you will ever need, and heavy enough to keep you out of trouble. The grip safety will prevent a dropped gun from going off, and the thumb safety works the direction your thumb does, and is manageable by anyone.

The extractor and locking design

The drawback is the extractor. The extractor is not actuated by a spring, as so many newer designs are. (And an even older Browning design.) The extractor is its own spring. As such, it can lose tension from hard use or bad ammo. When the extractor goes, reliability decreases. In the old days, we spent lots of time fussing over extractor tension, measuring it, adjusting it, and wondering why it changes. Some of us have better luck than others do. My friend Jeff Chudwin has been shooting large volumes of ammunition through 1911 pistols for over two decades. He was an early and frequent winner at Second Chance. In that time he has broken on average (broken, mind you, not just de-tensioned) something like an extractor a year. He keeps the ones he managed to hang onto in a small bottle, for the curious. In the same time I have broken two. I think. Maybe it was just one, and that other one I was thinking of was a gun I was just testing. Lest you think his guns are poorly maintained or built, Jeff is scrupulous about cleaning, and his guns get built by Ned Christiansen, known as the Master of Metal. Ned is even better at building guns than I am, and hasn't broken many extractors, either. All three of us are puzzled by this statistical oddity. In the 1990s, manufacturers started replacing the traditional 1911 extractor with an "external" extractor. External in that it is machined flush to the side of the slide, and is actuated by a coil spring at its rear. The latest of those arrived in time for this book.

The S&W 1911

Through the decades and the competition for the revolver market, the one main thing Colt had that S&W didn't was the 1911. S&W just changed that. They now offer a 1911 pistol with some improvements. The first is the external extractor. Held in by a pivot pin driven down through the top of the slide the extractor is now immune from the de-tensioning that bad ammo, abuse and the phases of the moon seem to induce in the original. The second is the firing pin block, which has been changed from the trigger-activated one of the Colt Series 80. The grip safety activates the firing pin block on the S&W. Some of us feel the whole firing pin block subject is a bad idea that should just go away, but it does seem to satisfy the bureaucrats writing departmental regs and state law who know little or nothing about firearms.

The S&W 1911 is stainless, with fixed sights, a 5-inch barrel and a non-ambidextrous thumb safety. In the modern world of 1911 use, you might wonder about fixed sights and left-side only safeties. For the occasionally rough-and-tumble world of law enforcement, fixed sights work fine. These are three-dot Novak sights, with the front sight in a dovetail. Should you wish to swap them for night sights, any competent armorer or gunsmith easily does the job. And those who want or need an ambi safety will no-doubt have their own ideas about which is "proper" and the odds are S&W will have selected the "wrong" one had they installed any particular one. The trigger is clean enough to be easy to use accurately (as we shall see) but heavy enough to keep you out of trouble, about five pounds. The frontstrap has vertical serrations to aid in gripping; the mainspring housing is flat, checkered, plastic and easily changed. (If you wish to have a lanyard-loop MS housing instead, you can) the grip safety is a high-ride and has a speed bump on the bottom to ensure positive unlocking when grasped. As a positive, the slide has forward cocking serrations. As a neutral (bureaucratic-requirement) feature, the barrel hood has a small notch so you can (theoretically) see if you have a cartridge chambered. It satisfies the requirements of some states without causing any problems, so I don't worry about it. The grips are black rubber with the S&W logo in them. The magazine opening is lightly chamfered. The stainless pistol is accented by having the controls and grips colored black. The serial number, model number, and "Caution – Capable of being fired with magazine removed" are laser-etched on the frame and slide. It comes in a blue plastic storage case with instructions, a fired case (more of the silly state requirements), trigger lock and two Wilson eight-round magazines.

Three full magazines, 7 yards, standing. I chickened out and didn't fire a fourth.

Those with an eye to design will look at it and declare "That's a Kimber." For those who haven't gotten the word, S&W has been doing the forgings for Kimber for some time now. It was only a matter of time (and maybe contractual agreement) before S&W started taking those forgings and making 1911s.

The S&W 1911 accepts standard magazines, fits in standard holsters, and works with all accessories, within manufacturing tolerances of course. My first chance to work with it was at a law enforcement firearms class devoted to AR-15s. After the first day's work, the instructors stayed at the range to get in some practice. I handed the S&W 1911 around and let everyone have a few runs with it. We had the usual miscellaneous ammunition supply you'll find at an LEO class; hardball and a wide range of factory hollow-points, including boxes of the expensive LE-only stuff that taxpayers pay for but never get to shoot. The pistol gobbled everything and worked fine except for one carton of hardball. We should not blame the manufacturer for the failures, because the storage history of that case of ammo was unknown. We had occasional failures to fire. The blame does not go to the pistol, for as you can see the firing pin struck the primer, and struck it hard. It was just a cautionary example of knowing your ammo and where it's been. That particular ammo was brought out for play precisely because it had been around too long and in the wrong places.

As for accuracy, I tried it out to see if the sights were "on." I fired on the standard drill target we use, a sheet of paper with three, 4-inch circles, each with one of the numerals 7, 10 and 15 in them. I used the "0" of the 10 as my aiming point from the 7-yard line. I placed a full magazine of hardball into the zero. I then placed a full magazine of Winchester 230 JHP-SXT Law Enforcement Only ammo through the same hole. Putting 16 shots through one ragged hole is not bad. Then we promptly pasted over the target to get on with shooting. So, I tried to duplicate it once I got to my home range. I tried three magazines (stretching my luck) standing at 7 yards, and managed to put them all through a single ragged hole.

What is the S&W 1911 missing that the cutting edge "cool gear guys" desire? First, a light rail. However, since the frame is stainless steel it is easy enough to have a good gunsmith attach one via screws or solder. It doesn't have adjustable sights. But many of us have found through the years that adjustable sights aren't all that necessary. (They sure don't seem to be necessary on this particular handgun.) I have a batch of 1911s (and other pistols for that matter) with adjustable sights, and I can't remember the last time I had to do some adjusting. What can't be moved is unlikely to move at an inopportune time, and cause problems. It doesn't have an ambi safety, but that is an easy fix. And it doesn't have a magazine funnel, but that is even easier to fix than the lack of an ambi safety.

1911 magazines

The heart of a pistol is the magazine. Even the best pistols can be made to choke if fed from poor magazines. The two that came with the S&W were Wilson magazines, known for 20 years for their quality and durability. You'd be well served by simply getting more of them. I also tested the S&W 1911 with magazines from Chip McCormick, Ed Brown, Mag-Pack and Mec-Gar. I used the pistol in several matches with Chip McCormick 10-shot magazines. In all the testing and match use, I've yet to have a malfunction except for those first few dud rounds with the bad primers.

The S&W 1911, and the magazines for it, all fit the holsters and magazine carriers I obtained for the book. As the 1911 has gained in popularity, the gear makers have kept up, making holsters, mag pouches and other gear for it.

1911's now come with accessory rails, for those who think that seeing in the dark is important.

The latest new features

One new item that is rapidly becoming the "must-have" is a light rail. Back when I started shooting, the holy grail of the combat 1911 was the ambidextrous safety. We found out it wasn't really the "must have" we'd thought back then, but it can still be a very nice feature to have at times. The light rail is the 2001 equivalent of the 1981 ambi safety. The idea is that with a rail attached to, or machined into, the dust cover of the 1911 frame, you can attach a tactical light when you need it. Most of the time you don't need it, but when you do, you really need it. Springfield Armory makes their 1911 pistols available with the light rail in some models. And for those building a pistol from scratch, Caspian can ship you a frame with the rail built-in. Just have your armorer or gunsmith build the rest of it.

Chapter 12

The Para Ordnance LDA

TO QUOTE JEFF Cooper, father of the Modern Technique, "I've been told the 1911 is making a comeback. Someone should tell them that it never went away." Indeed. The 1911 has been popular ever since it was introduced. However, it has also been a problem child for police administrators for nearly as long. The main attribute that makes it so attractive to the cognoscenti is the trigger pull. The trigger is also the very thing that makes it such a nerve-wracking proposition for management. You see, for the longest time revolvers were considered appropriate police sidearms because of the long and relatively heavy trigger pull. In a military context, the rules are different. (And will be for as long as the Armed Forces can keep Lawyers in the rear echelon.) After all enemy soldiers may be fired on, on sight, and without warning. A short and relatively light trigger pull is only a safety hazard to your own people, and with training, no hazard at all. In the law enforcement setting, criminals may not be fired upon on sight, without warning. Even the suggestion will create huge volumes of paperwork and disciplinary board hearings. (And rightly so.) Police management took advantage of the trigger pull of the revolver as a safety mechanism. Slight errors in judgment, or excessive trigger pressure, could be tolerated, as after all "the trigger pull is so long it takes a very large error to fire inadvertently."

The search for a suitable magazine-fed pistol for police use, for decades, pivoted on the desire to have a pistol with a revolver trigger.

The other desirable attributes of the 1911 kept it in contention; the slender grip for a heavy (to dampen felt recoil) frame, the large caliber, the extreme durability. Some police departments allowed or issued 1911s for not just the SWAT teams, but the regular patrol officers.

Having it all, the revolver trigger, the big caliber, the small frame, seemed for a long time impossible. Pistols that were offered for police use suffered when they tried to offer all, and many only tried to offer some. One example of trying to have it all was the S&W 645. It was a single-stack .45 pistol with their DA/SA trigger mechanism. Its problems were many. For having the same capacity as a 1911, it was larger, heavier, and had a bore higher over the hand than the 1911. The higher

bore offered more leverage to the recoiling parts, and for its size and weight it seemed to kick more than a 1911. The choice of going down in caliber was not attractive to the police officers. If they were "stuck" with a 9mm, which was and is basically a pistol equal to the .38 Special, then officers wanted more capacity. So, instead of having a sleek, easy-handling 9mm that held nine or 10 shots, they insisted on a pistol that felt like a 2X4 that held 15 or 17.

There was also a lot of work done on the "pistol with a revolver trigger" designs. Some trigger mechanisms are called DA/SA. Double action/Single action. They feature a first-shot trigger stroke that is long and heavy, followed by a light and short stroke, after the slide has cocked the hammer upon firing and cycling. These also came in two variants; the Hammer-Drop Safe and the Decocking Lever. The HDS features a safety (usually slide-mounted) that stays on "Safe" when released. The DL (usually frame-mounted) is spring-loaded and returns to the unset position once released. Other designs dispensed with the external safety, and had the mechanism re-set itself, and required another long trigger pull. Called DAO, or Double Action Only, they too came in two flavors. Some DAO pistols have a

The Para Ordnance LDA with a typical group. Double-action pistol does not have to mean inaccurate.

second-strike capability, others do not. A second strike capability (2S) means that in the event of a dud primer you can simply release and press the trigger again, and the hammer will strike again. A DAO pistol lacking the second strike capability (1S) requires that you either thumb-cock the hammer to reset the mechanism, or cycle the slide (thus also disposing of the dud round) to reset the mechanism. The Para LDA is a DAO with no second strike option.

And on top of everything else, some DA/SA-HDS pistols have the safety lever spring-loaded. While they look just like their DA/SA-HDS brethren, after you decock the hammer the safety lever springs back up in place when you release it. Why? For a few years, the idea of a pistol with a decocking lever instead of a safety lever had some panache. After all, who wanted to risk having the safety on when you needed it off? And training is an onerous chore some would rather avoid. The required routine when using a DA/SA-HDS is one of two methods; One, to press the safety down to decock, then leave it down and holster. On the draw, you must have trained yourself to push the lever up to clear the safety. The second is to push the safety down, and once decocked, push the safety up and then holster. On the draw, you needn't push the safety off. Then again, neither does the guy who is trying to grab your gun. To offer a decocking lever to the customers who wanted it, some manufacturers of DA/SA-HDS pistols came up with the spring-loaded option. So, for a while the pistol manufacturers tried to have it all. Well, most did. Some, like Sig, offered DL only or DAO only pistols. Glock offers their Safe action, which is a novel way of producing a DAO single strike mechanism. S&W for a while tried to be all things to all customers. They even made charts and slide wheels to allow you to determine what the model designation would be for a pistol, including its caliber, composition and capacity. While the mechanism could be made into just about any variant you could think of, the market wasn't there. The low-volume designs were dropped, and exist only as potential S&W Collectors Association Treasures for the future.

As a further picture-muddying option, some law enforcement agencies wanted magazine safeties, and others didn't. A magazine safety prevents a pistol from firing if the magazine is out. While the frames of S&W pistols lacking magazine safeties are so marked, if the pistol has been refinished since it left the factory the markings may be gone.

If you pick up a pistol you aren't familiar with, give it a good going over before you even think about loading it. The manual of arms for the safety may be something other than what you're used to. There have been more than a couple of accidents caused by ignorance (imagine that!) and even occasional deaths. Be careful.

Meanwhile, the 1911 kept on keeping on. In use by the military (at least until 1986, when it was replaced by the Beretta M9) and SWAT teams across the country, it kept offering power, accuracy, reliability and durability. If only it had a revolver trigger. Well, now it does. Sort of. The Para Ordnance LDA first came out in a high-capacity version, since that was what police wanted. But the true niche is as a long-stroke trigger in a single stack 1911. Now, it is possible to have it all.

The Para LDA uses a modified 1911 frame. The idea has been tried before. The Seecamp conversion of the 1911, back in the 1970s, was strictly a custom shop number. The Colt Double Eagle was a design-by-committee effort that impressed no one. To have the Seecamp, you sent your 1911 off, waited a long time, sent a big check after it, and then received a box in the mail. The Colt Double Eagle was a big, clunky pistol that in its early models allowed parts to fall off if you took the grips off.

The LDA trigger gives it away. This is not a single action trigger.

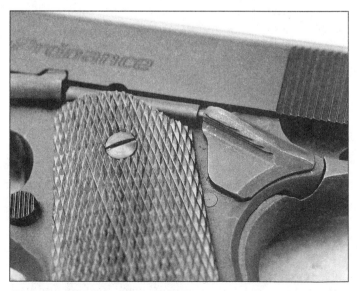

The 1911 controls are right where you expect them, and do what they've always done.

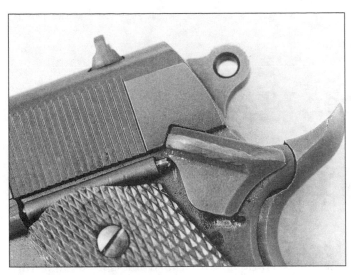

Safety on, hammer down. Hammer down is the only way you'll see an LDA

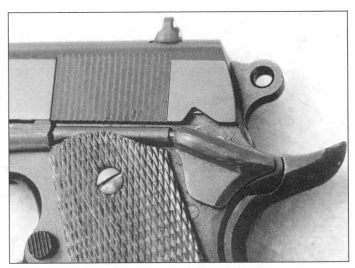

Safety off, ready to fire.

In operation the Para is simple but a bit different. First, you have to get used to the hammer never staying back. Second, it won't cycle at all unless you have the grip safety pressed in. Unlike DA/SA pistols, where the first trigger pull is long and heavy like a revolver, and the subsequent pulls are short and light, the Para LDA is always the same. If you cycle the slide back and forth, the hammer simply follows it down each time the slide closes. Not to worry, it isn't going to set off a primer. The hammer can't. In following the slide down it never delivers a blow to the firing pin. And even if it did somehow bump the firing pin, the firing pin is blocked from forward movement until the trigger pull activates the firing pin safety.

The Para LDA accepts all 1911 accessories that do not relate directly to the trigger system, so you can use 10-shot extended magazines, have a gunsmith change the sights to whatever you like, swap grips, or install a light rail. Indeed, you could go the whole route and pour $2,000 into an LDA and turn it into a tricked-out DA 1911. Of course, much of the expense would be wasted in competition, as both USPSA and IDPA do not allow many of the high-end custom gunsmithing options in Production or SSP shooting categories. But you could still do all that and not be treading in R&D territory.

The safety locks the mechanism, so when the safety is up pulling the trigger will gain you nothing. One thing to keep in mind, the safety will click up whether the mechanism is set or not, so trying the safety does not tell you if the pistol has been dry-fired.

In size, magazines and ammunition, it is simply a 1911 Government model. (Unless, of course, you have one of the more compact models.) As such, you can use any 1911 magazines you might have on hand.

The LDA I have has so far digested every type of ammunition I have fed it. The trigger pull is remarkably light and easy, and still long enough to keep the poorly trained out of some trouble. Its accuracy is quite good, and for those familiar with the 1911 frame the transition to the Para is not a problem. For duty work it will handle all the standard loads, and all the +P loads that you can hang on to during recoil. As a steel-framed government model the weight dampens felt recoil. As a competition gun, it has a great deal of promise. For use in USPSA Production Division, or IDPA SSP, where only DA/SA and DAO pistols can compete (no cocked and locked single-action 1911s need apply) your only concern is getting .45 ammo soft enough to be competitive in recoil against 9mm ammunition. Or just order an LDA in 9mm or .38 Super.

Chapter 13

Check Out The S&W 99

WHAT IS BLACK, plastic; chambered in .45 ACP, has a double-action trigger, and doesn't have a huge grip like the Glock 21? The S&W 99. Manufactured in partnership with the Walther firm of Germany, the S&W 99 is the answer to those who want it all; polymer, .45 caliber, a grip they can hold, and at least some parts made in the USA.

The 99 has some features that others, even Glock, doesn't have. First, the backstrap is changeable. The mainspring housing is a separate piece that can be removed and replaced. I find the flatter of the two is easier to shoot and more comfortable to handle. Next, the decocking lever isn't a lever but a button. On top of the slide, in front of the rear sight, is a large button/plunger. Pressing it down decocks the action. The DA/SA mechanism is a "restrike" DA, that is, if you press the trigger and hear a click instead of a bang, you can release and press the trigger again, cocking and firing the action again. On the Glock, if you get a click you must hand-cycle the action to be able to re-strike. (Of course, you're "re-striking" a fresh cartridge, which may be a good thing, but that is a different matter.) The de-cocking button brings the cocked action back to the long DA stroke, one that many police administrators

love or require. Up front, the slide has forward cocking serrations, and the frame has a light rail. The magazine release is a lever that has paddles on each side of the trigger guard. Instead of pressing in with your thumb, I find the easiest method of dropping the magazine is to use the trigger finger. Pull it out of the trigger guard and press down on the paddle. The slide hold-open lever is where we expect it, on the left side at the joint of slide and frame, where our right thumb can work it. The front of the

You can replace the backstrap for one larger or smaller.

The SW-99 in .45ACP is a lot more compact than you'd expect a hi-cap double action .45 to be.

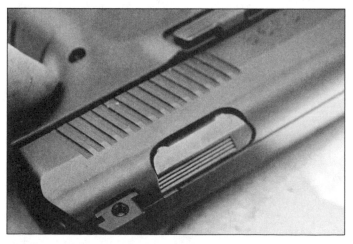

The de-cocking button is on the slide.

The SW-99 accessory rail accepts many things, like this Streamlight M3.

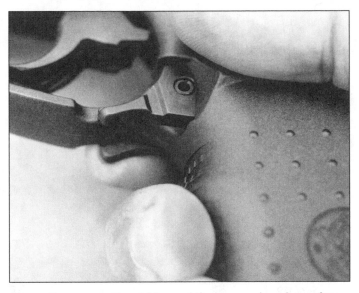

Press down on either side and the magazine drops free.

frame has rails for a light or other accessory, the feature soon to be required for every serious tactical or duty sidearm. If you need a light or a laser, the S&W 99 can hold one.

In function, the 99 works like any other pistol, with a tilting-barrel Browning lock, and many of the parts inside bear a resemblance to Glock parts. (No big deal, how many ways can you do the same job?) To take it apart for cleaning, unload the pistol and remove the magazine. Check the chamber again, then dry fire it. Do the Glock pinch, and ease the slide back, then pull down the disassembly levers on each side. Let the slide go forward off the frame. Pull the recoil spring out of its seat on the barrel, pull the barrel out and you're done.

The magazines are double stack, but with a long taper section, and a nine-shot capacity. I'm sure the taper is to allow for a slim frame on top, where the trigger mechanism has to pass around the magazine, and not some plan to keep the capacity down under an arbitrary figure. The magazine tubes are sturdy in appearance, and the lips that hold the baseplate on are bent outwards. In the event the Assault Weapons Ban of 1994 is allowed to expire, we can after Sept 14, 2004 attach a hollow magazine extension to

increase capacity past nine rounds. Adding another inch would probably get the loaded pistol capacity up to 13 or 14 rounds from the current 10.

In recoil the 99 is like any other .45, firm but not oppressive. It is not any problem to shoot passing qualification scores with it, although it is not as accurate as the S&W 1911 that I fired at the same range sessions. Part of the slightly lesser accuracy observed was probably me, and part was probably the pistol. The DA trigger mechanism just isn't going to allow the kind of precision that the single action of the 1911 will, and I've spent much of my range time over the last 30 years using one or another 1911. I'm just a lot more familiar with it, and will probably do better with any 1911 over any other pistol.

It never failed to fire (except for the previously mentioned rounds poorly stored and brought out solely as practice ammo) and is accurate enough to shoot a passing score on any course. For a holster, I

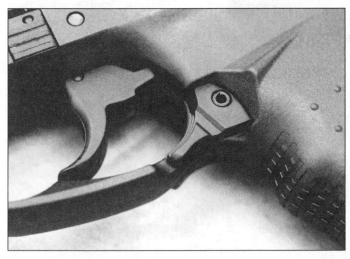

The mag release is a dual paddle.

The large and sturdy accessory rail of the SW-99. "Frame made in Germany" and the rest in the United States.

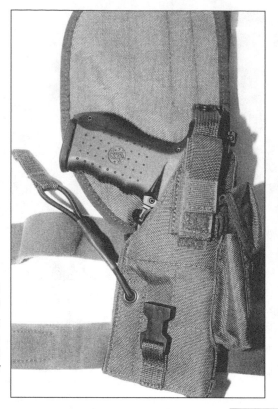

The SW-99 in .45 ACP fits Glock holsters like this LBTC NSW model.

The slide release is on the upper left side of the frame, for right-handed shooters. Note the frame scallop under it for trigger finger clearance.

found it would fit in many holsters marked for standard Glocks. Many other DA .45s, like the H-K USP, require a larger holster. If you have a holster for a Glock 22, you have no chance at stuffing a USP into it. The London Bridge Trading Company tactical thigh rigs for G-17/22 all accepted the S&W 99, as did the Shooting Systems thigh rig and belt holster. I had to let out the thumbstrap to accommodate the S&W 99, but that is no big deal. The mag pouches of the LTBC holsters would accept the S&W 99 magazine, but just barely. As for belt-mounted magazine pouches, that is a different problem and you should check to be sure. While the S&W 99 will fit in a holster designed for the Glock 22, a 40 S&W model (and the 9mm Glock 17) the S&W M-99 magazines will not always fit a pouch made for the Glock 17/22. You need to select a mag pouch for a double-stack pistol of larger size, like the Para Ordnance, Glock 20/21, or STI. The S&W 99 magazines were a snug but secure fit in the pistol mag pouches on the Special Operations Equipment Gear CQB vest. They also fit the accessory mag pouch from SOE Gear, but I had to let the Fastex strap out almost all the way on each. Once latched the magazine would stay. Check fit

A typical group fired with the SW-99 and .45 hardball.

before you buy. In the event we can expand capacity, you'll have to special-order mag pouches to latch onto your hi-cap S&W mags.

For someone who wants .45, but is stuck with choosing a DA pistol, the S&W 99 is more than a viable option, it is a handy and compact one.

Chapter 14

The Kahr Arms Pistols

KAHR IS A fairly new firearms manufacturer, and demonstrates that the open market and market competition dynamics are still viable and force improvements in products. Kahr began with compact, concealed-carry pistols of double-action only design. Their products were so well received that the lineup has expanded through the years. With this expansion and success came refinements and improvements. The latest Kahr pistol is a full-size 9mm single-stack meant to be used in the two competitive disciplines concerned with carry guns: USPSA Production Division and IDPA SSP Division. But our concern is with the backup pistols, the ones more likely to be tucked away in the web gear as a second or third gun, or carried by uniform officers as a backup gun.

In some circles, backup guns are viewed with skepticism and even contempt. Viewed by those with a mind to conspiracy theories as "drop guns" or "excuse guns". (Drop gun: If you shoot someone you shouldn't have, you simply leave the "drop gun" at the scene to justify your bad shooting. Anyone stupid enough to think they can get away with it in this day and age deserves to be behind bars.) For most departments, if a backup gun is simply a hassle, it is so because of recordkeeping, qualification and storage requirements. Some departments issue and mandate backup guns. And the Kahr pistols tested would serve well in that capacity.

PM9

The smallest of the polymer-framed 9mms from Kahr, it is small enough that I could only get two fingers on the frame when shooting it. The DAO trigger pull is heavy enough to preclude inadvertent firing, but not so heavy as to be a hindrance to accurate shooting. The magazine holds six rounds, with two magazines provided in the lockable hard case in which Kahr ships all their pistols. the PM9 accepts the longer magazines of the P9, so you could carry it with six- or seven-shot magazines, and reload with seven shots if you desired. However, packing the PM9 with a longer magazine inserted negates the compactness. The PM9 demonstrated 100 percent reliability with all ammunition tested, including all hollow-points. As a very small, quite light 9mm pistol, shooting the high-velocity Cor-Bon Pow'rball ammunition was less fun and more work, but nothing

The Kahr P9 and PM9

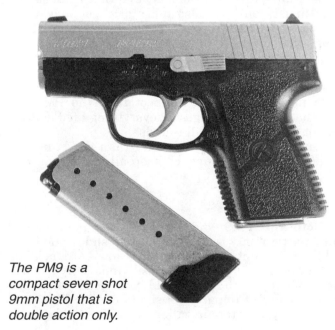

The PM9 is a compact seven shot 9mm pistol that is double action only.

The PM9, with its compact magazine, leaves your pinkie finger in the air. No accessory rail here, as the PM9 is meant to be a compact gun.

The P9 is getting big for a compact gun, but it is so flat and light it is still easy to carry and large enough to get a good hold of. Stainless slide and polymer frame, double-action-only.

Both the P9 and PM9 use a Browning-type lockup, and the sights are fitted in transverse dovetails.

like punishment. Given a sufficient supply of ammunition and a couple more magazines to shoot the course, I have no doubts about my ability to shoot a passing score on the state qualification course. At 10 yards offhand, I was able to easily fire a timed-fire group smaller than the palm of my hand. At maximum IPSC speed I was still able to keep all shots from a magazine inside the "A" zone. As a backup gun, it would ride well in an ankle holster, or clipped to the adjustment straps of a ballistic vest. As a backup for a SWAT team, the only problem is how to secure it to a tactical or load-bearing vest. I've mentioned the problem to the R&D people at Uncle Mikes, and they are working on it.

P9

The P9 is the bigger brother to the PM9, and the frame, while polymer, is long enough that I can get all three fingers on it. It also takes a longer magazine, holding seven rounds. With a chambered round, that brings you to eight total, enough for the P9 to be considered a viable off-duty or concealed carry gun. The slide and barrel are also another half inch or so longer, but it is the extra frame size that makes the P9 much more comfortable to shoot than the PM9. As with the PM9, the P9 digested everything I fed it, even the hot Cor-Bon Pow'rball rounds.

On target, it was even easier than the PM9 was to shoot compact groups, or keep all the hits in the "A" zone at maximum speed.

Common features

Both the PM9 and P9 have polymer frames, double-action-only triggers, stainless slides and good sights. The front and rear sights are both held in cross dovetails, so you can adjust windage by moving one or both of them. Should you need to adjust vertical point of impact, the sights can be altered or replaced by shorter or taller ones. The slide locks

open after the last shot is fired, and the slide stop lever is on the left side where you'd expect it. It is large enough to be easily pressed after a reload, but not so large it will get in the way during carry or the draw. The magazine release is at the rear of the triggerguard, set up for a right-handed shooter. The magazines drop free when released.

The Kahr pistols in general, and these two in particular, have many features that make them attractive as carry or backup guns. For those who are not enamored of the 9mm cartridge, they can also be had in .40, although you lose a round of magazine capacity in each when you step up in bore size. In the competition arena, the Kahrs become quite comfortable to shoot when fed target-power ammunition.

If you get one or both you won't be sorry. And as soon as I can figure a way to secure one to my SOE Gear CQB vest, Kahr will be added to the ensemble.

Chapter 15

A New Idea
For An Entry Pistol

THE JOB ISN'T easy. You have to go through the door (often after it has been pried, blown, sledghammered or kicked) and deal with the potential miscreants inside. You don't know if you will have to shoot or punch, kick or grab, and you'll always be yelling. What to take? A short rifle can be just the thing, but sometimes even a short rifle is too large. Ditto a shotgun or subgun. Sometimes only a handgun will do, as with the shield man on an entry team. He's got enough to do hauling the shield around, keeping it pointed towards danger, and not tripping over stuff. He doesn't need the extra hassle something with a shoulder stock can represent. Many departments simply mandate the departmental issue sidearm as the carry weapon on entry teams. Some teams have a choice. In many cases that choice ends up being a 1911 pistol, because of the self-selected nature of the team.

For many, having chosen a 1911, the selection then narrows to single-stack or hi-cap, custom or off-the-shelf, and caliber never enters into the equation. After all, isn't .45 the best?

I had thought that a particular idea I'd had was just a bit too much, until Ron Avery outlined much the same thing to me when we were both at the 2003 World Shoot in South Africa. During one of the breaks, he and I discussed the use of an IPSC Racegun as an entry gun. I know what some of you are thinking; everyone knows that a racegun is too expensive, too fragile, too specialized and too weird to be used as a law enforcement sidearm. And you may be right, if you simply consider using a competition gun without taking into account its use in the entry role. First, for those who don't shoot IPSC competitively, "what is a Racegun?"

One example would be the STI Competitor. A high-capacity .38 Super pistol with a red-dot sight (the example on hand has a C-More sight), a compensated barrel and built for high-speed accurate

For a long time the customary long gun, and chosen entry gun, of SWAT teams has been the MP-5. It has taken years to realize that it is just a 10-pound handgun with over-pentration problems.

Going to a .30-caliber rifle like this super-short G-3 exaggerates muzzle blast, and it weighs as much as the MP-5, for some terminal ballistic increase.

High-capacity, accurate, easy to shoot accurately, and it will feed any hi-tech hollow-point you can use.

The scope mount is secured to the frame; otherwise all the controls are traditional 1911.

shooting. Magazine capacity depends on length of the tube and baseplate and the caliber. (We will be discussing high-caps, not the 10-shot mags emasculated by federal law that may be obsolete by the end of 2004.) In .38 Super the STI magazines hold 18 rounds in the 126mm length, 20 in the 140mm, and 27 in the 170mm length. In .40 caliber, the capacities are 16-18-23, and in .45 ACP they are 13-15-19. Competition shooters have figured out ways to tune and adjust the magazines to increase those capacities by a round or two, but not always with reliable results. It is far better in the law enforcement world to have an 18-round magazine that always works, than a 20-round magazine of the same length that "usually" works. A factory load for the .38 Super or the 9X23 round boots a 130-grain bullet up to 1300+ fps. The red-dot sight makes target acquisition a high-speed affair. The comp keeps the muzzle down for quick follow-up shots. The high-capacity magazine relieves the operator of the worry of running out of ammo anytime soon. What are the objections against its use? One, they cost a lot. While a Racegun can be expensive, how does it compare to other firearms? A fully tricked out Racegun can cost from $1,800 to $2,500. Meanwhile, a department can get an AR, an MP-5 or a short-barreled shotgun for less. ($700 to $1,500) Or, a well-built "plain" 1911 for $1,000 to $1,500 Two, they can be fragile. I don't know about you, but team members I know who make it a habit to abuse their gear have said gear taken away. As long as a firearm can stand up to the "normal" team tactics and environment, it is durable enough. Such standard working impacts as getting whacked by other equipment, banged into door frames, car doors, vending machines, chairs, are all normal and expected activities. The only potential weak part of a Racegun is the scope. The most durable of the red-dots is the EO Tech scope, with its built-in cover. Put a Holosight on your Racegun and it will stand up to anything your other guns will. As for being dropped, all firearms will give up if dropped enough, but the EO Tech Holosight will stand up to

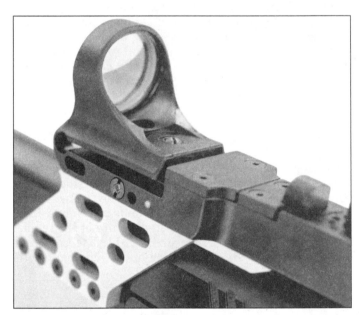

The C-More sight is proven after more than a decade of top-level IPSC competition.

more than other sights will. Some say it is too specialized. Well, the job, either in a practical match, or on an entry team is to diferentiate the "shoot" targets from the no-shoots, and engage them as quickly as possible while maneuvering through doorways, around walls, furniture and other obstacles. The job description sounds identical. The last objection is that the Racegun is commonly fed specially developed reloaded .38 Super (or some derivative thereof) ammunition. And after all, law enforcement uses 9mm, .40 or .45, right? Maybe I'd change, maybe I wouldn't. You can have your Entry/Racegun in any caliber, so it really isn't a problem.

There are some things about a full-blown Racegun that I'd definitely want to change before I started taking one on raids.

The Sweeney/Avery-Improved Entry Gun

By its very nature, you are giving up ballistic power in order to improve the compactness of the handgun. You can't have a handgun that hits like a rifle. Caliber may be departmentally selected: "You will use THIS caliber, as provided by THIS manufacturer, as issued by the department." Or you may be given some leeway in ammunition manufacturer, caliber or load selection. The competition choice of one of the .38 Super iterations will do many things for you. The factory loadings of .38 Super and 9x23 are hotter than 9mm +P+, and tread on the heels of the .357 Sig. For those who need it and can provide the paperwork for same, you can have the ammunition manufacturers custom-load armor-piercing ammo. (Don't ask me, or them, for the specifics, unless you're writing on departmental letterhead. It is unlawful to produce AP handgun ammo for civilian sale. And unlike the Assault Weapon Ban of 1994, which sunsets in 2004, this ban isn't going away anytime soon.) The .40 is a good cartridge, but what it isn't is adaptable. If it delivers just what you want, that's fine. But if you want more, it can't be stretched, pumped up or improved much, if at all. The 10mm is everything the 40 isn't, but the Ten has its problems. It can be a balky feeding round in some platforms. There aren't a lot of choices for loads. And it can be a handful to shoot. The top dog is the .45 ACP. It is what everyone who shoots a 1911-based pistol wants to be shooting. After all that is what the 1911 was designed to use. A good custom gunsmith, or the STI armorers, can make your Entry Racegun any caliber you want, but there are limits. As you go up in cartridge size, you get fewer cartridges in a magazine. And you can have calibers only within a breechface size.

The smallest breechface size is 9mm/.38 Super. There are those who will tell you that you can run a gun and interchangeably use .38 Super and 9x23. Maybe, but it isn't a good idea. The Super is a straight-walled case. The "23" is tapered. If you ream the chamber to fit the 9x23 and then use the smaller Super in it, you risk case ruptures. If you ream the chamber for a Super, the tapered (wider at the base) 9x23 may wedge cases tight and cause extraction problems. Get the gun chambered for one and don't swap ammo.

The next breechface size is the 10mm. Here, you can have the .40, 10mm and .357 Sig. As mentioned, the 40 is

The comp is a hazard, I'll admit. But there should only be non-team participants in front of the entry man.

A hot .40 will expand and not exit like this Speer Gold Dot, always a desirable effect in the close quarters of entry work. Many other bullets will, too.

limited, and unless your department strictly limits you to it, you should select a better caliber for the Entry/Racegun.

The largest is .45, and with it you can have .45 ACP, .400 Cor-bon, and others based on .45 ACP case.

The higher the operating pressure of the round (Super, Sig, 10mm) the more gas you have to feed the comp. The downside to an efficient comp is noise. If you are using a Super running at its maximum pressure ceiling, indoors, you are basically treating your ears to a rifle blast. The lower-pressure .45 ACP won't be so violent, but also won't feed it's comp as well. Somebody in the back is waving a hand and muttering "Get to it, Sweeney, which would you pick?" I'd go with a .357 Sig. It produces impressive

The ultra-short .223 is a handgun, but a clumsy one that is a poor bargain for terminal ballistics, handling and where do you get a holster?

The 9mm carbine is extremely controllable, but if you make it smaller to make it handier, you make it much harder to use effectively.

velocity, feeds a comp well, the reduction in magazine capacity is minimal compared to a Super, and the ammunition is readily available. With an Entry/Racegun in .357 Sig, you'd have 125-grain bullets at 1400+fps, and 18 to 22 of them in each magazine. And the extra modifications I'd make to the gun from Racegun to entry Gun?

Trigger pull

It is a rare competition shooter who is running an Open gun (the Division our Entry/Racegun qualifies for) with a service-weight trigger. It is common at matches to see trigger pulls between 2-1/2 and 3 pounds. Many Master or Grandmaster shooters run guns with the trigger pull less than 2 pounds. I would make sure the Entry Gun is a clean, crisp, 4-1/2 pounds. Not for durability, but in recognizing the stress of entry work. A competition gun, with the trigger properly tuned to 1-1/2 pounds, can go thousands of rounds between service calls. In some cases, tens of thousands before anything other than inspection is needed. But charging into a drug lab, not knowing what is on the other side, or what the footing is like, is not the place to be using an ultra-light trigger pull. Especially if anyone handling the pistol is wearing gloves. A competition-weight trigger pull is too light. You may cause it to discharge inadvertently (they don't "just go off") slipping and falling, being tackled by a suspect, or for any number of other causes. Also, a light trigger on just the Entry/Racegun creates training and operations problems. If your patrol rifle and shotgun or submachinegun have a 4-1/2-pound trigger pull or more, but your Entry Gun has 1-1/2 pounds, every time you transition from one to another you create more difficulty for yourself. I've seen it in training, and I've seen it in competition. At the old Second Chance combat shoot, many competitors would shoot in multiple events. I've seen the transition in both directions, with problems both ways. I watched one competitor switch from his shotgun, with a heavy gritty

trigger pull, to a competition 1911 with a light and clean one. On the start, his first shot off the rail with his handgun was into the ground 10 feet in front of him, the second was at the feet of the table, and the third was on the first pin he intended to shoot.

On another occasion I watched a competitor on the rifle range attempting to shoot the Light Rifle Pop and Flop. He'd been using his handgun all morning, and now he found himself only pulling his 5-pound rifle trigger for 2 pounds worth of trigger pull, the weight of his handgun's trigger pull. Needless to say, he was reacting to recoil that wasn't happening, as his rifle wasn't firing. You really don't want to be doing either of these examples in the middle of a shootout.

Clean and crisp 4-1/2 pounds is light enough for good work, but heavy enough to keep you out of trouble. Which leads to the next change.

Grip safety

The 1911 has a grip safety. Many competitors minimize or eliminate its engagement to the trigger bar. They do so in order to make sure they never draw and come on the target with a pistol that won't fire. They have their gunsmith pin the safety out of the way, or minimize the engagement so the slightest movement of the safety clears the trigger bar. On the Entry Racegun, I'd go the other way. I would increase the spring tension pushing the safety out and maximize the engagement. And to ensure 100 percent proper clearance when grasped, I'd have the speed bump on the bottom welded larger. Large enough that I would always depress the grip safety enough to ensure firing, each time I draw. If you go through enough doorways on drug lab raids, sooner or later you'll take a fall, have to wrestle with a

An entry pistol should have a light on it, and the Springfield XD already comes with a light rail. But getting a comp and red-dot sight on and XD might be tough.

The H-K MP-5 has extreme durability going for it. As long as you have a ready supply of extractor springs, it will never stop working.

suspect, or grab someone and run out while the building catches fire from the spilled solvents. Is there time to holster? Maybe. Ideally you'll have spent countless hours practicing re-holstering, and making sure the thumb safety is engaged in so doing. In any case, you want a dropped pistol to not fire and you want to be as sure as you can about that.

Lanyard

Remember the photos and artwork of the Cavalry during the first decades of the 20th Century? The lanyards? The idea was to keep the pistol with the rider. Well, they've come back. I've talked to more than one recent veteran who described themselves as so tired on ops that if they had not had their weapons tied to them they'd have left them someplace. A lanyard makes sure the pistol stays with you in the rough and tumble of a raid gone awry. What could happen? How about this: Just as your team busts the door down and rushes in, the dealer and his assistants decide to walk out for a break. There you all are, jumbled in the first room, you headed in, them headed out. You can't shoot, because no one has produced a weapon. But the movement has caused the lead person in each group to collide, and now it is

Lanyards are coming back. Blackhawk Industries makes a standard and a quick-detachable model.

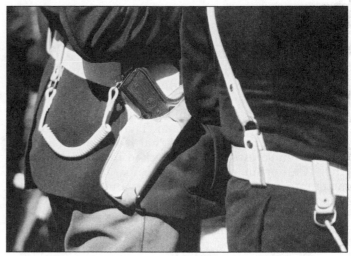

Lanyards are all over Europe. While lanyards are catching on Stateside, I don't think the white-finished leather gear will be.

a big wrestling match. With a lanyard, you know your pistol is staying with you. Lanyards have been all the rage in Europe all along. I'm not sure on any of my recent overseas trips I've seen a police officer that didn't have his pistol attached via lanyard.

Sight shield

In the rough and tumble, a sight can get banged pretty hard. In a competition, the extra weight will wear you down over the course of a match. But for duty, a sight shield can save your bacon. The EO Tech Holosight comes with a shield on it. Others will need one made.

Illumination

Last but not least, I'd mount a light on the Entry Pistol. Since it is a primary weapon of the operator it is issued to (or owned by) the light on it will probably be the primary light he has. Of course he'll have extras, maybe weapon lights, maybe a hand-held, but the light on the Entry Pistol will be his primary. So, mount a bright Surefire on it. STI can make a competition/entry pistol on any frame you'd like (at least any frame they make) and they make frames with light rails on them. If you've already got one, you can add a rail. If you don't, then you can order yours with a light-railed frame.

The STI Competitor

As the base for an Entry/Racegun, the STI Competitor would be great. For those who don't know, the lower half of the frame of the STI guns is a polymer. The three screws that hold the steel rails section to the polymer trigger/magazine section are designed to keep it tight. Unless you take the screws out completely it isn't going to come apart. The advantage to the method is that it allows a double-stack magazine in .45 without making the frame too wide. While the frame is not too wide for many shooters, that doesn't keep some competition shooters from making the frame even smaller. It isn't uncommon to see guns with the frame run against a belt sander to trim the grip area even more. (It voids the warranty to do so.) The particular gun I have on hand is a Trubore Competitor. The Trubore is a comp and barrel made as a single unit. Developed solely for import into California, the Trubore, with its integral comp, lacks threads. That is, most comped barrels are a regular barrel that is threaded, and the comp then screws in and is locked in place. However, the California Legislature, in their paranoid attempts to deny drug dealers and gang bangers silenced pistols, have deemed threaded barrels to be offensive to the law, and a crime to possess. (I'm sorry if I seem just a bit grumpy about this and other subjects, but the total technical knowledge of firearms that many legislators possess could be contained on a single page. With room left over.) To prevent their customers from being persecuted by the authorities, STI designed the Trubore barrel. In all respects except replacing the comp, it is simply a comped barrel. But a comped barrel that satisfies the authorities in California by lacking threads. The sight on this gun is a C-More. In use, it is like any other 1911 pistol, except that it is louder and the dot comes back down to the target faster.

At the range, I fed it some Cor-bon .38 super ammo, and over sandbags could easily shoot 4-inch groups. I suppose with less coffee that morning I could have done a lot better, but 4 inches at 50 yards is plenty good enough for a handgun. In a year of testing with it, I have yet to encounter a failure.

Accurate? This 25-yard group is just over an inch and a quarter between the farthest bullet holes.

Most entry teams spend many, many more hours practicing and drilling than they do minutes actually entering unfriendly locations.

Chapter 16

Springfield XD

IF SOMEONE COMES up with a new idea, soon competitors will be swarming in looking for a piece of the action. Lest you think this is a bad thing, consider the fix we'd be in if after Henry Ford's adoption of the assembly line (he didn't invent it, he just made it work) other carmakers just up and quit. We'd still be driving black cars, and we may have just now gotten around to electric starters, automatic transmissions and in-car radios. For all of his innovation and testing, Henry Ford was interested in the innovations Henry Ford was interested in. Competition is what really breeds improvement.

And much the same happens in the firearms field. When the Glock pistol came out, it was at first resisted. Once it became popular, then everyone else tried to make one with improvements and minor design changes.

One new maker is in Croatia, where they tested and modified a pistol until they had an improvement on the Glock. Imported at first independently, it was picked up by Springfield Armory, fine-tuned, and now is available as the XD. Like the Glock, the XD is a polymer-framed pistol with no thumb safety as the 1911 mavens are used to. Where it differs is the grip safety on the back. The XD also has a cocking indicator on the rear of the slide, so you can tell if the striker is fully forward just by looking at it. The extractor is in the upper corner of the squarish slide, and there is a loaded chamber indicator.

As a duty pistol the XD is right in with the rest, being offered in 9mm, .357 Sig and 40 S&W. It can be had in three sizes; full, compact, and ultra compact. They all have light rails, and Springfield offers a compact light to fit, the XML.

The XD comes with a light rail built into the frame.

The Springfield XD comes in three sizes (these are the largest and smallest) and three calibers.

The full-sized XD is much the same size as a 1911, holds more ammo, and already has a light rail.

Robbie Leatham shoots for Springfield, and makes the XD rock.

With a .40, he's on target with brass only inches away.

In competition, the XD is a serious contender, not the least for being in the hands of Robbie Leatham, perhaps the pre-eminent practical shooting competitor of our generation. (And perhaps even the next, too.)

The magazines come either in the emasculated federally mandated 10- shot version (unless the law expires as scheduled in September 2004) and high-capacity law enforcement-only versions up to 15 rounds. The XD fits any holster that a similarly-sized Glock (or other hi-capacity 9mm pistol fits) and judging from the durability of the sample sent me, will last many years of high-volume ammunition consumption.

In testing I was able to easily shoot a passing score on the state qualification course, shoot palm-sized groups at 10 yards in rapid fire, and keep all my shots in the "A" zone of a USPSA target shooting at maximum speed. The 100-yard, 10-inch gong on our rifle range is in serious danger, with my best session being three straight runs of 10 for 10 and several boxes worth of eight and nine hits for 10 shots.

For a black plastic pistol you don't have to speak German anymore. And you can have your XD in Green if you'd like. Just ask.

Springfield has a compact light for its compact pistol.

Chapter 17

Light And Lighting In General

The detailing of the tactics of light would fill this book. Covering all the variables, listing all the categories of situations, and the possible approaches would take many pages, many photographs, and is best done in a classroom setting. In fact, you can take classes on exactly this subject area, by contacting Surefire and scheduling time at the Surefire Institute. I'm just going to give you an overview, so you can begin to consider the possibilities, try a few tactics, and see if you need to schedule some time at the Institute. (The short answer: yes.)

Lighting conditions

Light is not always the same. Photographers can discuss light endlessly, the flat, sometimes harsh light of the studio, the "golden light" of the 15 minutes before sunset, bounced light, light temperature and fill light. For tactical illumination, we have daylight, dusk, moon and none. Daylight is just that: The bright light from the sun above the horizon, and in some places, above the vegetation. Even in daylight you may need illumination. A thick bush or heavy hedge can cast enough of a shadow that your daylight-adapted vision cannot see in. Leaving daylight to enter a building puts you in the position of losing the main illumination source, the sun. Dusk is the flat light of the day (morning and evening) when the sun is near the horizon, hidden by vegetation, or just below the horizon. You can see quite well for a long time into dusk, but any obstacle blocks light and requires artificial illumination. The moon, even if just a quarter, offers enough light for those with good vision and adapted eyes to see to maneuver. But unless it is full, the moon doesn't offer enough light to identify and acquire sights. Working indoors in windowless, lights-out conditions leaves you with no light. All illumination is artificial, and brought by you.

Operational conditions

Are you conducting a search and rescue? Search and apprehend? Detain and question? Or search and kill? Almost all law enforcement operations will be one of the first three. In search and rescue you want to light the night, create as much light as you can, to illuminate the terrain and advertise your location to those you wish to find and assist. Detain and question is another situation where the "wall of light" is best. You want the occupants of the vehicle you are making a felony stop on to not know how many you are, where you are, and feel uncomfortable looking in your direction. In a search and apprehend situation you want to find without being found until the time comes to overwhelm the suspect. You'll be using a no- or low-light travel and search, and then the wall of light at the moment of surprise. As for search and kill, it is mostly a military operational condition, and when night vision gear is involved, there may be no artificial illumination, at least, none in the visible spectrum.

Light as a weapon

Not as an impact weapon, but as a force multiplier. Bathed in the blinding glow of a powerful light, suspects or offenders have severely limited options. They can't face the light; their visual protection reflex is too great. They can't see intervening terrain, so movement is hindered. They can't tell how many opponents they face, so judging the odds is impossible. And they can't see if you have a weapon ready, or what it might be. They can try to go for a weapon, but you'll see the movement. If they charge, they may trip and fall, run into an obstacle, or find themselves on the receiving end of chemical restraints, less-lethal, impact weapons or even gunfire. Using light properly shifts the odds in your favor, affords you options you would not have, and gives you time and space in which to maneuver, think and prevail.

Travel in light

The best way to travel in light is to use artificial lighting as little as possible, so you do not give away your location, numbers and direction of movement. Travel quietly, with no "white light ADs" and use light as your tool to open darkened corners or rooms. Also be aware of light direction. You want all the light you use to be under your control, in front of you, and pointed away from you. Do not allow yourself to be backlit, by moving on a ridgeline or allowing yourself to be silhouetted against the sky. Backlit conditions simply alert the opposition to your location. If searching, control lights and lighting and avoid being backlit. If setting up an observation post, ambush site or pre-positioning a team prior to a raid, go to a location that affords you light control. That way, your target(s) will be backlit as they move through your area, or in the case of a team, you will be unseen as the suspects move into the designated apprehension area.

There is no such thing as too much

You can't have too much light unless your light is so bright, and the area illuminated is so reflective, that you get backsplash. Otherwise, you need more than one light per man, and enough to ensure that no one illuminated can stand to look in your direction. You need more than one light because even the best lights break. Even new batteries die soon enough (or right away). Once you have achieved sufficient lumen output to trigger the reflexive vision protection of "turn and squint" you need to maintain the advantage. You must make sure that every option is defeated. Turning and twisting don't help the offender if you have multiple lights on him. Sunglasses don't help if you've got hundreds of lumens at your disposal. And before his vision can adapt, you've moved in, searched and secured.

Light and move

If you're conducting a search and rescue, you can be a "searchlight." You can plant yourself in a high location and sweep the area with a powerful light, to observe all. If you are facing anyone else besides that lost person, anyone who may wish to escape detection, or resist apprehension, you cannot spend time lighting. Approach a suspected position to a safe point. Illuminate it, observe, turn the light off, move and reconsider. Consider what you saw, and who could have seen you. Move safely (navigation LEDs are very useful in this part of the process) to the next location that allows you to safely engage an unknown area, and flash again.

Operational readiness

Sometimes even unknown situations have to be handled with discretion. While searching an office on an alarm call, you cannot always be using the weapon-mounted light and the most aggressive tactics. First, you'll burn yourself out before you finish the building, your shift or your career. Second,

if the owner is there and forgot the alarm code, you'll find the Chief is not at all happy about a big local business owner being subjected to an aggressive search and detention. Finally, bad guys are bad guys in part because many of them are not very smart. If someone is stupid enough to break into a building and set off the alarm, they're probably making enough noise to be easily heard. Just step into the building, find a secure location, and listen. Once you've identified the direction of the noise, you can then approach and refine. Each leg of the approach gains you more information.

In a darkened building raid on known violent offenders, you operate as noisily, brightly and quickly as possible. One consideration you may need to consider, and train for, is the effect of NFDDs on illumination. If the flashbangs create too much smoke, or blow up too much dust, your hundreds of lumens of illumination may simply be spent creating bright clouds of visually impenetrable dust. Nighttime raids in dusty environments may preclude NFDD use, or require careful planning as to their deployment.

Spares

Not only should each team member have two or more illumination devices, there should be team spares and batteries. Particularly difficult is the military environment. I've talked to a number of soldiers and Marines who've dealt with modern operations, and the worries they go through are quickly and strictly ordered: "Do we have enough ammo? Do we have enough water? Will the batteries last? Are the bad guys where we thought they were?" Once the raid is done, and before the evidence crew shows up, the area must be secured, both for and from people, and to ensure there are no safety hazards. You carry the compact, powerful and "way cool and sexy" tactical lights for operations, but once the raid is over, bring out the ugly lights. You know, the ones that are clunky, painted yellow, work well in your garage when you're working on the car, and take up more room than you have on your vest.

Light is your friend

Unless someone gets the upper hand on you, light is your advantage. The bad guys are not known to carry expensive and bright lights. Practice, have a light handy, and if you can, get additional training. And keep spare batteries close at hand.

Chapter 18

Multi-Tools and Knives

THE ORIGINAL MULT-TOOL is the Swiss Army knife. The name has since become generic, indicating any knife that has more than one blade and additional tools besides those that cut. The original knives were just pocket tools to take care of the routine tasks that a soldier might require. Since they were very useful, and I'm a sure customer asked for "this or that" the knives grew, and turned into a multiplicity of models. You might consider it quirky to have a Philips screwdriver on a pocketknife, but the rear sight adjustments on Swiss military rifles use Philips head screws. And since every adult male is in the Swiss Army, they need a lot of screwdrivers for annual rifle qualification. As a traveler, I would not take a Leatherman in place of a Swiss Army knife; rather I'd take both. After all, the Leatherman doesn't have a corkscrew, and there are times when you need the corkscrew more than you need the pliers. With both in your luggage, you're covered. However, Swiss Army knives have limitations. The blades don't lock. A non-locking blade is not very useful beyond opening tape-wrapped packages or slicing fruit for lunch. If you want any more out of a blade, it must lock. Also, none have pliers. Perhaps in the old days there were fewer things that required pliers, but in today's world

it seems like everything that isn't digital needs sooner or later to be turned or tightened. And that brings us to the Leatherman tool.

The first time I heard about the Leatherman tool, and Tim Leatherman, I knew I was going to like it and him. Traveling in Europe in 1975, he was driving a cranky rental car. (Just driving in some European countries and surviving should be good for a testimonial dinner. Someday I may get to tell you about my driving experience in Turkey.) At times Tim found a scout knife or a Swiss Army knife were wholly inadequate. Once home he started designing and experimenting. Seven years later, the first tool was unveiled on the marketplace. I had one about five minutes after that. I still have it. However, Tim and the company have not stood still since then, and the variety of tools you can choose from has grown to nine, from the tiny Micra (which you can get in colors other than stainless steel) to the big Wave with enough tools to almost require a user's manual.

First, what is the attraction of a multi-tool? Basically, once you get past the "boy do I love a new gadget" mindset, a multi-tool saves space and weight. Space on your belt, or in your pockets or web gear, is not limitless. A tool with several knife blades, a pliers built in, with wire cutters and a few common screwdriver sizes, can take the place of at least half a dozen to up to a dozen tools. Let's say you need a Philips screwdriver to tighten a screw. Where is it? Which pocket, or is it in the tool kit? For a single job, the multi-tool is in the same place on your belt it has always been. Never, however, underestimate the attraction of gadgets or cool gear.

The drawback is that for each job, the multi-tool is not quite as handy or robust as the actual tool for that job. But, it doesn't weigh the many pounds that a tool kit would. If you were going to assemble something, and screw in and tighten two dozen screws, take the extra minute to go to the shop and get the correct screwdriver. But if you're in the field, and need to tighten one right now, the multi-tool on your belt can be a lifesaver. With the book to consider, and readers to update, I set aside my trusty original Leatherman to try the newest ones. Since this book is devoted to law enforcement and not comfortable traveling overseas, I tested the big ones and not the little ones.

The first multi-tool, the Swiss army knife. Despite its limitations, its good to have one in your gear.

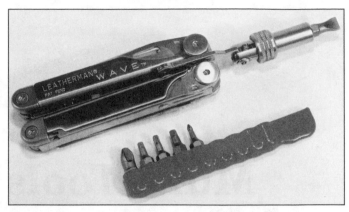

The attachment lets you use any socket tip, so you can assemble your own collection, tips that will fit what you commonly need tightened.

The Leatherman Wave, a toolbox in your pocket.

Wave

Yow, what a toolbox. It has 13 tools with 18 functions, and it still fits on your belt. The dual-use technology comes from things like having the file two-sided. One side is a diamond-coated file for use on metal (finishing sharpening a knife blade, for example), while the other side is coarser for softer stuff like wood and plastic. The file, like the two big knife blades and the saw blade, locks open.. The big four open without having to open the tool itself. Just find the one you want and lever it open. The plain blade is just under 3 inches long, and comes sharp enough to grudgingly shave hair. The serrated blade is also a fraction under 3inches, and makes short work of tape and boxes. The shipment that had the Leatherman tools also included about a dozen other boxes, half of them ammo. (My delivery driver gets quite a workout.) I opened the Leatherman box first, and using the serrated blade on the Wave, quickly sliced open the other boxes. Once emptied, the same blade made short work of turning said boxes into a stack of flat cardboard for recycling. Once at the range, I tested the saw blade by shortening some 1X2 target sticks. It took about 10 seconds to saw through the soft wood of the sticks. As a quick way to shorten a stick or two, the Wave is great. If I had to shorten a bundle for use in a match, I'd get a much bigger tool, which is the exact sort of demonstration of a multi-tools use and limitations. The only drawback to the files blade is that you can't use it to sharpen the tool in which it is installed. Otherwise, it is great to field-restore the edge on a knife that has gotten a bit dull. At the shop (or in the precinct house) you'd want to sharpen a blade with big stones and fixtures to properly maintain the angle. But in the field, when a blade dulls and you have to keep cutting, the diamond side would get you back in business. The outside tools need to be covered to protect your hand. The sheet metal stainless steel covers are fabricated with a larger radius than the box section of the

regular or classic Leatherman designs. When you have the tool open to the pliers, you have a grip with the corners more rounded, and easier on the hand.

Inside, the Wave has in one handle a large screwdriver blade, Philips screwdriver tip, can and bottle opener and lanyard ring. A notch on the can/bottle opener is the wire stripper. In the other handle are three smaller flat screwdriver blades and a scissors. The interior tools do not lock when open. However, to protect your fingers, once you've opened the tool you need, close the handles again and the handles will keep the tool from closing onto your fingers.

The pliers are classic Leatherman, short but narrow enough to be useful needlenose, with wire cutters in the jaws. The blade's wire cutters are for soft wire, like copper or aluminum electrical wiring. The hard wire cutters are the notch underneath the soft cutters, for cutting soft steel wire. If the wire is bigger than the notch in the tool, you really need to get a set of cutters intended for the bigger job. But for the wire wrapping ammo crates (for example), the hard cutter works.

And as if all this wasn't enough, there is more. The Wave (and all the other tools, too) has an accessory adapter to accept 1/4-inch hex drive tool tips. Open the Wave part way, and pull the handles apart so there is a gap between them. Slide the adapter down over the pliers and close the handles. But wait, it gets better. The hex base can be changed from straight to a 45º to a 90º angle. And since it is a standard 1/4-inch drive, if you need special tips, or replacement ones, any you get in the 1/4-inch size will work. I'd hate to have to assemble something from scratch with just a Wave and adapter (but it could be done) but if all you need do is tighten one nut or screw, the tool on your belt is a lot better than the toolbox back in the car or at the station.

Crunch

Sometimes you need more than just a needlenose pliers. Sometimes you need to grab a pipe, or leave the pliers clamped in place. For that, the Crunch is the ticket. The first thing you notice when opening it

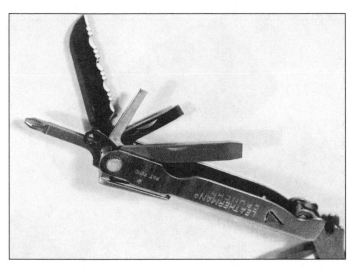

The Crunch has all the usual useful tools, but the real reason you get one is....

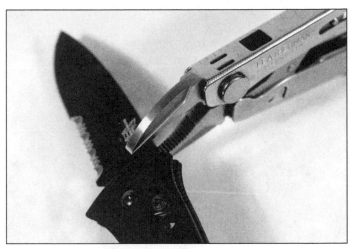

The Crunch locking pliers can clamp and hold, like this Benchmade knife for a photograph.

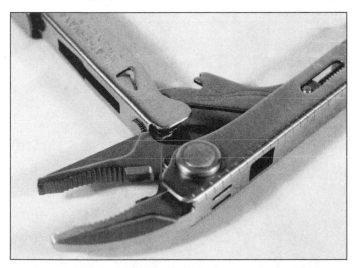

The locking pliers. You can use the Crunch as a light clamp, or to hold something as a third hand.

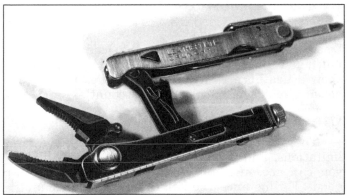

The middle pivot allows the two handles to be used as plier handles while still folding into a flat, rectangular package.

is that it doesn't pivot open like all the others. One handle swings down and away, like a parallel ruler threatening to come unhinged. The pliers' jaws are attached to the other handle, and spring-loaded. They also have the standard Leatherman soft and hard wire cutter jaws built in. Once the handles are opened, you clip the pivot end of the loose handle to the pivot tip of the pliers, and you have locking-jaw pliers. At the bottom of the pliers handle, you'll find an adjustment screw. By turning the screw out you open the jaws. With the jaws fully open you can grasp a 1-inch pipe, and clamp it on a 3/4-inch pipe. The price you pay for the locking feature is fewer auxiliary tools. The plier's mechanism takes up one of the handles, leaving only one for the other tools. On the Crunch you get six tips, a screwdriver blade with medium and fine file sides, a small and a medium screwdriver tip, a Philips tip, a lanyard loop and a serrated blade 2-1/4" long. The blade and the other tips have two safety features: they lock in place, and the handle design offers the Leatherman

Posi-Stop, where the closed handles prevent the tools from closing onto your hand or fingers.

With the adjustment knob, the locking release, and the pivot knob of the pliers jutting out of the handle, the Crunch isn't as sleek as the other designs. A small price to pay, I think, for the advantage of the locking jaws and the real-pliers-not-a-needlenose shape. One extra price you pay is the inability to use the 1/4-inch hex driver adapter. Since the pliers don't pivot, they can't clamp the adapter in place. To get around that problem, the designers at Leatherman made the access hole for the adjustment screw into the 1/4' hex driver. Remove the screw and the hex tips click into place in the handle. My only hesitation with it is that I don't like taking parts off. But since the introduction of hex tool tips to the equation means removable parts, I guess I can accept it.

One advantage to the Crunch is its thin profile. As flat as it is, you can take a Crunch, and a 1911 pistol magazine, and fit them both into a magazine pouch designed for a high-capacity 9mm pistol. For those who carry a 1911, the compactness is a boon. If you don't, then you just lash the Leatherman nylon case to your gear. In April 2003, there was a front-page photo of American soldiers crossing a bridge in

The adjustment nut on the end sets the pliers tip gap for locking. The lanyard loop is a nice touch.

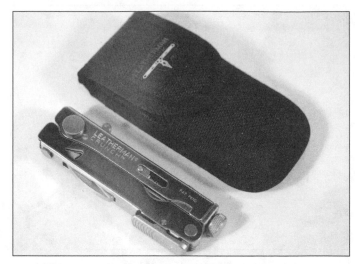

The Crunch fits the standard Leatherman nylon pouch, seen in a number of photographs from Iraq.

It's easy enough to attach a Leatherman case to your gear, with 550 cord, tape or cable ties.

Iraq. A close examination of the lead trooper (as much as I could zoom in on the digital file) seemed to show a Leatherman nylon case fastened to his load-bearing vest. These tools work for countless projects.

Other tools

There are countless copies; knock-offs, clones and imitations, and not all are bad. For a modest sum, you can get one, and modify it to your particular needs. For instance, the USPSA had a batch of multi-tools made with their logo on them. Included in the pouch were screwdriver tips, hex head and torx tips. What I did was to take the tips and, where possible, modify them. Where it wasn't, I replaced them. The tips now properly fit the grips screws on the pistols I use (1911, Beretta, Sig) for both the slotted-head screws and the occasionally found on 1911 pistols, Allen head screws. I narrowed and rounded the smaller screwdriver blade on the handle to fit the mainspring housing pin of the 1911. That pouch, with its modified tool, goes into my range bag for competition and teaching duties. If I have to do a quick strip and clean on a dunked 1911, Beretta or Sig, I've got the right tips on or with the tool.

Knives

As we consider this chapter, people are divided into two groups: knife users/lovers and non-lovers. Those who love knives can't get too many, too big or small, too many functions, or too sharp. Those who don't cotton to knives don't want to be near anything except a steak knife, and then it had better stay on the table. I've heard and read discussions taking it further, going so far as to discuss a "knife culture" where the blade is a preferred tool. I'm not so sure I'd go that far. While the right knife for the right job is to be desired, there are times when a knife is the wrong tool for the job. For example, as much as I like knives, I don't have any use for one when changing a tire or going into a gunfight. Many people who don't work in law enforcement carry a pocketknife of some kind. In the course of your day you may have to open a box, an envelope, cut string, twine or rope, or push a small part out of a crack or crevasse where it has fallen. For those jobs a small penknife or pocketknife will work fine. I have had one such knife for more than 25 years. It is a little Buck knife, stainless and linen Micarta scales, a model 503. It has been with me to four continents, a thousand competitions or training classes, three gun shops, a couple of dozen other auxiliary knives and a multitude of uses. I don't take it on trips any more, at least not when flying, as I don't want to risk it being confiscated as a "deadly weapon." Many police officers carry similar knives, for when flipping out a large, serrated, "tactical" folder might not be appropriate.

Knives are best selected for, and used in, particular jobs. If you're a hunter caping your deer or elk, you'll want a fixed-blade, drop-point knife with a thin blade

A Swiss Army knife and a gentleman's pocketknife are accepted many places. (Just not airports.)

The Wave fits nicely into a magazine pouch, for those who find a Leatherman is called for more often than a handgun reload.

and a razor sharp edge. If you're an airborne trooper clearing out some brush for your lines of sight to the path you're watching, you'll want a large, heavy-bladed kukri or machete. And if you're a police officer dealing with a recently-released felon who is trying to take your sidearm away, you'll want a knife that is plenty sharp and that you can get to with your left hand.

Many police officers are to be found in the "love a knife" group. If you were to grab a shift of officers (or a raid team) by the ankles and shake them upside down, you'd probably find a fine collection of knives falling to the floor. And a finer collection not falling because they've been properly secured or have stout clips on them. Ask those officers why they have all those big, sharp, and many times serrated, blades, and the near-universal response will be "in case I have to cut someone out of a seat belt," or "Cut down a suicide attempt."

OK, show of hands: how many have had to actually do just that? As expected, one or two. So, the real reason is? Besides opening boxes, packages, etc? Simple. Many police officers work in dangerous areas. Even those that don't work in high-volume precincts do work at hazardous jobs. And putting on the badge is like putting on a bull's-eye. Sooner or later, someone in the department is going to get into a fight that goes really, really bad. Or have a suspect attempt to take his or her sidearm away. The knife is the last tool before bare hands and bared teeth are what's left. Make no mistake; a knife can be a lethal weapon. In many jurisdictions it is considered just, and only, that. In a situation where lethal force is permitted or required, a knife will do if there is nothing else. It does not always have to be lethal force. But always in the backs of our minds is that comforting thought that it can be used to get us out of a bad situation. But in order to do that, it has to be a good knife. While a Swiss Army knife is great for opening bottles and taking care of minor emergencies, it isn't what any of us would pick as the backup to our backup gun.

When I began this now decades-long adventure in the firearms, equipment and law enforcement culture, knives were not as high-tech, nor as common. You could find a few officers on each shift that had a "buck folder" in a pocket or on their belt. But there were no belt clips, no high-strength alloys, no serrated blades, and no specialized tools, just a choice of "stainless" or "spring steel" blades. There was also an occasional officer who carried a switchblade he'd taken off a "JayDee" and carried because it was occasionally useful. Now, the choices are many, and can be almost overwhelming. And style is always a consideration. Just as you must select a knife that is appropriate to the intended use, and durable enough to withstand that use, you have to consider style. Not because selecting the wrong style will subject you to a merciless ribbing from your fellow officers (it will) but because you have to believe in it and like it or you will not carry it, and thus render it useless. I know officers (and competition shooters, and trainers) who insist on almost ugly, merciless tool-like looks from a knife. If it looks like something an Orc would carry, they're happy. Others insist on knives with flowing looks, more along the lines of something an Elf would carry. (To extend the Lord of the Rings comparison) Whatever you select must be something you are comfortable with, in performance and looks, or you will leave it home. And we all know what happens when equipment is left at home. Home is not where you need it.

But before we consider blades, we have to consider blade usage. Jeff Cooper once spoke a great line, oft-repeated, that "Owning a firearm does not make you a gunfighter any more than owning a musical instrument makes you a musician." If you carry a knife with the intention (even if that

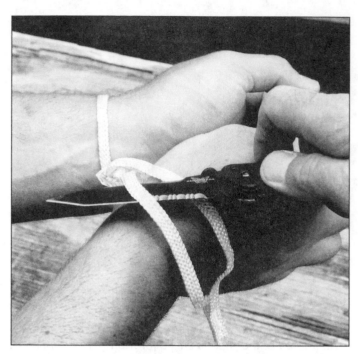

You need a training policy, or you might find officers using knives for things they ought not to.

intention is not publicly spoken) of using it in defense, you'd better get some instruction in how to use it. Using something in which you have no training could get you in trouble. Many police departments do not have a Use of Force policy concerning knives. Many do not even describe it in their Use of Force Continuum. The results of no training and no policy can be anywhere from unfortunate to tragic. Remember, unlike a firearm, a knife is a deadly force tool that is most often used in a non-deadly force situation.

But then, many departments have strange gaps in what is covered and what is allowed. One tragic case demonstrating the problem with no use of force policy on standard tools happened in Detroit. Two detectives attempted to apprehend a suspect on drug charges. The suspect put up an unbelievable struggle. Detroit then (and now) has no intermediate tools between bare hands and firearms. No batons, no chemical sprays, no electrical compliance tools. Detroit also had no Use of Force policy on flashlights. Struggling in the suspect's car, with no room to maneuver, and no visible stimulus to escalate to firearms, all the officers could do was continue striking the suspect with their flashlights. As one officer remarked during the trial "All I could think of was 'Why is he fighting so hard?'"

The suspect subsequently died. Whether he died as a result of the fight, or physical problems due to years of drug abuse, does not matter here. The department had no Use of Force policy regarding flashlights, and no training in their use other than as a source of illumination. As a result, and by definition, their use of the flashlights could not therefore fall within departmental guidelines. They are now in

prison as a result of the incident. Detroit still has no Use of Force policy regarding flashlights (and no chemicals, batons or electrical tools) but it does have a new policy on flashlights themselves; Small, light, and not physically useable as batons or impact devices. Small metal ones are OK, but nothing 3-cell or larger. The issue light is a special Streamlight, the 20XP, a rechargeable with a plastic body.

So, your department doesn't have a Use of Force policy for knives, but you're carrying one with the idea in mind that you may need it to get yourself out of a jam? You could be in trouble either way.

Here is another example, again from Detroit. (I hate for it to look like I'm picking on them, but I get the Detroit papers, have contacts in the PD, and I learned a long time ago not to discard useful information just because of the source.) The arresting officer found that the sleeves of the suspect's coat prevented him from applying the handcuffs. The suspect was also unhelpful in being secured, struggling and pulling her hands up into the sleeves of her coat. So the officer attempted to use his knife to cut her sleeves away. I can see some of you wincing already. But before you all rise in indignation, how many of you have cut the cable lock, or zip strips, used as lightweight handcuffs? And have you always waited for the departmental sidecutters? Or just used the serrated portion of your knife blade? She struggled, he found himself using a deadly-force weapon in a non-deadly force situation, and inadvertently cut her. She lost the tip of a finger. As you can well imagine, the ensuing headlines and lawsuits created quite a mess. As of this writing, the incident is still under review, and the officer may well be fired.

Even a cursory glance at any knife magazine such as Blade can set your head spinning. What to buy? Should it be custom, semi-custom or production? Do you want fixed or folding? What steel for the blade? For most of us, cost puts a serious restriction on our choices. It is entirely possible, if you buy a one-of-a--kind custom blade from a big-name maker, in exotic materials, with engraving, inlays and a Damascus blade, to spend thousands of dollars. No, that isn't a misprint or typo. You can spend $5,000 to $7,000 for a unique blade. I don't know about the rest of you, but paying twice the cost of a custom, tuned and tricked-out 1911, for a knife, is something I will do only after the Lotto win. That leaves production and semi-custom. A production knife is a standard item, usually produced by a company. A semi-custom is usually a knife you order from an individual craftsman. You select blade length, steel, grips (called scales) material, decoration, and then wait.

The variety of, and quality of, production knives is now so great you can get more just picking out of a catalog than you could from many semi-custom bladesmiths. By simply poring over the catalog of one of the big-name production knifemakers, selecting the type and size you need, the blade material, and scales type, you can have a semi-custom knife in short order. And makers such as Benchmade and Spyderco also can laser engrave your name, unit or PD logo, or other designs on the blade and sometimes the scales.

You can have semi-custom for the cost of production.

All that having been said, how do you select and test a knife? Unlike sidearms, where most departments mandate one or one of a few choices, knives are going to be individual-purchase items. First, a knife has to fit you, your hand, your uniform and the intended use. A big, Teflon-coated bush knife with a saw-tooth spine and a hollow handle for survival extras may be just the tool for a deputy in a rural county who has to hike once he gets to the end of the road. But it sure is going to look menacing strapped to a city officer directing traffic. And just how do you wear it so you can drive the squad car? For uniform officers and detectives, a folding knife will be the first choice. For team members a fixed-blade can be an option, but only so long as you can find a location on your gear for it. Even for entry or raid teams a folder can be more convenient. A blade does not have to be big to be effective. A 3-inch blade can reach vitals. Serrated looks cool, and does cut better. But the lack of serrations doesn't mean you're handicapped. And at the bottom of it all, the handle has to fit you. A handle too big, or too small, too flat or too round, means a knife that doesn't feel like an extension of your reach. Fondle all the knives you can, try the ones others like, and then select one for your hand.

Modern folders come with side clips. Those of us who date from the old days remember folding knives that rested in the bottoms of our pockets, or on our belts in leather sheaths or pouches. The pouches still work, and many a "buck folder" or Leatherman tool rides on duty that way. But side clips make carrying much easier. First, they fit in your pocket. Second, you can tuck one behind your belt, with the clip keeping it in place. If you are going to carry "back of the belt" you must experiment to find the right location. Otherwise, your own body movement will lever the knife out from behind the belt, where it will eventually fall off. And we all know that when it does, it will do so at one of two times: either maximum embarrassment (Judge: "Officer, what was that that just fell onto my floor?") or minimum chance at retrieval ("What was that splash?") Also, team members can clip it into a carry pouch on their web gear, the web gear itself, a pocket, holster or vest.

How to carry. The question is; tip-up or tip-down? My first tactical folder was a cheap, all stainless one that I gave to my Brother when it looked like he was going to be shipped out for the first Gulf War. (I also loaned him a Cold Steel Tanto, a Second Chance vest, and a lot of other gear. I got everything back but the folder, which stayed stuck in his pocket.) It was a tip-down design, and that was what I learned. It took a lot of practice to get used to the tip up carry and open method. The different methods are as follows, all starting with the knife in your right front trouser pocket, and a right-handed user:

Opening is simple in its basic method. Push the stud with your thumb to lever the blade open...
And keep going until it locks. But point up or down? You'll have to try to see what works for you, and then select a knife.

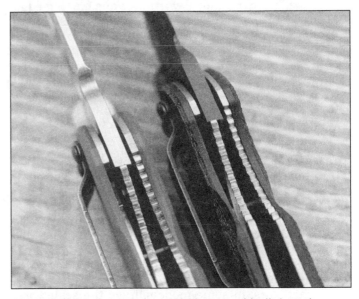

Liner locks are sections of spring steel built into the handle that snap over and catch the rear of the blade to lock it open.

Tip-down: As you reach for the knife, your right thumb slides the length of the handle. Once your palm bottoms out against the butt of the knife, you grasp and remove it. Your thumb then levers the blade open, with the grip already in your palm.

Tip-up: As you reach for the knife, your thumb stops partway down the grip, and then you remove the knife. To open, as your thumb works the blade your fingertips press the grips back into the palm of your hand.

In both methods, knifemakers have assisted your thumb by adding studs or levers to the blade, or in

What's legal?

What is and isn't allowed as far as knives go is even more varied from state to state, state to federal, and between police and civilian. And to make matters worse, some of the terms used are so archaic as to be useless. First, is the matter of length. Your state probably has a maximum length allowed for a blade. Right around 3 or 3-1/2 seems to be normal. And that is enough blade to be useful without being handicapped, or scaring people because you're packing a big knife. In many jurisdictions, there is a big difference between fixed-blade and foldingknives. As a civilian here in Michigan, a fixed-blade is definitely a no-no. If you're hunting, have a license, and are wearing a fixed blade knife when you stop off at the local party store "up north" then you'll probably be overlooked. (The responding officer, if one is asked for, will tell you not to forget next time, put it away, and by the way, how's the hunting?) Do the same in the Detroit suburbs and there will be someone waiting for you when you walk out, waiting with other questions.

Michigan prohibits double-edged knives. So, when you order an expensive folder, not only must the blade be less than 3-1/2 inches but also you better ask for the model with just one cutting edge. Many States have similar restrictions. Some prohibit any locking blade. So, your folder had better be a penknife, and not a locking blade.

Some designs have even more prejudice against them. A spring-loaded blade, a switchblade, is viewed with horror in almost every state. And federal law restricts their manufacture for interstate commerce. I once knew a fellow who had an extensive collection of military-issue switchblades and gravity knives (the blade comes out of the handle via gravity when the button is pushed) from the U.S. and many foreign services. He couldn't show his collection to anyone, because even though he was a decorated airborne trooper with a combat jump to his credit, they were illegal.

But where it really gets crazy is in how the laws are written. Did you know it is illegal in some states to own or carry a snee, a dirk, or a stiletto? Look all you want, you will not find a definition for any of those in the compilations of state law in most jurisdictions. Except for 19th century legislators, and knife collectors (who won't agree on all the definitions, by the way) the definition of what they are depends on the judge who is presiding over the case. If he or she feels that any knife fits that name, so be it. And remember, your actions and demeanor will greatly influence the chain of events. If you are at the local airfreight shipping store, and happen to pull out and open a folder that has a blade a fraction too long in order to open a box, it is likely no one will know, care, comment or raise a fuss. If you're acting like a complete pain in the butt, waving a penknife with a legal-length blade, you'll be hauled off by the local police for "possessing a deadly weapon."

So, if you are going to carry a knife, here's the drill: Know the law, both the laws specifically concerning carry and possession of knives, and the law concerning self-defense and lethal force. Consult your attorney to make sure what you read is what the law actually says. Then, make sure you take a class to know what you're doing when you need to do it.

---

the case of Spyderco fabricating the blade with a large hole. The loop over the hole is your lever point for opening.

Clip location determines which "handedness" a knife is. Hold the knife folded, with the spine up and the tip away from you. A knife made for right-handed use has the clip on the right side. A left-handed knife has it on the left side. It is difficult to open a right-handed knife with your left hand. Some manufacturers, in some models, have the scales pre-drilled and tapped so you can switch the knife from right to left-handed. (Some even offer extra holes to change from tip-up to tip-down.) Modern synthetics are very tough. If you are skilled, or know a machinist, you can often unscrew the clip screws, and drill and tap the scales to change a right-handed knife to left. Or tip-down to tip-up. However, if you mess it up, or something breaks, you are not likely to get it replaced under warranty.

If you are carrying your knife with the idea of using it to get you out of a gun-grab struggle, it must be a left-handed knife that you can reach with your left hand. (Assuming you are right-handed, and your right hand is clamped on your gun, keeping it in its holster.) A right-handed knife will be tough to open with your left hand. And if you can't reach it with your left, it might as well be in your locker back at the station. Some officers carry two knives, one for the daily chores and emergencies, and one for getting the felon off their gun.

Fixed-blade knives also require thought as to size, design, length and method of carry. Let's talk about carry first. If you are a uniformed officer, and carry a fixed-blade knife, you'd better find a way to carry it discreetly. As I pointed out before, a whopping big "survival" knife lashed to your belt is bound to raise comments. After a few citizen complaints, your Sergeant or Shift Supervisor will want to have a talk with you. Special operations team members do not have such worries. You and the team are standing there with rifles, submachineguns, shotguns, body armor and web gear, grenades and ballistic shields. Who's going to even notice what kind of knife you're carrying? (I would, but that's my job.) So most team members carry fixed blades in BDUs or web gear. The most popular locations are on the belt and on the front of the vest. The belt is handy, out of the way, and traditional. The only location to consider is on the strong side and behind the holster. You can even use some 550 cord to keep it close to the holster, and get it out of the way when you sit down. The bad place to carry it on your belt is in front of the holster. It seems convenient, but it is dangerous. If you trip and fall the knife is in front, and covers a part of the body that folds. It would be easy for the knife to flip away from your belt, and be in the way as you fall. Your body weight will drive the tip of the knife into your thigh, through the sheath unless it is super-tough like Kydex. Even if you have a Kydex sheath, and the knife doesn't stab you in the thigh, you will have the handle forcefully driven into your abdomen or ribs as the sheath hits your thigh. You will at the very least be badly bruised, and could even suffer internal bleeding.

The other location is on the vest. One worry is that falling could injure you. Unlike on your waist, where the knife can pivot away from you, or your bending at the waist, the knife on the vest can't pivot. At least, not if it is properly attached. Vest location leads to questions concerning point-up, point-down, or horizontal carry. The point-up method is way cool, and prone to loss of the knife. The point-down method requires that you lift the knife, perhaps past your shoulder, to remove it. Horizontal precludes loss, injury, and is an easier draw than point-down.

Serration or not?

The discovery/invention of the serrated blade was a great improvement in cutting ability. For tough, fibrous items like rope or plastic, serrated blades work much better than plain blades. So much so that some users prefer a blade that is serrated along its full length. Others prefer a serrated section for use when they need it.

There are two kinds of tests: Usability/durability, and test to failure. Since I do not like abusing and destroying fine tools, (and I really can't borrow items, test them to failure or destruction, and then send them back broken) I didn't abuse them and test them to failure. What is a "test to failure" kind of test? How does clamping the first inch of a blade in a vise and then seeing how far you can flex it before it breaks sound to you? That's what I thought. If I was representing a department or military unit adopting a knife, I'd certainly buy five of each of the likely candidates and apply that test. I'd also give all passing grades to knives that withstood up to 200 pounds without permanently bending or breaking.. Another test would be to hammer the spine of the knife to drive the blade through a difficult object. Or hammer the butt of it to drive the point into something hard. Other than finding out which knives will survive, the test proves little. One test that can be informative (but just as expensive as the others) is to see how much force a folding blade lock can hold. An unlocked or broken-lock blade can cut you, sometimes severely. (One of the two times I've been cut, was due to lock failure.) But again, getting five expensive folders just so I can subject the locks to weight and impact testing is expensive. Better yet, ask the manufacturer what tests he subjected his design to before embarking on production. If the answer is "none" perhaps you should move on. The big name makers are all sensitive to lock failure (hey, they use knives too) and make their locks as robust as possible.

Blade material

Steel rules. A knife blade must be hard enough to stand up to the rigors of cutting, but not so hard it easily chips or breaks. For the last few millennia, the material of choice has been iron or steel. For some applications, there are other materials. Divers and those special operations personnel who spend a lot of time in the water have started using Titanium. It has the virtues of very slow rate of corrosion, and non-conductivity. If you happen to leave it wet it won't rust, and if you happen to be cutting through something electrified, you won't get shocked. For the rest of us, the expense of Titanium is too great to make the lack of rust and electrical conductivity appealing. Appealing, yes, but not enough to reach into our pocket and buy one. Other metals aren't hard enough (bronze, for example) and some are too hard and thus brittle. A tungsten carbide blade would be harder than sin, hold an edge forever, probably chip too quickly, and be hellishly expensive to make. No, steel rules, with various alloying elements in it to change the hardness, flexibility, and ability to deal with wear. Steel manufacturers spend a lot of time, money and effort testing alloys and developing heat treatment methods. If you are a manufacturer of any product, not just knives, you have an almost overwhelming choice of alloys from which to select. There are some that all knifemakers seem to use, and specialty alloys that each individual maker selects. Steel is produced from iron by introducing carbon, and controlling the grain structure of the iron and carbon in the forging and heat-treating process. Additional elements used to alloy steel, for corrosion resistance, hardness or other properties include chromium, cobalt, copper, manganese, molybdenum, nickel, phosphorus, silicon, tungsten and vanadium. The current common selections in steel for knives include, but are not limited to:

Stainless

154CM The problem with most stainless steel is that by the time you alloy enough nickel and chromium with the iron to make it truly stainless, you have an alloy too soft to hold an edge for long. 154 has a high chromium content (14 percent), no nickel, and the grain and heat treatment add toughness to its edge-holding ability

440C A classic stainless, with a higher chromium content than 154CM (16-18 percent) and no nickel, high corrosion resistance at a slight loss of edge-holding ability.

H1 A chromium and nickel stainless (14 percent and 7percent respectively), with very high corrosion resistance and good edge-holding ability. Proper heat treatment alters the grain of the steel, making it harder, tougher, or both.

Carbon

The non-stainless alloys. In the old days we used to select knives with "spring steel" for the blade. Now blades are made with tool steel, for superior edge holding, corrosion resistance and abrasion resistance.

D2 A tool steel with a high carbon content, some chromium and a trace of nickel.

M2 A high-speed steel, commonly used in machining before the use of carbides and ceramics became common. Very tough, shrugged off heat in machining (thus its use in an earlier age) and will hold an edge very well. It has no corrosion resistance.

AUS8 A medium-carbon, high-chromium steel with traces of seven of the 10 alloying elements, AUS 8 is an Austenitic steel, with a controlled grain structure, good edge-holding and slight corrosion resistance for a non stainless alloy.

ATS55 A medium-carbon, high-chromium steel with traces of five alloying elements, it can be heat treated to a hardness that few other alloys can attain. It has very good edge-holding ability.

Damascus A method, not an alloy. Damascus steel is formed when two or more pieces of differing alloys are heated, forged into a sheet or bar, then folded and forged again. Also known as "folded steel." Damascus blades end up with the properties of both its component, so you can have a blade tough as the spring steel alloy and as hard as the tool steel alloy of which it is composed. It is very expensive and yet distinctive once the finished surface has been acid-etched to differentiate the component alloys.

Grip materials

You have to hold your knife, and in the old days we had two choices: wood or leather. Now synthetics rule the roost, and the choices also include colors.

Micarta The oldest of the new, Micarta comes in two types: paper and linen. In both, layers of the selected material are bonded with epoxy (think plywood) and when cured, machined to shape. Very stable, durable and can be dyed.

Carbon Fiber Woven layers of carbon strands are bonded with epoxy. Very durable, non-conductive and very light.

Epoxied wood Under enough pressure, epoxy can be forced right through the grain and pores of wood. The result is somewhat heavy, but very durable, and shows the grain of the wood.

The latest grips or scales appear in a dizzying array of synthetics, with a veritable alphabet soup of designations and names. (Steel makers and their alloys have nothing on the plastics industry. After all, you can trap stiffening materials in plastic, which you can't do in steel.)

G10® Compressed epoxy and woven glass composite is very strong and impervious to most solvents.

Noryl GTX® A glass-filled plastic that's lightweight and stiff.

Valox® A reinforced resin with the enhanced ability to accept dyes, so while many grips that are black are other materials, the ones in bright colors are often Valox or something like it.

Zytel® Lightweight glass-filled nylon is both durable and economical.

Kraton® This is a rubbery polymer, for non-skid grips and softer handles for comfort.

Kydex® An acrylic/PVC that has the virtue of molding into sheets, it is used for sheaths. Very durable, very cut-resistant, the sheaths are highly unlikely to be punctured and cut the owner.

For the book I subjected the blades to usability and durability testing. First I tested each to see if it would shave hair. For testing, I considered wood, rope, cardboard, paper and seat belt material as suitable materials. But what I used for long-term testing was garden hose. The genesis of the test was my failure at preventive maintenance last winter. I inadvertently left the garden hose out for the

Hey, I start a test, I don't bail on it. Cutting garden hose is lot more work than expected, but doesn't dull an edge very much.

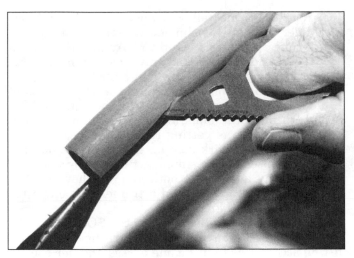

Here is the Kershaw cutting hose.

Michigan winter. This spring, the oldest section would not hold water. Stiff, brittle and hard to handle, it was useless as hose. But it was hard to cut. Oh-ho! So, to test the cutting edge durability of each knife, I sat down with a wooden backer and sliced short sections off the hose. Once I'd cut 100 times with each blade, I then tested it against a section of seat belt webbing. (After all, that is what we all say they'll be used for, right?) All except the Benchmade Rescue Hook. The hook is too small to slice off sections, so what I did was take the cut-off sections and slice them lengthwise with the hook. (while holding the hose with a pair of pliers, to keep my fingers out of the way.) Then, I tried shaving again. I wore each to the range for practice, and in training classes. I wore the folders daily, sitting and writing and going about my daily routine. I also tested the folders by opening them 50 times each day, until I was quite adept at (and thoroughly sick of) opening each. My enthusiasm for the hose-cutting test waned pretty quickly. Garden hose seems like some stupidly prosaic and inoffensive material, but when you go to cut it you find out it is pretty damn tough stuff. Even a razor-sharp blade has to be powered through. You aren't slicing bread. A cutting session would leave me dripping with sweat and quitting early before I got so tired I made a mistake and cut myself. While the hose is remarkably difficult to cut, it is not very abrasive, so cutting didn't take the edge off the blades. What it did was remind me to test some things before planning elaborate testing sessions, and to think before shooting my mouth off. But, the "need to know" over-rides an author's comfort, so I persisted and gained the knowledge.

My impressions of the knives, and the test results, follow.

Tactical Folders

Benchmade 910SBT Stryker

This one has a 154CM blade, the book spec reads 3.7 inches, but mine measures exactly 3.5" (good for

my home state of Michigan). The "S" is for the Comboedge, and the BT is the Benchmade proprietary BT2 black Teflon blade coating. The Comboedge is 1-3/8 inches of serrated blade, with a two small and one large serration scallop design. The blade is .126 inches thick, with a section of that thickness extending out almost to the modified tanto point. The serrations give superior cutting ability on tough or fibrous materials such as webbing, rope or net. The scales are G10, black, and the clip is on the outside for a right-hand tip down carry. The 154CM blade is hardened to 58-60 on the Rockwell C scale. If you need more wear or hardness, you can have it with M2 steel, hardened to 60-62 RC. You give up corrosion resistance to gain that extra hardness. The grips and Titanium liners are held together (and the blade secured in the mechanism) with torx head screws. The blade lever is a knurled wheel screwed to the top edge of the blade with another torx screw. The liner lock snaps into place with an audible click, and keeps the blade in place. The rear of the blade at the lock is machined on an angle, enough to let the lock snap into place but not enough to let the blade cam the lock out under a load.

It is sharp. Right out of the box I had no problem slicing suspended paper, cardboard cartons simply fell apart, and the hair on my forearm was easily shaved. Benchmade has a lifetime sharpening policy. Ship it back and they'll sharpen the plain edge free, check it out, and ship it back. Your only costs are the shipping charges.

In use, I found the Stryker rode easily in a pocket either in street clothes or uniform trousers, and would slide right in place in any web pocket or pouch designed for a single-stack pistol magazine. On the SOE Gear CQB vest, I could even fit the Stryker and a 1911 magazine in a pistol pocket. An alternate method of carry was to clip it to the hook-and-loop panel under a rifle magazine flap. One location that was very convenient was on the side panel tucked right behind the rifle pouch. By sliding it through the webbing used to secure a side pouch, the Stryker was out of the way but accessible to both hands. The only problem was getting it back. Once out, I either had to take the vest

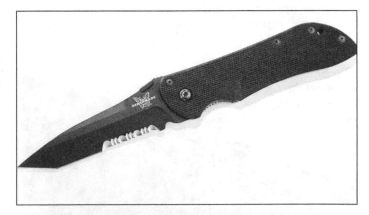

The Benchmade Model 910, the first to arrive and the one most often found clipped to my pocket.

The Benchmade 910LE-Trainer, an essential tool for learning how to handle and use a knife without becoming a mass of scars. And a great tool for adjusting web gear.

off, or have someone else put the knife back. The webbing is sewn so tightly I couldn't get the clip through without a struggle. Good for security, bad for "reholstering." Of course, if I need it in an emergency I have it. Once I don't need it, I can fold and drop the knife in a pocket until I can properly re-stow it.

The Stryker sliced 100 times through the garden hose without blade problems, (just lots of work on my part) and easily handled the seat belt webbing afterwards. It would shave at the start, but not cleanly. I think the difficulty in shaving was just the relative thickness of the blade. Once through the hose, it was slightly less able to shave, but still plenty sharp for anything else.

910T Stryker L.E. Trainer

If you want to get good, you have to practice. But how to practice with a razor-sharp knife? You can easily cut yourself learning to manipulate it, and training partners are very hard to come by if you are using live blades. Enter the Trainer version. Built just like the regular Stryker (and similar training models also mimic their parent knife) the trainer has red grips, to identify it as being dull. Well, dull isn't the right word. The blade is drilled through with three large holes, and the edge and tip are blunted so they can't cut. You can practice manipulation to your heart's content, knowing you can't cut yourself. You can also practice on a dummy, or with a partner, and not cause injury. Before you scoff at the idea, and

The Emerson Wave. The hook catches your pocket edge, and flips the blade open.

expense, let me tell you about my friend Chris Eder. He is a Benchmade dealer, and owns and runs Northwest Gun & Ammo Supply in Redford, Michigan, my old gunsmithing/stomping grounds. He had a customer pick up his new Benchmade folder, and in the process of admiring it and putting it in his pocket, used his leg to fold the blade back. A few minutes later, when he was getting ready to leave, someone noticed a dark spot on his thigh. He had cut himself in the simple act of putting his knife away, and hadn't noticed. (Yes, they are that sharp.) So, do you need a trainer version? After hearing that tale, I knew I did.

In the course of working with the SOE Gear CQB vest, trying different equipment arrangements and fitting accessories to it, I came across another use for the 910T: assembly paddle. If you are trying to fit straps, 550 cord, and pouch attachment webbing through the webbing attachment straps, you may find stuffing them through is work. The blunt tip and edges of the training blade are perfect. Now I will be the first to admit that that are less-expensive tools for the job (like tongue depressors and Popsicle sticks) but if you have the training blade (and you should if you have the knife) then it is the perfect tool. With a 910T and a Leatherman tool, you can assemble or re-fit just about any gear you own.

Obviously, cutting anything with a training blade is an exercise in futility. It wouldn't cut, and it mustn't cut, so I didn't bother trying.

Emerson Commander

Remember the comment before about those who prefer a flowing design, like that of the Elves? Well, the Commander has just that. The blade is 3.75 inches long, with serrations along the inner third of the edge. The blade thickness is .128 inches and extends half the width and almost out to the tip. The rear of the handle is ribbed for a non-slip hold, and the rear of the blade comes up for two reasons: grip and opening. The rear of the blade behind the

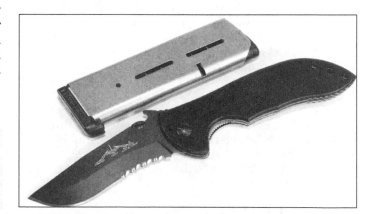

The Emerson Commander, a great-looking, sharp and extremely durable knife. The hook on top is "The Wave", the opening feature that lets you open the knife by hooking the wave on the edge of your pocket. It takes some getting used to.

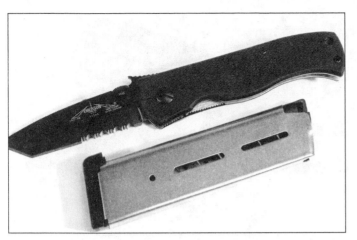

The Emerson CQB, the toughest and heaviest-duty tactical folder I've laid hands on. Were it any tougher I'd say it wasn't a pocketknife, but something to secure to your tactical vest.

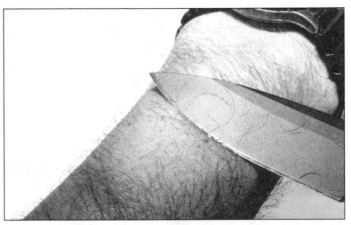

A sharp knife should shave hair. After all, that is what a razor is, right?

opening stud is the Emerson Wave. The hook of the Wave offers a fast-open feature. By hooking it on the edge of your pocket as you extract the knife you can flick the blade open. It is quite fast once you get the hang of it. It is also hard on your clothing. I can see blue jeans standing up to it long-term, but dress trousers aren't going to last long. The blade is 1-1/8 inches wide, and comes sharp. I mean sharp. Unlike the old days, where we'd get knives with something of an edge on them, and have to sharpen them ourselves (and some of us never got the hang of it) modern knifemakers ship knives that are sharp. As in hair-shaving sharp. Slicing hose was less work, and the edge would still shave once I was done. It made ribbons of the seatbelt material.

Emerson CQC-7

The CQC-7 is on the other end of the design spectrum: Orc-like. The tip design is a tanto or modified tanto, almost a straight section of steel with a tip that is just angled up from the cutting edge. Smaller than the Commander, with a blade only 3.25 inches long, and only 7/8 inches wide, the CQC-7 is still plenty capable of getting the job done. As with the Commander, the CQC-7 has the Emerson Wave, and non-slip serrations on the back. The edge is serrated for the inner third and had a bolted-on thumbstud just in front of the Wave. The blade thickness is .127 inches. The edge on the Emerson CQC-7 is a chisel grind. Instead of both sides of the blade being ground to the centerline (and edge), on a chisel ground blade only one side is ground down to the cutting edge, and the back is left flat. A chisel blade is more durable than a knife ground or hollow ground blade, and one thing Ernest Emerson wants on a blade is durability. A chisel-ground blade requires a slightly different sharpening technique, so if you get an Emerson with a chisel edge, make sure you learn and follow the Emerson sharpening method.

As with the Commander, the CQC-7 has a point-up side clip, so you don't have to pivot the knife as

You can see the cut in the back lock, to prevent the blade from being unlocked when you grasp it.

you extract and open it. But you must remember to slide your thumb all the way down the scale before extracting it or you won't be able to open it.

The chisel edge of the CQC-7 made it more work to cut the hose. The edge did not appreciably dull, but after the struggle of getting the thick, chisel edge through the hose 100 times I was ready for a tall cool drink and a nap. Afterwards it had not appreciably dulled, and would cut the seatbelt material with abandon.

Spyderco Delica

If the Stryker and CQC-7 are angular and the "look" you desire in a knife, the Spyderco Delica might seem a bit effete. You'd be wrong. The 3-inch blade is plenty long enough to deal with most anything you'll encounter, and the lines of the blade and handle would please those who favor flowing arcs and delicate proportions. Made of VG-10 steel, the Delica was, along with the Benchmade Nimravus, the sharpest knife I tested. The smooth portion of the blade (2 inches of the total blade length are serrated) shaved hair off my now nearly bald forearm with a single stroke. At .099 inches thick, the blade is tough enough to stand up to hard use, but delicate enough that you don't feel like you're trying to cut things with the sharpened edge of a thick slab of steel. The Spyderco trademark (besides the serrations) is the opening lever. Instead of bolting a knob or protrusion to the blade, Sypderco uses a large loop drilled through the widened blade. The result is a slightly flatter package that doesn't offer a point of abrasion in your pocket. The grips are FRN, molded in a single piece. The lock is a back lock, rather than a liner lock, and the locking access features a "dent" in the lock lever. Called the David Boye

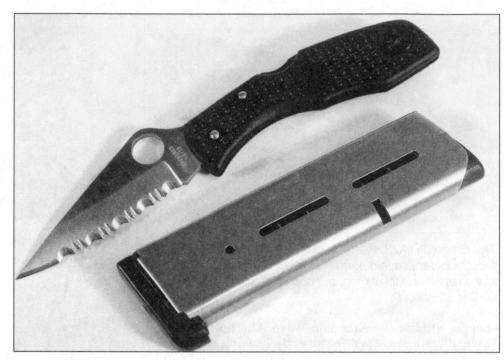

The Spyderco Delica is smaller than the others, but the blade cuts out of proportion to its size. For slicing through things, the all-serrated edge is great. The loop is the Spyderco trademark and image, used to open the blade instead of a stud.

dent, it reduces the possibility of your hand unlocking the blade when you grip the knife. The Delica rides point up, and the clip can be switch from right- to left-hand carry, but cannot be changed to point-down carry. The Delica carries like a lightweight, but is not at all a lightweight in performance.

The serrated edge of the Spyderco made sawing through a hose a relative piece of cake. By the time I got to the Delica, I was resigned to my Herculean labors, and found the serrated edge made the job a lot easier. I'm sure if the other blades had been all-serrated they'd have cut easier, too. For a small knife, and light construction, the serrations made it cut on this

particular test like a much bigger knife. Afterwards, it would slice n' dice seatbelt material easily.

Kershaw Whirlwind

The Kershaw line includes a series of folders that are known as their Speed Safe spring-assist designs. Unlike switchblades, which automatically open when you press a button or a lever, the spring-assist knives open as regular folders do, by levering the blade open via a stud. The difference is, once the Kershaw blade has opened past a certain point, the spring finishes opening the blade. Why would you want a spring-assist blade? (Or for that matter, an automatic?) In many emergencies, you may only have one hand free

The Kershaw Whirlwind, a spring-assisted opening blade. While not an automatic, it does pop open once you've pressed the blade far enough in its opening arc to let the spring help you.

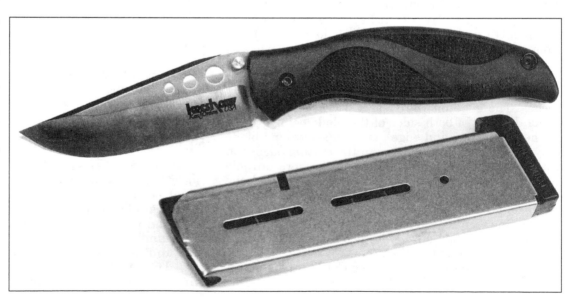

to open the knife. Automatics are useful in the military arena in airborne or waterborne operations. Stuck in a tree, a parachutist may only have one hand free to open a knife and cut the rigging. An extreme anxiety-inducing situation (and one I have not had the pleasure of being in) is being tangled in gear or rigging at the exit of an aircraft, or a sinking boat or chopper. In the former, the Jumpmaster or Crew Chief may be pushing and kicking to get the man free, but a knife to cut gear away is always useful. And if the craft is sinking, cutting your gear off may be the only way to free yourself. In a law enforcement situation, if you have one hand clamped on your sidearm to prevent its being grabbed, you only have one hand free to get your knife out.

The Whirlwind has a 3-1/4-inch 440A stainless blade, with a smooth edge. The blade is .120 inches thick, with the thickness going out 2-1/2 inches of the blade length. The edge is hollow-ground. The handle is Polyamide, black, molded in one piece. The clip is point-down, and the liner lock is set up for a right-handed user. The Whirlwind is one of the Ken Onion series of knife designs, and there are several models that closely fit the size and pattern of the Whirlwind, so if you want, for example, a blackened blade, or a reversible clip, one of the other models may be for you. The Speed Safe design is patented, and built into many of the Ken Onion designs. One, the Boa, uses a protrusion on the blade to let you use your index finger instead of your thumb to open, and even has a lock to prevent opening in your pocket. As a quick way to open, the Speed Safe design has a lot to offer. The big question many have, is "Is it a switchblade?" That depends. Under federal Law it is not. So, you aren't risking a federal felony by owning one. (Automatics, or switchblades, are Federally controlled, and allowed only, as far as the Feds are concerned, to active duty military personnel and law enforcement officers.) However (and there's always a "however" isn't there?) local laws vary. In some jurisdictions, the way the law is written, the Speed Safe is verboten. And in others, a Judge may have ruled that regardless of mechanical design, in his or her opinion it is a switchblade. A Judge did just that here in Michigan. The decision was overturned in the Appeals Court. So, if you want one, you have to do some homework. Check up on the legality before you get one. One way would be to check with a knife specialty store (hopefully one that carries Kershaw knives) or a gun shop that leans towards tactical gear, and ask them. If you get the word "yes" then be an upright customer and buy from them. After all, they did the work that gave you the information. Reward them for their extra efforts.

The Whirlwind as it came out of the box was not the sharpest knife received. It required a bit more effort to shave hair than some of the other. However, it sharpened easily and once worked over a bit took hair off without effort. The opening was a bit stiff at first, taking more force to cam past the spring point than other knives did to that point in their arc. Once I'd opened it a few hundred times it smoothed out, although it still takes a bit more force to get started than other knives do. The grip is nicely shaped, and the overall design is definitely in the "Elven" as opposed to "Orcish" design camp.

Cutting hose was just as much work as the others, and afterwards it easily cut the seatbelt material.

Benchmade 520

Just as I was wrapping things up, a box arrived from Benchmade. Inside was a prototype, the 520. The 520 is an axis lock without any springs. The axis lock is sturdy, positive, and accessible to both hands. Right or left handed, your thumb can reach the lock. The axis lock has until now been used only on the automatic blades. However, under Federal Law automatics are available to law enforcement officers and active-duty military personnel. All others need not apply. What Benchmade did was make their automatic without the spring, and more importantly, without any provision for installing the spring. The axis lock mechanism is very smooth in opening, and the lock snaps into place easily. The 520 has aluminum scales, and is a bit wider than the

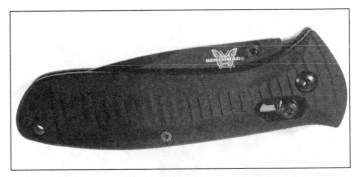

The Benchmade 520 prototype sent me. The scales are machined aluminum, and the lock is the button you see on the side.

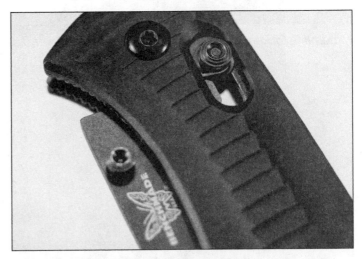

Closed, the spring-loaded lock lever acts to keep the blade closed, so you don't have to worry about reaching into your pocket.

synthetic-scaled knives. As for durability, with a steel frame and aluminum scales I'm not sure you could harm it. In bulk it is a bit thicker than others (I'm thinking of the 920 in particular) and I find it is just a bit too thick for daily trouser carry. However, tucked in the waistband behind a duty belt it disappears and can ride there all day long without a

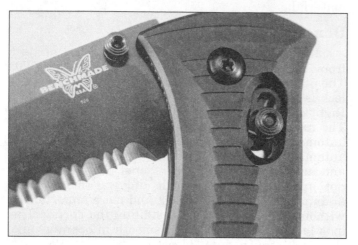

As you open the blade, the lock button cams back, then snaps forward to lock the blade in place.

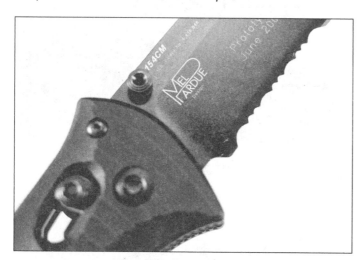

When it is locked open, the button snaps forward.

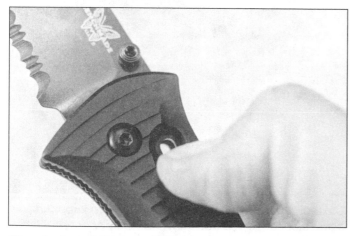

To unlock, pull the button back.

problem. One feature I particularly like is that the clip can be swapped from side to side. The scales and frame are pre-drilled so you can remove the clip and change sides, making it capable of carry for the left hand. The blade on the 520 sent to me is a drop-point of 154CM steel, 3.5 inches long. This one is a winner.

Fixed blades

While at a recent tactical officers conference, I had occasion to watch a number of teams practice bus assaults and other drills. Many had fixed-blade knives attached to their gear. One team in particular had every member so equipped, and the smallest knife was almost a machete. Why? "Hollow-core doors." When they deal with buildings that are cheaply constructed, they have found that a big fixed-blade knife is all they need to get inside. Cheap hollow-core doors, the doors on trailers and similar construction all yield to the prying force a big knife can generate. And if they are faced with an interior door in such construction, a sledge hammer is often too much; too much to swing and too much for the door. Those of you who have never had the "pleasure" of swinging a sledge against a cheap door, and having the hammer puncture the door without opening it, can relate. You can hurt yourself, if you are braced for the impact against a real door. You simply warn the suspects inside that something is up. And then you have to get the sledge out of the door, and still get the door open. So, for many jobs a big fixed-blade can be perfect. And after all, when in raid gear, you never know what you might need. Despite the weight you have to pack, a big knife can be a comforting possession. That said, my friend Ed Mohn of NIPAS EST tells me that the team equipment requirements in the beginning mandated a fixed-blade knife.

"We all carried big knives, bowies, tantos and others," said Mohn. "We found we never needed them, and when we had all stopped carrying them because of the weight we dropped the requirement. Leathermans do what we need done. Those, and a good folder."

Why not a big knife? Suppose your area of operations is The Projects. Every building is concrete block or poured concrete. All doors are steel fire doors, hung in steel frames set in the concrete walls. How much use will a big knife be? A big sledgehammer may not be good enough. So, whether a team carries a fixed-blade knife, and how big it is, depends on where you are, what you do, and how much weight you're willing to pack. Me, I tend to favor carring a fixed-blade knife AND folders. But then, I'm a firm believer in two lights, two guns and extra ammo, too.

140 Nimravus

The Nimravus is a larger knife than its 4.5-inch blade would seem to promise. The handles are textured G10, and is of full-tang design and construction, that is, the chunk of steel that is the blade continues the full length and width of the handles. The steel is left "proud" of the handles, so you can feel the steel regardless of your grip. The spine rises from the grip, and has machined

The Benchmade Nimravus, with a full tang (all steel under the grips) and made of M2 steel, cuts like everything is butter. (Well, except for garden hose.)

The sheath lock holds the blade in place. To remove the blade, lever your thumb against the lock. Once it opens, you..

Remove the blade. The lever locks against the thumb grooves on the spine of the blade.

serrations on the spine for a non-slip grip for your thumb. On the finger side, the grip and steel have a pronounced finger groove to keep your forefinger on the handle and off the edge. The blade is 1.3 inches wide at its base, tapering to 1.125 inches at the start of the smooth cutting edge. The blade is .116 inches thick, extending out nearly to the point. At the rear is a lanyard hole. The model I have, the 140HSSR, comes with an M2 blade, Comboedge and BT2 coating. The first thing I can tell you is that it is sharp. When I opened the box, I tested it by shaving some hair off my forearm. Using just the tip end of the blade, one pass had a one-inch square shaved clean as a razor. The catalog description is "modified tanto" but the blade shape looks to me almost like a spear-point and almost like a drop-point that would have a multitude of uses.

The sheath of the 140 is Kydex, made of two pieces riveted together and probably impossible to drive the knife through. (An essential requirement for anyone in an Airborne unit, who rappels, or who will be wearing it during strenuous activity.) The belt loop is reversible and removable, and the sheath body has lashing holes and a webbing loop so you can attach it just about anywhere. On the top is a thumb-lever lock and on the bottom is a drain hole. The thumb lever lock latches onto the serrations on the spine, and keeps the knife in place almost regardless of the force applied. Even with the lock unlocked (press it away from the blade to unlock) the knife clicks into its locked position in the sheath. The belt loop is removable by unscrewing two torx head screws and removing the loop. With the loop you can attach the sheath to belts up to 2 inches wide. With it off, the sheath lays flat on whatever web gear you've secured it to. If there isn't a convenient web strap, the holes let you use 550 cord to lash the sheath to web gear. Two locations I have found convenient on the SOE Gear CQB vest are the left side horizontal over the rifle pouches, or the right side vertical next the rifle pouch. By "over" I mean on the front of the pouches, using the hook and loop patches as the lashing points. The closed flaps protect he knife, but the handle is accessible. When the flaps are opened to grab magazines, the knife stays put. On the right, the webbing straps offer lash points for the sheath, the vertical carry is accessible to both hands, and the pouches fore and aft protect the knife. There up on the vest, above the belt, the knife is not in a position to cause injury during a fall.

Cutting the hose was a lot easier than other blades, but still work. Even though I was done before my coffee had a chance to cool, and I didn't have to pause and rest once in the 100 cuts, cutting was still work. The blade was not noticeably diminished in sharpness after the test, and cut seat belt webbing with abandon, and still shaved hair with a single pass. Unless I worked in or around water (assigned to the Power Squadron, for example) I'd go past stainless and settle on M2 as my blade material of choice.

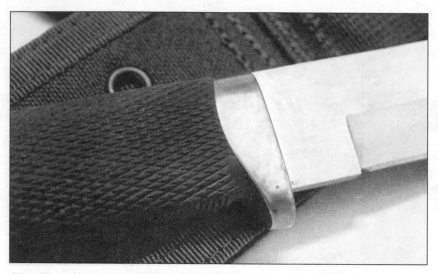

The Cold Steel Tanto grip is molded rubber with a checkered pattern.

Cold Steel Tanto

One of the original knives with the tanto point (at least as best I can recall, having gotten mine many years ago) the Cold Steel Tanto is a knife big enough to be used as a prybar. Mine is the regular steel, and my brother's is the San Mai laminated. At 5.75 inches long, 1.1 inches wide and .187 inches thick, the Tanto is a big, heavy blade capable of prying open almost anything. It is 11.25 inches long in total, with a brass endcap with a hole through it for a lanyard. The Cold Steel catalog delights in showing the abuse such a knife can take and still function. I have no intention of recreating such abuse. First, they already did it. Second, it voids the warranty. And third, it is

dangerous to do things like clutch it as an icepick and punch a knife through a steel drum.

I don't know if the edge comes hair-shaving sharp, as mine is many years old, has been resharpened many times, and I didn't try shaving with it back then. It has a smooth edge, no serrations, and the grip is a moulded rubber over the shank and filler.

One thing I didn't like about the Cold Steel was the sheath; Leather. Yes, leather is classic, but I want to be protected from my own knife when I'm doing such exciting aerobic exercises as falling down stairs, wrestling with perps or getting hit by cars. I set it aside for a long time until I could score a suitable scabbard, and I found one. Blackhawk makes two of their Airborne Deluxe sheaths: one for a 5.5-inch blade and one for a 7-inch blade. Outside they are made of Blackhawks NyTaneon nylon, and inside they are Talonflex. The Talonflex is a hard synthetic much like Kydex. It is puncture-proof. The outside also has a utility pouch, to hold a stone or other tools. A very useful combo is to pack a big fixed blade knife in the sheath, and a Leatherman in the outside pouch. As for attachment options, the back of the Blackhawk sheath has more methods than you can shake a stick at. There are four hook-and-loop fastener straps on the back, and a leg tie-down off the tip. The Airborne Deluxe can be worn on the belt, a vest, rigged to web gear, or with the optional drop strap on the thigh. On sheaths, blade length is all. The 7-inch version will

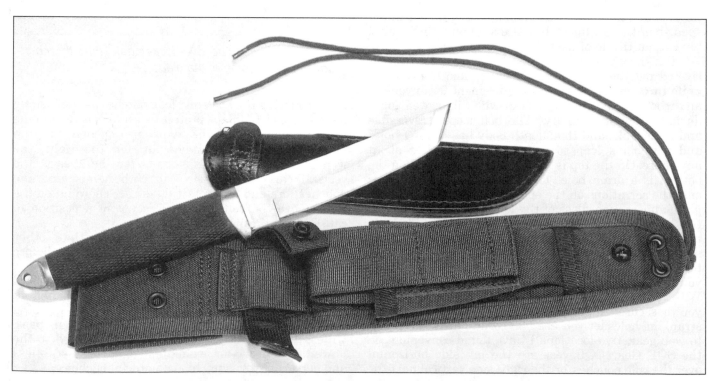

My Colt Steel Tanto, with its original sheath and the Blackhawk Industries Airborne sheath.

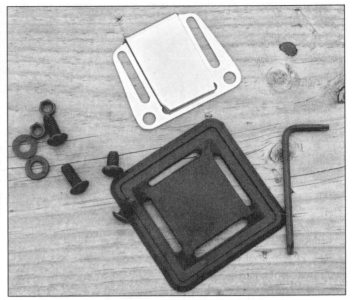

If you're going to attach your knife to something, you sometimes need hardware. Benchmade offers these and more.

The Benchmade Rescue 520 rides in the top flap of the SOE gear vest, clipped to the flap. If you open the flap for the rifle magazines, the 520 will still be attached. Ditto if the flap is folded up and secured to the Velcro above.

Sometimes you need more than one knife. The Leatherman Wave is in the pistol magazine pouch of the SOE Gear CQB vest, with a Benchmade above it.

accept the standard K-Bar, while the 5.5-inch one holds the standard issue U.S. Air Force survival knife. Once I had this, I could use my Cold Steel Tanto once again. The securing strap is adjustable, and the snap easy to secure or open. With the adjustable strap, and the 7-inch length, almost any blade will fit.

Attachment options

Unless you are wedded to 550 cord, there are extra options for attaching your knife or knives to your belt or gear. The Rescue hook can be bolted to the belt hook, which can also attach to the proper-sized pack lash tab. You can use an existing lash tab, or a four-sided belt/webbing tab. Just bolt the securing hook to the Rescue Hook sheath with (provided) bolts, and then click it on. The Nimravus sheath can be bolted to a Blade-Tech Tek-Lok, and then clipped to a belt, webbing, vest or pack. The Tek-Lok is large enough to

secure to a uniform belt or military pistol belt. Modern securing options have removed most of the old duct tape and electrical tape approaches to keeping your gear on you and off the ground. One approach I'm going to consult with my fellow gunsmiths on is to custom-machine aluminum plates, then drill and tap them. Slide the plates through the webbing on a tactical vest, and then bolt the sheath right to the plate. The old sheath of my Tanto is leather, and were I to use it on the job I'd acquire a kydex sheath for it from Blade-Tech. With impervious kydex as a material to chose from, no way would I continue using a leather sheath. With the Blade-Tech sheath I'd carry it on the belt, right behind my sidearm holster.

In addition to a hook for rescuing, the Rescue hook also has a notch milled to turn the valve on an oxygen bottle.

The Benchmade Rescue hook, ready to be attached to something.

One aspect you must take into consideration is access. If your knife is handy and easy to grab, and comes out easily when you snatch it, it will also do that for the offender. Pay attention to anyone who attempts to lay their hands on you, for they may find that your web gear is more than just a convenient handle for a takedown, they may find your knife.

The Specialty Blade:

Rescue hook

Remember the main use that police officers said they needed a knife for? Cutting seat belts? Well, Benchmade makes a cutting implement for just that. I hesitate to call it a knife, because the cutting surface is guarded such that it can almost only be used for cutting webbing, rope, seatbelts and the like. The Rescue Hook is a "Q" shaped chunk of 420HC stainless steel. The spine behind the hook has machined serrations for a non-slip grip. The hook is sharp (I made the mistake of sticking my fingertip in there to see just how much access there is. Not much access, but way sharp.) and will slice through seat belt webbing easily. The guarded edge prevents inadvertent harm (or undesired scaring) of the rescue subject. No one likes to see a big, serrated blade near their face while someone is trying to cut them free. With the Rescue Hook there is no worry of that. In addition to the hook, the tool has an oxygen bottle valve wrench built in, for EMT personnel, and a bottle opener. On the end is a slot for a lanyard. Should you wish, you can run a lanyard through it, and carry the Rescue Hook around your neck under your uniform or BDU blouse like dog tags. There is also a web belt pouch and a plastic neck sheath for carry. For the ultimate in one-location setups for your cutting needs, you can use the Benchmade attachment points on the Rescue Hook sheath and the Nimravus sheath to bolt them together and to

your vest or harness. One spot for either a big cutting tool and fighting knife, or your Rescue Hook. You won't fight off any attackers with the Rescue Hook (not even trying to use it as a brass knuckle) but if you are truly worried about getting someone out of a car (or cutting down a suicide victim quickly) then the Rescue Hook is just the tool you need.

And for those embarrassing moments at the precinct house when no one can find the sidecutters to cut off the cable ties used as disposable handcuffs? The Rescue Hook makes short work of them, with no risk at all of cutting the suspect. If you really do anticipate getting someone out of a car, you simply must have this tool on your belt or around your neck.

The hook sliced hose lengthwise with relative ease. Shaving is impossible, so I didn't try. If it ever dulls, (10 feet of hose cutting did not diminish its ability to handle seat belt webbing) the hook cutting edge is formed by a circular surface, and would be easy to sharpen with a round stone.

In all, the hose-cutting test proved to be a better test of my persistence than of the edge-holding ability of the blades. I had assumed that the rubber of the hose would be more abrasive than it turned out to be. All the knives tested passed it without a problem, and I have complete confidence that any of them could be called on to cut rope, webbing, hoses or cable ties as needed.

Care and maintenance

First of all, no maker is going to warranty a knife that you abuse. All knives are to be used as cutting tools. Using a knife as a pry bar, wrench, hammer or lever is not going to get you any sympathy or free repairs. "My dog chewed it" "My ex-wife threw it in the fire" or "I ran over it with my truck" are not going to suddenly make the warranty department break down and give you a new knife free. Using a knife as a chisel or punch risks breaking the tip, again not covered under anyone's warranty. And as for throwing it? You've been watching too many action movies. Damage caused by throwing is almost never covered.

Sometimes you need two blades. One for social occasions where observers can admire the engraving, and another for "social" occasions where you need to stay in one piece.

Keep your knife and sheath clean and dry. If you get it wet, muddy, bloodied or spill food on it, wash with a mild soap, warm water, and keep your fingers away from the edge while washing or drying it. You can probably run it through the dishwasher, but I'd ask each maker about a particular knife. Some handle materials may not like the experience. Keep your knife sharp. Use a proper stone, and sharpen by hand. Do not use a power wheel to sharpen a blade. It is far too easy to over-heat the edge, ruin the temper and make the knife essentially useless. (Oh, you can still sharpen a knife where the temper has been ruined. It just won't hold an edge very well, and may chip at the temper-loss area.) Do not disassemble a folder unless the manufacturer specifically gives the OK for it as a maintenance step. If you disassemble it, and can't get it back together, the manufacturer will charge you to reassemble it. If you break anything in the attempt, they will charge you for the new part.

What they will warranty is the edge. Benchmade and Spyderco will both re-sharpen your blade at no charge. All manufacturers will warranty their knives for defect in materials and workmanship. If you buy a knife with a specified blade material, and it just won't hold an edge, send it back. If it turns out the steel supplier shipped the wrong alloy, or someone on the shop floor grabbed the wrong stuff, you'll most likely get a replacement blade at no charge. But if you use your folder to pry the hubcaps off your car to change a flat, and break the tip, you'll only get laughed at if you ask for a new one. After all, you used a $150 high-tech tactical folder to remove the hubcaps, when the tire iron was right there? Were you crazy, or just showing off?

Get one or two. Carry them all the time. Get familiar with opening and closing them. And you'll always be prepared.

Chapter 19

First Aid

HOW MUCH IS enough? That depends. If you're a deputy on a department with a large rural area, making a raid on a meth lab tucked in an inaccessible spot near a National Forest, you're going to have to be packing a whole lot more gear than an Urban SWAT team bailing out of the team vehicle at the curb in front of the raided house. And regardless of which place it is, all of that gear will be carried on your back or on your belt. Part of that gear will be a lot of first aid stuff, since getting more once you're out there in the boonies won't be easy. Even in an urban environment, and if the vehicle is in sight, you must have the gear on you when you need it. Even when the vehicle is in sight, tactically it may as well be on the moon. During the Miami shootout, the FBI agents involved found out that the shotguns and body armor resting on the back seats of their vehicles were of no use. And worse yet, if someone has the vehicle covered with hostile fire, it is of no use to you except as a bullet magnet.

You need medical attention and supplies in two different categories, each with two different approaches: They are personal/environmental, and medical/trauma.

The supplies can be found in three levels of bags or pouches; 1) The personal treatment kit and the First Responder, 2) The range/tac team kit, and 3) The full-blown med kit, usually with the assigned EMS Technician or ER Nurse. In all three, the kit's existence is not protection, since training with the contents of the kit is needed in order for it to be of any use.

What do teams do for medical assistance when needed? Some do nothing some cross-train team members as EMS techs. I know of more than one department where the medical plan is this: If a team member needs medical attention, they apply a bandage and compress to the wound, bundle him or her into the back seat of a waiting squad car, and drive to the nearest suitable medical facility. (I am not making this up.) The better teams have a pre-planned route. In their defense, the lack of medical preparation is not an oversight on their part; parsimonious elected officials and administrations force it on them. At the other extreme, I know of teams with fully cross-trained members who are both fully trained and certified EMS techs or ER Nurses, and state-certified badge-carrying law enforcement officers. (That only takes from two to three years of schooling to accomplish.) In-between the levels of preparation go from letting the area EMS authority know there will be a team on a raid at a given location and time, to having an ambulance or EMS truck with a med team waiting down the block, who then drive off when the operation is done. What your team does depends on a lot of things. It depends on the budget. It depends on the desires (and sometimes whims) of higher authority. And it depends on the willingness to accept risk of the team members. If you are left on your own, you must balance the risk of not having any training or gear against the risk of being sued for having it, and not having enough of it, or not having the right training.

One step in the right direction to getting your team more medical protection is to join the

Your basic EMS med kit. (Courtesy Blackhawk Industries)

A personal first aid pouch is simple: load it with what you need, attach it to your gear, and forget about it until you need it.

International Tactical EMS Association. You can find out how other teams have managed their EMS needs and planning, and get information to use to get your department or agency moving in the right direction. You can also, through them, attend classes and training to augment your own skills and equipment, should you decide that the risk of taking on the responsibility is worth preventing (possibly) the avoidable death of a team member due to your training.

Personal/Environmental

I've heard more than one person refer to the personal bag as a "snivel kit" so I have to think the term is some sort of military shorthand or slang. Personally, I don't think keeping myself from bleeding on expensive equipment, getting infected, or impairing my ability to help the team falls under the heading of "sniveling" but then I've been wrong before. Part of the image problem with a personal kit is that treating gunshot wounds and knife wounds is sexy (in a bizarre, counter-productive sort of way) and basic maintenance isn't. What's in the kit, and where do you

A compass pouch or dedicated wound-dressing pouch with a dressing in it should be attached to your gear.

keep it? Actually your personal medical supplies are probably going to be in two or three different locations depending on what and how much you have. You'll need more than one if you expect them to be of much use. You'll need a small personal kit, an emergency wound dressing, and a re-stocking kit.

Location is easy. Your personal wound dressing goes where every member of your team keeps their main wound dressing that they carry. The easy way is to simply clip it to the upper web gear or vest on the left side, as is done in the military: Under the radio pouch, or just below the location your weapons stock rests when firing. Why the same? Simple. The main wound dressing is something that may well have to be applied to your wound by someone else. They must know how to find it. Since the basic uniform on a SWAT officer or infantryman has 10 pockets, and the tactical vest or web gear you're wearing could have that many again, asking your rescuer to frisk you looking for the "blankety-blank" wound dressing wastes time. Clip it where everyone else does, and leave it alone except to make sure the seal is unbroken. Make sure it is clearly marked.

The small kit can go where it is convenient and comfortable for you, since you will be the one using it. If you have enough waist room, clipping the pouch to your belt works. If not, then some place on your web gear or in a vest pocket will do. If you expect it to be with you every time you need it, and will not always be dressed in second line gear, attach it to some part of your first line gear, the stuff you'll always have with you. You can stencil a small red cross on it as a reminder, and as a guide if someone else needs something. Some things on the offered list may seem a bit precious, and others puzzling. The individual bandages, for one. You have an "oops" and you, you super-tough SWAT Cop you, you're going to put a bandage on? You bet. Cut your hand or a finger on a nail, piece of glass or sharp edge of a metal door, and the bleeding can make your firearm slippery. It can corrode parts of the radio you need to use. Blood can obscure radio, NVG or cell phone controls. The

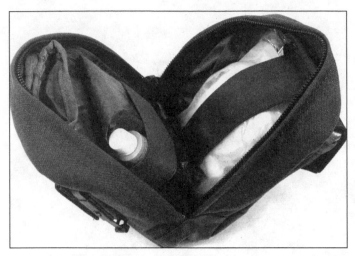

A personal medical pouch doesn't have to be big to be useful. (Courtesy Blackhawk Industries)

wound is a path of infection. If you've cut yourself, and the team isn't going in right away, put on the bandage. If you have the kit with you, you don't have to leave the team to get treated. Water purification tablets? OK, how's this: Your team managed to sneak around behind the suspect, but now he's moved and any ingress or egress will be observed. You're there for a few hours in the sun and getting thirsty wearing your all-black gear. Can you really trust the water from the rusty faucet in the back of the shed you're hiding in? You can with iodine tablets. (Or you lucky devils who planned ahead and bought a CamelBak with an in-line filter can just load up and sip away in peace.)

Sunscreen? Chap Stick? The fence you've hidden behind (Instead of the shed) offers no protection from the sun. Or, in both the previous gear example and this one, instead of being on an operation you're at a training facility: The water isn't potable. There isn't any shade, and the wind is hot and dry. (It is, after all, in the middle of nowhere.) Do you really want to make the drive home with chapped lips, sunburn and an urgent desire to know the location of every rest stop, just because you were too macho to carry a personal first aid kit?

The OC pepper spray decon wipe should speak for itself. If not, consider that anyone who is sprayed with OC may try to still close the gap and wrestle with those who did the spraying. The wind can suddenly shift, putting you downwind of your own spray. If your face has been swiped by the arm of the sprayed suspect, a decon wipe will be very comforting indeed. The baby wipes are simply a way to clean your hands without having to find a faucet and sink. For a quick wipe, before lunch, or in the field, they can be very useful. A Swiss Army knife can have knife blades, tweezers, a toothpick, and all the other gadgets that can make a long wait bearable. A handcuff key? You haven't lived until you get to the point where a suspect has to be uncuffed, and no one, even with 20 pockets and pouches full of gear each, has a key.

Personal First Aid Kit Contents

The following items will make up a good basic first aid kit: Adhesive bandages, small, medium and large. Antibiotic cream. Aspirin or non-aspirin pain tablets. (Better to have both.) Pepto-Bismol tablets. Water purification tablets. Tweezers, tick pliers, matches and a small, sharp knife. Gauze, medical tape, cough and sinus medicine. Rehydration packets in case of dehydration.

Pack a few packaged hand wipes or baby wipes, to clean your hands or clean a wound before putting on antibiotic and bandaging. An OC pepper spray decon wipe is one of those things that you'll never need, until you need it so badly your team members can't pry you out of the fetal position. Add a Swiss Army knife, real or knock-off, in place of the knife and tweezers, and a handcuff key. If you can find room for a first aid booklet, that's great. If not, then you'll just have to remember how to treat cuts, bruises, scrapes, blisters and insect bites.

The personal wound dressing should be the small or medium military dressing you can find at any gun show or in the pages of any surplus catalog.

The on-your-vest personal first aid kit does not have to be a big bag. If it is too big, you'll be tempted to leave it behind. Ideally the whole thing should not exceed the size/volume of a single rifle magazine. You can stuff a lot of the gear into a single G.I. compass/first aid pouch. If you need the whole lot, the Special Operations Equipment med pouch will easily hold it all. At 6 inches x 5 inches x 2 inches, the SOE med pouch is only 60 cubic inches, half the size of a lot of other med pouches, which generally run 120 to 130 cu in. If you only want personal stuff, the SOE is better. If you're carrying general stuff for the whole team, the bigger ones might be better.

The Pepto-Bismol tablets (or something like them)? It would be a shame to cut short your training session, or have the Team have to go on without you because no one really knows the answer to the burning question "What was in lunch?" Stomach upset can sideline you as much as a gunshot wound. And even if you can tough it out, do you really want the perpetrator to later file a suit against the department and you, charging "assault with a disgusting weapon" i.e., your soiled uniform?

The one that may be puzzling to some of you are the tick pliers. Actually tweezers, they are indispensable for getting ticks off of you. In some parts of the country you may never see any. In other parts, well, just be ready. My friend Jeff Chudwin has commented more than once on the "monkey ticks" in one training area his teams and classes work in, where the ticks are so big, "You can see them swinging down out of the trees towards you." You want to apply the insect repellant for sure, but if one tick gets through your clothes, applied anti-insect toxins and skin creams, you must have the right tool to extract it, or risk infection at the bite.

And the antihistamines are not just for those with allergies. Dust, pollen and powdered irritants like mold or fungus can cause breathing difficulties even in those who are not allergic. Select a brand or generic that does not cause drowsiness, and keep a few in your personal gear and the rest in the re-supply bag.

The big personal kit

What's in the big kit that isn't in the little kit? Insect repellant, hemostats and foot powder or cream and more of the stuff that is in the personal kit. The small kit should only hold enough for one or two treatments. The big kit, which rides in your gear bag in the vehicle, or in your rucksack on a rural deployment, contains the re-supply and a few extra items too bulky for the personal gear. From it you can top off your personal kit, or treat fellow officers who neglected to bring their own personal kit.

The big kit can have a large bottle of sunscreen, box of all sizes of adhesive bandages, etc. You can stock it with large wound dressings, the Israeli

The Israeli dressing is larger than the basic military wound dressing, but incorporates larger tie-down wrappings.

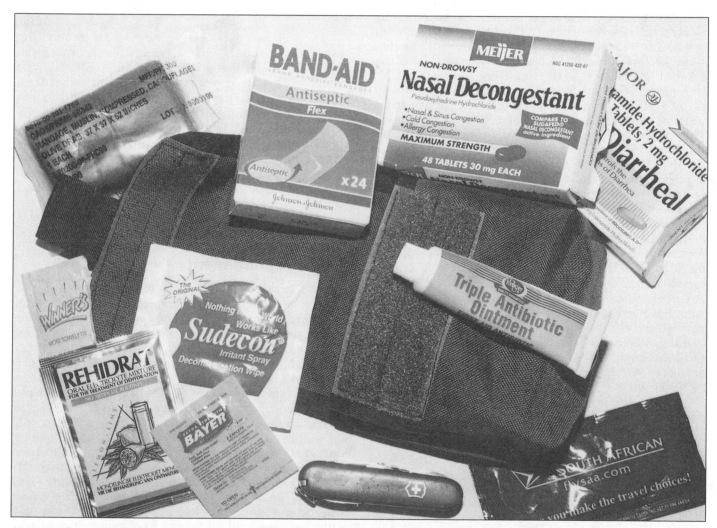

Your basic first aid personal kit should include all the things that make life easier, and allow you to treat and ignore minor training incidents. Obviously, you don't pack the cardboard containers the top items come in.

dressing, and a first aid book. Don't make it too big, you're just making it possible for you to re-supply, not transport an entire drug store with you to a callout. The hemostats are useful for many things besides clamping a bleeding wound. As in extracting a splinter or clamping a bandage out of the way while you tie the ends. The foot powder can make an otherwise unbearable training session at least bearable.

Environmental kit supplement

You need to plan for the predicaments that you suffer when on operations or training. Take those items you need rarely but boy when you need them, you really need them. How about dehydration? Or a chemical imbalance caused by excessive heat and water without supplements? I had the occasion to run into that in the Philippines. I was at the World Shoot in 1999, and the heat and humidity each day were both over 90, even though it wasn't the hot season. I made sure I drank plenty of water, bringing three liters each day and adding to them from the vendors. (Bottled water. I did not use ice cubes, nor eat fruit, or fruit drinks. I learned that lesson from shooters who'd gone the World Shoot in Brazil in 1993.) However, by Thursday (the shooting was a Monday through Friday schedule) I'd depleted my electrolyte reserves. Facing the hill on the hike out (we had to go a quarter mile through the surrounding shanty town to reach the buses at the road) I realized I would not make it to the top. Were I to try, the EMS techs would find me face down in the shantytown, no-doubt stripped to my underwear. I just turned to the waiting ambulance and told them of my predicament. They force-fed me a couple of liters of electrolyte solution, and made me rest. You can easily get powdered electrolyte solution at any drug store, and a packet mixed in a quart of water will quickly restore the electrolytes to any team member feeling the effects of the heat.

Deal with heat exhaustion, heat stroke or dehydration, by taking a moment and adding a few packets of the supplements to your gear. You can put an extra stash of them in the re-supply bag for other team members and for use on training sessions, as you are not likely to exhaust your electrolytes with the water you have on you. Add some flavoring, as many powdered electrolyte solution formulas have a "medicinally-yucky" taste. Yes, that is the correct technical/medical term. They can taste awful. A cherry, orange or strawberry flavor packet can keep you (or the victim) from gagging on the electrolyte solution.

The re-supply bag needs to be bigger than the personal pouch. A G.I. tool bag, or a small carry bag is plenty big enough.

The personal stuff is going to be used a whole lot more than the medical and trauma stuff. One of the reports back from the field in Iraq is that Navy Corpsman's bags are not loaded with enough of the personal stuff. Yes, they can deal with gunshots and shell splinters aplenty, but after a week in the field they run out of aspirin, antihistamines, adhesive bandages and the like. Your team may never have to deal with a gunshot wound, but you'll need the personal stuff on a weekly basis.

Medical

The medical supplement pocket of the re-supply bag contains the extras that particular team members might need. Yes, they should carry what they need themselves, but do you really want to be in the position of evacuating a team member because he forgot his bee sting meds or his insulin? I can hear someone in the back grumbling about that: "No way would I let someone on my team who needed those." Well, welcome to the brave new world of teams in the 21st century. If they can meet your stated (and task-relevant) team standards, you aren't going to preclude them because they are allergic to yellowjackets. You would be prudent to include extras of all such meds that your team members need. However, some will be prescription, and some may require additional proper training to use them. In the case of one of your team members needing such medical supplies, take the time to research their needs, the supplies and the training.

Trauma

Even if you are only going to be conducting training, you should have a trauma kit on you, or in your gear at the firing line or training site. No, you are not anticipating getting shot in training, but then if you were expecting to lead an uneventful life you wouldn't be training at all, now would you? As one experienced SWAT leader explained it to me, "You're spending a whole day around high-speed low-drag guys who all want to do it faster, better or more stylish than anyone else. And everyone is armed. Even if you don't get shot, what are we going to do if you fall off the rappelling tower?"

Pack or buy a trauma kit, and wear it. It can also serve as your First Responder trauma kit.

First Responder kit

The first responder is a basic trauma kit, for those who arrive when things are still happening, and which allows them to handle the situation for the critical first minutes of an emergency. The offender is down, but backup hasn't arrived, nor has the ambulance. Or, the offender and his victim are both down, and you have one wound dressing, your personal one. What to do? If there are multiple victims down, or several wounds to treat, the single wound dressing you may or may not have on you will not suffice. A small bag with just wound dressings and treatment options is just what you need. Rather than try to assemble your own kit, and go through two or three bags until you find one the right size, just ring up North American Rescue Products and order from them. I checked out two of their bags and found both well suited for the first responder or first-aid trained officer in an emergency.

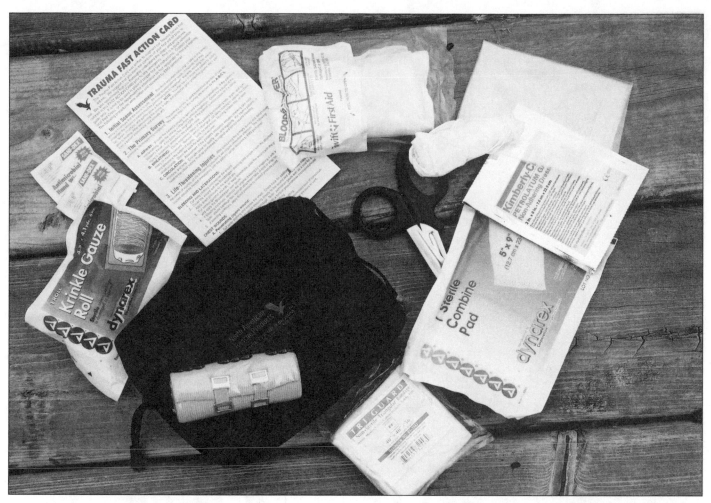

North American Rescue Products First Responder package, with enough first aid gear to treat several wounds.

Immediate Response Kit™

The IRK is designed and sized to fit in the cargo pocket of a BDU trouser, and has lash straps on the back to fit on a belt or be secured to a vest or pack. On the side is a clutch-purse type strap so you can quickly get it out of a pocket, or slide your fingers through so you can run, climb or grapple without having to drop it. The strap also allows you to quickly snatch it out of your patrol bag on the seat next to you in the squad car, and dash where you are needed while keeping your left hand open in case you need to hold something else or grasp something. Inside, the IRK has hand wipes for cleaning your hands before or after, a 5-inch x 9-inch combine dressing, Bloodstopper® dressing for large or deep wounds, krinkle gauze roll, 3x9 petrolatum gauze, a triangular bandage for restricting limb movement after wound dressing, a 17-foot Ace bandage, trauma shears, nitrile gloves, 8x10 plastic bag and a fast-action trauma card to remind you of the steps for taking care of the injured. (Hey, it may have been nearly a year since the last annual refresher and certification, right?) All of this gear is stowed in a bag of only 6x8x3. With the IRK you can treat several severely wounded, or a number of slightly injured victims. It can ride in a pocket, or be lashed to your

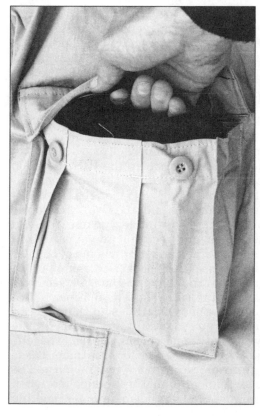

The NARP F-R package fits in a cargo pocket.

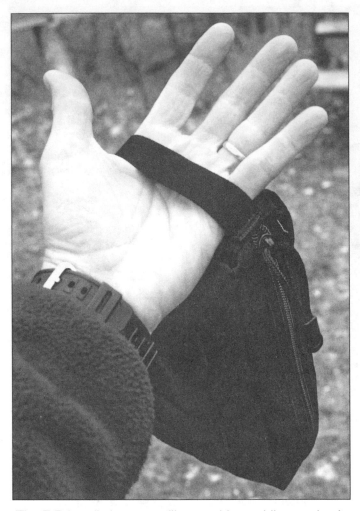

The F-R handle lets you still grasp things while carrying it.

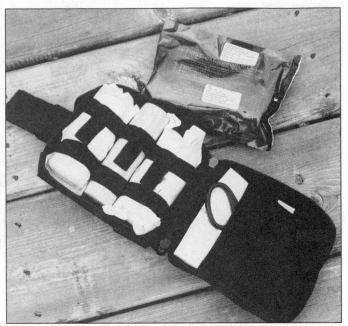

With the NARP Battle Pak and an Israeli dressing, you're covered for a lot of emergencies

tactical vest, or even kept in your gear bag in the patrol car. With it and your personal wound dressing, you are able to care for a number of victims until help arrives.

Battle Pack™

The BP is the next step up, and is not only stuffed with more items, but is designed as an equipment item and not just a pocket bag. The Battle Pack, in addition to all the items in the IRK, also has; two 2x2 gauze pads, a 2-inch fingertip bandage, a 3-inch knuckle bandage, four 1x3 bandages, four 3/4-inch x 3-inch bandages, and two antiseptic towelettes, all in a thigh-mount leg pouch. You can hang it from your belt and secure it to your thigh in place of a spare magazine carrier or gas mask bag. Or you can carry it in a pocket or pack, and snatch it out by the handle sewn on the top of the bag. Or, secure it to a load-bearing or tactical vest. The 6.5-inch x 7.5-inch x 3-inch bag has enough extra room that you can add extra bandages if you want, to augment the regular supply, or add items not on the list. There is also an external zippered pocket for treatment cards for particular injuries, to refresh your memory. The zippered sides extend around three sides, so when you open the bag it drops flat down your leg, making

You have enough room in the NARP Battle Pak bag to add gear, like an extra dressing, hemostats and a TraumaDex applicator.

all items accessible. The elastic restraints holding the dressings in place have finger tabs, so you can easily pull the elastic out to snatch the dressing free without a struggle. The kit allows you to treat minor injuries, such as small cuts, as well as do an emergency dressing on a major wound.

Both bags have extra room (the contents do not fill the bags to bursting) so you can augment both with extra items if you wish.

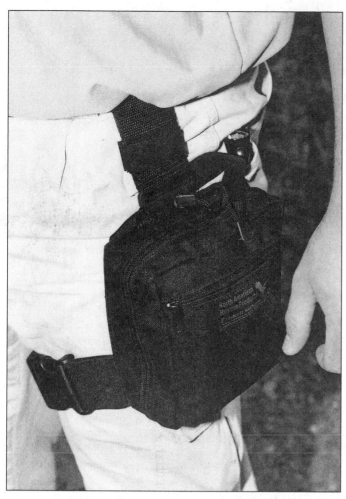

The NARP Battle Pak, rigged as the tactical thigh pouch. You can also secure it to a load-bearing or tactical vest.

Outside of these kits, the big item of interest is the Israeli bandage, a wound dressing that has an elastic backing built into it. Fellow Gunsite graduate Anthony M. Barrera, M.D. (aka "Doc Gunn"), who is quite taken with it, turned me on to the Israeli dressing. My only quibble (and it is minor) is that the dressing is large, and cannot be stuffed into a small med pouch. You must use a larger bag or pouch if you want to include it with the regular gear, or use a dedicated Israeli-only pouch or bag. However, with it the big advantage is that you do not have to apply a wound dressing and then use a separate ace bandage or tape to secure it. You can apply the bandage and secure it in one operation. For those trained in its use, it can even serve as a tourniquet. All the tactical EMS people I've talked to are enthusiastic about this bandage, and North American Rescue Products has them as individual items. (Go right to the manufacturer, not Israeli by the way, and you'll have to buy a carton of them.) If you do nothing else to prepare yourself, get one or two of these, and keep them where they will be handy.

In case you need additional products, North American Rescue also manufactures a whole line of casualty litters, spine boards, splints and ENT

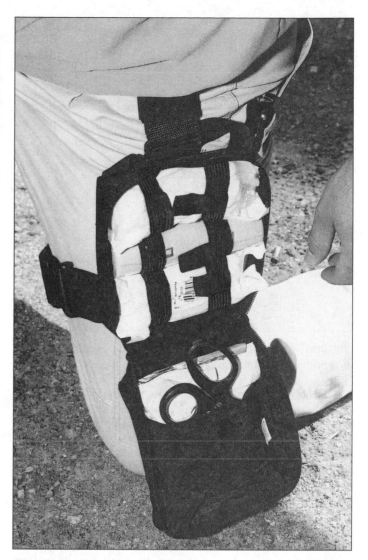

The Battle Pak open, ready to go.

Corpsman kits. They can supply you with bags, bags with kits, packs and decontamination systems. Their Reeves Sleeve II® spinal immobilization board is standard issue on all Navy ships, and you can't get much more accepted than that.

TraumaDex

One new addition to the basic trauma kit, or the First Responder kit, is TraumaDex. In reviewing the medical reports of battle casualties, an appalling percentage of the deaths servicemen suffered came from relatively simple wounds, usually to the extremities, where the bleeding could not be stopped. Death by gunshot or a knife wound does not have to come from a sucking chest wound. It can come from an arm or leg wound that bleeds copiously and cannot be controlled. A bandage and pressure will sometimes do the job, but a line of inquiry that has borne fruit is the external chemical application of clotting agents or additives. The Department of Defense has been encouraging research on these lines, and TraumaDex is the first one I'm aware of on the market.

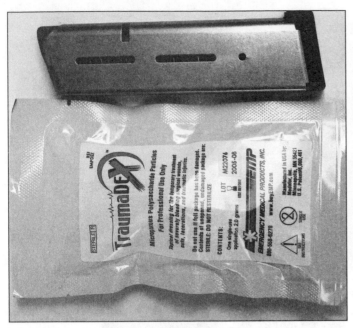

TraumaDex is an applicator with a topical dressing for speeding the coagulation of blood in a wound.

Clotting stops blood loss. As the blood is exposed to air, chemical reactions with blood components cause clotting. However, if the blood flow is too great, the clotting can't happen quickly enough to stop bleeding. TraumaDex speeds clotting, and slows and stops blood loss.

It is simple to use. TraumaDex is provided in sealed applicators. Twist and break off the sealant tip, wipe excess blood from the wound, apply the TraumaDex and then apply pressure with a bandage. In testing (You aren't going to believe this, but they managed to find volunteers who were cut and then had TraumaDex applied!) TraumaDex greatly increased the speed of clotting, and reduced blood loss. There are caveats; you should not apply it intravenously, nor on exposed brain wounds. It doesn't do much on sucking chest wounds but we have other solutions for that problem. TraumaDex on the skin doesn't do anything except absorb perspiration. And since TraumaDex has no human or animal proteins in it, there are no concerns over immune response.

Once the bleeding has been stopped, the ER Physicians can clean the TraumaDex out when they deal with the wound. Since it is derived from plant materials, there is no need to worry about infection from the source of origin.

TraumaDex comes in two sizes, a 2-gram and a 5-gram tube. Each is sealed in a foil envelope, to keep them sterile and away from humidity. The compound is very hygroscopic (attracts water) and if the seal is broken on the applicator, toss it and replace it.

A bandage and pressure has been the standard response to bleeding. The success rate of the standard approach is improved by using TraumaDex, which is now a regular item in my trauma kit, personal and first responder.

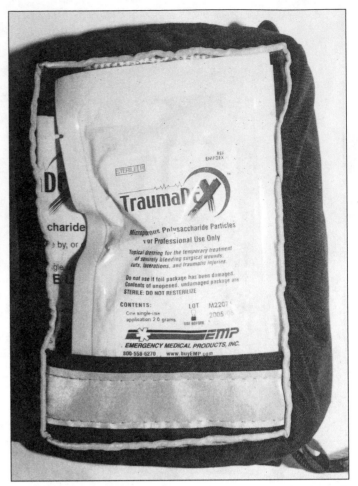

The EMP X-Pouch comes with a clear cover and reflector tape, or clear and low profile.

Xpouch

Rather than assemble a trauma pouch with individual items, and find a bag for same, you can start with the Xpouch and add items until the bag can't be closed. The Xpouch starts with TraumaDex, and adds a 4x4 gauze pad, an Asherman chest seal, two 3-inch x131-inch rolls of cling, a roll of dressing tape, a 5x9 combine dressing, trauma scissors, nitrile gloves and a bag seal. Once you've inventoried the bag, and added any extra items you might feel are needed, you zip it closed and apply the seal across the zipper tabs. Now, if it is opened the seal is broken, and you'll know. No need to worry about someone rooting around in your trauma kit looking for a bandage. The bag has enough room for an extra dressing or two, an extra TraumaDex applicator or two, or other items you may need in an emergency. The Asherman chest seal is particularly interesting. Designed by a Navy SEAL, it is designed to deal with a particularly troubling wound, the sucking chest wound. The sucking chest wound is where the puncture has entered, and deflated, a lobe of the lung. In addition to the bleeding, blood and ambient air can enter the chest cavity, preventing re-inflation of the lung. This situation is triply bad as a result: blood loss, decreased oxygenation, and impending

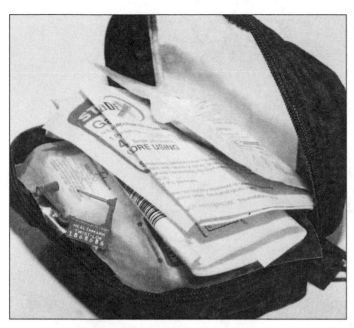

Break the seal, unzip the X-Pouch and you have a ready-to-go rapid responder kit.

over the injury location, and sealed to the skin. Once the subject arrives at the emergency room, the ER Physicians can remove it when appropriate.

The Xpouch comes in two styles, both with a hook-and-loop fastener panel secured to the back so you can secure it to your gear, gear bag, squad car or any place needed. One style is the hi-viz, with a reflector panel and reflective border around the clear cover. The other is the low-profile, all black except for the clear cover. The clear cover lets you instantly identify the Xpouch, and know which side is the top.

If you don't like the clear pouch, you can transfer the Xpouch contents to a container of your liking. Me, I keep them right where they started, so I don't have to recall under stress where the kit is, and what it looks like.

The Team Kit or Range Master Kit

Now it gets more complicated. While the idea of a team kit or range kit is simple, the training involved isn't. The purpose of the kit is to ensure that a team member can be treated until evacuated to the perimeter and an ambulance, or student or trainer in a class will survive and be treated until the ambulance arrives. The main intent is to deal with a gunshot or knife wound, but the injury may be a fall or caused by a falling object. Not all wounds are survivable, but the kit helps improve the odds.

The kit requires more than just basic training. If your department doesn't offers such training to every officer, then you have several choices. You can attend enough American Red Cross classes in order to get up to speed. Or you can attend a TacMed course such as

panic and shock from hyperventilation. The Asherman chest seal acts as a one-way valve for blood loss. Blood leaves, air cannot enter, and the lung can be re-inflated with effort. Once the sucking chest wound is controlled, the blood loss and the injury itself can be addressed. The Asherman chest seal has an adhesive backing, and once the seal layer is peeled away, the valve is pressed in place directly

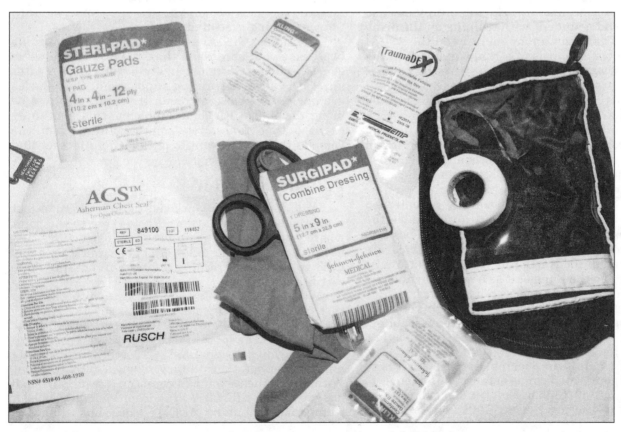

Bandages, TraumaDex, gloves, and the Asherman Chest Seal, to deal with thoracic perforations to the lung, a.k.a. sucking chest wound.

Big problems require big bags, and the training to go with them. (Courtesy Blackhawk Industries)

the one Gunsite offers from time to time. (Be sure you meet the pre-requisite training before applying for any advanced courses. Any good course will have pre-reqs, you will have to have gone through them, and you won't be able to catch up if you haven't taken them.) This is not gear you can just buy, read up on, and have ready. You must know what you are doing. One advantage a range master may have, is that if he is running a class, there is a chance that one of the two dozen students has emergency medical training more advanced than his own. Having a fully stocked bag on hand and a student with training on the firing line is a lot better than an ambulance "on the way." I recently read the synopsis of a range incident in the Marine Corps, where a Marine was struck by gunfire. When the shout went out for assistance, the first three Marines to arrive were two EMT-Certified Marines and a Navy Corpsman. With such a bag on hand, it would almost be like teleporting into an emergency room. In one of the Gunsite Shotgun classes I've attended, we had both an EMT and a Board-Certified ER Doctor as students. When the help is on hand, the kit can be a lifesaver.

One note on this kit is that nothing is controlled nor requires a prescription, so you can assemble the bag and have it handy even if you are not in a position to acquire prescription items. And, some items are already stocked in the North American Rescue kits, so you can assemble the Range kit as a supplemental bag or pouch with the North American bags attached.

Some might ask why pack this gear if you need extra training for it? Well, first of all, you should get the training. As in a Special Forces team, a law enforcement team should be cross-trained. Not to the full extent of the full-time member whose job it is to provide emergency medical assistance, but enough to get the team out of trouble. No, you don't have to be fully trained to the level of an EMS tech or an ER

Nurse, but more training is better. The idea is to be able to treat the immediate problem, stabilize the wounded, and keep them alive until you can hand them off to the ambulance crew. One way to build a range kit is to start with an NA Rescue IRK or Battle Pack, then add the personal and environmental items, and the items on the Range Kit sidebar. Pack them all into a medium range bag, suitably marked, and you're ready to go. Or at least, someone with proper training is ready to go.

The Range Kit, due to the size of the two saline bags, takes up more room than the other bags we've gone through. It is most likely a vehicle bag. After all, if it is a range/training supplement, the vehicles are likely to be close at hand. If you are going to be using the Range Kit as a supplement on a training exercise that takes you some distance from the vehicles then you'll want to pack it in a rucksack and assign someone to carry it.

Full Blown Med Kit

Well, for this one you need to do more than just some reading. As a matter of fact, to get to the point where you can be the guy giving the instructions, and not just another one following them, you'll probably need two years of training and experience and state certification

With the top-end kit you can deal with anything that comes along. Of course, at this level of training and experience, you are too valuable to go in with the entry team. The path to this level is a series of courses leading to an EMS Tech certification, state nursing cert, or the military medical tech training. With any of these, you can count on a good-paying, if busy life as an ER Nurse or a hospital or clinic job, or riding in an ambulance or EMS truck. Life will not be

To make sure no one has gone diving into your X-Pouch looking for a band-aid, you use the numbered seal.

dull and boring. My friend Ed Mohn of the NIPAS EST has members with this level of training and certifications on his team. (Lucky guy.) However, not many teams do.

Sealed packaging

Many of the items in the various kits will be sealed against the day they will be used. If you build your own, or replace items from wear and tear, training, or expiration dates, you may want to seal your own packages. One of my fellow Gunsite graduates used to work for the Air Force. At one time his job was stocking and packing survival vests for pilots. He took to using a kitchen vacuum sealer with which he heat-sealed the plastic bags in which he packaged items. The pilots might go foraging in the vests when bored during various classes, and he'd have to re-stock items early. Vacuum-packing them in plastic bags both protected them from the environment, and kept the pilots from helping themselves too easily. "It's a survival vest, not a

convenience store" was his comment on the situation. You might want to consider his approach. The plastic, serial-numbered seal of the Xpouch serves the same purpose.

Painkillers

Most of law enforcement patrol work is waiting, driving, walking, filling out reports and talking to people. A whole lot more of SWAT or Special Operations work is training. It isn't uncommon for a SWAT team member to spend 30 or 40 hours of each month on training. Now, some of that training is the 20 minutes devoted to reviewing Use of Force policy each Monday morning at the start of shift. Or the half hour each Friday spent inspecting gear and making sure buckles are tight, pouches don't have holes worn through them, and that all gear marked with expiration dates is within date.

But a lot of that training is range time, door and building-entry time, team time doing drills. And to get through a grueling day, we sometimes gobble over the counter painkillers. Well, we call them painkillers, but the technical term for them is Non-Steroidal Anti Inflammatory Drugs. Those whose stomachs can take it just keep washing down aspirin. Others use the non-aspirin painkillers, ibuprofen or acetaminophen. And how many know you can overdose on them? Oh, you won't start seeing aliens landing, or the second coming, no, nothing like that. You just suffer liver damage and every now and then someone dies. Every year, federal health officials report that some 160,000 people end up in the ER, and 16,000 die, from complications due to over-the-counter painkillers. (Made me start reading the labels thoroughly, that bit of information did!) OK, so reading the label just became more important. The slight problem is, you can get some painkillers from more than one product, and you might not think about it. So, you've got a cold, and you slug down a dose of daytime cold reliever. At lunch you have another, to stave off the cold and keep training. You feel a bit sore, from the exertion, so you gobble a couple of painkillers. It's OK, right? They're all just over-the-counter stuff, right? Maybe. It depends on what you took. If you took some acetaminophen for your cold, and some aspirin for your sore back, you're probably OK. (I'm not a doctor, and I don't even play one on TV, so don't take my word for it as an assurance.) Then again, the aspirin could irritate your stomach, and just increase the effect of the others. Mixing can be no problem, and it can be a serious problem.

But if you took Acetaminophen all the way, you could be over the recommended dosage. But wait, it gets better. If you take Non-steroidal anti-inflammatory drugs, (NSAID) and at the end of the day you hoist a few cold ones with the boys, you're setting yourself up for some real bad medical news. You see, acetaminophen when broken down by the body creates a toxin that harms the liver. In safe doses, the liver can counteract the toxin and get it out of the body. (The exact chemical mechanism is fascinating, but beyond the scope of this book.) The maxim with many poisons is; "dose makes the poison." Some poisons you can take a little and suffer no long-term effects. Others just kill you. The liver toxin is one of the former. If you have had a drink or drinks, your liver function is greatly diminished. The build-up of toxins from the overdose of the NSAID's could cause damage to the liver. Food also acts to buffer the liver from the toxin. So, if after a day of training, in which you've gobbled handsfull of painkillers, you have a couple of drinks at the restaurant before the food arrives you've just set up the hardest problem for your liver to deal with.

Solution? Not drink. At least not after training and taking over the counter painkillers. What are these NSAIDs? The big three are ibuprofen, naproxen sodium, and ketaprofen. The chemical trade name is not necessarily the name of the product on the shelf, especially if you're cruising the pharmacy at the big-box store looking for generics on the cheap. Read the labels and see what is what. And keep track of what you take, so we don't have to read about you. I had wrestled for some time with the rough draft of this chapter, trying to decide if I should keep it in or not. After all, do I want to be the chicken little who warns gruff, tough SWAT cops about a little stomach irritation from taking too many aspirin? Then I met James Etzin of the ITEMSA at the Michigan Tactical Officers Association annual conference. He knew of team members how had gotten into exactly the kind of problem I was writing about, and even knew of some who had gotten themselves into medical problems from using non-steroidal and steroidal drugs to train harder and ensure they made the team. And others who had taken "natural" supplements to improve performance and recovery from the stress of training. (Needless to say, landing in the hospital had a serious effect on their opportunity to join the team.) When it comes to doing things right, you need good medical advice, not the tricks and tips that you've been getting away with for years. If your department doesn't have the budget, perhaps someone on the team can reach out to a doctor or ER nurse who can answer questions and point you to the right places to get training. And I would also like to step up onto my personal soapbox at this point and rail against dietary supplements. Yes, some of them can help you. Some of them do no harm, and simply drain your wallet. But some of them can be detrimental. Just because it is "natural" doesn't mean it is harmless. Arsenic is a naturally found element, but that doesn't make it safe. The various "X" supplements, all variations of MaHuang or ephedrine, are all stimulants that can have adverse effects on your system. Even small doses for some people can cause elevated heartbeat, blood pressure and other more serious problems. Some natural supplements can cause excessive bleeding. As a result, some wounds and bruises heal more slowly with some supplements. Were you to ask him or her, there are good reasons your doctor will tell you to not take a whole range of supplements.

Take care of yourself. If you don't, it will be that much harder for the person who will have to later.

Chapter 20
Hydration

YOU MUST DRINK to live. While the word "dehydration" brings to mind rag-clad wanderers crawling through the desert, with vultures circling overhead, the build-up is more subtle, but the effects just as traumatic.

On a hot, dry day, if you spend time outdoors you'll be sweating. Even if you don't feel it, you'll be losing water. If you do not replace the water, your body slows down. Some slowing is an autonomic response to decrease the rate of water loss, and some is due to body systems not being able to get the water they need to work efficiently. If you do not drink enough water you will get clumsy, lose concentration, and get weaker. Lose enough water and you will be unable to move, and finally pass out. You can go days (weeks for some of us) without food. But go more than three days without water, and you're dead. When I first showed up at Gunsite, we arrived at the range to find drinking cups with our names on them. "If you're loading mags, you should be drinking water" was our introduction to getting along in the dry Southwest. We were encouraged to drink early, drink often, and drink before we knew we were thirsty. The advice worked, as none of us spent class

After a long day of training, or a long day waiting for the real thing, your skills could be diminished by dehydration.

Searching a building in Afghanistan, all six soldiers we can see clearly have Camelbak systems on. They also have knee and elbow pads, big knives and extra canteens. Nothing beats being prepared. (DoD photo)

time face down into the dirt from dehydration. In training and on operations, you should do the same.

Some water is clean and ready to drink. Most isn't. Those who operate in a city have the luxury of clean water from the tap. Typically during training and range work a supply of bottled water will take care of your needs. In most other instances water should be suspect. What is in water besides hydrogen and oxygen? Two things; chemicals and living critters. The chemicals might be heavy metals, pesticides, runoff from old manufacturing sites and the like. Yes, it is possible that your training area might not have these in the water, but you never know. The problem is, no treatment or filter you can carry will remove them. The only way to remove chemicals is distillation. If you're really worried, take samples from your training area to the County and have them tested. The living critters can be bad for you, but you can do something about them. The three kinds of water-borne pathogens are viruses, bacteria and protozoa.

Viruses

Hepatitis A and E, Norwalk virus, poliovirus, rotavirus and echovirus are all bad little critters. So small they can't be filtered out, you can only treat your water by boiling or with chemicals. Worse yet,

there are no treatments once you've caught them. You simply have to tough it out and get on with life. That is, if you are a big tough operator. They can be deadly to the immuno-compromised or elderly.

Bacteria

The list is long, and the most common include E. Coli, Campylobacter, Shigell, Vibrio cholerae, salmonella. All are nasty to get through, and all can kill the weak, immuno-compromised infants or the elderly. They can survive in cold water for days to weeks. The good news is that they can be filtered out, or killed by chemicals or boiling. And, the ailments can be treated. Depending on which particular one you have (you need the specific prescription drug for the specific disease) erythromycin, tetracycline, Trimethoprim-sulfamethoxazole, chloramphenicol, or one of the fluoroquinolones will get you back on your feet. But all are prescription drugs, each is specific, and your doctor will have to test you to see which is appropriate, so you can't just stock up your first aid kit just in case.

Protozoans

Giardia lamblia, cryptosporidium, and entamoeba histolytica are the nasty little devils of the bad water

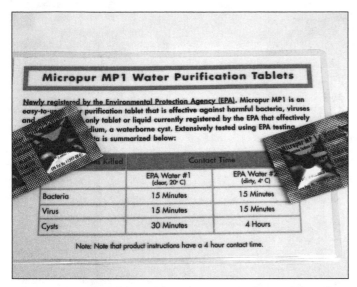

To make suspect water clean, one option is chemical treatment. These Micropur tablets will kill anything in the water that might make you sick.

The Katadyn Hiker is a compact filter that can provide lots of clean water. It is small enough to fit into a three-magazine rifle pouch, or disappear into a medium rucksack.

set. Protozoans are microscopic denizens of the deep (and shallows) that have hard shells. The shell makes them resistant to chemical treatment, but Giardia (the one most people know about) and E. histolytica (the cause of amebic dysentery) can both be killed if you follow dose instructions. Cryptosporidium in particular is tough to kill with iodine or chlorine treatments, essentially brushing its teeth in the stuff and grinning back at you. They all die after boiling, and their large size (typically 10 times the size of the pores in a good filter) makes them easy to filter out.

I can see some in the back getting restless. "We drink city water, and our training site has clean water on it." Uh-huh. So, there you are doing your annual wilderness training, and just after filling your canteens you come around the bend of the stream to find a new beaver dam. Guess what beavers do in the water? Everything. Guess where a lot of these pathogens come from? That's right, fecal contamination. Or, how about you round the bend and find a deceased critter right in the stream? (Happened to me one year hunting. Luckily I treated my water.)

Chemical treament

The old standbys are iodine and chlorine. Tablets or droplets, added to water to kill the pathogens and assault your taste buds. Using the recommended dose of either gets you chemical-tasting water. Halving the dose with iodine and doubling the standing time can remove most of the taste, but does nothing for the looks. Adding chemicals to silty water does nothing to improve the looks. But both do produce water that is safe to drink. Easier and more sure are tablets, like the Micropur MP1 from Katadyn. While high enough amounts of iodine and chlorine will put the skids to even tough bacteria and virii, the cysts of cryptosporidium are a lot tougher. The EPA tests products, and wouldn't you know it, they have test water standards. (Allowable amounts of silt, mud,

organisms, etc. Our tax dollars at work.) The Micropur tablets are relatively unaffected by temperature and clarity of water, making water safe in 15 minutes. Temperature and clarity had an effect on the cyst test, taking 30 minutes to make room temperature and clear water safe. When the temperature was dropped to ice-cold ($4°$ C) and made muddy, it took four hours. Compared to the results for iodine and chlorine (summary: never) four hours sounds like fast work to me. The Micropur tablets come in individual foil packets, each good for a liter of water. If you're looking for easy and safe, then tablets get the job done. Of course, the tablets aren't going to get that mud out of the water. Filtering can make it safe and clean.

Katadyn is an old and respected name in water filtration. You can get a filter of almost any size from them, from a pocket-sized one to tide you over walking back from a broken-down vehicle, to one big enough to supply the needs of an expedition into the wilds. For a lightweight filter that is easy to pack but can be counted on to supply water enough to last you through an operation, try the Katadyn Hiker. The basic unit is lightweight and compact. Roughly a cylinder of 6.5 inches x3 inches x2 inches it would fit into a corner of a rucksack and hardly be noticed. You could even stuff it and it extra gear (tubes, bottle adapter, pickup nozzle, o-ring lube) into an accessory pouch secured to your rucksack or vest. With it you can filter a liter a minute (or so, depending on how fast you pump). The Hiker has a replaceable filter unit. Unlike the ceramic filters, the replaceable one lasts for about 200 gallons (less if you're pumping someplace really bad like the bayou) but replacing it gets you back to easy, pure water. The ceramic filters can be cleaned, but they suffer a few drawbacks (at least drawbacks by our standards here): they cost more, they weigh more, and they are somewhat more fragile. If you are acquiring a water filter "just in case" for your gear to be used when an operation goes

Camelbak hydration systems are compact, easy to wear, and carry a whole lot of water.

The Camelbak Stealth (and many others) has comfortable shoulder straps.

bad, why get one more fragile and more costly? And if you are going to stash it away against future need, you don't have to worry about the storage (and sitting in the trunk of a car) durability of the Hiker.

In use, the Hiker couldn't be simpler. Hook the intake tube to the bottom inlet, and the out tube to the top. Drop the intake into the water source. Keep the inlet off the bottom of the pond or puddle, out of the silt or sludge. There is no point in shortening the useful life of the filter by simply sucking up and straining out sand and muck for the bottom of your source. Pump a dozen times to clean any dust or odd taste out of the filter. Attach the bottle adapter, or hold the outlet to your bottle or canteen. Then pump water into your bottle. When done, pull the inlet out of the water, pump the unit dry, and put it away. When you get a chance later, disassemble it and let it air dry so you don't have funky odors from storing it wet.

Canteens or water bottles stuffed in a pocket will do for training. On an operation, a canteen may be too bulky or clumsy, and you have to reach around to use it. You may even have to put down what you're holding to drink. There is a solution. The original product was Camelbak, and so quickly has it been adopted as a product that the name is in danger of becoming a generic label. The Camelbak rides on your back, roughly between your shoulder blades, and you drink

via a tube that runs over your shoulder. The origin? The designer and owner of the company used to be an intensive care nurse, and he also rode in 100-mile bicycle races across Texas. (And I used to think I'd done some crazy things in life.) After almost wiping out while riding and trying to wrestle a water bottle off the bicycle frame, he came up with an idea: He took an IV bag and some tubing, and rigged the bag to rest on his back so he could drink from the tube. As an immediate result he noticed increased performance (both for not having to slow down to drink, and being able to drink more) and lots of interest. The transition to military and law enforcement uses was not planned. The focus had been on the extreme sports community. But it didn't take long for the extreme military community to find out about it. (After all, a lot of the special operations military unit personnel participate in Ironman races and the like.)

There are now many models to choose from, and the latest (and in some areas highly desired) option is an in-line filter. In many locales, water is not good. Indeed, in many places water can make you sick. Treating water requires either chemicals or a filter. With a built-in filter, just fill the bladder and go.

The advantages of the Camelbak are more than just the cool factor. First, you can carry more. A large bladder is 100 ounces of water. That's a lot. I drank that much each day when I was at the World Shoot in the Philippines in 1999, and South Africa in 2002. The weight is also better distributed than it would be on your waist. Three one-liter canteens on your waist is a lot of weight to be jostling around. The weight of the Camelbak is between your shoulder blades. Also, to drink from the canteens you have to pull one out, open it, drink, and replace it. With the Camelbak just locate the tube and bite on the valve. And a Camelbak will not be in the way (at least the flat ones) with a properly designed backpack or rucksack. If you need both water and cargo, you can get packs

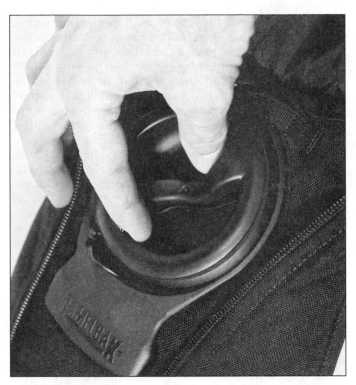

The fill spout is large on the new Camelbaks, and screws down tight to be waterproof.

The tab on the bottom is to hold the reservoir so you don't splash water all over you and your gear while filling.

(Camelbak and others) with an internal pouch to hold the Camelbak bladder.

OK, so it holds a lot of water, and it is easy to carry. Why change from a bunch of canteens? The access port is big, big enough that you can shovel ice cubes into the reservoir on a hot day, to keep your water and you cooler. You can stick a hand in the reservoir on some of them when cleaning, to scrub all the corners. A reservoir tough enough that it won't burst if you sit on it or fall backwards and land on it when it is full. The valve is a bite-and-sip design, so you don't need to use both hands to drink. If you rig it to be close to your face you don't even need one hand. The valve has a lock on it so you can close it and not worry about the valve dribbling your water out onto the ground if you happen to set your pack down on it. And the quick-disconnect design of the tube, valve and reservoir means you can change to other valves, or take it apart for cleaning. If you find that after a summer of use the reservoir has gotten funky from the

U.S. Navy personnel on the line for familiarization fire with a .50-caliber machinegun. The shooter has a Camelbak on, as well as a grin. (U.S. Navy photo)

The Stealth is a low-profile hydration system.

wearing a vest, you have to go with two other models, the Storm or the Pakteen. The Storm is a 100-ounce reservoir in a cover that has lash points to secure it to a vest. You simply secure it with strapping or 550 cord to your vest, and then wear it on your back as part of the vest, in the normal Camelbak location. The Pakteen is a canteen replacement, meant for either a shoulder blade carry, as with other Camelbaks, or on the web gear replacing a canteen. It is "only" 50 ounces and can go on your pistol belt, but with the Camelbak tube and valve. In an extreme environment, you could use both Storm and Pakteen, but you'd be better off working out a method of carrying lots of extra water in a vehicle or vehicles.

The benefits of Camelbak technology (Holy cow, I'm using the word "technology" to describe a canteen. Drag me kicking and screaming into the 21st Century, as I have too many old habits to go easily.) are many. The new Omega reservoir has a huge opening, making it easier to refill without spilling water all over the unit. Many covers are insulated, to keep your water cooler longer. The reservoirs now incorporate the new Camelbak silver ion treatment, which reduces or eliminates mold and mildew growth. The treatment is incorporated into the reservoir, so it doesn't wear out or get used up. The hydrolock lets you shut off the valve so you don't have to worry about leaks from inadvertent pressure on the valve. The valve is attached with a quick release system that lets you swap it for a new one, change to a valve for use in a respirator, or disassemble it for cleaning. But best of all, is the Velcro strap management. The ends of the straps have Velcro flaps that let you roll up the excess strap and secure it. As soon as I saw that, I said to myself "they better patent it, or someone else will steal it." Well, the patent application for Camelbak is in the works even as I write this.

I will admit I was reluctant to switch to the Camelbak when I first saw it. (More of the same reluctance I had with Surefire lights: "Expensive" "Bulky" "What I've got works." I was wrong. In the classes I was accustomed to stuffing water bottles in my cargo pockets, or leaving a bunch of water bottles in a cooler on the truck. The problem I ran into was that I always seemed to quickly finish the water I had, and was too busy to walk back to the truck for more. By the time I'd realized I needed water, I was already dragging, slow and tired. The first time I

water in your area, you can freshen it with baking soda or sanitize it with household bleach. The reservoir is separate from the case, so if you want to stash the reservoir in a rucksack you can.

I am wearing the Camelbak Stealth as I type this. Despite the bulk of two liters of water, I can comfortably sit at my desk and write. One slight drawback is that the integral design of the Stealth, with its carrier cover and its shoulder straps, does not mesh well with a load-bearing or tactical vest. It is designed to be more compact and thus fit you in cramped places or under a vest or body armor. I just can't get it to ride under my vest and not have the multiple sets of shoulder straps get tangled up on each other. If you want the Camelbak options while

The Big Bite valve is much better than any other valve. Get it if you can. The on-off switch keeps your Camelbak from leaking if something rests on the valve.

used a Camelbak I found I stayed fresh the whole day. Even when I had to go back and refill it (The main range for one of the classes is asphalt paved. A real cooker.) I stayed fresh. After all, a refill meant I was good for the rest of the afternoon. It only took one time for me to be a convert. Don't wait, and don't let the seemingly high cost deter you. Get one. Get one now, and be sure and wear it. In hot weather, you're going to need a quart of water an hour. Pack it comfortably.

Can you drink too much water?

The latest medical inquiry has found that yes, you can. However, the circumstances in which you can drink too much water do not apply to us. Not in training, and not on operations. Excess water has to be removed from the body through aspiration, perspiration and micturation. When you exceed your body's capacity to replace the sodium lost through these processes, you end up in a condition known as hyponatremia. Hyponatremia can lead to seizures, respiratory failure and even death. Hyponatremia occurs in marathon runners, long-distance hikers and those who compete in Ironman competitions, who excessively hydrate. The top athletes don't get it because they run too fast to stop and drink until they slosh. It is the medium to slow runners, those who take a long time to finish, who are at risk. By

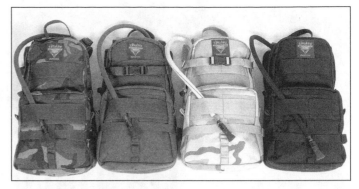

Blackhawk Industries, under their Hydrastorm line, is not to be left out of the hydration wars. They have a dizzying array of sizes, colors and options. (Courtesy Blackhawk Industries)

stopping at every station, and drinking until they can't drink any more, to prevent dehydration, these competitors are actually driving their body in the opposite direction. They force their body to work harder getting rid of the excess water, deplete the sodium (and other chemicals needed) in their system, and suffer. Is this a risk for us? No. The risk of having a memory lapse, or judgment lapse due to partial dehydration is far greater than that of hyponatremia.

Chapter 21
Ballistic Testing

HOW WILL A new cartridge work in the field? How will a new bullet design perform? Ammunition manufacturers and hunters have it easy. If you have a new design, issue the ammunition to your employees and have them use it on the next deer hunt. Or sign up for a guided hunt. You can get good data back in a short period of time. That approach is not open to law enforcement. Officers cannot schedule shootouts. And shooting critters is not always relevant to the law enforcement scenario. In the old days, you wouldn't believe what people used as test media to prove or disprove cartridges. Blocks of soap, blocks of a product called ductseal, which is/was (I don't know if it is made any more) a plastic-like clay stuff used to seal pipes. Experimenters also have used water-soaked newspaper, phone books, magazines and sawdust. Shots have been fired into tanks of water. You name it and someone used it. Then someone got the bright idea of using gelatin. However, all was not rosy. What temperature? What percentage of mix? How to produce it? Extensive testing produced the annoying conclusion that all three changed how bullets performed. Change the temperature and you change penetration and expansion. Produce the gelatin incorrectly and it was just so much yucky-tasting glop. Dr. Martin Fackler worked up a process of brewing it, and a set of specs for using it, that produced repeatable results. Once you are able to reproduce a test, then it was possible to compare products at different times and places. Without reproducible results, every experiment produces nothing that could be compared. After that it was a matter of determining just what the testing was actually showing. That produced a lot more argument, but the method itself is easy to describe. It just takes time, equipment and product. You can find a lot more

Testing in water gives you a good preliminary read on what gelatin will do to bullets. But not on what bullets will do to gelatin. If it won't pass the water test, it won't pass the gelatin test.

Ballistic gelatin is tough stuff, it isn't your flavored dessert gelatin.

discussion of it on the International Wound Ballistics Association web site: www.iwba.com

Making the gelatin and storing it properly is a fussy process, but unless you follow the instructions properly, you will not get consistent results. You will also not get result consistent with other experimenters.

Testing the bullets in gelatin requires another set of standards, and an appreciation of the scientific method. All details of time, date, temperature, humidity, indoors or out, distance to targets, velocity of bullet all must be recorded. Ideally you want all testing on every session to be with the muzzle a set distance from the gelatin. If not, then specify the distance, and the reason for it. For example, testing rifle calibers at 15 feet and 100 yards is relevant. Rifles can be used at both (and farther) distances. Testing handgun cartridges at 100 yards has only a slight relevance, and farther, practically none. Unless you are the U.S. Border Patrol, which has a lot of experience with handguns being used (not by choice) at rifle distances.

The test results have been used to rank the "stopping power" of various handgun, rifle and shotgun loads. The way to rank has been done in both possible directions: comparing what the gelatin does to the bullet, and comparing what the bullet does to the gelatin.

What the gelatin does to the bullet

The early softpoint and hollowpoint bullets suffered from one problem: The manufacturers were accustomed to bullet designs that worked at rifle velocities. What works in a .30-caliber rifle bullet hitting the target at 2,400 fps does not necessarily work in a .45-caliber handgun bullet striking the target at 800 fps. Gelatin formulated by the Fackler method was intended to reproduce the impact resistance of pig muscle, which is close to human muscle. (Testing on pig cadavers is socially accepted, though viewed as odd in some circles. Testing on human cadavers is something you don't talk about outside of medical or ballistic circles.) By using gelatin as a test media, bullet designers were able to

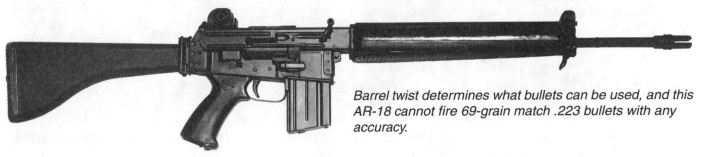

Barrel twist determines what bullets can be used, and this AR-18 cannot fire 69-grain match .223 bullets with any accuracy.

A tough, deep-penetrating bullet will go 15 inches into ballistic gelatin.

Gelatin gives repeatable results from testing bullets, even if the results are not exactly what happens in people.

design, test and adjust bullet construction so the bullets would consistently expand at the velocity ranges handguns could produce. The designers could also test the results velocity changes would create. Some designs would actually penetrate less as velocity increased. The extra velocity was simply expended on the bullet. Other designs might increase penetration as velocity went up. Using gelatin, designers could find out through testing that some designs were not suited for defensive use because they broke up so quickly that they could not be depended on to penetrate to a depth sufficient for reliable incapacitation.

What the bullet does to gelatin

The logical conclusion to developing gelatin as a test medium was to replace live trials. In hunting rifle bullet design, designers can make a new design, go to a hunting ranch, and shoot a few game animals as part of the testing process. Handgun bullets intended for defensive use cannot be similarly tested. Using gelatin is an attractive option. Using gelatin, bullets can be tested for depth of penetration, size, shape, volume and stability of the wound track. All the parameters can then be recorded.

What to do with the results of both approaches is where the real arguments begin. The two sides fall into two camps: "High-Velocity Incapacitation" and

"Deep-Penetration Incapacitation."

Both view blood loss as the mechanism of incapacitation. The High-Velocity camp views velocity, even at the expense of some penetration, as adding to incapacitation. The Deep-Penetration camp feels that only by severing large blood vessels can blood loss be accelerated, and the shallow penetration of the high-velocity approach is a poor trade-off.

What is "Good enough?"

Everyone agrees that more is better. The problem is, you cannot get more without cost. A .44 Magnum obviously creates a larger wound track through gelatin than a .38 Special. You don't need a degree in criminal science or ballistics to see that. But the .44 Magnum is a bigger gun with more recoil and muzzle blast. And it is possible to have too much of a good thing. As an example, 9mm, .40 and ,45 full-metal-jacket bullets penetrate too well for law enforcement use. Despite the political objections of some politically motivated police administrators and chiefs, hollow-point rounds are a better choice. If you were thinking that "a little more isn't that much" a short example is in order. Many hollow-point bullets will not penetrate any deeper than 12 to 18 inches in gelatin. They do much the same in people. A 9mm, .40 or .45 full-metal-jacket bullet is capable of penetrating 48 inches of gelatin. There are not a lot of people who are 48 inches thick. Mas Ayoob has recorded a number of police shootings using full

The hardball on the left plowed through 3 feet of gelatin and was luckily captured by a spare test vest. The two hollow-points went 16 inches. Over-penetration is a concern, and rightly so.

Out of the longer barrel of this H-K, the same .45 rounds will penetrate more (hardball) and less (hollow-points). The extra velocity makes the difference.

Many rifle bullets break apart at close range, as the impact velocity is too great for their construction. Breakup can be a good thing or a bad thing.

metal jacket bullets where the fired bullet struck the offender, exited and subsequently struck an innocent bystander. Misses are bad enough, but to have hits pass through and strike bystanders is inexcusable.

Enough penetration without too much is a contentious issue. And then there is the problem of incidental barriers. The bad guys do not stand still. They do not always stand in the open. Sometimes in order to strike the offender, a police officer has to fire through the obstacle the bad guy is using for cover or concealment. Asking a bullet to penetrate a barrier and still expand in the bad guy is a tall order, but manufacturers try. And the FBI has a series of tests. After the 1986 Miami shootout, the FBI got very serious about testing bullets, cartridges and firearms. They developed a series of test protocols to find out what bullets did. Some argue that the FBI insists on

Another handgun round passes the FBI protocols, at least for bare gelatin. However, at 14.5 inches in bare gelatin it may come up short in the later tests.

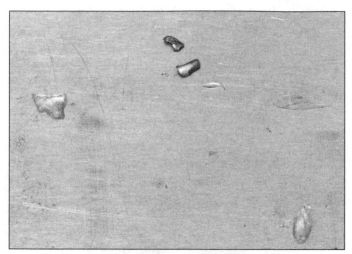

At the 12-inch mark, some rifle bullets only have fragments left to contribute.

Bonded-core bullets do not break up, and are more likely to work through incidental barriers such as vehicle doors. However, they are not a good choice for entry work, as you want bullets to break up in interior walls.

too much penetration, and tests against barriers that are too difficult. One aspect of the scoring system is that a bullet that does not penetrate a full 12 inches in ballistic gelatin has been deemed a failure. One might argue that point, as a .45 hollow-point that has passed through incidental barriers, heavy clothing, expanded and stopped at 11-3/4 inches of gelatin could hardly be called a failure. Perhaps it would have been better to have come up with a scoring system that down-rated but not failed such a bullet, so comparisons could be made of those that fell short.

The FBI test protocols are nothing if not thorough. Check out the sidebar

Two blocks will stop a lot, but not some hardball.

FBI Test Protocols

Test Event 1: Bare Gelatin

The gelatin block is bare and shot at a range of 10 feet measured from the muzzle to the front of the block. The bare gelatin test is a standard so the FBI can compare their test results with other, published and provided test data. As an example, if the FBI test shows that XYZ bullet penetrates 14 inches in bare gelatin, but published data from a state police agency shows the same factory load only penetrated 10 inches, then something has changed between tests. Perhaps it is a newer or older bullet design, the velocity differed, or something else changed. As a benchmark, the bare gelatin test provides a reproducible standard.

Test Event 2: Heavy Clothing

The gelatin block is covered with four layers of clothing: One layer of cotton T-Shirt material (48 threads per inch); one layer of cotton shirt material (80 threads per inch); a 10-ounce down comforter in cambric shell cover (232 threads per inch); and one layer of 13-ounce cotton denim (50 threads per inch). This simulates typical cold-weather wear. The block is shot from 10 feet, measured from the muzzle to the front of the block. Not all shooting incidents happen in the summer, or in warm climates. Amazingly enough, some hollow-point bullet designs do not expand when fired through heavy clothing. It turns out that cloth cut from the garments can clog the hollow portion of the point, and the plugged bullet becomes a non-expanding bullet. As a result of this, some departments that have cold climates for much of the year favor .45-caliber handguns. After all, even if it doesn't expand, it is still a .45 bullet.

Test Event 3: Steel

Two 6-inch square pieces of 20-gauge, hot-rolled steel with a galvanized finish are set 3 inches apart. The

In cold weather, the hollow-point may be plugged and not expand. Then, the .45 has an advantage, since it is already big.

gelatin block is covered with light clothing (Light clothing is one layer of cotton T-shirt material and one layer of cotton shirt material and is used in all subsequent test events) and placed 18 inches behind the rear piece of steel. The shot is made at a distance of 10 feet measured from the muzzle to the front of the first piece of steel.. The steel is the heaviest gauge steel commonly found in automobile doors. This test simulates the weakest part of a car door. In all car doors, there is an area, or areas, where the heaviest

obstacle is nothing more than two pieces of 20-gauge steel. A highway patrol agency would be very interested in what bullets might do when they encounter a car door or trunk panel. As a vehicular society, we spend a lot of time in and around cars. So do officers and their clients. The interesting thing is that many bullets do quite poorly against sheet steel, and even those that do well in this test fail when additional obstacles (as are commonly found in vehicles) are in their path.

Test Event 4: Wallboard

Two 6-inch square pieces of 1/2-inch standard gypsum board are set 3-1/2 inches apart. The gelatin block is covered with light clothing and set 18 inches behind the rear most piece of gypsum. The shot is made 10 feet, measured from the muzzle to the front surface of the first piece of gypsum. This test event simulates a typical interior building wall. Wallboard testing turned up the disparity between 5.56mm and 9mm bullets, and that the disparity was contrary to accepted wisdom. 5.56 bullets break up quickly, while 9mm bullets penetrate. Even hollow-point 9mm bullets can over-penetrate if the wallboard has clogged the hollow and prevented expansion.

Test Event 5: Plywood

One 6-inch square piece of 3/4-inch AA fir plywood is used. The gelatin block is covered with light clothing and set 18 inches behind the rear surface of the plywood. The shot is made at 10 feet, measured from the muzzle to the front surface of the

Ballistic gelatin has to be calibrated according to IWBA specs, or the results can't be compared properly. Here, the airgun calibration is being administered.

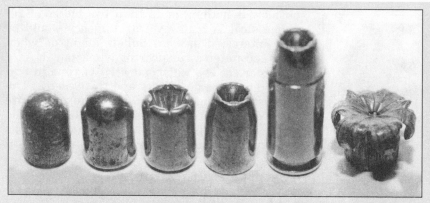

The Speer Gold Dot bullet in its various stages. Left to right: core, plating, punch, shape, loaded round and expanded into gelatin.

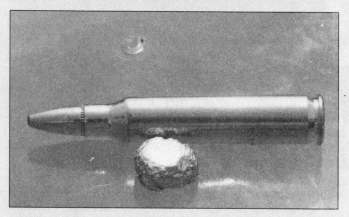

The new bonded-core rifle bullets do not fragment in gelatin.

plywood. This test event simulates the resistance of typical wooden doors or construction timbers. This is a step up from wallboard in housing construction, found in some walls, many doors, and a test of the bullet at the next level of resistance.

Test Event 6: Automobile Glass

One piece of A.S.I. 1/4-inch laminated automobile safety glass measuring 15 inches x 18 inches is set at an angle of 45 degrees to the horizontal. The line of bore of the weapon is offset 15 degrees to the side, resulting in a compound angle of impact for the bullet upon the glass. The gelatin block is covered with light clothing and set 18 inches behind the glass. The shot is made at 10 feet, measured from the muzzle to the center of the glass pane. This test event with its two angles simulates a shot taken at the driver of a car from the left front quarter of the vehicle and not directly in front of it. On this one I have to take a slight disagreement with the FBI. For a sharp bunch, I'm surprised at the "compound angle" aspect of the design parameters. If you tip a piece of glass (or any object) back 45 degrees, you have a 45-degree angle of attack. You can rotate that piece of glass to any other range (provided you've rotated it around the axis of the firearm bore) and you haven't changed the actual angle of attack. You've just made it harder to hold the piece of glass. If you tip it back 45 degrees, and then tip it to the side 15 degrees,

you simply have a piece of glass tipped more than 45 degrees but less than 60, depending on the location of the tipping point and the line of the bore. It would have been far simpler and easier to reproduce to just mandate a single tipping angle and leave it at that. The glass test is a very difficult one, as glass is very hard and abrasive at bullet velocities.

Test Event 7: Heavy Clothing at 20 yards

This event repeats Test Event 2 but at the range of 20 yards, measured from the muzzle to the front of the gelatin. This test event assesses the effects of increased range and consequently decreased velocity. Just in case anyone was worried that handgun ammunition would lose too much velocity in the additional 50 feet. Most will lose very little, perhaps 50 to 100 fps. The velocity loss may be offset by the greater stability of the bullet in flight, having settled down from its release from the muzzle.

Test Event 8: Automobile Glass at 20 yards

This event repeats Test Event 6 but at a range of 20 yards, measured from the muzzle to the front of the glass and without the 15 degree offset. This shot is made from straight in front of the glass, simulating a shot at the driver of a car bearing down on the shooter.

In addition to the above-described series of test events, each cartridge is tested for velocity and accuracy. Twenty rounds are fired through a test barrel and 20 rounds are fired through the service weapon used in the penetration tests. Two 10-shot

Glass is very hard on bullets. And curiously, it is hard to differentiate between calibers just by the hole they make in glass.

groups are fired from the test barrel and two 10-shot groups from the service weapon used, at 25 yards. They are measured from center to center of the two most widely spaced holes, averaged and reported.

The FBI is very thorough, but the results are available only to law enforcement agencies. They will not release the data to the public.

What bullets should you use? The newest generations of bullets have been tested thoroughly, and you could hardly go wrong selecting a known name. What I advise my customers who carry is to try all they can afford, and once they have tested enough to be sure a load is utterly reliable, to use the load that shoots most accurately in the gun they carry.

What is stopping power?

Stopping power is the crux of the issue, and one most prone to contentious arguments. Ideally, we would record all the information from all the shootings, and sift through the information to determine what cartridges and bullets work the best. The most famous attempts at that are the stopping power studies conducted by Evan Marshal and Ed Sanow. However, political and legal realities prohibit a proper scientific analysis. First of all, the reports of shootings are held as proprietary information by the police agencies that investigated them. Many reports can find their way to Evan and Ed only after being edited to remove any information that might let them be traced back. Second, despite being thorough, there are not standards to ensure reproducible comparisons between reports. One report might simply have check boxes for range such as "1-2 yards" "2-4 yards" "Greater than 4 yards" while another has it measured to the inch. Third, all reports are filtered through the participants. Memory is not photographic, and

A flat surface cannot have a "compound angle" it can only have an angle of incidence. Tipping the plate makes the bullet's job more difficult.

participants may wish to emphasis certain aspects to avoid legal problems.

And since Evan and Ed have to keep all reports that come their way confidential in order to protect their sources, their data cannot be viewed by other researchers who may uncover new or different conclusions.

On the other hand, the measurements that come from ballistic gelatin only lack a certain real-life verification that many of us seek. Will the question ever be answered? Probably not to everyone's satisfaction.

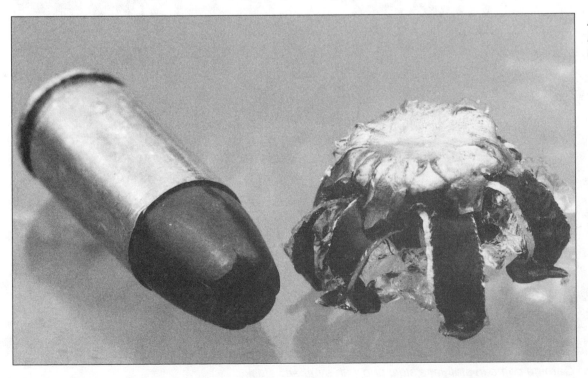

A properly designed bullet expands and does not exit.

Chapter 22
The Patrol Rifle

A RIFLE IN a patrol car is nothing new. In fact, a rifle as a law enforcement officer's tool is not new either. Town Marshals on the Old West kept rifles handy. After all, not every cowboy who rode in for a night of drinking and fighting brought only a handgun with him. A number of rifles started showing up in patrol cars after the riots of the 1960s. Detroit was one such city, issuing or allowing the carry of M-1 Carbines. The catch was, they could only be transported in the trunk. Officers who work in sunny and dry climates might be surprised to know that trunks leak. Any DPD officer who kept his own carbine in the trunk, and didn't wipe it regularly with an oily cloth, soon learned about rust. And what of the departmentally owned carbines? Many rusted into oblong red lumps of useless ordnance.

The modern use of and desire for the patrol rifle puts some police chiefs in a quandary. The line officers want them. Some citizens want the officers to have

them while some don't want the police to have anything that looks aggressive. Many modern rifles do look "aggressive." A black assault rifle is not what some people envision "Officer Friendly" carrying. However, modern rifles have the black plastic for reasons of durability and reliability, and excessive anxiety over cosmetics is a sure prescription for failure. There are some few wooden-stock solutions, but they all have drawbacks. But first, what is a Patrol Rifle?

The desirable traits of a patrol rifle for departmental issue (and here we'll combine the rifles used for patrol, perimeter, entry and raids, and some tactical uses) are; that it be light enough to not be a burden; durable enough to stand up to years of issue, weather, use and training; reliable enough to function for certain when needed despite abuse, neglect or weather; accurate enough that a fight-stopping hit can be certain when used by a trained

Newer versions of the Carbine come in stainless steel and with synthetic stocks.

The patrol rifle is entering law enforcement use in a big way, and the AR-15/M-16 is leading that wave.

If a patrol rifle can't be fired effectively from awkward positions, it isn't much use.

The 5.56mm is "just right" for many users. The FN 5.7 is new, and may prove to be a success, but the big .308 is just too much for much police work.

operator; powerful enough to stop an assailant, without being so powerful that it intimidates new or small officers; simple enough in operation that annual training can keep officers trained in its use; reasonably inexpensive for initial purchase and regular maintenance. And the least tangible, but vitally important factor is that the officers to whom it is issued have confidence in it.

For personally-owned weapons, there are a few extra traits that matter. It must fit the officer who owns it. There should be no sharp edges, corners, hooks or protrusions that can injure the owner.

And whether the rifle is department-owned or personally owned, it must be stored in the patrol car or cruiser in a secure but easily accessible location, secure from theft and not exposed to the elements. If the experience of the FBI agents in Miami in 1986 has taught the law enforcement community one thing, it is that weapons in the trunk or back seat, in the next car or on the next officer might as well be on the moon when they are needed. If an officer can't grab it as he exits the vehicle, he probably won't have it when needed.

What are the likely weapons called on to be a patrol rifle, and why? Do they possess the desired traits listed above?

AR-15/M-16

This is the first rifle thought of in modern usage. Despite its Vietnam-era reputation as an unreliable bullet hose, the AR is the embodiment of the modern patrol rifle. The polymer furniture, aluminum alloy receivers and oxidation-resistant finish on the steel parts make the AR quite resistant to the elements. It can shrug off years of being handed out, taken to the cruiser, carried for a shift, and turned back in. A day of rain on perimeter won't turn it into a mass of fuzzy red oxide. Abused or neglected AR's can show casual accuracy, but then any rifle would so treated. A rack-grade M-16 (the AR is simply an M-16 without the ability to fire full auto or multi-shot bursts) with good ammunition can easily group under 2 inches at 100 yards. The better-tuned examples can do under an inch. The ergonomics of the M-16 are excellent. The safety can be reached without taking your hand

Contrary to much myth, the bullets from a 5.56 do not over-penetrate. This tip was dug out of the front block of gelatin, less than 18 inches of penetration.

This original A-1 M-16 is plenty good enough for patrol work, but don't confused it with a 600-yard target gun.

off the pistol grip. The stock may be a bit short for taller officers, but shorter is easier to deal with than longer. The sights are good, and durable. It has low recoil, and the noise of the muzzle blast is not so great as to impede training. The noise is bad enough to harm hearing, so all training must be done with hearing protection. The 5.56mm cartridge, while faulted by some, has a good track record of getting the job done. And as a bonus, the cartridge can be "tuned" through bullet selection. For use by a

No rifle is useful without a supply of ammunition. And ammo in the car is no more useful than ammo in the precinct.

highway patrol agency, deep-penetrating bullets that hold together through glass, like the Hornady TAP rounds, penetrate cars. For entry teams in an urban setting, more-frangible rounds that will break apart on interior walls make it safer than 9mm weapons.

While it is easy to mount a scope on an AR, it can be a bit more difficult to use than expected. The resulting height of the scope over the stock on most rifles leaves the cheek unsupported, and aiming more difficult.

What the AR has going against it is looks. It looks like an "assault weapon" and as such, some chiefs will not allow their issue or ownership on duty. They don't want their officers getting out of a car looking like they've responded to a complaint in downtown Beirut. The events of September 11 have changed that to a large degree, but many chiefs simply switched from a "no rifles" policy to a "no black rifles" policy.

The current issue version of the M-16 is called the M-4. It differs from earlier versions mainly in that the barrel is 14.5 inches long. When it came out, the selected barrel length was quite puzzling. Why not simply go to a 16-inch barrel? What advantage did the 14.5-inch tube offer? The answer was simple; at 16 inches the barrel forward of the sight base is too long to secure a bayonet. Trim the barrel to 14.5 inches and the standard bayonet now fits. As the bayonet is rarely utilized in law enforcement operations, the shorter barrel offers no advantage. And as a disadvantage, the slightly shorter length lowers muzzle velocity and increases muzzle blast.

AR-18/AR-180

After Armalite (the original company, not the current one) sold the rights to the M-16 to Colt, Eugene Stoner went about the problem in a slightly

The ideal (if bare) patrol rifle. A shorty (16.5-inch) barrel, telescoping stock, and light weight.

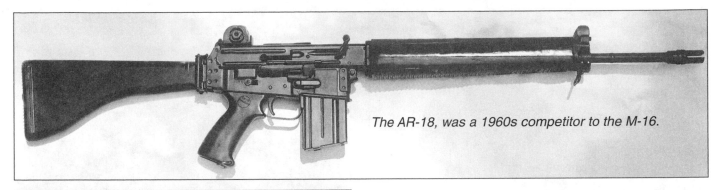

The AR-18, was a 1960s competitor to the M-16.

A bone-stock M-16A1 marked for easy identification.

different manner. The AR-18/180 can be called "an M-16 with an AK gas system." Instead of the direct gas impingement system of the M-16, the AR-18/180 uses an operating rod powered by the gas port drilled into the barrel. Instead of the M-16's forged and machined aluminum receivers, the AR-18 uses stamped and folded sheet steel assemblies. Aluminum forging was not common in the early 1960s, but sheet steel fabrication was. The fly in the ointment: while Armalite was trying to sell their new design, the U.S. Government was giving M-16s away like prizes in cereal boxes. The original Ar18/180s are collector's pieces, and while their magazines look like standard AR-15/M-16 magazines, they aren't. The current model uses a polymer lower receiver and uses standard Colt magazines. The design (old or new) does show promise, but will need to prove itself. The one useful feature of the old design not carried over to the new is the folding stock.

M-14/M-1A

The M-14 is an improved Garand, chambered in 7.62 NATO. It uses a 20-round box magazine, and has a gas system that is an improvement over the Garand. The chief attraction is the power of the cartridge. While some have reservations about the ability of the 5.56mm to get the job done in a fight (I don't) no one complains about the effectiveness of the 7.62mm. The cost of that power is a heavier rifle, and greater recoil. Recoil that isn't oppressive or objectionable, but enough to slow down follow-up shots and make it more difficult to get all officers qualified. The attraction is greater for officers in a

Some shooting stances are meant for long-term comfort, not rapid fire. This trooper in Afghanistan is covering the approach of others in his unit, to search the cave. (DoD photo)

The flat-top carbine allows for easy mounting of optics, like this EO Tech Holosight.

The AR-18 came with the three-prong flash hider much like the old M-16 flash hider.

The AR-18 had a scope clamp built in.

The AR-18 folded, making it very compact.

rural environment, or those dealing almost exclusively with vehicle stops. The 7.62mm retains its power farther downrange than the 5.56mm does. The 5.56 can be a marginal fight-stopper past 200 yards, while the 7.62 has enough effectiveness to solve problems out to 600 yards. And for close-range penetration (like vehicles) the 7.62 is much better. The last car I had the pleasure to shoot up, that caused a problem, was a 1976 Chrysler New Yorker. In summary, nothing would reliably get through the doors except .30-caliber rifles. Not 12-gauge slugs or buckshot, not 5.56mm green-tip AP, not 9mm AP, nothing. The .30-06 and 7.62mm both perforated (through and through) the passenger compartment from any angle that didn't include the engine block. That level of performance is what gains the M-14/M-1A its adherents. The only difference between the M-14 and the M-1A is that the latter was originally manufactured to be semi-only, and therefore is not an NFA weapon. As such it is civilian-legal in all the rational states of the union.

Ruger Mini-14

The Ruger is also chambered in 5.56mm like the AR series, and offers all the advantages thereof. What it has going for it for many administrative officers is that it isn't black and it doesn't have a pistol grip on the stock. The wooden stock of the Ruger is a weakness. I've seen AR/M-16 rifles dropped onto concrete (accidents, we weren't trying to prove anything) that were none the worse except for the scuffmarks. They didn't break anything, and didn't lose their zero. (Change point of impact of the bullet.) Back when I was doing general commercial gunsmithing, one of my regular customers was the Michigan State Prison System. They would bring or send in their "Minis" for service. The stocks were often cracked, but not broken. I can only assume that swapping a stock was so easy that the broken ones were replaced in-house. And replacements must have been cheap enough, because they never were interested in my offers to epoxy-reinforce the stocks with threaded rods to keep them from cracking or

The M-14, or Springfield M-1A, is very accurate, but too large and heavy, and has too much recoil, for patrol work.

Full-metal-jacket bullets often do not deform, and thus usually over penetrate. They can be poor choices for law enforcement.

While the recoil of the .308 can be heavy, an accurate rifle is always desirable. Fifty yards offhand. (Why can't I shoot like that when the instructors get together?)

breaking in the future. Kept in the towers and armory of the various prisons, the Minis didn't suffer too much from the weather. But any wooden-stocked rifle may have problems from the stock warping with changes in humidity, temperature or heavy weights sitting on them in the trunk of a car.

The other shortcoming in maintenance was the gas system. The gas system of the AR/M-16 is self-cleaning, and the bolt and carrier is easily cleaned. On the Mini-14, the gas system is clamped to the barrel at the end of the forearm. The four cap screws that hold it together are on very tightly, and not meant to be removed by the operator. One rainy day at the range or out of the patrol car on a deployment, or a batch of mildly corrosive surplus ammo, and the

gas systems would start seizing. Removing the cap screws quite often meant deforming them, and thus replacing them. Once the system (with small parts, easily lost) was put back together, it was simply waiting for the next rain to fail.

In durability, the rear sight of the Mini-14 is fragile. The sight blade has no protection from impacts. The sight mechanism on the adjustable sights is not rigid, and the play in the parts makes it tougher to shoot accurately. The front sight is a plain blade, with no protection. It can be worn from racks or gun cases to be shiny and tough to use.

The Mini-14 magazines lock into the rifle in much the same manner as its design model, the M-14. Each magazine must be rocked into and out of the rifle. The magazine change must be done with one hand holding the rifle while the other grasps the magazine and its latch. Rock the magazine forward, and then pull it out. Inserting the replacement requires hooking the

The Ruger Mini-14 is a nice lightweight duty rifle.

The wooden stock is a weakness, but the Garand-type safety (in the trigger guard) is good.

The Ruger rear sight is fragile and exposed.

The Ruger magazine catch is behind the magazine, and not as easy to manipulate as the AR-15/M-16.

front retainer into the rifle, then pivoting the magazine up and back to lock it in place. On the AR, one hand can be pressing the release button while the other is reaching for the replacement.

Heckler & Koch G series

The H&K G rifles started with the G-3. After WWII, the West German Army was kept small, and not allowed to manufacture (or rather, have manufactured for it) anything in Germany. The G-1 and G-2 were Belgian FN-FAL models built for the German Army. H&K, when the time came that Germany was allowed firearms manufacturing again, used a design that had been developed at the end of WWII. The locking mechanism is the "delayed blow-back, roller-locked" system. A shaft that bears on two roller bearings connects the bolt head and the bolt body. When the mechanism closes, the roller bearings are cammed outwards, and rest in recesses machined in the barrel extension. When the round fires, the thrust of recoil is borne by the roller bearings in their recess. The thrust is transferred to the bolt body, and as it recoils it allows the rollers to cam out of the recesses. Once the rollers clear the recesses, residual chamber pressure blows the action open and cycles the bolt. The delayed blow-back, roller-locked system is very reliable.

As if all that wasn't revolutionary enough, the rifle was made of heavy-gauge sheet metal stampings, folded, shaped and welded together. The barrels are hammer-forged, the stocks molded plastic. The only machined parts are the bolt assembly and some trigger parts. The G-3 was made select-fire with options being safe, semi and full. The semi-only 7.62mm rifles are called the H&K Model 91.

Parts interchangeability on the G-3 was amazing. You could swap any assembly with any other rifle and things would work. The cost, however, was great. First, it is heavy. The G-3/91 (in 7.62mm) and the corresponding H&K 93 in 5.56, are somewhat (the 7.62 is a pound more than an M1-A) to a lot (the 93 is 2 pounds more than a similar AR-15) heavier than comparable rifles. They are not, however, unique in being heavy. An FN-FAL is also heavy. The really

The H-K G series rifles are heavy and expensive, even though reliable and accurate.

A short-barreled .308 is loud, heavy, kicks hard, and can be tough to shoot a qualifying score with. But they are popular.

amazing thing about an H-K rifle is the ejection. The residual chamber pressure blows the action open. The bolt, as a result, travels back very quickly. So quickly, in fact, that the empty brass only has enough time to begin tipping out of the ejection port before the bolt has brought it to the rear of the port. The brass is caromed off the rear edge of the ejection port at high speed. H&K brass comes out hot and fast, and travels far. And ends up with multiple creases. To aid extraction, the chamber is fluted, and hot gases flow back between the case and the chamber walls. Also, the brass striking the ejection port puts a heavy crease in the brass. The German Army had no interest in reloading (nor does any army, for that matter) so the mangled brass was not a problem. For those contemplating reloading, or turning brass over

The H-K UMP comes from the same design imperatives that the G-36 did. As much polymer as possible.

The FAL is long, and heavier than an AR.

The FN-FAL gas system is adjustable. The first thing I'd do once it is adjusted properly is paint it in.

Some safeties on the FAL can be reached, and others are too much for those with small hands.

to a reloader to stretch the budget, brass fired in an H&K rifle is a real impediment.

One technical aspect, in the interests of safety, that can be a problem, is the trigger pull. The original specifications called for a loaded rifle, with the safety off, to withstand a fall of 25 meters onto soft earth without discharging. As a result of the need to pass the test, some rifles can have heavy and gritty trigger pulls, making training and qualification difficult.

Heckler & Koch G-36

The G-36 is not like any of the previous "G" series rifles. Instead of heavy-gauge steel stampings the G-36 is made of polymer built onto and integrated with a steel skeleton. It has a built-in optical sight and carry handle, and rates very high on the "cool looks" scale. My experience with it totals a few hours on three separate occasions, and personally I don't like it. The optics are difficult for me to see through. The stock flexes under recoil. It is reliable and accurate enough for the job. One contact I have on the Washington Capitol Police told me they had to struggle to get them to work well enough, and had to install Aimpoint sights to be able to aim. Knowing my contact, the "get working well enough" refers to the ergonomics and the sighting, and not the reliability. Had he found it unreliable, he would have used much more colorful language to describe the process. If your department buys and issues them, make sure your officers can handle them properly. (But then, you should do that with any rifle, right?)

FN-FAL

The FN-FAL is the evolution of the SAFN-49 rifle that had its design beginnings before WWII. The designer, Deudonne Saive, fled Belgium ahead of the approaching German Army, taking the blueprints with him to avoid such a revolutionary rifle falling into their hands. After the war, FN (his employer) and he evolved the design into the FAL. The original intent was to make a rifle chambered in a cartridge good enough for the Infantry, without the excessive recoil and range that the .30-06 produced. The attempt failed when the U.S. Army refused to consider any cartridge with less power than the one they already had. The result was the FAL being altered and chambered for the same cartridge as the American M-14, the 7.62 NATO. Was it successful? It went on to be adopted by almost every country in the free world that wasn't getting free weapons from the United States.

Rugged, reliable, and reasonably accurate (it is very tough to turn into a tactical marksman rifle) the FN-FAL suffers from two faults that are unforgivable; it is long and heavy. The barrel can be shortened to make it handier (but never as handy as an AR) but it is heavy. Then again, chambered for the robust .308, a bit of weight is not a bad thing. The sights are not as easily adjustable as the M-14, but the gas system can be easily adjusted to use any ammunition that will chamber.

FN-FNC

The FNC was the result of FN trying to come up with a 5.56mm rifle to compete with the M-16. Early in the M-16's use, it was felt to be fragile and unreliable. In the long run it proved to be easier to improve the M-16 than come up with a replacement. The FNC is now out of production, and the semi-only examples are collector's items. (Like almost every other rifle in this list, I had a chance to purchase an FNC at one time, but needed the money more for things like rent and groceries. I should have learned my lesson sooner, and lived in a cheaper place and kept my waist small.) The FNC used AR/M-16 magazines, so feeding it is no problem. To see one in the movies, watch the dynamic and heart-stopping shoot-out scene in the movie "Heat." The rifle Al Pacino is using is an FNC.

The Steyr AUG magazines clip together for fast reloads. Clipped together they don't fit standard ammo pouches. The two on the right will fit in a three-mag pouch. The three on the left will fit in a gym bag.

Steyr AUG

The Steyr is unlike any other rifle on the list. The design is a bullpup, with the action is stuffed back into the buttstock. The whole idea of a bullpup design is to make a full-sized rifle fit a compact package. The advantages are obvious; compact size for handling and storage, less length to catch on objects or offer opponents a lever for attempted takeaways. The disadvantages are not all apparent. First, a bullpup presents a problem of what to do with the empty brass. Since the shooters face is right over the action, the empties are ejected from directly underneath your face, on the opposite side of the receiver. Which means you can't shoot it left-handed. The Steyr gets around this. You can disassemble it and rebuild it as a left-handed rifle. But you can't do that in the middle of a shootout. The short length and weight-in-the-rear design make most bullpups neutral or butt-heavy in balance. And the muzzle is closer to the shooter, and therefore louder.

The Steyr AUG (Universal Automatic Rifle in German) is more than just a bullpup. The housing the parts are assembled into is a polymer shell. Many of the trigger mechanism parts are fiberglass-reinforced polymer. The barrel is changeable in a matter of seconds. You can literally go from a 16-inch to a 20-inch to a 24-inch with attached bipod in a few seconds, without even (in an emergency) removing the loaded magazine. And the carry handle has a built-in low magnification scope with a sighting ring. Lastly, on the select-fire version, the trigger is the selector. Press back as normal for single shots, and yank the trigger vigorously to over-ride the mechanism into full auto fire.

The AUG does not use M-16 magazines. However, the Steyr magazines are unbelievably durable and reliable. The Australian Army adopted the AUG and found they had to make some changes. Their Marines and Special Operations teams found that their sand was very fine, and could cause the dual operating bars to bind in their housings after an amphibious operation. Modifying the bars solved that problem. They also found that they had to change the scores for qualification. The old course had been based on soldiers firing the FN-FAL, and with the new rifles in 5.56mm and using a low-powered scope, scores skyrocketed. Without changes, they would have had everyone in the service scoring as Expert.

Durable, reliable, accurate and easy to use, the Steyr AUG is a love it or hate it rifle.

SA-80

The SA-80 would serve well as a military equivalent of a lesson by example that MBA programs are so fond of. (We shouldn't be too harsh on the British on this one, after all we did it twice: with the M-1 Carbine and then the initial introduction of the M-16) The SA-80 is a bullpup with all the vices and few of the advantages of the design, with other problems thrown in. Field experience has shown it to be fragile (parts falling off or failing), unreliable (the Ministry of Defence blames that on poor maintenance) and have marginal accuracy (still a problem of unknown origins). In general the SA-80 is viewed without enthusiasm by the troops. The basic problem stems from a parsimonious acceptance procedure. Once the design seemed "good enough" it was pushed into production. Once in production, any changes were deemed "too expensive and unnecessary" and turned down. Rarely seen in the U.S., and thus a collector's piece, it is not a viable option as a law enforcement patrol rifle.

FN 2000

Designed and built by Fabrique National, the 2000 is another bullpup, but one that overcame the faults of the earlier rifles. The two big differences in operation between the 2000 and the others are ejection and the replacement forearm. The 2000, instead of ejecting the

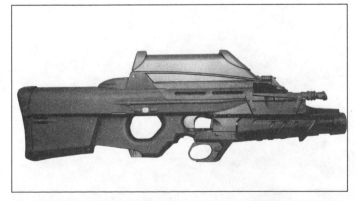

The FN 2000 may be the future of police carbines. It sure is compact and easy to shoot.

The M-1 Carbine is a holdover from an earlier time. While it can be effective, there are much-better carbines to be had.

empty brass out one side or the other, takes the empty brass and stuffs it down a tube towards the muzzle. Once you've fired a few rounds, the empties collected in the tube begin gently dropping out the front. If you pause and point the muzzle down, they'll slide right out. Hence it is a bullpup that can be switched from one shoulder to another without modifications. The forearm clips onto or off of the rifle. It can be replaced with a single-shot grenade launcher, a light mount, or anything else that can be fitted with the mounting hardware to clip to the rifle. The scope is clamped in a mount that is covered by the same polymer shell that covers the mechanism. As a result of this approach, it can be exchanged when damaged without having to withdraw the whole receiver from service, as with the AUG. It can also be changed to a different scope if desired. Time will tell if the reliable and accurate FN 2000 can cut some space for itself in the market.

M-1 Carbine

This is another wooden-stocked rifle, selected by many departments because it is not an aggressive-looking rifle. As such, a dropped carbine may suffer a cracked or broken stock. And wood can warp. Before the collectors started poring through the supply, carbines could be had relatively

inexpensively. As the supply of original ones dries up, and collectors snap up the rare ones, the price has risen. The Carbine suffers from multiple faults as a patrol rifle. First, its cartridge, the .30 Carbine, is not as useful as the 5.56mm. In a soft-point or hollow-point version, the carbine bullet can be a fight-stopper. However, neither of those two versions can penetrate body armor. In the full-metal-jacket version, it suffers from both a lack of stopping power and over penetration. And many shooters have heard tales for years of how the carbine was unreliable in the Korean War.

The magazines often do not fall free when the release button is pressed, requiring the use of both hands on the reload. Overall, there are much better choices for duty rifles than the M-1 Carbine.

The sights are very useful and sturdy.

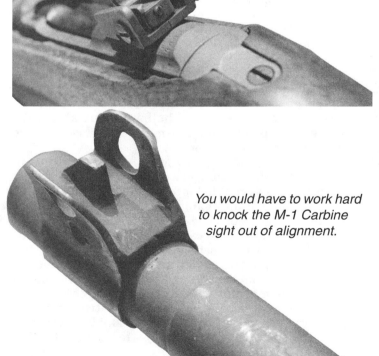

You would have to work hard to knock the M-1 Carbine sight out of alignment.

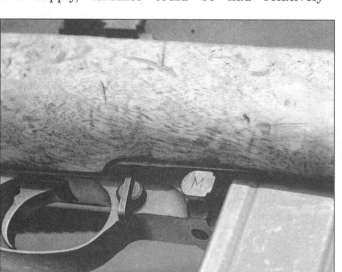

Here is the M-1 Carbine safety and magazine release.

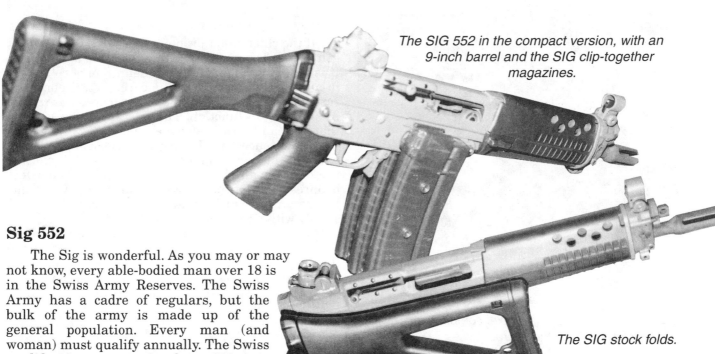

The SIG 552 in the compact version, with an 9-inch barrel and the SIG clip-together magazines.

Sig 552

The Sig is wonderful. As you may or may not know, every able-bodied man over 18 is in the Swiss Army Reserves. The Swiss Army has a cadre of regulars, but the bulk of the army is made up of the general population. Every man (and woman) must qualify annually. The Swiss qualification course involves 300-meter shooting with iron sights. The Swiss held off adopting the 5.56mm NATO round until they could have one accurate enough for the qualification course. And they wanted a rifle to match it. The Swiss know how to make precision-machined equipment, and the Sig rifles show it. They are durable, accurate, reliable and ergonomically designed. But they are imported. While your departmental armorer can pick up spare parts at a gun show if need be, Sig spares can only come from across the Atlantic. Ditto magazines. The Sig magazines are durable, reliable, and they even clip together so you can handle them as pairs or triplets. (Although fitting them into a magazine pouch that way can be tough.) But you won't be able to buy a bushel of them on the surplus market. As a departmental weapon, with factory-supplied tools and service, it is a great choice. As an individual one, the few that are on the market are so ferociously expensive (not many were imported for civilian purchase before the importation regulations were changed, shutting off the supply) that you could buy several ARs, and enough ammo to wear them out, for the cost of a Sig.

Besides reliability and ruggedness, the Sig 552 has another feature that endears it to trainers and administrators. The selector switch can lock out full-auto fire. The lever on the side of the receiver is simple. Open the receiver, turn the lever to cover the "30" and then close the receiver. Now, all that will show is the safe and numeral 1. The position dots painted onto the receiver also let the shift commander, supervisor or anyone else who cares to look, know just what status your selector lock-out is in.

Bought on departmental letterhead, as departmental property, they are not too expensive. But users don't have any options for seeking outside armorers work or modifications.

The SIG stock folds.

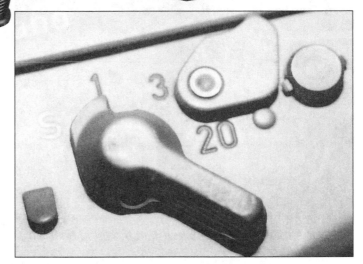

The selector can be left open, so the rifle can fire burst and full auto.

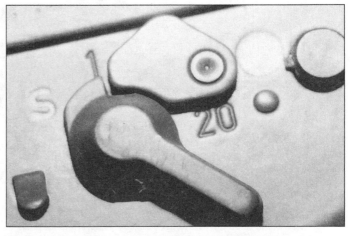

Or be locked out, so the choices are safe and semi.

The SIG sight is sturdy, adjustable, complex and exquisitely finished. In other words, Swiss.

AK-47

If the chief had a problem with ARs, then he isn't going to go for an AK. The AK has some advantages. It is reliable. Indeed, the very definition of reliability in a rifle is an AK. While the carbon steel parts can rust, the bore is chrome-lined and so even a furry red AK is going to function. The tolerances are so large that you can literally swish a muddy AK around in a ditch, and shoot it. However, its disadvantages are many in the law enforcement role. First, the stock is too short for any but the smallest officer. The safety is unreachable without taking your hand off the rifle. Where an AR can be changed from "safe" to "Semi" simply with a push of the thumb, to do the same with an AK you have to let go with one hand or the other. When it comes to ammo, the common chambering of the AK, the 7.62x39, offers two choices; cheap and dangerous or expensive and safer. The imported ammo is corrosive, and has steel jackets or cores. As such it will over penetrate. Using domestic, metal-

The safety is also the dustcover.

The AK safety can't be reached with the firing hand on the pistol grip.

The now-common AK-47. Not the first choice of very many firearms instructors, or chiefs.

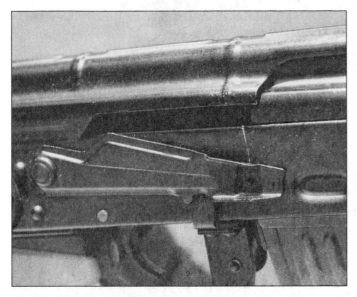

Open, the safety is off.

The AK and SKS have the same sight system, a sturdy front...

And a notch rear forward of the action.

jacketed ammunition alleviates the penetration problem some but it is still over-penetrative indoors.

The sights are not good for LE work, although plenty good enough for military applications. Mounting a scope on it to overcome the iron sights is not easy, and often not any more satisfactory than the irons were.

SKS carbine

The SKS suffers mainly from a low ammunition supply (it has an attached 10- round magazine that must be reloaded via stripper clips) and marginal reliability. Most of the examples seen in the U.S. are Chinese, manufactured as inexpensively as possible and sold so cheaply they are almost disposable rifles. Chambered in 7.62x39, it suffers from all the faults of the AK in that regard.

Galil

The Galil is a product-improved AK, designed and built by the Israeli Defense Force. The most-common standard of maintenance of small arms in Israel could be best described as benign neglect. As a result, any firearm made or issued must be utterly reliable. The Galil is that. The AK safety is improved by linking a thumb lever on the pistol grip to the big AK safety, so you can push it to fire without removing your hand from the pistol grip. The magazine catch has not been changed; so magazine changes require both hands. More accurate than the AK, the Galil can be had in either 7.62mm or 5.56mm. In 7.62 the rifle is large for patrol use. In 5.56mm it tends to be heavy.

The 9mm choices

The big advantages of the 9mm carbines or submachineguns is the reduced cost of ammo and the ability to use the guns on indoor ranges. Some departments mandate 9mm carbines for fear of over-penetration or excessive range. Both are wrong, but some cannot be convinced otherwise.

Heckler & Koch MP-5

For a long time the MP-5 was the standard shoulder weapon that all entry, raid and special operations teams used. It is reliable but heavy, being a G-3 design descendant chambered in 9mm Parabellum. The safety is the same "can't reach it unless you have thumbs like an orangutan" H&K design. As a result, some teams' standard procedure is to enter with the safety in the "fire" position, but with the trigger finger outside of the trigger guard. (A policy that gives me the willies.) The MP-5 is accurate and utterly reliable, although they do tend to go through extractor springs faster than other designs. The MP-5 uses H&K magazines that are extremely reliable and durable. The curved ones are newer, and more reliable than the straight ones.

In layout, the MP-5 is not the most compact SMG. The magazine well is in the front of the receiver, with the mechanism and trigger assembly behind it. Utilizing the H&K delayed roller blowback system it is reliable but long and heavy. The slightly bulkier design actually makes it easier to shoot well than other SMGs, as it is more like a rifle than they often are.

The MP-5 still has a use, especially where a suppressed weapon is called for, but it has fallen out of favor, replaced by 5.56 rifles, mainly due to the weight-to-power ratio. For the same weight, and an only slightly larger package, you can have a 5.56 rifle instead of a pistol-caliber carbine.

Uzi

The Uzi is an early design for the Israeli Defense Forces, and was the first successful design with some revolutionary features. The magazine well is the grip. The bolt is designed to project forward over the barrel, adding more mass and placing part of that mass forward of the chamber and of the pivot point during recoil. Utterly reliable, the Uzi suffers from its design imperatives as an easy-to-produce military weapon. It fires from an open bolt; so precision shooting is more difficult. The top of the receiver is removable for disassembly, so attaching a scope or red dot sight is not possible. It is very compact with a folding stock, but is even more difficult to shoot precisely that way. With a fixed stock it is easier to shoot accurately, but becomes almost the heaviest and bulkiest of SMGs.

Colt SMG

The Colt SMG is an M-16 modified to work with 9mm ammo. The changes are slight, and rifles can be rebuilt from one to the other. The Colt uses magazines modified from Uzi magazines. The Colt modifications are to change the magazine catch to a location that works with the AR magazine catch, and a spine in the rear of the tube to hold a bolt hold-open tab. Original Uzi magazines with the Colt magazine slot milled in them still function, but will not lock the action open when empty. The Colt has a reputation for marginal reliability, but every one I've ever used worked 100 percent of the time. The magazines do have an annoying tendency to spew ammo if dropped. The solution to that is to either not drop them, or carry spares.

The big advantage to the Colt SMG is that the manual of arms and manipulation, is the same as that of the AR/M-16, so training is made easier with both in stock. Changing from a Colt SMG to an AR, or vice versa, is a lot easier than going from a Colt to an H&K, or any of the others.

Ruger PC9GR

The Ruger Carbine is a blowback 9mm built to be about the same size as an M-1 Carbine, with inoffensive lines. It uses Ruger handgun magazines, and as a result commonly has only a 10- or 15-round capacity. The sights are not easy to adjust and can be knocked out of zero. While reasonably reliably they are not as durable as other carbines or patrol rifles.

Ruger also offers an SMG of a modified Uzi design, but with a better folding stock.

Kel-Tec Sub 2000

As a stand-in for a regular SMG or carbine, the Kel-Tec can be great. (There is a chapter on it later.) As a full-time carbine, I have my reservations. I haven't had a chance to do the years of range testing I like before adopting something. My friend Jeff Chudwin has had the earlier version for many years, his is still going strong, but he uses it as a back-up carbine that rides in his gear bag.

Which model is best? Many will work for patrol use, some better than others. As time goes by and field experience accumulates, the AR/M-16 is shaping up as the new standard. This is partly due to a wide supply of spare parts and accessories and partly due to ex-military personnel being familiar with it, but mostly due to the virtues of the design. The last of the faults and shortcomings of the design were corrected more than 20 years ago, and the occasional manufacturing problems are easily dealt with. For length of service with the Armed Forces the M-16 has already surpassed every other shoulder weapon. However, it has a long way to go before it passes the benchmarks of the Browning-designed M-2 .50-caliber machinegun, and the 1911 pistol. Both are still with us, even though "better" designs were supposed to have supplanted them years ago. Even if those two icons disappear tomorrow, the M-16 will have to be in service until the year 2048 to pass the M-2, and until 2055 to pass the 1911. It has beaten all comers to this point, long since passing the Lee-Enfield and Mauser rifles. Some might argue that the .38 Special S&W revolver still has it beat, as it started before the 1911 and is still going strong in some circles. But we will ignore them. Of course, the real record would be that of the Brown Bess, the British Army musket. Introduced in 1712, it wasn't replaced until the 1850s, when rifled muskets came into use. That would put the M-16 record date in the first decade of the 22nd Century. I wish I could be around to see if it makes it.

Shotguns

The traditional law enforcement long gun has been the shotgun. It is traditional for a number of reasons. First, law enforcement activities happen at what Jeff Cooper calls "conversational distances." While much military work goes on at a distance too great for the voice to be heard, almost none of the police work happens at that range. After all, if you aren't close enough to tell someone that they are under arrest, you are rarely in a legal position to be shooting them. (Precision riflemen aside.) Law enforcement rarely requires sustained fire, so a large-capacity rifle is not often needed. And, back when hunting was more common, and a high percentage of police officers came to the job from the military, you could count on almost all of them knowing how to use a pump shotgun.

The shotgun still has a place in law enforcement.

The only one of these not shifted markedly from the past is the distance. In an age of high-capacity everything (handguns, rifles, shotguns) in the hands of police, perpetrators and in the movies, is there a place for the shotgun? Yes. It still has a great deal of fight-ending power ("stopping power" Terminal ballistics", whatever you wish to call it) in a compact and easy-to-use package. The trick is knowing the limitations and strengths.

Limitations

The shotgun can be bulky. Even a short-barreled pump gun can be a handful for a smaller officer. Hand a typical police 870 with an 18-inch barrel to a woman who is only 5 feet tall, and you'll have problems getting her to qualify. The buttstock should also be shortened. Two sizes, short and shorter, will accommodate everyone. It is easier for a tall man to use a stock that is a bit too short, than it is for a short woman (or man) to use a stock that is too long.

The shotgun recoils a lot. The ammunition manufacturers have been made aware of that, and have come out with "low-recoil" or "tactical" loads. The result is a 12-gauge that shoots more like a 20-gauge. The reduced recoil does come at a price, and that is velocity. However, the typical 12-gauge buckshot load has so much power that cutting back a bit does not make it very much less effective. While shotguns can be ported to reduce recoil, porting is not recommended for a "street gun." Ports reduce felt recoil by diverting the propellant gases. The diverted

The problem with shotguns is they are always running out of ammo. You need a ready supply, and a tactical thigh rig can do that. (Courtesy Blackhawk industries.)

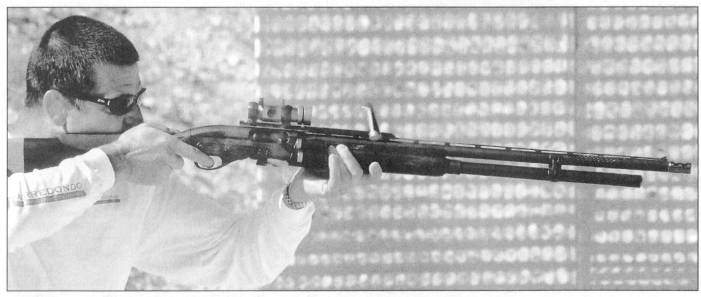

In competition, shotguns get longer, and sport porting, optics and many gadgets.

This is the Neostad, a new and unique shotgun from South Africa. My friend John Flentz demonstrates the pump-forward action.

The two tubes on top are the magazine tubes. The barrel is the bottom one.

gases have to go somewhere. In a crowded shooting situation, it is bad enough being close to the muzzles of fellow officers. But to be in the path of the diverted gases of porting or a compensator is a miserable place to be. You could injure someone. (No ports or comps on rifles, either.) Recoil can also be dampened with a good recoil pad. Instead of the hard plastic or steel buttplates of old, a soft rubber or synthetic pad can take enough of the sting out of shooting to make it possible or even fun to qualify.

Everyone has an opinion about patterns and choking. The two divergent theories are: more spread and less spread. The more spread theory is that by making the pattern as large as possible you increase the potential of hitting the target. The problem is you also increase the potential of hitting other things and people, too. And, the pattern quickly spreads out so much that your hits become random, and you don't place enough pellets on the target to effectively stop a fight.

The less spread idea is to keep all of the available energy in the pattern, and on the target, so you cause incapacitation as quickly as possible. The problem is, you then have to shoot the shotgun much the same way you would as a rifle: by aiming, and not merely pointing. The military spent quite some time and effort trying to make shotguns the replacement for rifles, and demanded a level of performance in patterning that would guarantee at least one pellet strike on a man at 100 meters. That requires a "pattern"

not much more than 4 feet at 100 yards. There is no choke around that will do that with anything, let alone buckshot. They had to give up once it became clear they were asking the impossible. However, a good choke on a good barrel will often keep most of the pellets in a buckshot load in the "A" zone at 25 meters. And it is possible with a good barrel to keep all slug shots on a silhouette at 100 yards.

Another decision that can raise arguments and tempers is the choice between pump and auto. The pump is the "never-fail" choice, or so its defenders will say. I've seen pumps fail, and seen those pumping them fail. The advocates of the auto point out it doesn't need force to work since it works itself, at which point the pump advocates will bring up the delicate nature of many gas systems. Any self-loading firearm will need maintenance; the shotgun just needs a bit more than the rest. My brother and I had no problems getting our Remington 1100 shotguns to go through the Gunsite shotgun course. We simply spent each lunch break of the week breaking down our guns and cleaning the gas system. Were we being too fussy? No, in every course I've been to at Gunsite I've spent some or all of the lunch break each day cleaning my firearm. I'm there to learn to shoot, not learn to deal with malfunctions caused by not cleaning. One old canard that must be put to rest is the notion that the pump is faster than the auto because "the shooter doesn't have to wait for the bolt to cycle." I shot in the shotgun class at the Second Chance combat shoot. We hosed bowling pins as fast as possible with shotguns loaded with

The Neostad field strips quite easily.

buckshot. I set or tied the records in both categories; pump and auto. And my pump times could not catch my auto times. Anyone who tells you a pump is faster doesn't know how to shoot. Or they're using some load that deliberately slows down the auto.

The last controversial choice is sights. Bead, open sights or ghost ring? Traditional shotgun shooters will tell you everything can be done with a bead. Yes, but... Yes, but it takes a lot of practice, it isn't easy, and sometimes it isn't fast. The open sights many shotguns are shipped with are much better. For those willing to spend some time learning, the new ghost rings can be very fast, quite accurate, and an easy transition for those who learned on an aperture sight on a rifle. With the quick development and adoption of red-dots and optics for carbines, it won't be long before shotguns can be equipped with similar sighting systems.

The shotgun isn't obsolete, it just needs the right extras and its operators the proper training.

Chapter 23

Improving the AR-15/M-16

THE MOST COMMON long gun on SWAT and
entry teams used to be the MP-5. The shortcomings
of a 9mm weapon are discussed elsewhere. Recently
the AR-15/M-16 has rapidly increased in popularity
as the weapon of choice for these operations. While
quite useful in its stock form, the AR, like any
product, can be improved. Not all improvements are
equally useful for all applications, and not all
"improvements" are actual steps forward in utility.

In its stock form, the AR is well proportioned and
quite ergonomic. Which is what you'd expect, since
those were some of the design intentions. However,
things have changed since the Armalite design was
first shown the light of day in the late 1950s. There
are many things that can be done to improve its
handling or ability to take accessories that were
never thought of back when Ike was President. I do
not consider reliability as something that needs
"improving", but rather something that is an
absolute. The AR or any other rifle must be
absolutely reliable or it is not a suitable platform to
be improved upon. No amount of extra gear will turn
an otherwise unreliable individual weapon into
something you would want to use in a sticky
situation or on a raid. Reliability must be 100
percent or the rifle is not useful. Improvements in
the AR fall into six main categories: Aiming, lighting,
handling, accuracy, slings and magazine storage. The
seventh category you must attend to is magazine
selection and maintenance.

*Not all malfunctions are rifle or magazine-induced. This
factory round was never going to fire (the primer is in
sideways) and caused a qual-course failure. Always,
ALWAYS check every single one of your duty rounds
before loading them.*

Aiming

An inherently accurate rifle with no sights is
little better than a shotgun. Without some way to
take advantage of the accuracy potential, it remains
potential and not actual. Aiming improvements come
in two ways: a trigger that is good enough, and a
more-precise aiming system. I say a trigger that is
"good enough" because some shooters, competitors

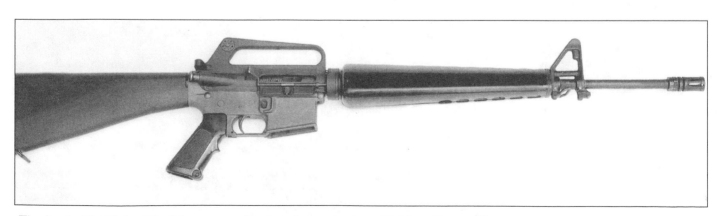

The basic M-16A1, while it has some shortcomings, can be a viable police carbine

Competitive shooters will experiment and develop new gear in order to win. My friend Jake Kempton with two sights on his rifle.

and team members chase the perfect trigger without putting said trigger into the context of its use. A USPSA Grand Master running through a 3-gun match may be well served with a light, (how does less than 2 pounds sound?) crisp (no creep or backlash), target trigger. But a raid team going through the door of a clandestine drug lab with that same trigger is asking for trouble. A clean, reasonably crisp trigger of 4-1/2 pounds is plenty light enough. A trigger with no creep isn't needed, provided the creep isn't "jumpy", that is, you can feel it clicking through its travel. A long smooth "creepy" trigger is just what the Sig 550 series often have, and the Swiss manage to qualify annually with it out to 300 meters. Trigger feel is difficult to describe and relatively easy to feel. Once you feel one that is "good enough" you don't need a description.

As a result, a Match or two-stage trigger system is wasted on a patrol or raid rifle. If you are using an AR as a Tactical Marksman Rifle, then you need a trigger good enough to shoot to and beyond the departmental standard. But on an issue patrol rifle, a light target trigger is asking for trouble.

The iron sights that come on the rifle are plenty good enough for much work. In the course of teaching, I have had occasion to arrive at a National Guard base, and the class has access to the 300-meter computer course. In it, the hit-sensitive targets pop up, and whether you hit them or not they eventually fall. If you hit them they fall immediately. When the course is done, the computer spits out your score. I have fired 20 hits on 20 target exposures more than once, and with iron sights as well as scopes and red dot sights. (Each target will register

The AR/M-16 can be built into a small-caliber precision rifle. Here my friend Jake Kempton of Accuracy Speaks is working over some 600-yard plates.

Some find laser sights useful for aiming. They also work as intimidators. Who wants to keep up their unfriendly activities after seeing the red (or green) dot? (Courtesy Surefire)

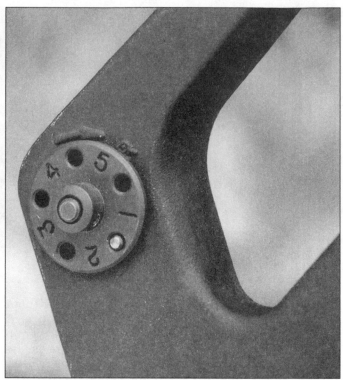

The A1 sight is adjustable, but not easily so. This is an advantage in keeping unauthorized idle hands from messing with your zero.

all hits until it has fallen. I have taken advantage of that mechanical/electronic quirk to post a hit "score" of 27 hits on a 20-target exposure run. On one occasion, my friend Jeffrey Chudwin and I teamed up on a target run to post a hit "score" of 37 hits on 20 target exposures.) For many law enforcement uses, well inside 100 yards, iron sights will work just fine. But when "better" is available, many will take advantage of it. Mounting a scope or red dot sight on an AR greatly improves hit potential. The temptation is to press the advantage too far. A high-powered scope can be a detriment when trying to engage close targets at high speed. And battery-dependant red dot scopes can fail in bitter cold, or be obscured in rain.

Lighting

Much police work happens at night, and in buildings with little or no illumination. Modern manufacturing buildings are made with as few windows as possible. Windows cost money to buy and install, and act as conduits for heat loss. A call-out to a manufacturing building may mean a windowless location with the lights out. (Might as well be a cave in Afghanistan, or the hold of a ship for all the illumination present.) In the old days, using a light meant one hand on the light and one hand on the weapon. For a rifle or shotgun, that was a tough job. Since the early days of duct tape and hose clamps (I'm not kidding, we used to do just that) inventors and manufacturers have come up with many solutions. Some are "good enough" and inexpensive. Others are the best you can get and, while pricey, worth it.

If you have any chance of ending up in a dark place with a patrol rifle in your hands, you simply must have some means of illumination at your disposal.

Handling

The "one size fits all' approach of the military when it comes to weapons is an unsatisfactory one for law enforcement. Not all officers are the same size, and not all can effectively use the "best" weapon as determined by the 6-foot, 4-inch Chief Range Officer. If you have any doubts about that, ask the FBI. They

ended up in court over their weapons policy and training procedures, lost, and had to change both.

In particular, the AR stock, especially the new A2 stock, can easily end up too long for some officers. Also, storage in vehicles can be a problem with a full-size AR/M-16. Shortening both the stock and barrel can make the rifle easier and more effective to handle. Also in the handling department is weight. It is all too easy to add accessories to the rifle, and end up with an overly heavy rifle that you simply can't carry around all day. The best rifle in the world is of no use if it is so heavy that when the time comes, you can't lift it.

Accuracy

Inherent accuracy is dependant on the ammunition used and the barrel quality and condition. Use of the wrong ammunition in a barrel can lead to poor or non-existent accuracy. Use of a poor quality barrel, or poorly maintained barrel, can lead to loss of accuracy. A good rifle, with a good barrel, fed new factory ammunition suited to the barrel can easily deliver groups an inch or smaller at 100 yards.

Slings

As my friend Jeff Chudwin has said many times, "A sling is a holster for your rifle." Without a sling, you can only devote one hand to operations other than firing the rifle. You can't properly deal with a suspect, haul someone to a safer location, utilize your sidearm, or haul a heavy object without putting the

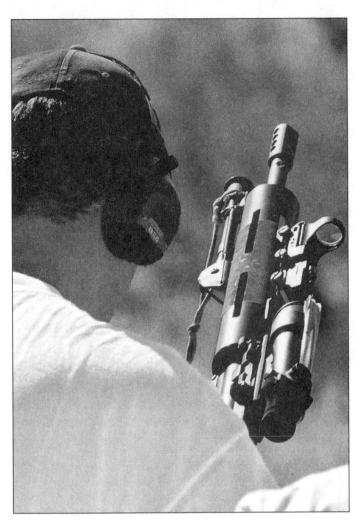

Another two-sight approach, a C-More for close and fast, and optics for long and precise.

A dab of paint can ensure your rifle stays zeroed and free from idle hands.

rifle down. Trying to do any of them one-handed can end up with you getting hurt, or hurting yourself. A proper sling lets you carry the rifle ready, but not in your hands or acting as an obstacle. It lets you quickly sling and swing the rifle out of your way.

And a proper sling isn't acting as a potential hook, to catch on any stray object you might run past or need to dodge around.

Magazine storage

A vest full of loaded magazines is of no use if it is in the trunk of the patrol car or back at the station house. Often an officer who rolls up on a call, or has to deal with an active shooter will have only the ammunition that is on his person when he exits the vehicle. A spare magazine on a belt is cumbersome, even if there is enough belt to fit it on. Many officers have decided that the best way to keep a spare magazine on hand is to attach it directly to the rifle.

Setting up a patrol rifle (our subject rifles will be several different ARs, to show various configurations) can be somewhat expensive. If you show an admirable lack of restraint you can easily end up adding half or more of the cost of the rifle to it with accessories. But the end result, if you are prudent and careful, will be a rifle with a greatly increased utility.

Aiming

The basic sights on an AR are pretty good. If you are going to rely on the "irons" then you need to establish a good zero, and make sure your sights cannot be changed without your knowledge. AR sights come in two lengths and two flavors. The lengths are the 20-inch barrel, or full-size, and the 16-inch or shorter barrel, the "shorty." The flavors are the A1, the "flat knob" original rear sight, and the A2, or adjustable rear. To further confuse the issue, the original front (A1) is a tapered post, with five detents, and the A2 is a four-sided straight post, with four detents. And they are interchangeable, so you can find a rifle of either length or rear sight with an A1 or A2 front post.

Zeroing is straightforward. From a stable shooting position, you adjust the sights so that your point of aim and your point of impact coincide. The problem is your line of sight is straight, while the bullet trajectory is curved. You can only have the sight line and trajectory curve coincide at two points. Which two? The military method is simple: coincide at 25 and 250 meters. The military method of aiming is simple. At any distance, aim for the enemy soldier's belt buckle. At any distance out to 275-300 meters you will (potentially) strike him with a disabling blow. The problem for law enforcement use is that it is extremely rare for a patrol rifle to be needed much past 100 yards. (Rare in the military context, too, at least outside of desert engagements.) Due to the height between the bore and the sights on the AR, with the military method at distances less than 25 yards the bullet strikes below the line of sight, and beyond 25 it strikes above. For a law enforcement officer who has to take a shot at a partially obscured bad guy, the question of "under or over, and how much?" can be crucial. For law enforcement use, the competition method is preferred. I call it the competition method because that is where I developed it. My friend Jeff Chudwin calls it the police method, for that is where he developed it. The practical shooting competition zero is a 100-yard zero. The bullet is under the line of sight out to 100 yards (gradually rising, decreasing the difference) and then passes over and stays above the line of sight past 100 yards until it falls back down to the line of sight again. The long-range effect is to make the second coincidence of line-of-sight and arc-of-trajectory only 250 yards away. The extra 50 yards/meters hardly matter for law enforcement use (or competition) but the known "hold under" out to 100 yards makes closer shots much easier to make.

Every time Jeff and I go to make sure all the rifles in a class are zeroed, we end up practically tearing our hair out over the frustration. It isn't that getting a rifle zero is that hard, but when you have two dozen shooters trying to zero, things go wrong. When zeroing your rifle, do not hurry, and do not settle for "close enough." Use a solid rest. Shoot slowly and carefully. When you have to change the group location, change one direction at a time. Shoot a group, then adjust the up or down. Then shoot another group, and adjust the left to right. Theoretically, you could do them both, but scopes and iron sights do strange things when you start adjusting them. Once you're sure it is zeroed, fire another group just to be sure.

Once zeroed, you have to make sure the sights don't get changed on you. You'd be surprised (or maybe not, if you've spent time in a police station or precinct house) at how many people will idly turn sight knobs back and forth out of boredom. The trick

Here is the GG&G A2 sight, with its locking button in the down position. The locking button is the round button between the sight hinge and the sight adjustment screw.

is to paint the sights in. Painting in is nothing new. Long-range target competitors do it to make sure they know what their basic zero is, and can return to it. In practical/defensive rifle use, the paint is simply a blob of viscous paint in a bold color. Jeff likes bright orange. I've used orange, yellow, light green, light blue, whatever is handy. Model paint works well, and degrease the metal before painting. You only need a blob the size of a match head or smaller. Apply the paint across the bridge or gap between the sight knob (or the sight base of the front sight) and the receiver.

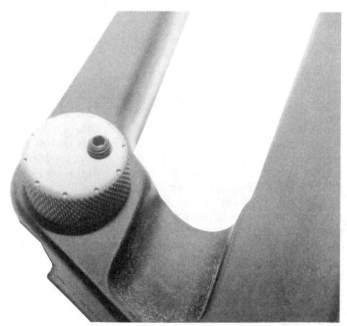

The Ace Ltd. locking sight knob. Once zeroed, tighten the allen screw down.

The GG&G sight in the up and locked position. Locked up, it can't be inadvertently knocked down or partly down.

An EO Tech Holosight mounted on a flat-top, to co-witness with the iron sights.

The paint must adhere to both knob and receiver. If the idea of painting your rifle with bright colors clashes with the perceived need for camouflage, I don't think the bad guys are going to spot you due to a tiny fleck of orange paint. If someone takes it upon themselves to fiddle with your sights, you have immediate evidence in the broken paint blob. If changed, you can get back to a very close setting by adjusting the knob until the two paint parts line up. You can check at the next range session.

Another approach is the Ace Ltd. custom knob. You can get them in plain black or a number of other colors, but they are all the same. The Ace Ltd. knob replaces the adjustment knob or plate on your rear sight. Once you have the rifle zeroed, you tighten down the Allen screw that is in the knob, locking the knob in place. If you have to change your zero, loosen the screw, make your adjustments, then tighten it again. Once it is locked, you don't have to worry about a merry prankster or someone who is bored cranking the knob around for amusement.

In the A1/A2 rear sight controversy, two questions always come up: "Which is better?" and "Can I change to the other one?" Better? They both work. The A2 is easier to adjust and zero, but also easier to adjust and lose a zero. The A1 is harder to adjust, but supposedly more durable. The only sight part I've ever broken was the leaf spring for the aperture setting, which is the same on both sights. You can't turn an A1 into an A2, although you can install a Rapidex knob to make zeroing easier, or install the Ace Ltd. knob to adjust and lock. You can partly turn an A2 into an A1, by installing a windage screw and plate from the A1 onto an A2. I can't see any advantage to it, though. As for the greater durability of the A1 over the A2, while I'm sure it exists, the only sight part I've seen broken by someone else was an A1, and the roll pin holding the adjustment plate on had broken. The plate stayed on the rifle, and turned when you went to adjust the rear sight. But there was no movement of the sight, and no change in point of impact.

Flat-top rifles

To make scope mounting easier, manufacturers offer "flat-top" rifles, where the carrying handle has been designed away, and the top of the receiver is built as one long scope mount base. The problem is,

The EO Tech Holosight (AA version) mounted on the Bennie Cooley adjustable front rail.

An EO Tech Holosight that took a hit from a paint training round during force-on-force training. The operator didn't even notice until the scenario was over, and the sight still works.

The Aimpoint mounted on the A.R.M.S. SIR.

The test fixture at the EO Tech assembly plant, with sights ready for their trip through the G-machine. They get jolted hard enough to turn us to jelly, so recoil isn't going to bother your sight.

The Aimpoint sights, as adopted by the U.S. Military.

what to do if the scope breaks? Use the iron sights? But it doesn't have any. The carrying handle, with its rear sight installed, can be carried as a backup, but that isn't always a viable tactical option. The carrying handle is bulky, adds weight to the load, and takes time to install. Better yet is a folding rear. The GG&G A2 Improved sight is just the ticket. It folds down out of the way so you can clearly see the red-dot scope or optics. If you need it, you flip it up. The sight has a detent that keeps it standing until you press the detent and fold the sight out of the way. It doesn't do any good to have a folding sight that folds at inopportune moments. One additional aspect of the folding sight and red dot optics combo is the ability to "co-witness" your sights. Once you've zeroed the irons and the optics, you can compare them. With the red dot on and the sight standing, you aim through the irons as normally. You should see the red dot resting on the tip of the front sight. If it isn't, make note of their relationship. (It happens, though rarely, and is usually a product of the shooters eyesight.) If in training or on an operation one of the sights takes a heavy impact, check the alignment. Dot on, sight up, check the lineup. If they still agree, the sight that was hit survived the impact. If they don't, the one impacted is probably now wrong, switch to the other and get on with things.

In the early days of ARs, and trying to mount scopes on them, getting a flat top wasn't easy. One

The A.R.M.S. mount clamps right to the SIR, or to any picatinny rail flat-top or sight mount. While this mount is Aimpoint-specific, A.R.M.S. makes similar mounts to hold just about anything else you need mounted to your rifle.

The Surefire M-900 on an A.R.M.S. SIR assembly.

approach was to saw off the handle, mill the top flat (and level with the bore, the difficult part) and then secure a scope base to the flattened receiver. I did a few that way. Now, the cost of a new receiver is less than the labor I charged in the old days. If you really feel compelled to have a flat top, buy a new flat top receiver and have your parts swapped over. Don't pay to have your receiver milled.

Red dots

Once an item found only on the IPSC competition ranges (and early on roundly denounced as "not practical, not tactical" and my favorite, "not cool") red dot sights are now accepted sights. The Army buys truckloads of the Aimpoint sights. Competition shooters realized their advantage right away, and soon were mounting every sight ever offered on any gun they needed in a match. And right away, sights were breaking. The durable ones survived in the marketplace. The rest are now shrapnel. When considering any red dot sight, you have to be aware of their shortcomings. They need batteries, they must be mounted securely or they are useless, and they can be at the mercy of the weather. The batteries and secure mounting are obvious. Everyone knows of at least one deer hunter who missed his buck because his scope was loose. But weather? Bitter cold drains batteries. And rain, dew or mist can make many red dot scopes un-useable. The standard method of operation for a red dot scope is for the beam generated by the tiny laser or light to be projected forward and reflected off an interior surface. Your eye sees the reflected dot. You align dot with target, and shoot. However, if the optics of the scope are beaded with rain, covered with dew or fogged from humidity, all you'll see is a glowing red screen. The dot is diffused and useless.

One scope is not so affected. The EO Tech Holosight does not reflect a laser out and back, it fires its laser into a microscopic grid made up of many images of the reticle you see. The result is a three-dimensional image that your eye sees and your

An M-4 set up with A.R.M.S. SIR, Rase stock, Aimpoint and GG&G rear irons. All it needs is a sling and a Surefire M-900 light to mount on the bottom rail and it is ready for duty.

brain reassembles into the image of the reticle. If any part of the screen is not obscured, you see a reticle image. I've even seen Holosights with the screen punctured that still functioned well enough to use properly. If your operations are subjected to rain on a regular basis, look into the EO Tech.

The Aimpoint CompM2 is the current selection for our Armed Forces. (I saw lots of other sights in photos from Iraq, but the CompM2 is the one the government buys) The CompM2 and Comp ML2 differ in one respect: night vision equipment. The M2 has four settings (the first ones when you turn it on) for NVG optics. If you use a regular red dot scope with night vision gear, the dot is too bright. You may damage the NVG, and even if you don't you can't do any aiming that way. The too-bright red dot "blooms" in the field of vision of the night vision optics, causing the screen to become a useless green blob. The 10 switch settings include four NVG settings and six visible optics settings, one of which is "extra bright" for use in harshly lit locations. The ML2 settings are off, and nine visible settings, one of which is extra bright. That's right, the M2 is never off. The battery is good for 10 years just sitting at the lowest setting, and a thousand hours at higher settings. The adjustments are half an inch per click at 100 yards. Not very precise, but you aren't using this sight on a tactical bolt-action rifle at 800 yards. With half-minute clicks your group cannot be centered more than half an inch from the dot at 100 yards, which is a smaller margin of error than most shooters can hold. As for weatherproofing, the M2 and ML2 have been tested to 100 meters underwater. A little rain isn't going to inconvenience the sight operation.

In use, you should clamp the Aimpoint to a rifle that has a flat-top receiver, using an A.R.M.S. throw-lever mount. You can use a base and ring assembly in the carry handle, but the height over the bore will cause you to be shooting with your cheek off of the stock. Alternatively, you could use a Bennie Cooley offset rail.

A.R.M.S. SIR

You have to have some way of attaching the red dot (and other gear) to your rifle. Mounts that clamp a scope or red dot on the carrying handle are usually unsatisfactory due to height. They take the already high line of sight (compared to the bore) and make it higher. They also put the line of sight so high that it becomes difficult to look through the scope and keep a proper cheek weld. Without your cheek securely pressed against the stock, aiming is even more difficult. Your head can move independently of the rifle. (The Bennie Cooley adjustable rail solves many of those problems.) A flat top AR with the top machined as a scope mount, the Picatinny or M-1913 mount (soon after 1913 turned into the Weaver base) is great, but short. Some scopes have a length such that you can't get the rings to clamp around the scope and then have them attach to the receiver. A longer rail is needed. Also, the use of lights, targeting lasers and other accessories requires some sort of attachment method.

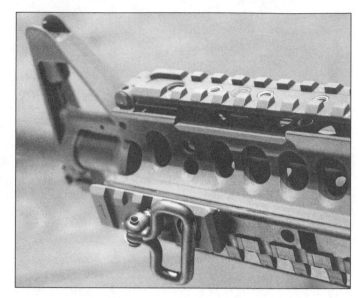

The left side of the A.R.M.S. SIR, showing the sling mount and the top rail. The forward part of the rail is hinged and removable to allow mounting a PEQ-2 or PEQ-4 laser targeting designator.

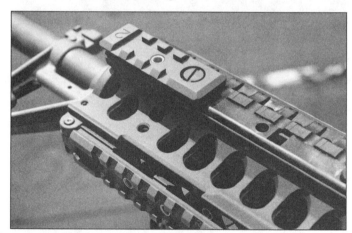

The right side has another small rail where you can mount a sling swivel (for left-handed shooters) a light, laser, just about anything.

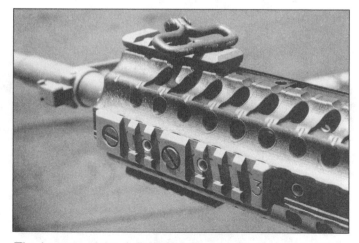

The bottom of the A.R.M.S. SIR, with the lower picatinny rail for mounting a light.

A.R.M.S. solved that problem with their SIR™ system. The Selective Integrated Rail replaces the forearm, clamps to the receiver rail and allows you to attach almost anything you want to the rifle.

Installation is relatively simple. First, select the appropriate length. You cannot use a carbine-length SIR on a full-size rifle, and vice versa. The "C" and "M" models differ in requiring removal of the delta ring and parts. (The C does not, the M requires removal) Then follow the directions.

The real value of the SIR (not that the rest of the functions aren't useful and worth the price) is the length of the top rail. With the top rail extending the length of the rifle from the rear of the receiver to the front sight, you can mount anything you need. First, a rear iron sight is needed. If you don't use the A.R.M.S. rear, you can install a GG&G A2 Improved. This sight locks up and won't get folded just when you need it. Forward of that, mount a red dot such as the Aimpoint M2 or the EO Tech Holosight. If your department issues, or you have and have need of it, mount a Night Vision optic, and forward of it the red-dot (with NVG capability, of course) sight. Remove the NVG unless you need it, and leave the zeroed red dot in place. With the NVG you'll also need an Infra Red light, so one of the rails gets dedicated to take an IR weapon light from Surefire. In the military context, PEQ-2 or PEQ-4 laser target designator also gets clamped on. I've seen them on top and on the side.

Bennie Cooley rail

What if your department issues regular-upper rifles, and won't allow modifications? How can you get a scope or red dot sight on without ending up with a line of sight a foot over the rifle? The typical method is to use a rail that attaches in the carry handle, but extends forward, and down to the handguard. The drawback to these mounts is the non-adjustable nature of the rail. If your red dot scope sits high or low, the dot is in an odd place, or near the edge of the tube. The Bennie Cooley

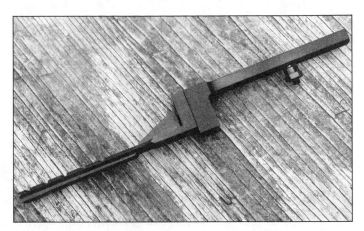

The Bennie Cooley rail, adjustable for red-dot optics.

rail is in two pieces, with a dovetail fitting. Once the handle part of the rail is secured, you clamp your red dot into the front part. Turn on the dot, and loosen the dovetail locking screws. Adjust the front rail up or down until the dot is centered in the tube and coincidental with the iron sights. Tighten the locking screws and fire at your zero distance to fine-tune the red dot zero. If you want a red dot sight, but not up on the carry handle (and you can't remove the handle) then the Bennie Cooley rail mount is the best thing going.

If you switch scopes, to one with a different diameter or base height, you can adjust the rail to the new scope. You can change it if you are issued (or buy) a different rifle. For scopes or dots on a standard rifle, the Cooley Rail is slick.

C-More

Combining a red-dot optic and irons for backup, the C-More flat-top AR sight is one compact and useful system. The C-More is a laser sight using a reflector screen reminiscent of the optical sights on WWII fighter planes. The image of the dot appears in the screen, and you simply (as with all red-dot sights) place the dot where you want the bullet to go. (Within range and trajectory adjustments, of course.)

The Bennie Cooley adjustable front rail allows you to move the optics up or down to get the dot co-witnessed with your iron sights.

The C-More flat-top sight. The thumbscrews on the side secure it to the receiver. The rear sight is a fully functional A2 version.

The integrated iron sight is an A2 rear with windage and elevation adjustments. The red-dot has its own adjustments, so you can zero them independently of each other. Or zero them to the same range and then use the co-witness capability to check and make sure they're still where you left them.

The C-More attaches to the flat top with two thumbscrews. There are models to fit handles, pistols, models without the iron sights, models for all uses. Once secured, you'd be best off using model paint to paint the knobs in, so you can be sure they haven't loosened or the sight been removed and replaced.

The C-More is quite durable, having been extensively tested in IPSC competition since I saw the hand-cut prototype at the 1991 Steel Challenge. It is capable of withstanding as much ammo as your barrel is, and then some. The C-More is used by some of the top IPSC competitors, and their practice routines and match schedules encompass tens of thousands of rounds annually. You aren't going to wear yours out merely via ammo consumption.

Lighting

Half the time, it is dark outside. And some places indoors, it is dark as soon as the power is off. Illumination is essential. The best way to have illumination for your rifle is to have illumination on your rifle. You can attach a light of some kind to your rifle with an adapter, or you can use a dedicated mount that replaces some part (usually the forearm) and contains a light. One approach for the first method is the GG&G Sling and light Combo. This is a front and rear set of sling swivels, and a light mount. The front clamps around your front sight assembly. "Clamp around" is a poor description for the precision-machined adapter and mount base that fits inside the front sight housing. On the rear, the adapter blocks clamp through the lower sling slot of a telescoping stock. The beauty of the rear adapter is that the sling is now on the same plane, and in the same orientation, as the front sling. Rather than simply looping the sling through the rear stock slots,

The GG&G Sling and Light Combo, on the light mount rail side, the right side.

and ending up with a sling that is on the side at the front but on top at the rear, they line up. Then it is a simple matter to use a scope ring to fasten a light to the base. A light like the Diamond Products, with a pressure tape switch that you can turn on by pressing it will work well. Another compact light that will fit is the Laser Devices six-volt light with pressure switch, clamped on the GG&G rail with a one-inch picatinny ring mount. If you don't want a side-mount sling, then just use the front mount for your light and the regular sling swivels.

You can also use a Surefire Millennium Universal Systems Weaponlight, with the built-in clamp on the body of the light. Secured to the GG&G rail it offers more light than many others do. The beauty of the GG&G combined with a light is that you can easily move it from one rifle to another, and it doesn't require

The GG&G SliC rear sling swivel in place.

The Surefire M-500 light replaces the handguards, and uses a multi-battery assembly cage to hold the power in place.

any weapon modifications. If your department issues a rifle, but doesn't allow any permanent modifications, then this is a viable low cost solution.

If you want lots of light, then you have to either go with a big, heavy Surefire Millennium, or an integral light mount. On the AR, that means the Surefire M500, M510 (for 20-inch rifles) or the M900. The 500 and 510 are replacement forearm units. You have to remove the upper or lower handguard of your rifle and replace it with the Surefire unit. The M500 and M510 have a pivot switch to turn them off and prevent inadvertent illumination. On the rear of the handguard is a pressure switch for momentary lighting. Up front is a rocker switch to turn the unit on and leave it on. The pivot switch locks out both the pressure and rocker switches. New on the 500 series are navigation lights. Behind the rocker switch is a pressure switch for the navigation lights. In front of the rocker switch are LEDs. (Your choice of red, white, blue or infrared. Don't get the IR option unless you've got night vision optics to see through.) When you press the navigation switch, you get just enough light to move around without stumbling, but hopefully not enough to let the bad guys know where you are. The 500 series are set up for right-handed shooters, with the light and pressure switch on the right, and the rocker and navigation switches on the left. You can mount the 500 or 510 in place of the bottom handguard, putting the light on the lower left.

The M-900 requires a picatinny rail somewhere on the rifle, preferably on the bottom of the lower handguard. The A.R.M.S. SIR fills that need nicely, and provides room to locate other equipment as well. The M-900 also has navigation lights, momentary switch and lockout switch, and has the benefit of being removable. You don't need illumination all the time. When you don't need it, you can remove and store the M-900. Just be sure you grab it when you might need it (or keep it on your person) so it will be available. The Surefire 500 and 900 can offer up to 500 lumens of illumination, enough to make anyone who is subject to it reflexively turn away and close their eyes.

Handling

Handling comes down to four things under your control: length of the buttstock, weight and balance on the front end, the pistol grip, and the safety/selector lever. If you are average height, and pick up an AR-15A2 or M-16, with the new, longer buttstock, it feels pretty good. However, add a Kevlar vest, suspenders from web gear, gloves and a helmet, and that A2 is going to start feeling clumsy. Add a light on the front end and it begins to move like a truck. If cold weather requires more clothing, the stock can quickly end up so long it is difficult to use. What to do? The first thing is to change the buttstock. Go back to the older A1 length, 5/8" shorter. Better yet, go with an adjustable stock, with three or four positions. The change from the A2 to the A1 stock is simple, unscrew the upper buttplate screw, slide the old off, the new on, and don't lose the little spring in the rear of the receiver. To change from the fixed

The SliC in use, and a Fobus railed handguard with a Falcon vertical foregrip in place.

stock to the adjustable you have to replace all the stock components, internals as well. For that you'll need instructions and a buffer tube wrench. Best to let your armorer or a gunsmith make the change for you. With the new stock you can change the length until it is correct for the way you are dressed. (Note: if the Assault Weapons Ban of 1994 is allowed to sunset in 2004, you can afterwards change any rifle this way. If it is not allowed to sunset, even a police officer cannot add a telescoping stock to a rifle manufactured after September 13, 1994.)

One way to get weight off the rifle, and adjust length, is with one of the Ace Ltd. Stocks. The ARFX is lighter than a standard stock, and has a foam rubber sleeve to cut down on vibration to your face. It replaces the existing standard stock and has provisions for attaching slings. If you need something shorter, the entry version is 2-1/2 inches shorter. For lighter, the ARBT "Boom Tube" is lighter, and adjustable. For the lightest possible stock, go with the AR-UL, the Ultralight. It shaves 9 ounces off the weight of the standard AR stock. Nine ounces may not seem like much, but it is 9 ounces of weight you can devote to something else, without increasing the starting weight of your rifle.

At my latest class, one of the students was an officer from the Chicago area. At around 5-feet, 4-inches tall, and with a 54-inch chest, there was no way he was going to shoulder an A1 or A2 stocked rifle. He used a telescoping stock, with the stock collapsed into its "storage" position. There, he could shoulder it and use the sights. On the front end he had a Surefire M-900, locked as far back as he could and still get his thumb between the Surefire and magazine well housing. It was altogether too short for me, but it worked fine for him. He would have been well served by the entry-length Ace Ltd stocks.

Only shortening the barrel or replacing the barrel with a shorter one can change the front of the rifle. If you have a 20-inch barrel, it can be shortened, but not

The standard grip. Hard plastic, slippery, with a finger hook that mostly gets in the way.

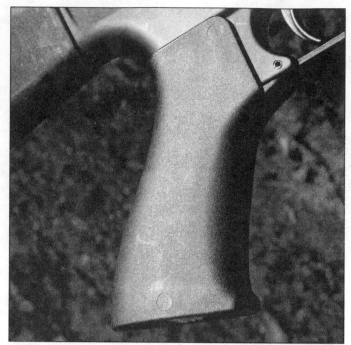

TangoDown LLC makes the Battlegrip, nicely contoured and it also holds batteries. They have just come out with a textured grip.

easily. To do it properly and replace the flash hider requires removing the barrel and turning it on a lathe. It may be less expensive (depending on how much it costs for replacement barrels) to simply swap to a 16-inch barrel. A barrel shorter than 16 inches is not advised. If the rifle was originally manufactured with a barrel longer than 16 inches, and in semi-only, making it shorter than 16-inches turns it into a Short-Barreled Rifle, a specific category under the National Firearms Act of 1934. To make the change requires paperwork, and approval from the ATF, and cannot be done at all in some States. You also lose performance and increase muzzle blast by going less than 16 inches in barrel length. If the rifle left the factory as a select-fire rifle (i.e. an M-16) then making the barrel shorter than 16 inches doesn't change its status. It is already an NFA weapon.

The best patrol rifle is a shorty carbine, a 16-inch barreled model with telescoping stock. (Again, speaking of AR-15/M-16 rifles.) So how to improve the rest of the handling? The pistol grip is an area of compromise. The original grip was not selected after an arduous design process intended to produce the grip most comfortable to most troops. It was what felt good at the time. Better grips for fast handling have come along since then. One is from Falcon Industries, the Ergo grip. Designed along the lines of the MP-5 pistol grip, it offers a more comfortable grip with a better angle than the stock M-16 grip. Another is the Battlegrip from TangoDown LLC. The Battlegrip has a small compartment that takes stored batteries. If you depend on a red dot sight, a spare set of batteries right with the rifle is comforting. TangoDown also offers the Battlegrip in a smooth and a textured

version, after feedback from the recent Iraqi war. A replacement grip is easy to install. The grip on the AR/M-16 is held on with a screw with either a single slot or an Allen key head. If it is a screwdriver slot, just use a long screwdriver with a blade thick enough to catch and not bind. Allen screws are a bit more difficult in that the hollow of the grip is a bit deeper than many standard Allen wrench extensions. Underneath the grip is the spring and plunger for the selector lever. Do not lose them, and be sure to return them in their original placement when installing the new grip.

For those who use ARs as precision rifles, a more filling grip may be called for. Sierra Precision makes a hand-filling grip with finger grooves and thumb rest. If your job is to lay out in the sun for long periods of time until the shot is called for, the Sierra grip may be just the thing.

On the front, you can install a vertical foregrip. The easiest way is to install a forearm like the A.R.M.S. SIR, or a Fobus handguard, where you can clamp a foregrip or illumination unit like the Surefire. Some shooters like foregrips, some don't, and others don't care one way or the other. If you need light, they're the best way to get it. If you need the leverage, then get one.

Left-handed shooters have the option of either using their trigger finger to operate the selector, or installing an ambidextrous safety lever. While useful, an ambi safety can cause handling problems. I, for one, have a grip where my hand rides high enough that the offside lever on an ambidextrous safety lever gets in the way. If you plan to install an ambi safety, try one on another rifle before you lay down your

The cover is tight, water-resistant and keeps your batteries safe.

money and install one. You may find one or another particular model is not comfortable for you.

Accuracy

Accuracy in an AR requires a good barrel and good ammunition. (And sights and trigger, but we've covered those.) Do not expect your rifle to shoot well with whatever was cheapest at "The Import House of Ammunition, No One Beats Our Prices." While cheap surplus can be useful in practice, and can stretch the training budget, sooner or later you simply must dial in and check your zero, and check function, with what you will really use. The temptation of surplus can be great for individuals and departments. Premium ammunition such as the Hornady TAP round can cost a dollar a shot. It can become very expensive for an officer or department to hold annual practice and qualification, if that is the issue ammo. However, you must fire enough of it to make sure it works and that it hits to the sights. If you don't, then false economy will cost the department dearly when the resulting problem of accuracy or reliability surfaces. A few dollars saved by exclusively using surplus for training, and issuing something else for duty will cost the department many thousands (or millions) of dollars in legal costs and settlements. And cost you many nights sleep and much anguish.

Factory-produced ammo or commercial reloads can deliver as much or more accuracy as you need. It isn't unusual for a box-stock new AR to deliver groups of an inch or less at 100 yards with Black Hills, Remington, Winchester or Federal ammo. If you want better than that, you have to spend money on two fronts. You need better ammo, and you need a

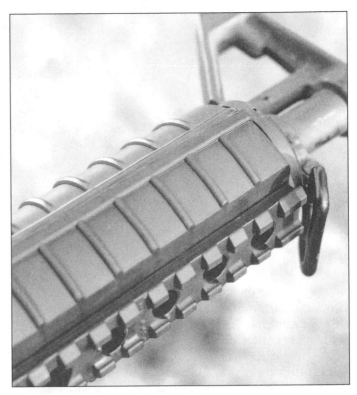

The Fobus railed forearm. You can mount one underneath for a light or vertical foregrip, one above for a light, or both for multiple options.

better barrel. The better ammo is easy: move up from 52- or 55-grain ball (full metal jacket) to 69-grain match hollow-point bullets. Depending on how you or the department buys ammo, the change can easily double your ammo costs. The change also comes with additional costs. The 69-grain bullets will not shoot accurately in older barrels. (More on that shortly.) The 69-grain bullet, despite its greater weight, does not penetrate chance obstacles any better then 55-grain bullets do. But it may over-penetrate inside a structure. And even rack-grade M-16s or vanilla plain AR-15s can have plenty of accuracy.

Bullet construction can be selected for the job at hand. An entry team can select/be issued more frangible bullets, bullets that will disintegrate on interior walls and not endanger others. Officers detailed to a roadblock, or who work on the highways, can be issued rounds with a bonded bullet that will penetrate auto glass and sheet metal. While the differing rounds probably will shoot to different zeros, they can all shoot accurately. And once your rifle is sighted-in with a particular cartridge, you must not assume every other round will shoot to the same point of impact. (They may, but there is no guarantee.)

Improving the barrel usually means replacing it. One approach to improving a poor barrel is to employ a fire-lapping process on it. The idea is simple: use bullets coated with very fine abrasives, fired through the bore, to smooth the barrel. While it can improve an average or poor barrel, it will not do anything to bring useful life back to a shot-out bore. If your rifle is inaccurate because the bore is rough, using

Although some match barrels are not marked, a good barrel is clearly marked with chamber and twist rate. This DPMS barrel is a 5.56 chamber (not .223) and the twist is the most useful, one turn in 9 inches.

something like the David Tubb FinalFinish can improve it. If your rifle is inaccurate because it has already had 10,000 bullets fired through it, replacing it is the only thing that will help. Where the Tubb FinalFinish does help is in keeping the bore clean. A rough bore fouls faster than does a smooth one, and loses accuracy sooner. When it comes time to clean, a rough bore takes longer to clean than a smooth one does. A lapped bore keeps its accuracy longer during a shooting session, and requires less effort to clean once the practice I over.

And always the questions are: how long, and how fast a twist? Barrel length is simple: As long as you can handle, and as short as you need. The two real choices are 16 inches or 20 inches. The 16-inch barrel will handle better in a vehicle, plane or boat. The 20-inch will deliver higher velocities. Longer than 20 inches does not gain enough to be worth the length (and weight) and shorter than 16 loses too much velocity and adds too much muzzle blast. For entry teams who work in very tight quarters, an 11.5-inch barrel can be handier, but with extra costs. The shorter barrel loses velocity. At short range, the loss isn't much, but if one of the team has to take a longer shot, the velocity loss can decrease stopping power. The shorter barrel has much greater muzzle blast. And, the shorter barrel can affect reliability. As soon as the bullet passes the gas port, gas is vented back to work the action. Once the bullet passes out of the muzzle, the gas pressure in the barrel rapidly drops. In a 16-inch barrel, the bullet is still in the bore for 9 inches past the gas port. In the 11.5-inch barrel, that distance is halved. The difference in gas pressure dwell time can be enough to make some rifles unreliable with some loads. The difference depends on the burning rate of the powder and how much is used. In an attempt to make such rifles more reliable by feeding them more gas, some armorers mistakenly

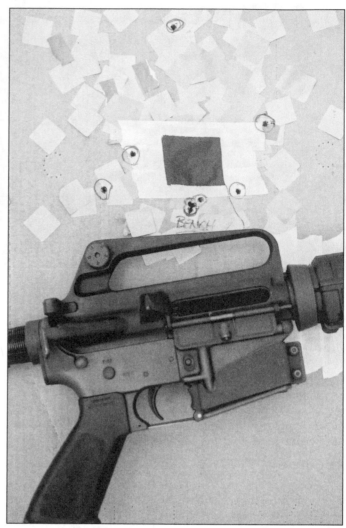

A barrel with a twist rate of one turn in 12 inches cannot be depended on to shoot heavy bullets. This rifle shoots 55-grain M193 just fine (the small group) but not SS109 (the individual bullet holes) at 50 yards.

open the gas port. Invariably, even if it works it makes the rifle even harsher in recoil.

One option is to go with the 14.5-inch barrel that is found on the current-issue M-4 carbine. The barrel was selected for its ability to accept the standard bayonet, not for ballistic or functioning reasons. Any barrel shorter than 16 inches turns a rifle into an NFA weapon, requiring much paperwork. If the rifle is already a select-fire (M-16) then the barrel change isn't a problem. On semi-only AR's, it can be a real paperwork hassle.

In the end, the rifle selected usually has a 16- inc barrel with short handguards. Even for tall shooters, who have to "choke up" on the handguard, it is a handy and viable selection.

Barrel twist is important. The accuracy of a rifle is derived mostly from the spiral grooves cut into the bore, that impart a twist to the bullet. The gyroscopic forces keep the bullet point-forward and allow it to shrug off turbulence in the air through which it passes. How much twist is "enough" depends on many things, primarily the bullet length. Since length and weight are linked, we speak of a bullet and its weight with an associated twist rate. Twist is measured by how many inches of bore (or bullet travel) is required for one full rotation. In the early Armalite rifles the twist was one turn in 14 inches, 1/14 or 1-14. As the rifle was refined (hurriedly, marginally and under severe time pressures) the twist was found wanting. In extreme cold, or with a slightly worn bore, the groups opened up too much for the testers and those deciding how much was "enough." The twist was tightened to 12 inches, 1-12. It allowed the 55-grain full metal jacket bullets (the M-193 load) to be fired accurately, although at the loss (too much, some felt) of some wounding potential. Until the early 1980s 1-12 was good enough. In the interests of increasing accuracy, especially long-range accuracy, experimenters had used longer and heavier bullets. The most radical experimenters had used barrels with a 1-7 twist. When it came time to update the M-16, that rate was selected. One reason was it allowed tracer rounds to be fully stabilized for the full distance of their burn. Since this was some 700 meters, and the tracer bullet looks like a little #2 brass pencil, the twist was faster than needed for other bullets. The new M-855 bullets are 62 grains in weight. However, since they had a steel tip, they were longer than other bullets of the same weight, and needed a faster twist than the 1-12 of the older rifles. (The Winchester 63-grain soft-point is very blunt for its weight, making it shorter than the 62-grain M-855, and thus useable in some, but not all, barrels with a 1-12 twist.) Target shooters have since taken advantage of the faster twist to use bullets up to 80 grains for long-range competition. The bullets are so long they can't even be fed through the magazine, and have to be single-loaded.

As a compromise, some manufacturers settled on barrels with a 1-9 twist. The 9-inch twist is fast enough to stabilize bullets up to the weight and length of the 69-grain match bullets, but not so fast as to preclude the use of the old M-193 55-grain bullet. But the 1-9 barrels are not fast enough to stabilize the long, 80-grain target bullets.

This leaves AR barrels (and all rifles using the 5.56mm cartridge) in one of three groups: 1-12, 1-9 and 1-7. The 1-12 barrels can utilize the old loading, the M-193, and commercial loadings of bullets with the lighter weights of the 5.56mm bullet diameter range: 40 to 60 grains. Some 1-12 rifles will shoot the Winchester 63-grain soft-point ammunition well, others won't. The 1-9 barrels will shoot everything, from the 40- to the 69-grain bullets, with a promise of good accuracy. The 1-7 barrels will shoot heavier bullets well, but sometimes do not shoot the lighter bullet accurately. Why? When a bullet is fired, it is pushed down the bore and rotated around its center of form. When it is released from the muzzle, it wobbles for a millisecond and then settles down to rotating around its center of gravity. A short bullet fired in a too-fast twist barrel can have its flaws magnified by the excess rotation. When it is released

The Giles sling from The Wilderness.

from the muzzle, it may yaw too much before settling down, and not all will settle down pointing in the same direction. The differences may be small, but accuracy is a function of reducing small differences to even smaller differences.

Changing barrels on the AR-15/M-16 is simple and straightforward, and any departmental armorer can handle the job on most rifles. Simply decide what length, weight and twist you need, and send a purchase order to DPMS or Brownells, and you'll have barrels and instructions. There will be a small percentage of rifles that will resist an easy barrel change for one of a host of obscure reasons. If the barrel change does not go well, send it to a pro for de-bugging.

Slings

A sling is a means of carrying your rifle without using your hands. The standard military sling is simply a means of carrying the rifle like cargo, out of the way. As a tactical carry method, the traditional sling isn't very good. We've spent many hours on the range and at home practicing sling presentation from the traditional sling. Giles Stock took care of that problem. Giles is a retired officer from Phoenix, and was for a long time an Instructor at Gunsite. His starting point was the Israeli sling, and the military modifications from it. The Israeli sling is simple: a long strap tied/taped around the buttstock at the sling swivel, and then tied/taped/lashed or wired to the front sight assembly. The rifle rests horizontally, and depending on how much strap you use, as low as at the waist. Better than the old method, but not all that great now.

The improvements Giles made were to fabricate the buttstock end so it secured to the stock without the need for tape, and on the front of the handguard without having to be secured to the front sight assembly. The big problem with attaching the sling to the sight assembly is that it can block the sights. If the sling bunches up, it can block your view. The attachment straps of the Giles sling also placed the sling on the side of the rifle. In the Israeli method, you have to have a lot of strap to have enough slack that you can shoulder the rifle to shoot. By mounting the sling on the side, you need less slack to shoulder and fire. Less slack means the rifle rides higher on you, and is less in the way in vehicles and doorways. The Giles Stock sling is available from The Wilderness, and comes in two models: fixed and adjustable. Make your choice based on what kind of stock is on your rifle. The particulars of the stock design do not allow a universal mounting strap for the buttstock, so you have to specify which one you need.

For those with telescoping stocks on their ARs, the GG&G Sling Thing or Sling 'n Light Combo offers a great sling setup. The rear unit bolts to the buttstock, using the lower sling slot on the moving portion. The front clamps in the opening of the front sight housing. The SliC has an additional base on the far side of the front assembly. That is a section of picatinny rail. Once the SliC is on, you use a scope ring or mounting base to clamp your light to the rail. As with the Stock sling, the GG&G unit puts the sling on the side of the rifle.

The Wilderness makes a sling that goes on the GG&G side adaptor plate. Available now for both fixed and telescoping stocks, the adapter goes between the stock and the rear of the receiver. The adapter has a ring for a sling. Actually, there are several adapters, some with rings on both sides, and some with loops for fastening clips for those who favor the bungee type slings. You can get just the GG&G plate and lash your own sling to it, but The Wilderness sling offers something most slings won't: a quick-detach buckle. Pat Rogers, long-time NYPD officer and Marine, and Instructor at Gunsite, tells me that the quick-detach is a required item for U.S.M.C. issue. Apparently, it isn't unusual for Marines to be working around water. And if a Marine happens to fall in the water then being able to quickly jettison excess gear can make the difference between getting back to the surface in time, or not at all. Another advantage of The Wilderness sling comes from its single-point attachment. Those with vertical

This M-4 has a single-point sling on a GG&G adapter plate. It also has an EO Tech Holosight, backup iron sights and a Surefire M-900 light.

grips on the forend of their rifles can turn the rifle so the ejection port side is towards the body. That leaves the forend grip poking out where the left hand can grasp it. The twist carry is much faster than trying to dig your left hand under the rifle to grab the front grip to present the muzzle end towards an offender.

One aspect of sling use that must be considered in the tactical or patrol use is how to store the sling when the rifle isn't on you? You cannot dash off with a sling-equipped rifle, leaving the sling dangling and flapping in the breeze. The first object to hook the sling will snatch the rifle out of your hands, and may even cause you injury. You can stow the sling with a large rubber band, or masking tape. Collect the excess, and fold it up on the forearm. Then band or tape it down. When you need the sling, grab and yank the sling out from its band or tape, and then put it on. While stowed slings are not as important to a team (you have time to get the rifle out of the rack or carry case) for a patrol officer it can be very important. Without a properly stowed sling, the mess of radio microphone, seatbelt, and rifle sling may strangle you as you try to call for backup, get out of the car, and grab your rifle, all at the same time.

Magazine storage

Sometimes you need more ammo. You've used all that was in the rifle, and the problem is still with you. Or, your magazine is damaged, and you need another. Both situations have, and will, occur. In the Miami shootout of 1986, one of the FBI agents across the street from the collided vehicles fired his S&W 9mm until the magazine was empty. He then transitioned to his backup gun, a snub nose revolver. After one shot, ("This isn't going to do the job" he thought) he holstered his revolver, picked up the 9mm and reloaded it. The biggest gun is the best gun, until it is flat out of ammo. In the Northridge, California shootout where the two bank robbers were dressed head-to-toe in body armor, one of the responding LAPD officers who was in a position to bring fire on one of the assailants found his rifle wasn't working properly. The feed lips of the magazine were damaged, and the force needed to strip a round out of the magazine caused it to feed very slowly. "So slowly I could see the bolt moving." Without a spare magazine, he had to fire at the rate the rifle allowed, and not at the rate the situation demanded.

Spare magazines (loaded, of course) are as vital as the weapon. But if the belt is full, where do you keep them? You keep them on the rifle. The trick is, keeping it handy but out of the way. We have four methods available; Redi-mag, Mag Cinch, Rase and stock pouch. All four are ambidextrous, working for both right- and left-handed shooters.

Redi-Mag

My friend, Jeff Chudwin, was an early convert and enthusiastic proponent of the Redi-Mag system. So much so that he even convinced the Big Sky Rack Company of Montana to build a special roof rack (Called the "Olympia Fields PD Model") to store an AR with a Redi-Mag on it on the ceiling/headliner of a patrol car. The idea of the Redi-mag is simple: a spare magazine well on the rifle. To make it requires some precise metal stamping, and a bit of work to get it installed. But once on, it is an excellent system. The Redi-Mag is a sheet metal (tougher than it sounds) assembly that clamps around the magazine well of the lower. Part of the assembly is another mag well. The linkage of the assembly is an additional magazine release, positioned adjacent to the existing one. Once clamped around the receiver, pressing the magazine button on the receiver releases the magazine in the receiver, and the magazine held in the Redi-Mag. The rear of the Redi-Mag clears the bolt hold-open. When the bolt is locked open, pressing the hold-open lever behind the Redi-Mag closes the bolt. Jeff likes to increase access to the bolt hold open lever by fabricating an extension from an empty 5.56mm case. (If there is one thing firearms instructors have access to, it is fired brass) In response to inquiries, the Redi-Mag people now make a bolt hold-open extension lever. It clamps on the existing lever, and provides access to close the bolt by the customary method of slapping the left side of the receiver with the palm of your left hand.

In use, the Redi-Mag is simple. When you need to reload, reach up with your left hand and grasp both magazines. Press the magazine release button and draw both magazines down. Move your hand to the right to line up the second magazine, insert it and press it home. Then place the first magazine in a pocket or your empty magazine pouch. Alternately, if you need to reload quickly, grasp just the left magazine and press the magazine release button. Let the first (right) magazine fall free, remove the second one, insert it in the receiver mag well and press it

The Redi-Mag is a steel assembly that fastens to the side of your rifle.

The Redi-Mag is another mag well right next to the original. Drop the old, remove the new, move it over and insert it. What could be faster?

The Redi-Mag in use. When you want to reload, reach down and grasp the spare mag. Press the mag button and let the old mag fall free while you extract the fresh one and move it over to the magazine well.

Mag Cinch and their "why didn't I think of that" product. The magazines must be offset (right-hand one lower) so the right-hand magazine doesn't interfere with ejection or the dustcover door opening.

home. If you've fired to slide lock, slap the bolt hold open lever to close the bolt.

The Redi-Mag also allows "ammo-select" where you have one type of ammunition in the right-hand magazine, and another in the left. One choice would be relatively frangible ammunition for an entry team, backed up by tactical penetration ammunition in the left. Indoors, the relatively frangible entry ammo will not exit your adversary (or is much less likely to) and will break up on interior walls. If the team chases the suspects out of the rear of the house and finds them attempting to escape in a vehicle, the frangible ammo will not penetrate the sheet metal, and do poorly on the glass. A quick change of magazines to the tactical penetrating ammo will allow them to effectively return fire into the vehicle.

The downside of the Redi-Mag is bulk. You have to find room in the vehicle, and the storage racks at the stationhouse may not take the rifles with Redi-Mag on them without some rack modifications. A small price to pay.

Mag Cinch

The Mag Cinch is one of those "why didn't I think of that?" products. In design, it is simply a set of straps and positioning clamps that secure two magazines together. I know what you're thinking "I can make that" or "My wood block and duct tape assembly works as well." Well, you would be wrong. First, the strapping is easy, but the clamps aren't. The trick is positioning the magazines far enough apart so they clear the receiver bumps, but not so far they are clumsy. Second, getting straps tight and keeping them tight isn't easy. As for the duct tape

routine, ever try to clean old duct tape adhesive off of magazines? It isn't any fun. And I had a set of duct-taped magazines fall apart in the middle of a match once. It didn't hurt my score enough for the second-place shooter to catch me, but it was embarrassing. And in real life it could have been more than just a bit of an inconvenience. Mag Cinch makes their assemblies for just about any rifle or SMG that uses detachable magazines. The trick in putting one on a set of magazines is in positioning the left magazine higher than the right. If you make them level, the right-hand magazine may interfere with ejection when you're firing from the left magazine.

As with the Redi-Mag, you have to make sure your car racks have enough clearance for the pair of magazines. Unlike the Redi-Mag, you don't have to worry about storage racks in the station house. Once the magazines are out, your rifle is like any other and will fit standard rifle racks without a problem.

Rase

The Rase stock replaces the standard stock, and holds a spare magazine horizontally and tucked up out of the way. The cutout of the stock is a friction fit for your spare magazine, with a spring-loaded retainer on the receiver end. To use, pivot the lever as far forward

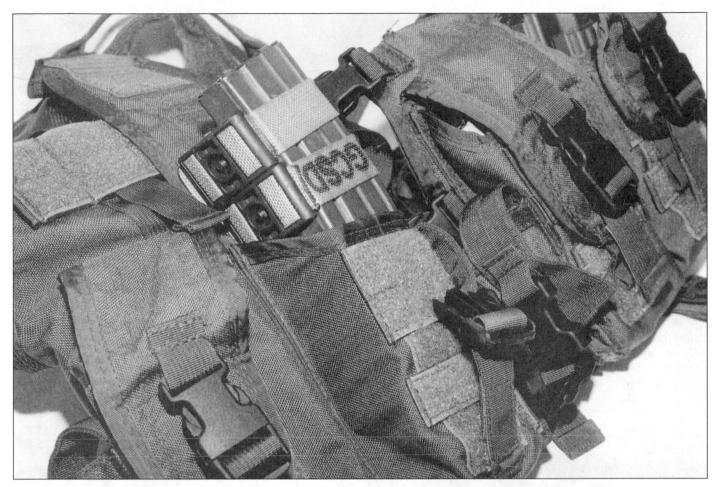

One drawback to the Mag Cinch is that a pair of mags won't fit in a two-mag pouch. You need three-mag pouches to accept the assembled mags.

as it will go, and insert a loaded magazine with the feeding end to the buttplate, and the cartridge tips up. Press back until it clears the lever, and then swing the lever down to lock the magazine in place. In use, reach back with your forward hand and place the web of your hand against the spine of the magazine. With your fingers riding along the magazine, slide the web of your hand forward until it has pressed the retaining lever clear. Clutch the magazine and pivot the bottom down out of the stock. Pull the magazine out of the stock and forward towards the magazines well. (While this is going on, you have already pressed the magazine release button to drop the mag, or wait until the spare magazine arrives, to do a tactical reload) Pivot the magazine in your hand to orient it towards the magazine well, and insert.

The Rase stock replaces the standard stock, and there is no way to fabricate such a design with a telescoping stock. For one thing, the telescoping stock latch is in the way. The design is also capacity-dependant. If you have a stock built for 20-round magazines, you can't fit a 30-round magazine in it. If you have a 30, the 20-round magazines will simply fall out.

The Rase does not create storage or vehicle rack problems. And for those who find a standard stock is comfortable, useful, and in some departments,

The Rase stock holds a spare magazine out of the way. The stocks are capacity-specific, so you must get one for your 20-or 30-round magazines but not both.

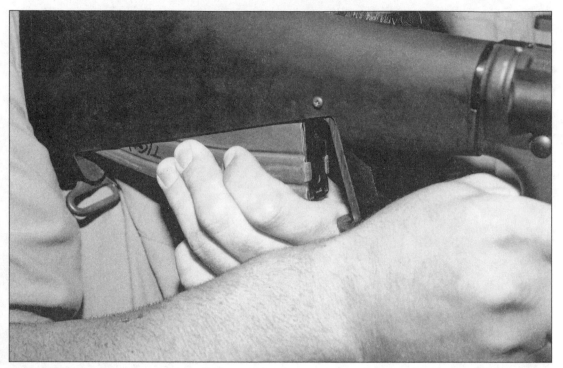

The Rase stock takes the place of the old fixed stock. When you need more ammo, reach back with the left hand and use the web between thumb and forefinger to push the latch open.

The stock pouch on a telescoping stock. Some move around, get the Blackhawk...

And then rig it so the buckles prevent the pouch from rotating on the buffer tube.

required, it works very well indeed. If you need an extra-short stock, such as a telescoping stock can provide, then the Rase will be too long. (Can't have everything, although we try.)

Stock pouch

The idea is simple: take a belt pouch and fasten it to the stock. As with simple ideas, the trick is in the details. And as with other methods, duct tape is a poor substitute for adequate planning. For fixed-stock rifles, the attachment is simple, a pair of webbing straps, one of which is also secured to the sling swivel. By securing it on the sling swivel, it stays back out of the way, and doesn't pivot around the stock. On telescoping stocks, the swiveling is much more of a problem. The pouch I have, from

Blackhawk, stays put. (Sliding pouches are the main reason Jeff is do down on them.) The securing trick is to position the buckle of the rear strap, the one that goes through the sling slot, so it is tight against the stock and won't allow any movement. In use, simply reach back and unfasten the flap, extract the magazine, and reload. The stock pouch has some drawbacks. First, it restricts shouldering. If you've set it up for a right-handed shooter, you can't switch to the left shoulder. The pouch is in the way. Second, on telescoping stocks, it uses the sling slots and precludes using a sling.

Magazine selection and maintenance

It would seem to be simple: buy new magazines, treat them right, and you're all set. If only it were so. Magazines in the AR universe are not a uniform product. They look identical, and some will work in every rifle. Some won't work at all. And there are the maddening ones that work reliably in some rifles, and marginally in others. The test protocol is simple, and all it takes is ammunition, a rifle, range time, the magazines and the willingness to use up some of your rifle barrel's service life.

First, check to see that the magazine inserts smoothly without binding. Then, does it drop free? If not, don't use it. Or clearly mark it as practice/training only, and not for duty. Insert again, and work the operating handle. Does the bolt lock open? If not don't use it or mark p/t. Once the bolt is locked back, does the magazine drop free of its own weight? If it does, you're on to the shooting. If it does not, you have yet another practice/training magazine.

Load five rounds. The oddest and most puzzling malfunction in the AR is the "bolt-over-base" failure, where the round does not feed up fast enough or straight, and the bolt rides over the cartridge, gouging twin tracks in it. It usually happens near the end, so test with five rounds. Fire the five, and see if the bolt locks back. Try it several times, and keep an eye on your magazines until they've been fully proven. In classes it is common to load magazines with five or 10 rounds only, to test as much as possible for the bolt-over-base problem. Once you're satisfied, then load it up to 20 or 30, its maximum capacity. Fire five rounds, reload the magazine and continue. A magazine with a tired or weak spring will have problems lifting the full weight of ammo. Repeat until you're satisfied.

Once you have a supply of tested and reliable magazines, mark them. You can use something as simple as colored electrical tape, or stencils and spray paint. Mark them well enough that if you drop one you can identify yours from the others. At a

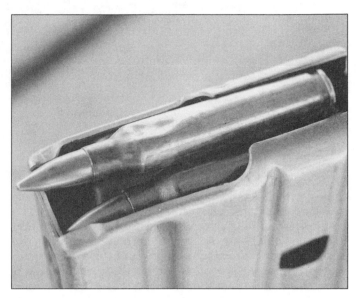

The result of the bolt-over-base failure. It isn't easy to correct once it happens, and the fault is usually with the magazine.

match or in a class there will be many others with rifles and magazines, and everyone wants to get their own magazines back. In a shooting incident, you'll be able to identify yours once the evidence technicians have finished marking, diagramming, photographing and sealing everything in plastic bags.

Recalcitrant magazines can be improved or salvaged by replacing the spring and follower. The newest and improved versions are the green USMC follower, and the "red" spring. The bright green

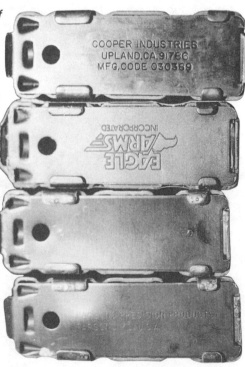

Keep track of your magazines. These all work in my rifles. The only way to know for sure is to test them. Once tested, don't lose track of your magazines.

The dented magazine on the right does not work, can never be made to work, and should be kept only as an example of what happens if you don't regularly check your gear.

follower is less likely to tip within the magazine body, and will lift the stack of rounds straight. The red-dyed spring is heavier and stronger, and lifts the stack faster and more reliably. You can get them from MagCinch, or from Specialized Armament Warehouse.

Magazine strings

A secure magazine pouch holds a magazine so well that even if the flap is open it won't fall out. The Blackhawk Omega Enhanced tactical thigh pouch is one example of a secure pouch, and the SOE Gear CQB vest is another. The problem arises from trying to wrestle a secure magazine out of the pouch. There are two solutions; traditional and Mag Cinch. The traditional method is to cut a section of 550 cord and melt the ends. One securing method is to slide the baseplate of the magazine partly off, insert the cord, and close the baseplate, trapping the cord in place. I don't like this method, as the mag tube and/or baseplate must to flex to accommodate the cord. Instead, I lay the cord in the grooves of the tube, and wrap stout tape around the whole works. The melted knobs on the ends of the 550 cord keep it from pulling through. The tape can be removed to clean the magazine, and the tube and baseplate aren't altered or flexed. The Mag Cinch solution is their MagPul, a moulded rubber cap that wraps around the base of the magazine, taking the place of the tape and 550 cord.

In use, you simply grab or hook the 550 cord or MagPul and pull the magazine free of the pouch. If you're using a triple-mag pouch to hold two magazines taped or Mag Cinch'ed together, you may not need a pull, but only testing can determine that. You may have grasping room, or you may not. But a triple pouch with three individual magazines stuffed

in it will not allow for finger room to grasp the first one. You will probably on need to modify one magazine. Once you've removed the first one, and assuming you need more, the second and third magazines will be easy enough to grasp that you probably don't need a string or MagPul on them.

Reliable function

The AR depends on proper ammunition and good magazines (as well as a certain level of maintenance) to function reliably. One shortcoming the system has is extraction. As designed the extractor is weak. It will slip off the rim of a stubborn cartridge. The Armed Forces have improved the extractor performance, first by adding the little plastic buffer you see inside the extractor spring. Later, they stiffened the buffer. Currently, the toughest and best is the black buffer. However, you can still make improvements. One

A magazine marked with my initials, and with a 550 cord as a magazine pull jammed under the baseplate.

The new bright green followers replace recalcitrant black followers, and often solve the problem of unreliable magazines. But test to be sure.

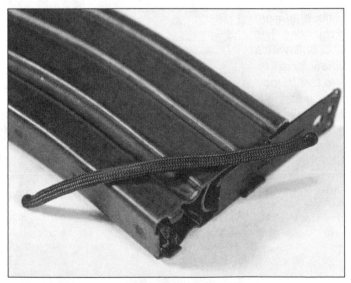

You can secure your pull strings by wedging them under the baseplate, not my favorite choice.

A better solution is to tape the 550 cord down in the tube groove, using duct tape or 100 mph tape.

You don't have to have pulls on every magazine, just one per pouch to make it easier to get that first one out.

method is to install the "De-Fender" (MagCinch carries them) The D shape of the part fits over the extractor spring. When you reassemble the bolt, the D-fender adds extra resistance to the extractor, allowing it to stay hooked on a case rim. Another approach is to replace the spring with a heavy-duty extractor spring from Specialized Armaments Warehouse. The SAW spring is much heavier, and turns a reluctant rifle into a reliable one. You might think that more is better. Well, in this case you'd be wrong. Do NOT use both at the same time. If you do, you'll make the extractor so difficult to operate that the rifle may not close on a chambered round, as the bolt doesn't have enough force available to it to pivot the extractor over the rim.

A bare AR is a plenty good enough tool with which to win a fight. But anything you can do that improves your chances of coming out on top, and coming home in one piece, should be seriously considered.

The AR-15/M-16 extractor with a mil-spec extractor spring and black buffer. Next to it is a S.A.W. extra-strength extractor spring. On the left a spring with a De-Fender installed.

Chapter 24

Pistol Caliber Carbines

IF POLICE DEPARTMENTS across the country are storing their 9mm submachineguns in the armory in favor of 5.56mm patrol rifles, why care about 9mm carbines? After all, why have a carbine/rifle that is really a shoulder-stocked handgun, with marginal power, excessive penetration, short range and an inability to penetrate body armor? Why, indeed? The reasons are simple and obvious: The ammunition costs less, the muzzle blast is less, in a heavy weapon the recoil is moderate, and the lack of penetration is an advantage. The decreased penetration of 9mm allows for use in indoor ranges that would not allow 5.56mm. You think steel is steel, and any backstop can stand up to 5.56mm ammo if it is good enough for 9mm? Incorrect. Many older backstops are not rated for rifles, and rifle use will quickly damage the backstop plates and make the range unsafe. Also, the use of a 5.56mm indoors can be quite oppressive. The muzzle blast quickly becomes tiring. Tired shooters do not shoot well, nor do they learn well.

However, any backstop design that can stand up to regular use by 9mm handguns can take the abuse dished out by 9mm carbines. Depending on the barrel length and the load used, a carbine will add 50 to 200 fps to the velocity a handgun generates. The extra 2 percent to 5 percent is not enough to over stress the steel in the backstop. And the 9mm carbine is not without its advantages in the field, too.

The advantages

Ammunition cost. While the average shooter feels the effect of increased cost, a department can be crushed by it. Bought in wholesale quantities (or in some locations, bought from the "State Bid," where the State buys in huge quantities and passes the lower cost on to local departments) the price difference between 9mm and 5.56mm can be great. For this comparison, I looked up the prices available on the current State Bid ammo lists, for practice ammunition in 9mm hardball compared to 5.56mm full metal jacket. The cost savings

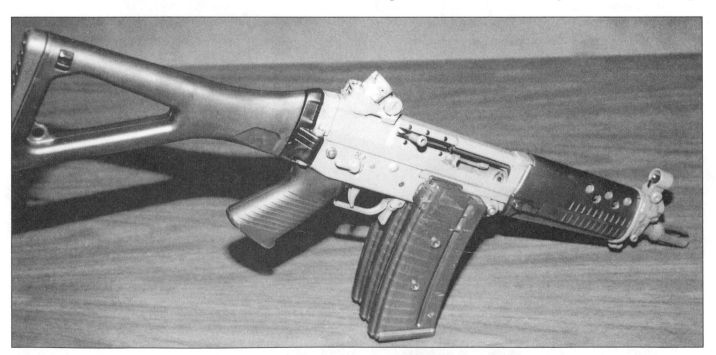

The Sig 552, in the carbine version, is as handy as any sub-gun. But with a short barrel (under 12 inches) it, like any other 5.56mm, is impressively loud.

Left to right, the FN 5.7mm, a 9mm and a 5.56. The 5.7 in the FN P-90, is intended to replace the 9mm while having nearly the terminal ballistics of the 5.56mm.

Pistol calibers, in the FN 5.7, 9mm, .40 and .45.

is $50/thousand rounds. ($95/M vs. $145/M) Lets us use a department with 20 sworn officers, where the chief decides to use 9mm carbines as practice rifles. Since they can use the indoor range built as part of the new precinct house/ police station 15 years ago, they can practice quarterly instead of annually. Quarterly practice consumes two magazines, for a total of 60 rounds. Annual state-mandated qualification, done with the 5.56mm carbines, takes another 60 rounds, but that cost is a fixed cost, regardless of the practice sessions or calibers.

The regimen of quarterly practice is a better one to maintain skills, and is also less work than an annual refresher of the same amount of ammunition. Twenty officers, 60 rounds each, four times a year, each officer fires 240 rounds, and the total comes to just under 5,000 rounds of ammo. A savings of $250 in ammunition costs. You may not think that $250 saved is that much in a municipal budget. However, the same ammunition expenditure, devoted to 5.56mm ammunition, would result in those 20 officers only firing 41 rounds per practice session. (And that assumes the indoor range can handle 5.56. If it

cannot, then there is no quarterly practice, only annual.) More practice is better. An administrative consideration of annual-only qualification that you may not have thought about is manpower. You, as the chief, can't pull all your officers off the streets to do annual qualification at once. (And even if you did, you couldn't get them through 240 rounds in one day and have meaningful practice.) You'd have to re-schedule the three shifts and pull one or two officers off their shift at a time. Or have them shoot on a day off, and pay them overtime. With three shifts of five or six officers, finding the manpower to do a single-day practice and qualification becomes a Herculean task. With an indoor range and 9mm carbines, you can do practice and handling drills before roll call. And while the scheduling becomes easier with a larger department, the cost savings of using 9mm mount.

Muzzle blast. While a 5.56mm rifle is superior in many regards for patrol, perimeter and entry work, the increased performance comes at the cost of extra muzzle blast. Outdoors, shooting a 5.56mm carbine simply require standard hearing protection. Indeed, depending on where you are, simple foam plugs are adequate. At my home range, with close-by walls, berms and buildings, the reflected sound is enough to require headphones/earmuffs and sometimes both plugs and muffs. Indoors is another matter entirely. Indoors, plugs and muffs are barely adequate. The oppressive blast from a 5.56mm round, when indoors, is reflected onto you so you absorb the sound not just through your ears, but also via bone conduction from your skull and jaw and through your chest. Even accomplished shooters can find indoor practice tiring, and prone to developing a flinch. However, sometimes firing indoors can't be avoided. In the week proceeding my writing this chapter, the wind chill when I got up each morning varied from a high of 9°F to a low of -16°F. Outdoor practice under such conditions is more a test of endurance than a means of increasing skill. Unless

The SMG is cheap, durable, reliable, heavy and not something you can easily mount optics on.

your location is in one of the southern tier of states, you have similar problems with the weather. Outdoor once-a-year practice and qualification becomes even more difficult, since not only are you having to wait until the warm months, when you do your scheduling is complicated by competition for every other warm-weather activity, too. And unless your department owns the range, you have to work out the schedule with other departments in the same fix.

The Beretta 93 is a three-shot burst pistol with a shoulder stock. It is not a general-issue "carbine" but rather a very specialized tool.

A 9mm indoors is a 9mm. Handgun or carbine, there isn't that much noise, compared to a 5.56mm. The lowered noise makes it easier to coach shooters out of bad habits, encourage good ones, and work in improving skills. The lower muzzle blast also reduces the chances of a shooter developing a flinch. A flinch is one of the worst habits to have developed, and one of the toughest to get rid of. Telling a new shooter they have to have both plugs and muffs is not a good way to introduce them to a new weapon. And not insisting on using both is a sure way to develop a flinch.

Recoil. The 9mm has slightly less felt recoil than a 5.56mm. It isn't much different, but it is less. Combined with the decreased muzzle blast, the 9mm is much more accessible to the new shooter than a 5.56mm. At one time or another during patrol rifle classes someone will point out that a 5.56mm can be tamed by using a muzzle brake or compensator. Well, yes. The problem is, you are not eliminating the blast and recoil, you are diverting it someplace else. That someplace else is usually the shooter next to you. The more effective the comp, the more likely it is to make the shooter next to you hate you. Outdoors, the "pop" of a 9mm carbine, especially in a 16-inch barreled model, is so small that you might be tempted to shoot without hearing protection. Don't do it! The muzzle blast is so slight it is no impediment to teaching a new shooter

Penetration. The lack of penetration is a good thing, and not just indoors. While it is a requirement for many indoor ranges, it is useful on outdoor ranges. In the development of the Modern Technique, and the practical shooting competitions that came

A Beretta 93, Colt 9mm, and a Glock 18. All fire 9mm, but only the Colt can produce longer-range accuracy in a general issue setting.

from it, IPSC shooters re-introduced the use of falling steel plates. Lest you think falling plates are a new invention, I have reprints of shooting magazines from the 1890s. One article concerns turkey shoots, and the difficulties the organizers had in finding turkeys to shoot at for their matches. They settled on a hinged steel plate they could shoot with their rifles. When hit, it fell over. The hinge allowed it to be easily re-set. The rifles they used were not like what we're using today. A target rifle suitable for a turkey match in 1890 would launch a lead bullet (no jacket) at a leisurely for a rifle velocity of 1,200 fps. A .44 Magnum at most, and in many instances what amounted to a .38 Special rifle. The 5.56mm will squirt a jacketed bullet at 3,100 fps. There are hardly any steel plates that can stand up to that kind of velocity. A 9mm, however, will not damage most steel. If you use falling plates, or non-falling and painted steel, for practice, they will stand up to years of use by 9mms. One session with a 5.56mm, and most plates would be ruined. As a training tool, the immediate feedback of a falling steel plate speeds up the learning cycle better than any other method. Do "it" right, and the steel falls. Do "it" wrong, and the steel doesn't fall. Simply turning them loose on a falling plate rack can turn shooters who otherwise don't get any charge or fun out of shooting into enthusiastic shooters.

And if you do need penetration, the 9mm can provide some. By using armor piercing ammunition (banned for civilian/commercial production and sale) your department's 9mm carbines can penetrate body armor. A spare magazine, marked with paint or tape, loaded with the special rounds, can provide penetration when it is needed. Conversely, over-penetration can be a problem in operational use. Indoors, a 5.56mm bullet will destabilize and tumble when striking building components. A standard 55-grain jacketed bullet launched from an AR or M-16 will be destabilized by the first wall, break up in the second, and be essentially harmless after that. A 9mm jacketed bullet fired under similar circumstances will continue through the building until it strikes something substantial like an electrical box or metal pipe.

As an issue carbine for patrol use, the 9mm carbine does have some advantages. It can be had in versions that are not so obviously military as the various 5.56mm carbines. Some police administrators are quite sensitive to the use of "machineguns" in the public view. Something that looks more like a common hunting rifle finds favor in their eyes. The issues of noise and recoil carry over to patrol use. Ammunition and magazine commonality can be had with the correct selection of pistol caliber carbines. While the idea of "the spare magazine" can be over-done, it is still comforting to have magazine commonality between weapons. Knowing that your sidearm and carbine not only use the same ammo, but the same magazines, makes it easier to pack "enough" ammo

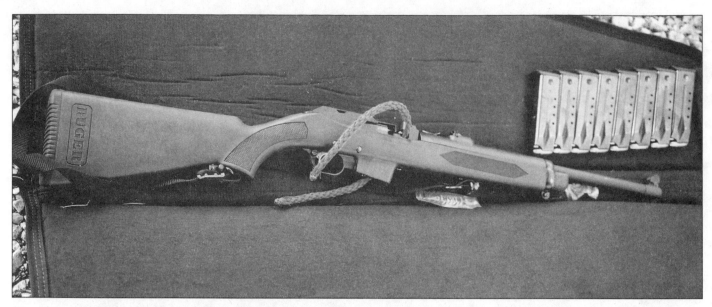

The Ruger PC-9 (or PC-40) can be a low-profile police carbine, but it has durability and accuracy drawbacks. Great for indoor practice, though.

The Beretta M-92, if backed up by a 9mm carbine, (especially one that takes Beretta magazines) is the issue for many departments and can be part of a viable sidearm/carbine combo.

auto fire at close ranges, starting with the selector on "safe" can be as fast or faster than selecting to "full" or "burst" and firing.

Which 9mm carbines?

The first consideration is commonality in operation and controls with the issue 5.56mm carbines. Practicing with one weapon, and then issuing a different one for use on patrol, is not the best arrangement. Ideally, you would want the two to simply be different-calibers of the same model. That way, practice with the controls, sights and magazine changes would carry over from one to the other. But the ideal is not always possible, and some practice is better than none.

The H&K MP-5: The symbol of SWAT teams for many years, the MP-5 has declined in use for a number of reasons. (Some covered in the patrol rifle chapter.) While some parts are not as durable as the receiver/sum of the parts (extractor springs must be regularly checked and replaced on high-use weapons) the MP-5 has an enviable record of reliability. It is heavy, coming in at 10 pounds loaded with spare magazine and light, it lacks a bolt hold open device (at least one engaged when the magazine runs dry) and the safety/selector require the thumbs of an orangutan to use. The sights are adequate. The stock is either the solid one, which is comfortable but bulky, or the telescoping one, which is compact but not comfortable to use. It is quite accurate, as H&K

and keep track of where it is. Also, more of the pistol caliber carbines are available in semi-auto only versions than the 5.56mm, and many police administrators desire that semi, and semi-only, weapons be issued. On that subject I am in complete agreement. There is an occasional need for full-auto fire in the military context, but none in law enforcement. You aren't going to need suppressive fire on even a high-risk traffic stop. While a full-auto or burst option might rarely be useful on a raid, getting to it isn't worth it. On a raid, you are going through the door with the safety on. (If you aren't, you are absolutely not going to be going in behind me!) In the event you need to fire, and perceive the need or desire for full-auto or burst fire, by the time you a) decide b) select c) aim d) fire, you could have simply pressed your safety to "fire" on your semi-only carbine and fired the three or four needed shots. Fast, aimed, semi-

The H-K MP-5 has been the standard carbine for SWAT for many years. It is being phased out in many departments by 5.56mm carbines, but it can still be a reliable and relatively inexpensive practice weapon.

makes good and highly durable barrels. The magazine change procedure of the MP-5 is different than the other manufacturers' carbines, but identical for other H-K products. Once the MP-5 runs dry, you reload by grasping the actuating knob with your left hand, racking it back, and turning it up into the hold-open notch. Grasp the magazine with your left hand, with your thumb on the magazine latch paddle. Squeeze the paddle forward as you pull the magazine down. Remove the old magazine, and insert the new one until it locks in place. Reach up and over with your left hand (tilting the MP towards your left hand) and slap the actuating knob out of its notch and thus allowing the action spring to chamber a round. It can be done quickly, but you don't know if you're out of ammo when running an MP-5 (or other H&K weapon) until it goes click instead of bang.

If your department issues the H&K 93, or the G-33, in 5.56mm, then using an MP-5 as an indoor practice weapon makes sense. If the issue patrol carbine is an AR-15/M-16, the lack of control commonality can make training problematic. The MP-5 is available with a number of different trigger housings, allowing you to have the option of the original safe-semi-full, or with later housings, burst,

or burst or full, or even semi-only. The civilian-market H&K 94, while a semi-only carbine, is not much of an option. First, as a limited-production item, and H&K, it is an expensive collectors' piece. As a result of the Assault Weapons Ban (and import restrictions) I've seen high-mileage 94s on sale for as much as $3,500. Better to go to H&K directly (as a department) and get an MP-5 with a semi-only trigger assembly for the current wholesale or department-direct price. (On the order of $625) Also, the 94 will have a 16.25-inch barrel, instead of the more compact 8-inch barrel of the MP-5. As a training item, the longer barrel won't matter. But as an issue item, trying to wrestle the longer model out of a squad car is a hassle.

AR-15: Colt came out with their 9mm carbine in the mid 1980s and promptly ran into a marketing conundrum. The 9mm worked, it fit a perceived (and shooter-expressed) need, it was cheap to shoot, and it wasn't hard on range equipment. But everyone wanted 5.56mm rifles, or so it seemed. Shooters were so eager in the mid 1980s to get 5.56mm ARs that they would track down the parts and assemble their own. (I made a decent part of my income as a gunsmith back then correctly assembling and

This is the new H-K UMP submachinegun. Mostly polymer, available in several calibers, and a durable if quirky weapon to fire. (In .45 ACP I can feel the stock flexing under recoil.)

debugging other people's attempts at AR building.) The 9mm languished. Colt sold a bunch to the U.S. Government, competing with the MP-5. Those who bought them wanted them so their training with M-16s would be reinforced when using the Colt 9mm. Colt has since been barely able to keep the doors open and the lights on. Between those who know the value of the 9mm, and the collectors who want pristine Colt rifles, finding an original Colt 9mm is tough. There are conversions that allow you to turn a 5.56mm rifle into a 9mm, by swapping the uppers and using an adapter for the magazine well. The big advantage to using the AR in 9mm is that practice with it directly reinforces lessons learned and skills needed for the AR-15/M-16 in 5.56mm. The controls, sights and magazine changes are all the same. The Colt 9mm suffers from one drawback, its magazine. The Colt uses a slightly modified Uzi magazine. The basic Uzi tube was changed to include a bolt hold-open tab on the follower. (Uzi magazines can even be modified to work in a Colt, and still work in an Uzi. But they won't lock the Colt open when empty.) However, the magazine is viewed as a weak point in the Colt. Drop a loaded magazine and you're likely to see anywhere from a few to all of the rounds squirt out. I have always wondered, is this a problem with Uzi mags? Since Uzi owner are unwilling to let me drop their magazines on concrete in order to see, I have not yet found an answer. As long as you don't drop your magazines a Colt/conversion 9mm carbine is great for practice. An AR is what your armorer

The Colt and the Uzi can use many of the same magazines. Why the Colt mags have a bad rep and the Uzi magazines do not is a mystery.

228   Pistol Caliber Carbines

The Beretta CX4 shows a lot of promise.

makes it. While he can't legally turn an AR into a select-fire 9mm SMG, he can "de-tune" an M-16 to semi-only for departmental use. (The BATFE will still consider them to be machineguns, but they will function as semi-only until the armorer switches them back.) And the various conversions are built to go onto semi-only AR-15 lowers, and not M-16 lowers. You have to either locate the proper select-fire parts to convert an M-16 into a 9mm submachinegun, or be a good gunsmith and not just a parts-swapping armorer. But it can be done.

Kel Tec: The Kel Tec carbine is unique in several of its design aspects. First, it folds. The receiver is hinged in the middle, and the folded carbine is compact enough to store in a surprisingly small package. Despite its compact size stored, it unfolds to be long enough to meet many state requirements as well as the Federal requirement for barrel length and overall length. As a result, it is "just another rifle" and not a Short-barreled Rifle under the law. A second unique aspect is the magazine well. The magazine well is the pistol grip, so your handgun reloading practice carries over to the Kel Tec. In addition, the well is replaceable, so the Kel Tec can use one of the common handgun magazines as its feeding device. Your department carries Glocks? Then the Kel Tec with the Glock grip will take your magazines. Beretta? Sig? Ruger? With the correct pistol grip, you can use any one of them. (But not all of them.) With a full 16-inch barrel, you get all the velocity your 9mm ammo delivers. While the Kel Tec doesn't carry over in handling or operation with any of the 5.56mm carbines, more practice is more practice. The Kel Tec is strictly a semi-only carbine.

The Ruger PC9: Here is an interesting option for those departments issuing Ruger Mini-14 rifles, or even the M-1 Carbine. It is a blowback-operated carbine that feeds from Ruger magazines. The stock design is that of a traditional rifle, with rifle sights. The Ruger PC9 is a semi-only carbine.

The Beretta CX4: The newest kid on the block, the Beretta is specifically designed for the training/patrol rifle role, and will garner a lot of interest by competitors who want to shoot in pistol caliber carbine matches. (Yes, they exist.) The CX4 Storm is a blowback 9mm, 40 or .45 carbine. The exterior is positively racy looking, coming from Guigiaro Design. The CX4 accepts standard Beretta magazines, but the situation is not quite as straightforward as you might hope. There are two models for the 9mm, one that uses the 92 series magazines and one that uses the Cougar 8000 series. In .40 caliber there is a model for the 96 series, and a model that takes the magazines from the 8040 Cougar. In .45, there is only one, using magazines from the 8045 Cougar. All take only the full-size magazines, not the compact ones. On the good side, the internals are changeable, If you want a left-handed version, just disassemble and swap the cross bolt safety, magazine button and bolt handle. And, the CX4 has optional picatinny rails for mounting scopes, lights, and vertical forearm/weapon lights. This is a very promising carbine.

Kel-Tec SUB 2000: The Sub 2000 is the improved model of the old Sub-9. Instead of the all-metal construction of the Sub-9, the Sub 2000 uses polymer. I don't know which formulation they use, but the Fiberglas-filled polymer seems tough enough.

Folded, the SUB-2000 is a compact package that measures just about a foot and a half.

The Sub-2000 is one of those "Why didn't I think of that" ideas. Simply described, it is a pistol-caliber carbine that is hinged to fold in the middle, right at the chamber. The barrel and chamber, forearm and front sight are in the front half, and the pistol grip, magazine well, bolt recoil spring and buttplate are in the rear half. The trigger guard is the lock that keeps the halves together when opened. Unlatch it and lift the muzzle, and you can fold the forward half up and back until it locks to the rear half. To unlock, press the latch above the buttplate towards the action and you unlatch the front sight assembly from the buttplate. Swing it forward and down, and when the trigger guard snaps into place you're ready to load and go.

The really trick part of the design is the pistol grip. Since it uses standard handgun magazines, and the pistol grip is the magazine well, then the design can be made to accommodate different pistol magazines. Your department issues (or you carry) a Sig? Your Sub-2000 can use the same magazines. Ditto Beretta, Ruger, Glock, S&W and Kel-Tec magazines. However, the Glock pistol grip cannot be changed, where the others can. So, if you have both Beretta and Sig pistols, you can swap your Sub-2000 back and forth. You can have the Sub-2000 in either 9mm or 40 (but you can't swap from one to the other) and you can have the buttstock and forend in black, green or gray. The metal can be blue, parkerized or hard chromed.

The bare carbine can be upgraded by attaching the picatinny rail for a light, a scope mount, laser, stock extension (for those with really long arms) and spare magazine holder.

The Kel-Tec SUB 2000 in a model that accepts your sidearms magazines, is one very viable pistol caliber carbine, and a compact one too.

The SUB-2000 differs from its predecessor by being mostly polymer. The crossbolt safety, below and behind the ejection port, is set up for right-handed shooters.

In use, it is simple. With the Sub-2000 opened and locked, insert a loaded magazine. Underneath the stock tube is the operating handle. Grab it and pull it back, then release and let it go forward. The handle reciprocates with the bolt, so you must not place your hand back there, or allow any equipment to get in the way. You can be injured, and the equipment damaged. And, the carbine will not properly cycle, which could be embarrassing in a gunfight. The safety is the cross-bolt button above and behind the trigger. Press it across to place on "fire." The aperture rear sight is automatically raised as you opened the rifle, sight through the rear, and align the front as you would any aperture or ghost ring sight. Aim and fire. To stop, take your finger out of the trigger guard, push the safety to "safe" and point in a safe direction. To unload, remove the magazine then operate the bolt to extract the chambered cartridge. If you wish to lock the bolt open, the operating handle slot has a notch cut in it. Pull the bolt back, the press the handle to the side into the notch. Ease it forward and the bolt will stay open.

The recoil is a bit snappy. However, the empty carbine weighs only 4 pounds, so a slightly sharper than "normal" recoil is to be expected. Once experienced, it is not a problem. Compared to a Colt SMG at 8 pounds or an H&K MP-5 at 10 pounds, the Sub-2000 should be expected to feel a bit sharper. The empties are ejected briskly and 10 to 12 feet to the side (9mm) but not so forcefully that they would present a hazard to others. The bolt does not have an automatic hold-open when the magazine is empty, but this also is no problem. The MP-5 does not, and many Colt SMG's lock open only occasionally when empty. Magazines are easily inserted, and drop free when the magazine button is pressed. While the brass deflector keeps empties out of the face of left-handed shooters, the gases blown out of the ejection port can sometimes be felt.

The big advantages of the Sub-2000 are the compactness of its folded condition, and the ease of aiming and firing for accurate results. Folded, the Sub-2000 is only 7 inches by 16 inches. You can easily stuff it in a gear bag, to ride on the passenger seat of a patrol car. Opened, it is 30 inches long. Since it uses standard pistol magazines, you can use the magazines from your sidearm, or keep a spare (even an extra-capacity) magazine attached to the carbine in the gear bag. When needed, it is quickly removed, opened, loaded and ready. With a standard magazine installed, it holds up to 17 rounds of 9mm, and you can fire from a low prone position. With an extra-capacity magazine, you can have 25 (Beretta) to 33 (Glock) rounds loaded, and follow-up if you need to reload, with pistol magazines. In accuracy testing, it was easy to keep all shots on a 10-inch steel plate at 100 yards offhand. The desire for a carbine in the patrol car comes in part from the North Hollywood shootout, where the offenders used rifles and body armor to keep the police at a distance. Using a handgun in a rifle fight, at rifle distances, is not an efficient approach, and entirely likely to end up with a disbursement of survivor benefits. However, a pistol-caliber carbine that can be brought into play in a few seconds evens the odds quite a bit. From prone, I was able to score hits on head-sized plates at 80 yards 75 percent of the time.

It would also be useful for the officer who has a regular patrol rifle in the car, as an issue carbine to backup. Example: rolling up on a situation, you bail out with your patrol rifle, to be met by the off-duty officer who called it in. With the Sub-2000 in your gear bag, you have a patrol rifle and a pistol-caliber carbine on hand to deal with the problem, rather than a patrol rifle and an off-duty snubbie. For the size, weight and cost, the Sub-2000 is an excellent option to add to your bag of tricks in a lethal force situation.

One question that comes up is reliability and durability. (OK, two questions.) I was introduced to the Sub-2000 in its earlier incarnation as the Kel-Tec Sub-9. Jeff Chudwin was one of the first to get one, and he has put thousands of rounds through his without a problem. He finds it dependable enough that he packs it in his gear as a backup, and if you knew him you would realize what a compliment that is. I have not put thousands of rounds through mine

A 50-yard group with the issue sights and Zero 9mm ammunition.

yet, but it has not failed yet. As for parts breakages, neither Jeff nor I have broken anything. From time to time I hear rumors of broken parts or recalcitrant guns, but have not been able to trace them back to their source. But then, if you were to mention any firearm at all to a group of shooters, competitors or police officers, at least one of them would be happy to regale you with tales he's heard of that particular one (regardless of which you mention) breaking or malfunctioning.

As a spare rifle, or an issue to backup, how would I set up the Sub-2000? I would first select one for the pistol magazines issued. Considering the accuracy mine delivered, I would not go with a scope or red dot sight. The bulk isn't worth the accuracy improvement. I would however, attach the light rail, and keep a Streamlight M-3 on it. I would use a loop of elastic, like a load-bearing vest or gear securing strap, and place it around the forearm. I would then use it to secure the carbine magazine. The strap can't

go around both halves or you can't open the folded carbine. And it can't go around the lower, or it will interfere with the reciprocating bolt handle. I would keep a high-capacity magazine on the rifle. If I needed to go prone, I could select a spare off my belt. If I needed the volume (a rapid-responder situation, for example) I'd use the hi-cap first, and reload off my belt as needed.

The folded carbine would then go in the gear bag to ride in the passenger seat in a one-officer car, or tucked out of the way in the passenger compartment in a two-officer car. (And of course, the vehicle is always locked when left unattended, as per Departmental SOP.)

The 16-inch barrel of the Sub-2000 potentially adds velocity to the cartridge. However, many 9mm loadings are balanced for 4- and 5-inch handgun barrels, so the extra barrel length does not give as much boost as you might think.

Chapter 25

Springfield M-1A Scout Rifle

IS THERE NO one who doesn't know the story? The M-1 Garand, after nearly 20 years of on-again off-again development, was rolled out just in time for WWII. And you could say it won the war. Or, at the very least, brought back a lot more GIs than would have otherwise come home in one piece. However, as good as it was, it had some drawbacks. The round was too powerful. Designed for an age when a rifle company had no other supporting fire, and had to solve all problems themselves, it was accurate and powerful enough to deal a lethal blow at 1,000 yards. At the end of WWII, anything 1,000 yards out was dealt with by artillery fire, not rifle fire. The eight-round en-bloc clip was limiting. It limited firepower, and it created supply problems. The ping it made when ejecting the empty clip is more myth than real problem. But only having eight rounds, and needing to reload another entire clip if a GI was down a few (or didn't know how many he had) was a problem. And the only way to see how many rounds were left in the rifle was to eject the remaining rounds, reload, and then count how many were lying on the ground.

So, the Ordnance Department spent nearly 15 years, a ton of money, rigged the tests, and came up with the M-14. The result was basically an M-1 Garand that fed from a 20-round box magazine, had an improved gas system, and used a slightly shorter but pretty much the same power cartridge. "Introduced" in 1957, production was so low that during the Berlin Crisis of 1961, the Berlin Brigade was still issued Garands. (That got some people in hot water.)

TRW, then a manufacturing firm and now the credit check people, decided to get into the business of making service rifles. They invested a bunch of money and went about the problem as one of making a precision-machined product, not just a rifle. They invested in new, precise, multiple machining stations, predecessors to today's computer-controlled milling stations. They considered the investment as part of their cost to enter the market, and serve the country. Despite under-bidding their competition, they were soon making money on each rifle, due to the early delivery and quality production bonuses on the contract. And then, in 1963, in one of his lesser sins, James McNamara, the Secretary of Defense, shut down M-14 production to focus on building M-16s. (A new, and different fiasco.)

The M-14 was immediately relegated to surplus status, hauled out for special uses like being built into sniper rifles, or issued to Naval vessels for mine control. But despite its drawbacks, many loved it. Loved it basically because it delivered what the M-16 couldn't; power and penetration. And as such it has never gone away. Back in the 1970s, Springfield Armory, the private gun maker, began production of the M-1A, a semi-auto only clone of the M-14. The government Springfield Arsenal had been closed, by the same Secretary McNamara, in 1968. SA

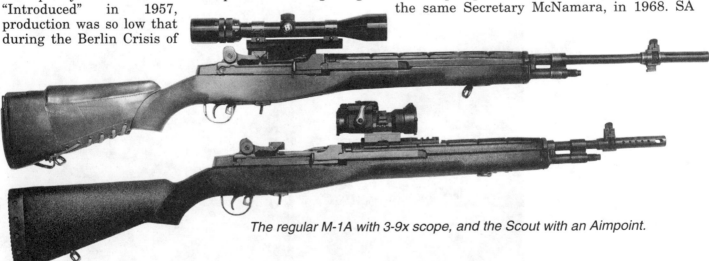

The regular M-1A with 3-9x scope, and the Scout with an Aimpoint.

made it for Service Rifle competitors who wanted a rifle of their own, and couldn't arrange long-term loan of a government-owned rifle. The ATF has a curious attitude about select-fire weapons: "Once a machinegun, always a machinegun." There are no modifications into semi-auto status you can make to the receiver of a machinegun that will preclude it being always considered a machinegun. However, were you to make a new rifle to the same configuration as that altered machinegun, it is kosher. As a result and example, if you take an M-14 and use a surface grinder to remove the selector pivot from the receiver, it is still a machinegun. However, if you use that same surface grinder to make a new receiver out of a block of steel, to the identical dimensions as the milled-pivot M-14, it is a kosher semi-only rifle. I'm not saying it is rational, just government policy.

Civilian shooters could own an otherwise identical rifle to the M-14 for Service matches, and not worry about the paperwork needed to own a "machinegun."

Fast forward to the 21st century. Service rifle matches now use AR-15s or M-16s since gunsmiths

The M-14 (and now M-1A) replaced the en-bloc clip of the Garand with a box magazine.

and shooters have figured out how to keep them accurate to 600 yards. But for some applications, the M-14/M-1A still rules. For all of its positive attributes, the AR still lacks power. For a highway patrolman or a deputy in a rural county, where it may be necessary to engage targets at distance or behind hard cover, the 7.62mm rifle rules. And the Springfield Scout is the one to have. Other than being semi-automatic only, the regular Scout differs from the original M-14 in three ways: the barrel is shorter, to make it handier, the stock is synthetic for

One thing not changed from the Garand was the rear sight.

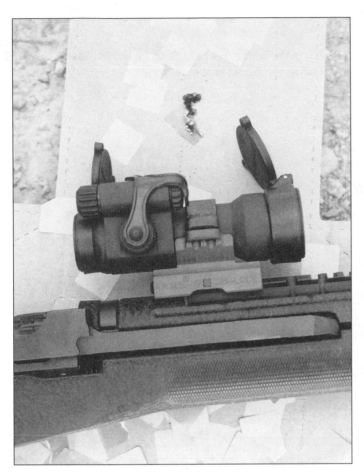

Five rounds offhand at 50 yards to check the zero. I guess it is still on.

durability, and the barrel has a scope mount on it for a scout scope or red dot optics. For parts and accessories, the M-1A accepts all items that were designed or made for the M-14, including magazines, slings, and the regular scope mounts.

Short barrel

Yes, there is some velocity loss due to the shorter barrel. However, analogous with the .45 ACP, the power the cartridge generates is not due solely to velocity. The .7.62mm bullet is three times the weight of the 5.56mm while only giving up some velocity to the smaller cartridge. The shorter barrel is much handier in exiting a vehicle or doing a building search, and reduces the muzzle-heavy feel of the balance. As an added bonus, the change in federal law, the Assault Weapon Ban of 1994, caused Springfield Armory to change the flash hider. Flash hiders aren't allowed, so they changed it to a muzzle brake. When I first looked at the brake, I thought "Oh, so they had to change it. Well, it doesn't look goofy, so O.K." Then when I first fired it, I noticed right away that the muzzle stayed down. As for flash, the flash is not greatly increased over the mil-spec flash hider, but that isn't much of a problem in police work. One item missing is the bayonet lug. Deemed an evil implement by the AW Ban of 1994, it had to be eliminated in order to pass muster with the law.

Synthetic stock

Original stocks on M-14's were wood. While reasonably durable, wood has some drawbacks. One is that in severe conditions wood may deteriorate. The greatest objection is that in order to make the stock durable enough for military use, the wrist of the stock (the area the firing hand grasps) has to be thick; too thick for comfort for some users. By changing to a synthetic. The wrist can be as thin as needed for comfort, and still be strong enough for use. Additionally, changes in point of impact due to temperature and humidity changes do not happen with a synthetic stock. Synthetic stocks can be easily painted to match the operating area. A deputy in the Southwest can easily spray-paint the stock of his rifle to match the brown, tan or gray of the county in which he works.

An additional feature and virtue of the use of synthetics is that if you need illumination, you can bolt an adapter rail to a synthetic stock. The crude method would be to drill the stock and bolt it on with wood screws or something like them. The elegant method would be to have a machinist or gunsmith turn threaded inserts that could be epoxied into the stock, and bolt the rail down with machine screws. Once the rail is on, a Millennium light could be clamped to the rail.

I elected not to undertake such a modification, as the kind folks at Springfield /Armory had sent me the rifle on loan. I'm sure they'd be impressed by my enthusiasm, design skills and workmanship, but I'm also sure they'd insist on payment for what had become my rifle.

Scout rail

The big difference (any M-1A can be dropped into a synthetic stock, and many gunsmiths can shorten a barrel) is the scope mount. Rather than mount the scope over the receiver, the rail is forward of the action, out on the barrel. Based on the scout rifle concept introduced by Jeff Cooper, the forward-mounted scope (with the proper optics) allows for

The Scout rail clamps around the barrel.

 Modern Law Enforcement Weapons   235

The Aimpoint with an A.R.M.S. throw-lever mount secured to the Scout rail.

aiming and firing with both eyes open. Scout aiming is much faster, and does not preclude peripheral vision as part of the aiming. The drawback is that you cannot have much magnification. Most scout rifles are built with "no-power" or 1X scopes, up to 1-3/4X magnification. But since most engagements are well within 100 yards for law enforcement (and even much military work) not having a lot of magnification is not a drawback.

In fitting a scope, you simply need either a scope with a built-in base to clamp to the picatinny rail, or an adapter to hold the optics in place. To test the M-1A, I tried two optics; the Aimpoint and the EO Tech. In comparison, I ran handling and field accuracy tests against my scout rifle, a bolt action FN Mauser action with a Burris 1-3/4X scout scope on it. The tests are not exactly fair, as the FN rifle is built to fit me, while the Springfield is the standard out-of-the-box Scout rifle. However, the advantages of the FN are small, and exist only for the first shot. For follow-up shots, the Springfield Scout had it all over the bolt-action rifle. (As you would expect.)

In the testing, the adaptability of the Special Operations Equipment CQB vest proved quite useful. The magazine pouches that usually held a pair of 30-round AR magazines comfortably held one 20-round USGI magazine for the Springfield. In total, the vest would store 80 rounds in magazines, with another 20 in the rifle. If you've run out of 100 rounds of 7.62mm in a law enforcement setting, and the problem still exists, you're just going to have to depend on your sidearm until the rest of your team can extricate you

The muzzle brake works. And isn't objectionable to other shooters on the line.

The Springfield M-1A Scout compares well with a Gunsite-inspired Scout.

from your predicament. Or throw you more ammo. For a rural deputy the rifle in the car, with a loaded vest nearby (or in the trunk, if that's what the Sheriff dictates), means that in a matter of seconds you can have a powerful, accurate rifle with lots of spare ammo.

One question that came up in the testing was "Can you have the scout sight, and still mount a regular scope on the rifle?" A qualified yes. The M-1A/M-14 receiver was designed from the beginning to have a scope-mounting capability. The left side of the receiver is drilled and tapped, and there are locating grooves to secure the scope base once tightened. Also, there are improved scope mounts that use two screws, one of which secures to a replacement stripper guide. The idea is to have a spare, higher-magnification scope at hand, so if you need long-range accuracy you can bolt the scope on and be ready. The receiver-mounted scope, while interfering with the scout scope, is not blocked by the forward optics. The problem is, you can't depend on pinpoint accuracy with the newly secured scope. While accurate, the point of impact shifts with each installation. Minute differences in positioning of the scope mount each time it is

Why .308 power? Because sometimes you need it. After this we used tape to hold the gelatin in place.

A bonded .308 bullet penetrated 14 inches.

tightened down means you can have a change of an inch or more in group location. If you want accurate long-range shooting, you have to secure the scope, then sight it in, and have it ready. But if you need the scout sight, you need it right away, with no time to take the other scope off. Mechanically it works, but as a practical matter you have to select one or the other. Unless you are lucky enough to have a rifle that happens to return to zero each time the scope is removed and replaced.

If you want power, in a handy package that delivers fast firepower, the Springfield Scout is a definite contender. That reference to "rigging the tests" earlier? The Army Ordnance Department most definitely did not want to adopt the competing T-48 rifle. (The FN-FAL.) Years of development had gone into both rifles. Standard tests showed the two rifles to be comparable in accuracy and reliability. With the formation of NATO, all countries were attempting to settle on uniform ammunition and weapons. The decision was not easy to make, and so minor differences were used as pretexts to select the "American" rifle over the "European." Basically, that the M-14 was a quarter-pound lighter, had a few less parts, and could be made on existing M-1 Garand machinery. The weight was inconsequential, the extra parts mattered not at all, and as for the "existing machinery" advantage, as soon as mass production was started it was found to be not true. We went with the M-14, and the rest of the world went with the FN-FAL. So what else is new?

For those who want the power, or feel the need for the range of the bigger rifle, the Springfield Scout can deliver in a compact-enough package.

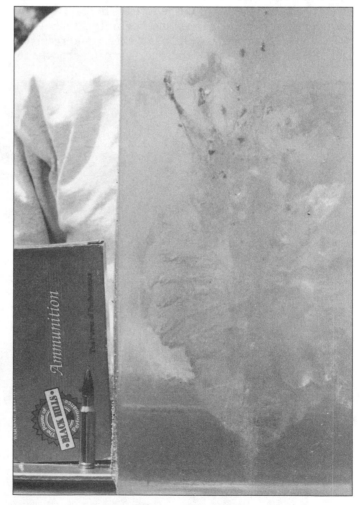

The Black Hills specialty load "penetrated" about ten inches, with some pieces going deeper.

Chapter 26

Myths Of The Rifle, Or: Things "Everyone Knows" That Just Aren't True

YOU'D THINK THAT in the 40 years since the AR-15/M-16 has been in service, the myths and misconceptions would have all been debunked. Unfortunately not. There are still some oldies being offered as "sage advice" and some new ones that seem reasonable, but aren't. In the interests of keeping things straight, here are the misconceptions I could find, whether they are true or not, and the reasons they may have gotten started.

The 5.56mm Is A Buzzsaw

And conversely, for some reason, it is also both a marginally penetrating light little bullet, or an over-penetrating armor-piercing bullet.

Boy, keeping this one straight is tough, even for some who argue all sides. Yes, there are some who argue that the 5.56mm is a tumbling, death-dealing saw, that it fails to penetrate vegetation well enough, and that it also goes right through cars. Their argument depends on just what part of their firearms decision-making they are trying to justify or defend. In order: The death-dealing buzzsaw. This one comes from the old belief that the 5.56 bullet tumbles in flight. I even had my high-school buddy, then a Captain in U.S. Army Armor, tell me this one. The earliest ARs had a barrel twist of one turn in 14 inches. It was just enough to keep the bullet stable in flight. The barely-stabilized bullet, upon striking an object, would begin to tip. The result was a 55-grain

The sights are high above the bore. If you do not pay attention, what you see is not always what you shoot.

The "penetrates too much" 5.56mm bullet actually comes up a little short to some observers. This bullet tip was dug out 14 inches in.

theoretical example to illustrate the point: If you issued 9mm full metal jacket handgun ammunition to a group of superb marksmen, all of whom take great pains to get as close as possible before firing, and place every shot right through the sternum of their opponents, that 9mm ammo will get a pretty good reputation as a fight-stopper. It would be an unwarranted reputation, for the results are due to the users and not the ballistics. Early AR-15s issued in Vietnam (before general issue) went to the best troops, with predictable results.

Penetration depends on a number of things. Among them are velocity, bullet shape, bullet construction, target construction, and the distance to the target. More velocity generally means more penetration, until the velocity becomes too great for the bullet's construction. At a high enough velocity, any bullet will begin to break apart. For the 5.56mm, the threshold is in the area of 2,600 fps to 2,700 fps. That means that within 150 to 200 yards the bullet will tumble and then fragment once it penetrates a soft object.

Penetration of a hard object is aided by velocity, as the 55-grain jacketed bullet of the M-193 round going 3,150 to 3,200 fps can burn through steel before the bullet is destroyed. However, in non-homogenous barriers, velocity works against the 5.56mm. Interior walls, for example often cause bullet fragmentation and breakup within a set of interior walls.

bullet going through the target sideways. The effect on the target (people, after all it was Southeast Asia, ca. 1963) was out of proportion to the recoil of the rifle. However, in the adoption of the AR-15 to become the M-16, the slow twist was found to be a little too marginal. A worn bore, or use in severe cold of the Arctic, could result in an inaccurate bullet. As many in the military had fresh memories of biting cold nights on a ridge in Korea, a loss of accuracy in cold weather was not acceptable.

The newer twist allegedly eliminated the "buzzsaw" aspect of the 5.56mm wounding mechanism, but didn't. What changed? Perception and use. Perception in that once it was general-issue there were plenty of instances that could be observed and noted. So, the extraordinary instances taken as gospel were seen as not true. And with general issue came general marksmanship. Then none at all. A

9mm vs. 5.56mm

The big differences in penetration are interior walls and body armor. The 5.56 will cut through body armor except for armor designed to stop rifle rounds. The 9mm rounds will rarely do so. Inside a structure

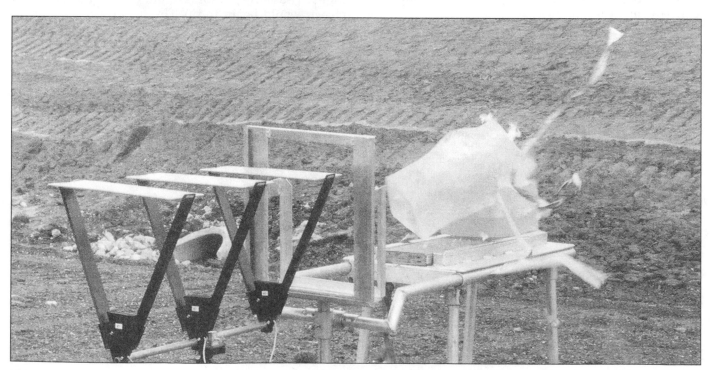

You can't make gelatin jump like this with a .223/5.56mm. No matter what magical bullet you use.

it is just the opposite. The stoutly constructed 9mm trundles through wall after all, since its velocity is not great enough to break up the bullet unless it strikes a hard object like a thick-walled pipe. The 5.56mm, with its relatively great velocity, causes bullet disintegration beginning in the first wall.

It is counter-intuitive, but indoors the less penetrative of the two rounds is the 5.56mm.

All AR/M-16's are alike

Velocity depends on barrel length, and short barrels can cause enough velocity loss as to make the 5.56mm wounding mechanism uncertain. The very sexy ultra-short barrels, 10 inches or even 8 inches, can cause muzzle velocity to be below the fragmentation threshold. Barrel twist can restrict ammunition election, as the slower twist barrels cannot be depended on to shoot heavy bullets accurately.

The Magazines are bad

Well, some are. I have heard that there are only two sets of tooling for the fabrication of AR-15/M-16 magazines in existence. And that these tooling sets simply get shipped from one manufacturer to another as each in turn becomes the low bidder or scores enough points for hiring this or that group. That may or may not be true. What is true is that some magazines are not reliable. However, it is not so

With the right bullet, the .223/5.56mm can do a creditable job of penetrating chance obstacles. But it is no powerhouse.

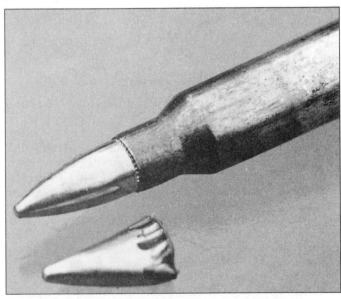

Starting at 52-55 grains, the largest piece is generally 20 grains once the movement stops.

Some magazines are bad, most are good. Once you've tested yours, mark them. Don't loan them. Keep them safe.

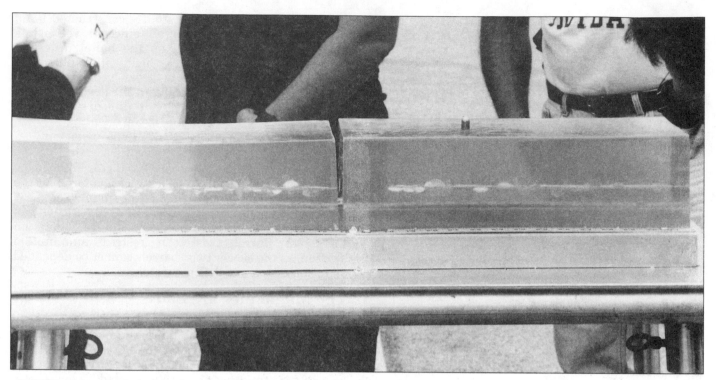

.45ACP, 230-grain fmj, went 36 inches in a straight line and it would have kept going if we hadn't caught it in a bulletproof vest draped on the back.

simple a subject that you can simply say "Stay away from X, always use Y, and test Z before you depend on them." They all have to be tested. I have seen various lists of the "these are bad" variety, and it never fails that I have some on the list. And mine have always been reliable. The basic AR magazine is an aluminum tube with an aluminum baseplate, plastic follower and steel spring. The magazine tube can be damaged or bent. The feed lips can be damaged. It can be assembled incorrectly.

The solution is simple: keep a sufficient supply on hand. If you are going to work each day with a rifle and five magazines, buy extras. Ten extras would be good. That way you'll always have a supply on hand, even if your range magazines are full of mud, and your backups are apart on the bench being cleaned. Test all your magazines. Mark them with your name, initials, department or some other identifier, and number them. If you start to see malfunctions at the range, you can quickly determine if it happens just with "#3" or with all of them.

Once you have yours tested and marked, do not loan them.

On variant of the "magazines are bad" is the '30-round magazines are bad." The 20-round magazines are indeed bullet proof. If yours are the old straight 20s, and not the new curved 20s, then you probably have great magazines. They tend to be reliable and durable. They are compact, and since everyone wants 30s, you can often get the old 20-round magazines at less cost than the newer 30s.

Load the magazines down

The idea is to load only 18 rounds in a 20-round magazine, and 28 in a 30. This is a mixture of truth and fiction. One part of the problem is that some 20-round magazines will accept 21 rounds, and some 30-round magazines will accept 31 rounds. These over-loaded magazines will not seat in the rifle when the bolt is forward. If you lock the bolt back and seat the magazine, the bolt may not have enough force to strip the top round off and fully chamber it. And, some magazines occasionally malfunction when loaded fully. As I mentioned before, none of mine have done so. You must test your magazines. My friend and experienced police trainer, Jeff Chudwin, is quite emphatic on this point. So much so that he advocates only 20-round magazines for law enforcement (the 20s have a much better track record

In the .223/5.56mm, velocity is key. Federal M-193 is hot stuff, and works well.

Resting on the handguards you won't see any change in the point of impact from offhand.

for reliability and durability than the 30s do) and then only loading 18 rounds in them.

Here's the secret: If you're willing to test, and test thoroughly, your magazines, treat them right, and never loan them, then load 30. (or 20) If you have to use issued magazines, or you can't test your magazines, or you are in the habit of loaning them to others, only load 28 (or 18) in them.

Barrel against barricade

Resting the barrel against a hard object is supposed to cause a complete loss of accuracy. Well sometimes yes, and sometimes no. As with all things, it depends. If you have a skinny-barreled rifle, and you rest the flash hider against a brick wall or concrete curb, you might have a marked loss of accuracy and a shift in point of impact. Then again, maybe not. If you're shooting a heavy-barreled rifle and only have the front sight assembly or bayonet lug resting against a wooden rail or post, you aren't going to lose much accuracy. Or you might. At close range it may not matter at all. On this subject you will have to do some experimenting.

I experimented with my heavy-use AR, my "take to class and loan to students" rifle. It is a lightweight, 1-7 twist and chrome-lined, Colt barrel, installed in an Olympic Arms upper and lower. It shoots just over 1-inch groups at 100 yards, and never fails. (When the barrel finally gives up, and I have to replace it, I'm not sure what to expect, as the barrel is the heart of any rifle, particularly the AR.) I first rested the

The starting group, an inch and a half low. (As it should be.)

handguards on a barricade and fired a group to determine zero at 25 yards. As expected, the shot were a tight cluster an inch below the point of aim. I fired at 25 yards only because I did not expect 100-yard groups to be on target, and I didn't feel like walking down and back for unmeasurable results.

Resting on the bayonet lug had no effect...

On the group fired that way. If anything, it is smaller than the handguard-rest group.

The next step was to rest the bayonet lug on the barricade and fire a group. As near as I could tell the resulting groups were no larger, nor in a different location, than when I rested just the handguards.

Next, I rested the barrel itself, just in front of the bayonet lug, on the barricade. The groups were marginally larger, and in much the same location.

Finally, I rested the flash hider itself on the barricade. Imagine my puzzlement when the groups fired were just as small as the best of any other position, and in the same place!

Exasperated, I fired the last position again, except instead of simply resting the weight of the rifle on the barricade, I pressed down to stress the barrel as much as possible. The "success" was limited. The group center shifted up 2 inches, but the group fired was the smallest of the day.

I then rested the barrel in the corner of the window of the barricade, and pressed down and to the side as hard as possible, while squeezing the handguards into the windowframe as much as possible. The group fired was average in size, and shifted an inch away from the window corner I was resting in.

In all, what I proved was that my rifle, at least, is unconcerned about contact with objects. Yours may be more picky about what it rests on, and only testing will determine its tastes.

Magazine against the ground

Every rifle is different. I tried five of mine, with half a dozen magazines, and couldn't get any to malfunction. However, I have seen rifles that repeatedly malfunctioned when the magazine rested on the ground. As with the problem of having a barrel against an object, you will have to do some experimenting on your own.

Resting the barrel is supposed to be a bad thing, but the group fired...

Isn't so bad. It might be half an inch high. And it might not be.

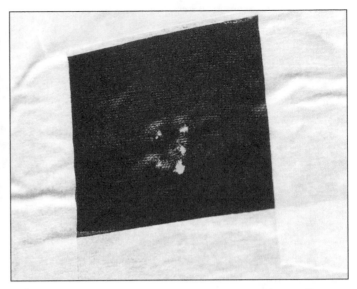

A group change. It is higher, but is one of the smallest groups fired.

Resting the flash hider on the barricade had no effect, so I leaned heavily on the rifle the next time, and got...

And finally moved the group a bit. Not much, it is still an inch and a half low, but now is maybe an inch left. The bottom of the square is the aiming point.

Resting the barrel against the barricade window and pressing hard (I've photographed it this way, but actually rested pushing down and to the right. I couldn't get the camera over to show the test position.)

Tight sling

This one is real, and is a variant of the barrel against the wall problem. One of the problems long-range match shooters had with the AR was a tight sling causing the barrel to flex, or changing the harmonics and changing point of impact or accuracy. But long-range target shooters are accustomed to using a sling so tight that they gauge their time on the line by watching the tips of their sling hand fingers turn blue. If you're using a tactical sling and have it pulled tight, it won't change the point of impact. (After all, it is secured to the receiver, not the barrel.) One solution for target shooters was to use a heavier barrel. The best solution for target shooters was to use a new forearm assembly. The target forearm is a tube under the handguards, to which the sling is attached. The sling never touches the barrel. For accurate fire in a tactical setting, a solid prone or rested prone will serve well, and be faster than a tight sling. Remember, the target shooters are firing at targets 600 yards away, and do not want to have to worry about another variable that adds a couple of inches to their calculations. (A couple of inches of accuracy at 600 yards is not one of the problems of an entry team.) Some rifles are affected more than others, and only testing will tell the tale.

Proper prone is supposed to keep the magazine off the ground.

And if you rest the magazine, bad things happen. Not always true, you must test for yourself.

246   Myths Of The Rifle, Or: Things "Everyone Knows" That Just Aren't True

An AR with optics can be very accurate. This holosight-equipped AR has no problem dropping the 300-meter targets.

Since the nearest 600-yard range is a goodly driving distance off, and the difference between sling and no sling is likely to be much smaller than my grouping ability at that distance, I didn't test my rifles. Then again, if resting them on a wooden barricade didn't change the point of impact, can I generate enough sling tension to matter?

The new M-16 is a 600-yard weapon

Well, yes. Of a sort. One problem with using an AR out at 600 yards is that the velocity has long-since dropped below the fragmentation threshold. It will simply poke a hole through things. Thus, it will not have much stopping power. The other problem is range estimation. At 600 yards, an error of range estimation of 25 yards could cause a miss by a foot. At a rifle match, the target distance is known. (Most, anyway. Some few matches have targets at unknown distances, but the competitors don't use 5.56mm rifles in them.) At a High Power match, the targets are 600 yards away, plus or minus a yard. If not, someone is in trouble. A gentle 10 mph breeze could push your bullet 3 feet off the target. No, while 600 yards is a distance in which a competition can be held, for real life work, it is strictly 7.62mm rifle territory.

The 5.56mm has too much range

This is just wrongheaded. The 5.56mm has as much range as it needs. If you miss your target any bullet has too much range. An errant bullet is an errant bullet, whether it travels 200 yards before coming down, or 2,000. And very few have a maximum possible distance of only 200 yards. Even the lowly .22 rimfire has a maximum possible range of over a mile. They are all dangerous if mis-handled.

The AR-15 and AR-18 have the same design of internals, and neither is easy to covertly convert to full-auto fire.

They are easy to convert to Full-Auto fire

Ahh, the "paper clip" conversion. I've heard of it, I've even heard three or four garbled descriptions of how it's done, and I'm unconvinced. The conversion line is the shooting equivalent of the fad diet that never goes out of fashion, even though no one loses weight on it.

The AR-15/M-16 is a mature piece of technology that works as intended, reliably and effectively. Learn its limitations, and if you want more gun, get more, don't try to make this gun what it isn't.

Chapter 27

FN Special Police Rifle

SOMETIMES A SINGLE precision shot is called for. To do the job to the high level taxpayers and the courts expect, a trained marksman using a superbly accurate rifle is assigned the task. Why the marksman? The nature of the job of law enforcement is to stop bad people from doing bad things. At times the people are very bad. An example would be the two men who were robbing armored cars in Miami, the ones the FBI found and attempted to apprehend. They were in the habit of robbing the armored car by waiting until the door was open, and then shooting the guard to start the robbery. Unfortunately, the FBI did not have, nor would have had the time for a tactical marksman when they made their vehicle stop that precipitated the shootout. A more general example would be a distraught family member holding the family hostage. Or an armed robbery where the perpetrators hadn't time to escape and found themselves surrounded by the police. When faced with threats to "let us go or we'll kill the hostages" the law enforcement community has found accurate rifles useful. In those situations, the marksman has to place his shot precisely so as to ensure bystanders and innocent victims are not harmed. The usual "behind the shoulder, a third up from the belly" level of accuracy that is good enough for deer hunting is totally inadequate for the police marksman. Within a quarter-inch of the intended point of impact, within a 100-yard distance, is more like it.

The typical tactical rifle is a bolt-action with a scope, in a large caliber. If the perpetrator has to be shot to prevent injury to others, a large-enough caliber to do the job must be used. But it can't be too large. In one of the "Dirty Harry" movies Inspector Harry Callahan was on the rooftop waiting for the 'Frisco Sniper, with a .458 Winchester Magnum in hand. The .458 magnum is an elephant gun. Why? Because it looked good in the movies, and the character of Inspector Callahan always carried the largest caliber available for the job. In real life, the caliber selected is almost certainly going to be .308 Winchester. Why? It is powerful enough to incapacitate the offender with one shot, while not being so powerful as to be difficult to shoot. (The .458 is not for the weak of heart or shoulder.) The .308 has a proven track record of getting the job done. And, it is accurate. The ammunition manufacturers have spent a great amount of time and money developing superbly accurate match-grade ammo for competitions and military snipers. A cartridge that is accurate to 800, 900 and 1,000 yards is likely to be accurate at 75, a more common law enforcement engagement distance.

And a superb rifle for that job is the FN Special Police Rifle.

Many tactical rifles are built on the Remington 700 action. Part of the reason for its selection is availability. The 700 can be found almost everywhere. Part of the reason is that the Marine Corps selected it for their sniper rifle, and for many, the Corps can do no wrong. And part of it is that the 700 action, being basically a cylinder, is easy to place in a lathe and machine the action parts and mating surfaces to exact and

The FN Special Police Rifle 5, with dedicated suppressor. Yes, you can quiet down a .308 a great deal.

The Special Police is built on a blueprinted action, with everything straight and square from the beginning. Here it is shown with its Badger ordnance scope mount.

Screwed on or off, there is no change in zero on the FN-SPR 5

agreeing dimensions, known as "accurizing". Thus, it is (relatively speaking) easy to find a gunsmith who can create an accurate rifle.

The FN SPR is an accurized rifle right out of the box that is not a 700 action. The FN is built on a selected and accurized Winchester controlled-feed action. The originator of the Special Police, Jim Owens, a retired Marine NCO who spent a great deal of time working in, and finally running, the Marine Sniper program, insisted on and got a special manufacturing and assembly cell in the Winchester plant for his product. The customary route is for the department acquiring a rifle to send it to a specialty gunsmith for the accurizing work. Then, the rifle must be bedded in a stock, have a scope installed, tested, zeroed, and the package built up with sling, bipod, case and log book. Rather than acquire a rifle, and find a gunsmith to rebuild it, a police department can get an FN-SPR complete with scope, drag bag and carry case, ready to go. FN did this by building that special assembly room in the plant that makes their Winchester M-70 actions and rifles. The special assembly room machines receivers to precise dimensions and ensures the mating surfaces are perfectly located and mated. They fit hammer-forged chrome-lined match-grade barrels, bed the action, test fire and ensure accuracy, all before shipping to the customer.

The stock is a synthetic, with the buttstock adjustable both for length of pull and cheek rest height. Rather than building a stock to a particular officer, the stock can be adjusted to the issued officer and left that way. If the rifle is later re-issued to another officer, the stock can be re-set to his (or her) proportions. The stock is also set up for quick-detachable slings, which can be installed on either side or the traditional bottom of the stock locations.

The trigger is the superb Winchester M-70, which can be adjusted for almost as light a trigger pull as

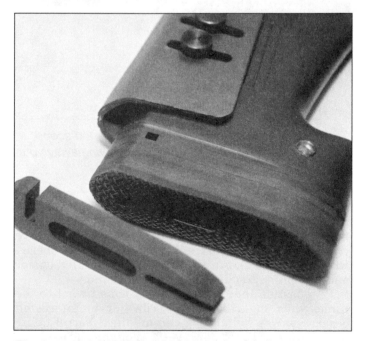

The buttstock is adjustable for length of pull.

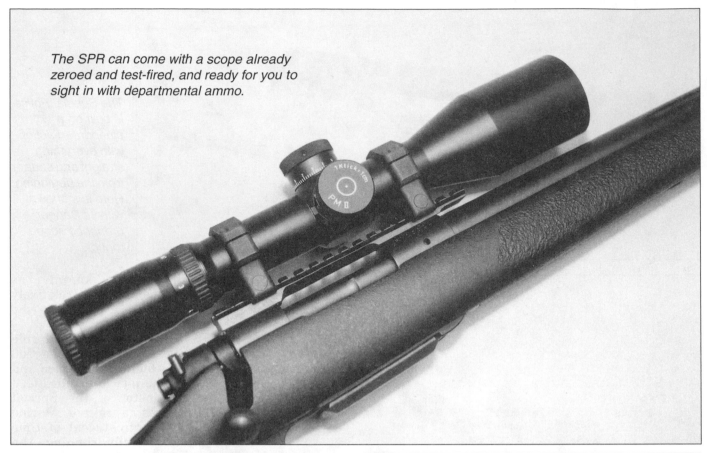

The SPR can come with a scope already zeroed and test-fired, and ready for you to sight in with departmental ammo.

The cheek rest is adjustable for height.

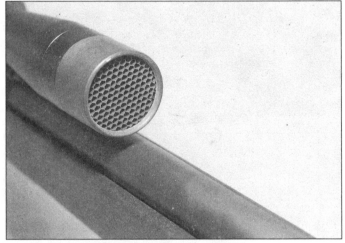

The barrel is free-floated, and the grid over the scope prevents reflections off your own optics giving away your position.

anyone would ever desire. The M-70 trigger is a model of simplicity and durability. With the M-70's one spring and two moving parts you can't make a trigger that is less prone to problems, while being capable of a superb pull. The best setting is a clean and crisp 3 pounds, light enough to not be a hindrance to marksmanship, but heavy enough to preclude inadvertent discharge.

The rifle is fed by means of a detachable magazine. While the separate magazine allows for quick ammunition selection (you can switch from match hollowpoints to bonded-core vehicle penetrators to AP glass-shattering ammunition in mere moments) the best part of the magazines is the administrative loading and unloading. Rather than the typical unloading methods of either racking all the rounds through the action or unlatching the magazine floorplate and dumping the ammo onto the floor or ground, the marksman can simply remove the magazine and extract the unfired chambered round. Loading and unloading are faster, safer, easier and less prone to damaging unfired rounds.

A question that came up every time I went to the range with the rifle, or described it to interested observers, was "what is a chrome-lined barrel doing in a sniper rifle?" The very thought of using a

The sling is a quick-detach model, and can be installed right, left or centerline of the stock.

Top-end sniper scopes come with windage, elevation and focus knobs.

chrome-lined bore seemed contrary to accurate shooting. After all, chrome-lining is what the military does for M-4 carbines and machineguns barrels. Well, FN has figured out how to make a superbly accurate barrel that happens to be chrome-lined. The increase in service life, and the decrease in cleaning effort is well worth their time and money in R&D. Don't let the thought of a chrome-lined barrel put you off. And don't even think for a moment that you'll "improve" the accuracy by removing the factory barrel and replacing it with a cut-rifled, expensive match barrel from a custom maker. You won't.

What is the result? I had the chance to test an A-4 FN-SPR, and what a joy it was. The rifle came nestled in its hard case suitable for shipping and tough enough to survive even the most sour baggage handler. Inside was the rifle wrapped in an Eagle drag bag, the rifle fitted with a Leupold tactical scope. To test it, I went to the range and set up on the shooting benches, using the Harris bipod that came with the rifle. In the military, bipods are hardly ever used. The Marine sniper program does not include

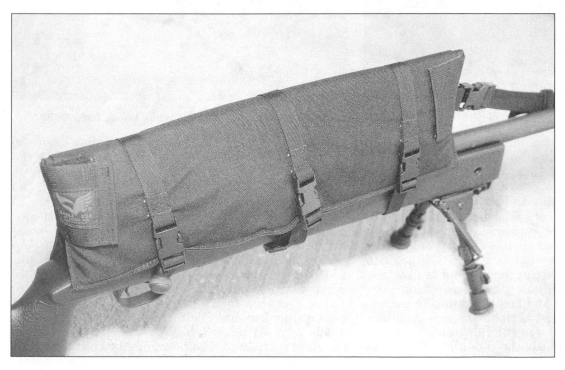

If it comes with a scope, it comes with a scope cover.

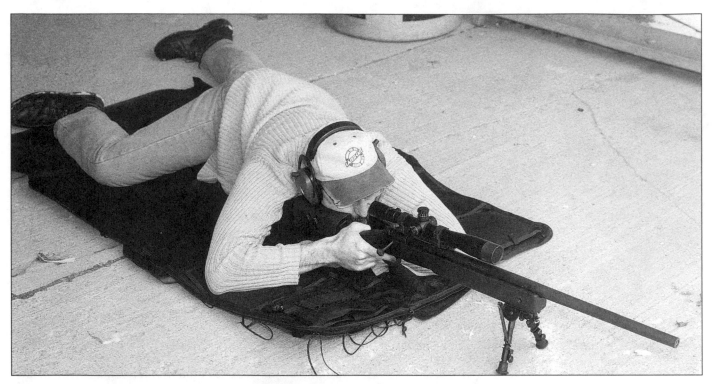

On the shooting mat, punching tight groups or hitting distant plates was easy.

The Black Hills was accurate. 100 yards, half an inch.

Black Hills, 165-grain Nosler Ballistic Tip, even better.

their use, simply because Marines are expected to spend much of their time so hidden in the brush, grass, forest or swamps that you can't find a sniper and his assistant unless you're standing on them. A bipod is a hindrance while sliding through the grass in a ghillie suit. If he needs support, the Marine will use a rucksack, bedroll, convenient log or lump of earth. A police marksman is more likely to be lying on a rooftop, without a rucksack, and a bipod can mean the difference between success and failure.

The range conditions were anything but conducive to a fun day and small groups. There was light snow, solid overcast, temperatures were in the mid-20s, and the wind was coming from the right. The only good things about the conditions were that

the wind and light didn't change, so I didn't have to be constantly recalculating my hold. I tested the Special Police with a selection of match ammo from Black Hills, Winchester, Remington and Federal, and was easily able to shoot groups under an inch. In fact, I was able to consistently shoot half-inch groups. Better yet, the individual ammunition zeros did not shift from type to type. I've seen and shot rifles that would shoot tight groups, but would shift the point of impact as much as a couple of inches when you changed from one brand to another. Later, I had a chance to try some field shooting at steel plates from various distances and positions. In the shade of a convenient bush, with a rucksack as a shooting rest, I was able to easily hit whichever steel

Federal, with sierra Match Kings, another sub-half inch group.

A laser rangefinder allows you to dial in your scope precisely.

plate I wished. Only when the shooting problem depended on my ability to read the wind did I start missing. After all, a 6-inch plate at 400 yards does not allow for very much error in calculating wind drift. But 400 yards is far beyond law enforcement engagement distances.

In all, the FN-SPR is an exemplary sample of the tactical marksman rifle for law enforcement, and you cannot go wrong acquiring one.

Laser rangefinders

But how far is it? You'd think, with the average engagement distance for law enforcement at 75 yards, knowing how far wouldn't matter. You'd be wrong. Remember, the law enforcement marksman is attempting to strike within a quarter-inch or less of his intended target point. A compact rangefinder like the Nikon 400 is plenty good enough to do the job. For the few hundred dollars it costs (as opposed to the $3,000+ of the first Leica models, beautiful but too expensive to let rain get on them) you can know with certainty exactly how far it is to the target.

Documentation

When someone gets shot, there will be an inquiry. When someone dies as a result of gunfire in any situation where the police are involved, there will be an inquiry and almost certainly legal action. The mindset of "somebody owes me" after any tragic

incident seems to be more and more the norm. When the inevitable inquiry arrives, the police marksman must have all the questions answered ahead of time. To do so, every range session is (or should be) documented. The log book should list everything relevant, from time of day and direction fired, to weather, and even how many times the rifle had been fired since the bore was last cleaned. What rifle was fired? What ammunition, including description and production lot numbers. At what distances? In what conditions? And what were the results? Otherwise, there may be trouble.

Trial Lawyer: Officer, you fired when it was freezing, with a light snow falling, from a distance of 82 yards, with a crosswind of 10 miles per hour, and firing down from a third-story window. Have you ever done that before?

Officer, consulting his log book: Yes counselor, I have. On October 17th of last year, I fired a practice session in almost the exact same weather conditions. In May of that year I fired a series of range sessions from a number of different elevations. And I have provided the targets fired on those days.

If possible, save the targets. If not, a properly marked target that is photographed can serve. Also, all training, the subjects covered, notes taken during the training, and books and articles read should be documented. You can't be too thorough.

Chapter 28

Long Gun Light Methods

WHEN IT COMES time to juggle a long gun and a light, there are two methods: a weaponmount light and all the unsatisfactory methods.

The weaponmount lights are simple: A Surefire M-900 or M-500, a Millennium, or something secured in a bolt-on mount to a picatinny rail. With the light secured to the weapon you can control light, weapon, recoil and not feel like you're at the circus tryouts for the juggling acts.

The two non-weaponmount methods that offer a modicum of support are the Harries adapted to a long gun, and the Ayoob adapted to long gun. In the Harries, you hold the light just as you would in the handgun Harries technique, and rest the forearm of the rifle or shotgun on the back of your wrist. The advantages are that it is the same as the handgun method, so if you've learned the handgun Harries technique you can adapt to the long gun method. And it lets you (if your wrist has the flex) to keep the light pointed out even when you have the muzzle in low ready. The disadvantages are the same as the

The best long gun lighting method is to have your light attached to your weapon. Like this Surefire M-900 on a Fobus handguard.

Or this A.R.M.S. SIR as a place for your illumination.

The Ayoob adaptation. If you have big hands or a narrow light, this can work.

The Harries adaptation for long guns. It is tiring, but gets the job done.

handgun Harries; it is tiring, and it does not let you use your off hand to control recoil when firing. In the Ayoob adapted, you hold the forearm as usual, with the light clamped under your thumb. With a light with a side button, you use your thumb to turn it on and off. With a Surefire you can if you have large enough hands keeps your thumb on the momentary button. The other method is to adjust the tailcap so

that it is as close to being constant on as you can get it without actually being on. Then by squeezing the light against the forearm you can turn it on and off

The Rogers adaptation, using the two smallest fingers to stay indexed to the rifle.

With a "C" cell light and big hands, you can make the Ayoob adaptation work.

by adjusting the pressure. The advantage is that you can use your off hand to control the long gun. The disadvantage is that you cannot point the light without also pointing the muzzle.

The third method is to handle the long gun one-handed and use the neck hold or FBI method to light independently.

The best arrangement is to have two lights, one a hand light on a lanyard, and the other a weaponmount. During the searching, you use the hand held to scan and inspect. When you need the weapon, let go of the handheld and let it fall on the lanyard. Bring up the weapon, and when you grasp the forearm you press the momentary tape to hold the light on as you shout commands and acquire a sight picture. Unless you're searching in a situation where contact is expected and imminent, and then you'll be working just on the weaponmount light.

The "squeezecap" method. Again, you need large hands to do this.